The Critical Handbook of Money Laundering

Petrus C. van Duyne • Jackie H. Harvey
Liliya Y. Gelemerova

The Critical Handbook of Money Laundering

Policy, Analysis and Myths

palgrave
macmillan

Petrus C. van Duyne
Department of Penal Law
Tilburg University
Tilburg, The Netherlands

Jackie H. Harvey
Newcastle Business School
Northumbria University
Newcastle upon Tyne, UK

Liliya Y. Gelemerova
University of Manchester
Manchester, UK

ISBN 978-1-137-52397-6 ISBN 978-1-137-52398-3 (eBook)
https://doi.org/10.1057/978-1-137-52398-3

Library of Congress Control Number: 2018938551

Cover illustration: Digital Vision / Getty Images

This Palgrave Macmillan imprint is published by the registered company Springer Nature Limited
The registered company address is: The Campus, 4 Crinan Street, London, N1 9XW, United Kingdom

To my patient partner, Elise, and my daughters,
Freya and Machteld – Petrus C. van Duyne
To Simon, Rachel and Ellen – Jackie H. Harvey
To my family – Liliya Y. Gelemerova

Preface

Most scholarly handbooks are written for an educational aim: to spread knowledge. That is a lofty objective. However, with the present work this was not the primary aim. We were driven by a simpler knowledge objective: after many years of working in the field of anti-money laundering we still had the feeling we did not understand it properly. Of course, we were well informed of the many technical and policy aspects and had published widely about them. But yet we had the feeling that we had no comprehensive grasp on the manifold relationships and interconnections of the many facets. Likewise we were baffled by the many statements about the alleged threat posed by money-laundering which did not appear to mitigate over time. Indeed, irrespective of the putting in place of an ever more powerful apparatus against money-laundering and an intensified control of international compliance, we never observed a lessening of the warnings against the laundering threat. That gave us a feeling of working on a puzzle with many missing pieces (or including those from another puzzle), while the manufacturer, the FATF, presents us an impressive picture on the lid. Is there a mismatch and where? This gave the drive to *know* in the first place: to analyse the facts and determine and discard what appeared to be non-matching myths.

From this angle the field of research looks vast but is by hindsight simple, as long as one wants to keep it simple. Soon there appeared one piece which remained difficult to integrate in the whole: terrorist finances. First, it is technically not laundering. Secondly, the amounts of reported terrorist financing are relatively low. Nevertheless, in the FATF documents money-laundering is repeatedly concatenated with terrorist financing: ML/TF with the only effect of creating a kind of lengthy empty mantra-drone. As this work is not dealing with empty mantras, we left TF out.

Writing a handbook on a changeable phenomenon due to its dependence on changes in politics, may have the consequence of needing a regular update. This handbook may provide a solid foundation for such updates, for example, regarding emerging illegal profits related to climate change: environmental or 'agro-laundering', or to the relatively new cryptocurrencies. If this work can contribute to such updating it would serve as a useful and dynamic knowledge product.

The Hague, The Netherlands — Petrus C. van Duyne
Newcastle, UK — Jackie H. Harvey
Manchester, UK — Liliya Y. Gelemerova

Contents

List of Acronyms

AML	Anti Money Laundering
AML/CFT	Anti Money Laundering/Countering the Financing of Terrorism
APEC	Asia Pacific Economic Cooperation
APG	Asian Pacific Group on Money Laundering (also the Asian/ Pacific Group)
APGML	Asia/Pacific Group on Money Laundering
BIS	Bank for International Settlements
BSA	The United States Bank Secrecy Act of 1970 is the shortened reference for The Financial Recordkeeping and Reporting of Currency and Foreign Transactions Act of 1970 (31 U.S.C. 5311 et seq.)
CAD	Canadian Dollars
CAM	Criminal Asset Management
CC	Criminal Code
CDD	Customer Due Diligence
CEMAC	Communauté Economique et Monétaire d'Afrique Centrale (Economic and Monetary Community of Central Africa)
CFATF	Caribbean Financial Action Task Force (FATF Regional Style Body)
CFT	Countering the Financing of Terrorism
CIA	Central Intelligence Agency
CMIR	Currency and Monetary Instrument Report
CoE	The Council of Europe
CTRs	Currency Transactions Reports
DEA	Drug Enforcement Administration
DNFBPs	Designated Non-Financial Business and Professionals
DoJ	United States Department of Justice

DPA	Deferred Prosecution Agreement
DYMINIC	Dynamic Multiple-indicators Multiple Causes, a statistical technique for determining explanatory variables for the size of the shadow economy
ECOWAS	Economic Community of West African States
EFCC	Nigerian Economic and Financial Crime Commission
ESAAMLG	Eastern and Southern African Anti-Money Laundering Group
EU	European Union
EUROPOL	European Union Agency for Law Enforcement Cooperation
FATF	Financial Action Task Force
FATF-AR	Financial Action Task Force – Annual Report
FCA	the United Kingdom Financial Conduct Authority
FDI	Foreign Direct Investment
FinCEN	the United States Financial Crimes Enforcement Network
FINTRAC	Financial Transactions and Reports Analysis Centre of Canada
FIU	Financial Intelligence Unit
FSAP	Financial Sector Assessment Programme (jointly run by the IMF and the World Bank)
FSRBs	FATF- Style Regional Bodies
G-7	Group of Seven (Forum of seven countries to coordinate economic security and energy policy Canada, France, Germany, Italy, Japan, the United Kingdom and the United States)
G-9	Group of Nine (A group of nine Northeastern European nations that would meet occasionally to discuss matters of mutual interest.)
G-20	Group of Twenty (Central forum for international corporation on financial and economic issues comprising 19 countries and the EU)
GABAC	Action group against money laundering created in 2000 by the Economic and Monetary Community of Central Africa
GAFILAT	Financial Action Task Force of Latin America (Formerly GAFISUD)
GAFISUD	Grupo de Acción Financiera de Sudamérica - Financial Action Task Force of South America against Money Laundering (Later changed to GAFILAT)
GATS	General Agreement on Trade in Services
GATT	General Agreement on Tariffs and Trade
GDP	Gross Domestic Product
GIABA	Groupe Inter-gouvernemental d'Action contre le Blanchiment en Afrique (Inter-Governmental Action Group against Money Laundering in West Africa)
GNP	Gross National Product
HSBC	The Hongkong and Shanghai Banking Corporation

IBRD	International Bank for Reconstruction and Development (also referred to as the World Bank)
ICRG	International Cooperation Review Group within the FATF
IMF	International Monetary Fund
Interpol	International Police Organisation
IRS	United States Internal Revenue Service
KYC	Know-Your-Customer
LEAs	Law Enforcement Agencies
LIBOR	London Interbank Offered Rate
MCDR	Modified-Cash-Deposit-Ratio
MENA	Region Middle East and North Africa region
MENAFATF	Middle East & North Africa Financial Action Task Force
MERs	Mutual Evaluation Reports
MIMIC	Multiple Indicator, Multiple Causes (see DYMINIC)
ML	Money Laundering
ML/TF	Money Laundering/Terrorist Financing
MLRO	Money Laundering Reporting Officer
MONEYVAL	Committee of Experts on the Evaluation of Anti-Money Laundering Measures and the Financing of Terrorism (formerly PC-R-EV) within the Council of Europe
MVTS	Money or Value Transfer Services
n a	Not Applicable
NCCT's	Non-Cooperative Countries and Territories
NDLEA	Nigeria National Drug Law Enforcement Agency
NFIU	Nigerian Financial Intelligence Unit
NNC	The Dutch Central Catalogue for libraries
NOK	Krone
NPOs	Non-Profit Organisations
NRA	National Risk Assessment
NZ	New Zealand
OC	Organised Crime
OCC	United States Office of the Comptroller of the Currency
OCGs	Organised Crime Groups
OECD	Organisation for Economic Co-operation and Development
OFC	Offshore Finance Centre
OFE	United States Treasury Department's Office of Financial Enforcement
PCMLTFA	Canada Proceeds of Crime Money Laundering and Terrorist Financing Act 2000
PC-R-EV	See MONEYVAL
PEPs	Politically Exposed Persons
POCA	United Kingdom Proceeds of Crime Act 2002
RBA	Risk Based Approach
RCMP	Royal Canadian Mounted Police

RICO	The United States Racketeer Influenced and Corrupt Organizations Act 1970
SARs	Suspicious Activity Reports
SEM	Simultaneous Equation Models/Structural Equation Models
SSRN	Social Science Research Network - Research database
STRs	Suspicious Transaction Reports
TF	Terrorist Financing
UK	United Kingdom
UN	United Nations
UNODC	The United Nations Office on Drugs and Crime
US	United States
USA BSA	US Bank Secrecy Act (BSA)
WGEI FATF	Working Group on Evaluations and Implementation
WGTM FATF	Working Group on Terrorist financing and Money laundering
WGTYP FATF	Working Group on Typologies

List of Figures

[illegible] of Figures

List of Tables

1

Money-laundering: a global issue and scarce knowledge

1.1 Introduction: why this book?

Writing a book on a subject that surfaced 25 years ago looks like writing a contemporary history book. Given that the subject, in this case money laundering, is still perceived to be an acute problem, there is nothing wrong with looking back and raising questions about what happened, what went well and what went wrong.

The initiative to do something about the profits of crime, more than three decades ago, was not a one-off event. It has continued to develop up until the present day and indeed, is still evolving. Therefore, it is appropriate to look back in time as well as to look around in the present and wonder what was the original state of knowledge about this phenomenon and what is its present 'state of the (knowledge) art'. We expect that a quarter of a Century of policy implementation provides a suitable time span for surveying what happened with this new anti-laundering supervisory and law enforcement regime. This comprises the accompanying ideas and concepts as well as the empirical material which should have been unearthed in the course of combating this menace. Given the variety of stakeholders in the field, one would also expect a multitude of insights, narratives and a great deal of data.

Naturally, given the importance of the subject, one would expect that all this has already been brought together in one or more comprehensive volumes, leaving us only the task of updating. However, that is not the case. It is true that many eminent studies and monographs have been published since money laundering became a global political issue. We will discuss these in later chapters. But it is also true that notwithstanding all these efforts, there is

P.C. van Duyne, J.H. Harvey and L.Y. Gelemerova, *The Critical Handbook of Money Laundering*, https://doi.org/10.1057/978-1-137-52398-3_1

still much fragmentation of data and little unity in concepts, with the exception of the idea that money laundering is a serious threat (even if there may be some rare dissidents). However, the shared agreement about its threat is a shallow one, covering many opinions on the nature of crime-money. Does imply gross proceeds or net profits; saved money due to economic and financial crime? Nobody can spell out the real nature of the threat or make a substantiated statement about its size: "how much?" Addressing this question is bound to lead to disagreement because the underlying question "Where are the (validated) facts and figures?" has not yet been properly addressed. Addressing this issue may also reveal a variety of assumptions that are not shared by all participants in this undertaking. For example, the economic (macro) approach works with different assumptions than the behavioural, empirical approach.

This contrasts with what one may reasonably expect if one would, as a layman, for the first time learn about the gravity of a threat which has loomed for decades above our heads without becoming smaller, but also without 'coming down'. This justifies some suspicion: can it be true that a threat that has endured for decades has still failed to materialise? Such circumstances taken together would in other situations be sufficient to lose faith in the threat predictions. Strangely enough this is not the case with the subject of money laundering. Despite this non-occurrence, empirical observations on these doomsday scenarios are few and far between. Remarkably, though its 'non-occurrence' has been put forward and challenged, such as by Ferwerda (2013) or Reuter (2013), it has rarely been picked up and debated politically. In terms of Popper's (1969) philosophy of science: in the absence of "conjectures and refutations" there is no real debate. Perhaps this circumvention of debate may be the best way to uphold faith in the tenets of the anti-money laundering policy. Whether this is the case has never really been properly made explicit. And as the philosopher Wittgenstein remarked: "*Wovon man nicht sprechen kann, darüber muß man schweigen.*"[1] So, for the time being we maintain the faith aspect as it is. Later in this work our hypothetical layman will return and haunt us with plain questions about policy tenets, such as "What is all this good for?" We will then see whether we have collected sufficient material to answer him with facts instead of faith.

From the threat perspective mentioned above it is worthwhile bringing facts, concepts and opinions together in one narrative which is not about one particular point to be proven and others to be rejected. Rather the aim is to put together views, concepts, facts and findings and analyse them to the bone. Views can contain truths, half-truths and myths; empirical findings and their interpretation can be valid, biased or spurious. All that has to be brought to light and narrated. We think it is time for such a narrative.

---

[1] "What we cannot speak about we must pass over in silence" (Wittgenstein, 1922; translation 1960).

1.2 Where did the global anti-money laundering narrative start?

The international anti-money laundering policy is considered to have been 'cemented at the summit meeting of the Heads of State of the G-7 in Paris in July 1989. It followed from previous initiatives, including the US Bank Secrecy Act of 1970.[2] The 'G-group' is an informal gathering of Heads of States, Prime Ministers, Ministers of Finance or their delegates of the most important industrialised countries. These meetings started in 1973 in the White House with five participants. Given the informal nature of these gatherings that number has changed at each subsequent event. At present there are 20 members and consequently we speak of the G-20, though it is still as informal as when it was the G-7.

In 1989, the leaders of the industrialised world came together to discuss a wide range of subjects. There were 11 issues on the agenda[3] and money laundering was just a sub-subject of the last one: drugs issues, of which the last two sections were devoted to criminal assets recovery and the creation of a financial action task force respectively.[4] It looked like the proverbial mouse coming out of the mountain. It would prove to become a mouse with a long, never-ending tail. Interestingly it was the only outcome of this meeting that crossed the memory threshold of history. This first meeting and the actions arising from it will be re-visited in Chapters 8 and 9.

The delegates of the attending states expressed their usual 'grave concern' about the phenomenon of laundering money originating from drug trafficking. Growth in drug trafficking in the 1980s was conjoined with 'laundering' in the minds of officials. It is from here that the imagery of a serious global financial threat was put forward. However, after a quarter of a Century that threat is still not substantiated. Taylor (1992) considered this imagery as seri-

---

2 Strengthened by the US Money Laundering Control Act, 1986; the UN convention against illicit traffic in narcotic drugs and psychotropic substances, 1988, the 'Vienna Convention'; and the Basel Statement of Principles, 'Prevention of criminal use of the banking system for the purpose of money-laundering' (1988). Also see the discussions in Chapters 7 and 9.

3 The range of discussion points was very broad: from the international economic and financial situation to international cooperation against AIDS with the situation of the poorest and heavily indebted countries discussed in between.

4 "Convene a financial action task force from Summit participants and other countries interested in these problems. Its mandate is to assess the results of cooperation already undertaken in order to prevent the utilization of the banking system and financial institutions for the purpose of money laundering, and to consider additional preventive efforts in this field, including the adaptation of the legal and regulatory systems so as to enhance multilateral judicial assistance. The first meeting of this task force will be called by France and its report will be completed by April 1990." Item 53 of the final resolution in the 'key Sections of the Paris Communique by the group of Seven', Paris, 16 July 1987 and published in the *New York Times*. Available at http://www.nytimes.com/1989/07/17/world/key-sections-of-the-paris-communique-by-the-group-of-seven.html?pagewanted=all. Accessed 11 December 2017.

ously misleading.[5] Apart from that, this proclamation attracted much attention and it looked as if a new threat had been identified: not only by the seven industrialised countries present at that meeting, but by an ever-growing number of countries.[6] When such a 'grave concern' is being expressed persistently by world leaders it is to be expected that the international political community will lend its unrestricted support – and so it did.

As a matter of fact, the initiative of the G-7 was no surprise. There was a confluence of political decision making to outlaw money laundering. In this policy development the USA took the initiative with the US Money Laundering Control Act in 1986, which followed the Bank Secrecy Act of 1970. It used its political leverage to put drug related money laundering on the international agenda of the UN, leading to the Vienna Convention in 1988. In the same year the Basel Committee on Banking Supervision issued a statement warning banks and other financial institutions against being "unwittingly used" in the processing of crime-money. As discussed below, in 1990 the Council of Europe issued a Convention on Money Laundering[7], followed by the European Commission Directive in 1991.[8]

With so much confluence the question must be raised whether there was a real acute criminal, financial or economic problem caused by the purported drug-money 'wave'? There is no contemporary evidence to underline this view. As a matter of fact, the US administration thought it had a drug-money problem caused by the cocaine boom and related finances in the 1980s. But given the US drug history, this was not a suddenly emerging issue to be addressed with so much emphasis *now* (Van Duyne and Levi, 2005; ch. 2).

There are many stories about wealthy organised crime figures from the 1920s onwards. Some of whom knew how to handle their ill-gotten funds during the prohibition era, mainly derived from organised bootlegging. After the abolition of the prohibition many crime-entrepreneurs arranged a settlement with the Inland Revenue Service and converted their illicit commerce into upperworld enterprises. An example of this 'gentrification' is Joe Kennedy, the father of the president of the US (Kessler, 1996). Others, the most famous of them Al Capone, learned to know the Inland Revenue Service in a less favourable way and ended up paying dearly. Other gangsters came under financial attack as well (Abadinsky, 2003). On this front the legendary Mayer Lansky earned his fame as a professional criminal money manager (Lacey, 1991; Gelemerova, 2011). Hence, the issue of 'criminal

---

5 For the history of deception on the drug portfolio see Van Duyne and Levi (2005, Ch. 1).

6 In the first year of its existence the following countries joined the FATF: Sweden, Netherlands, Belgium, Luxembourg, Switzerland, Austria, Spain and Australia. (FATF Annual Report, 1990-1991; p. 4).

7 Council of Europe Convention on Laundering, Search, Seizure and Confiscation of the Proceeds of Crime (September).

8 First Money Laundering Directive.

money management', later called laundering, was not a new phenomenon or threat in the 1970s and 1980s. However, systematic knowledge based on facts and figures was not available. Reports aiming at presenting crime-money as a national and global threat were to a large extent based on anecdotes and 'expert' opinions. (We will elaborate on the issue of systematic empirical underlining later.)

As we will discuss in chapter 2, the subject of money laundering had been worked on politically, step by step, for years. When we abstract from the first relevant US attempt to control the flow of the proceeds of (primarily tax) crime by the Bank Secrecy Act of 1970, the major breakthrough was brought about by the US Money Laundering Control Act of 1986. From that enactment onwards, the USA initiated a relentless internationalisation of its anti-money laundering policy. Three major achievements have been mentioned already. In 1986, money-laundering had been brought to the fore in the UN Congress' resolutions concerning transnational organised crime. Two years later, the UN agreed on what became known as the Vienna Convention against drug trafficking.[9] It criminalised the laundering of drug money although the term 'laundering' was not specifically mentioned. Given the importance of this history the subject is revisited again in Chapters 3, 4 and 7. In December 1988, the earlier mentioned Basel Committee on Banking Supervision issued a number of principles to prevent the abuse of the financial system for laundering purposes: the Basel Statement of Principles.[10] The streams of anti-laundering policy were now converging indeed. Finally, in 1990, in the same year as the publication of the (first) FATF report, the Council of Europe issued its anti-laundering convention (entering into force in 1993). The European Commission could not but follow suit and in 1991, the first money laundering directive was adopted.[11]

Against this background one can say that the subject of anti-money laundering was everywhere 'in the air' and not as something indeterminable. As will be discussed in the chapters on literature, taken together, one could observe the fruits of a well-planned targeting policy that ultimately led to the 1989 G-7 summit and the establishment of the FATF. As the unfolding of the anti-money laundering policy reached higher stages, the tone and the rhetoric became more shrill: Levi (2003) pointed at the 'evangelistic zeal' of the proponents as if many still had to be convinced or 'converted'.

---

9 UN Convention Against Illicit Trafficking in Narcotic Drugs and Psychotropic Substances ('Vienna Convention'/19 December 1988).

10 Basel Statement of Principles on the Prevention of Criminal Use of the Banking System for the Purpose of Money Laundering ('Basel Statement of Principles' 12 December 1988).

11 Council Directive 91/308/EEC of 10 June 1991 on prevention of the use of the financial system for the purpose of money laundering [Official Journal L 166 of 28.06.1991].

> Van Duyne experienced the USA evangelising the 'happy laundering message' in the beginning of the 1990s, when a delegation presented the USA Money Laundering Control Act to Dutch police officers and representatives of the Dutch Ministry of Justice. The interest was not only raised by a technical explanation of the law but also by pictures and press clippings of happy sheriffs next to shining cars they had confiscated, their happiness being enhanced by the prospect of shared confiscations between police forces, including those abroad.

As will be seen, this evangelistic drive had some grounds. While nobody will openly favour money laundering, not all governments or financial institutions were as equally eager to become involved in all aspects of the 'crusade' which the FATF (with the IMF and the USA agency FinCEN behind it) intended to unleash. Every country had (and still has) its favoured financial blind corners, in particular concerning significant corporations who really matter within the national economy. For example, one may wonder how many 'suspicious activity reports' failed to have been filed about wealthy Russians and Nigerians buying property in West London.[12] Or the 'caviar diplomacy' of the Azerbaijan president and his wife, as has come to light after a number of years of banking and, allegedly, making questionable payments in the UK and elsewhere in 2012-2014.[13]

1.3 A sense of urgency and accumulation of knowledge

As already indicated in the introductory section, there is little accumulation of knowledge from empirical sources, despite all the political expressions of 'grave concern'. There are empirical research projects, such as by Unger and van der Linde (2013), but these are also hampered by lack of reliable data, having to make use of 'proxy data' instead, or make far-reaching and apparently unsupported assumptions (Walker, 1995). These are discussed further in Chapters 7 and 8.

This state of affairs proves to be a systematic historical shortcoming (Van Duyne, 2004). For example, there are no time-series going into aspects such as the annual increase of 'available' crime-money.[14] Until the present day we still have to rely on wild and imprecise, if not wrong, estimates and extrapo-

---

[12] "Why are rich Russians so obsessed with buying up London property?" Stephen Moss, Friday, 9 May 2014, *The Guardian* on-line. Available at: http://www.theguardian.com/cities/2014/may/09/rich-russians-buying-london-property-real-estate; "Wealthy Africans spending almost £4million on London property every week as they snap up some of the most exclusive investments in the capital". Emma Glanfield, 27 October 2014, available at: http://www.dailymail.co.uk/news/article-2808556/Wealthy-Africans-spending-4million-London-property-WEEK-snap-exclusiveinvestments-capital.html. Accessed 5 February 2016.

[13] UK at centre of secret $3billion Azerbaijani money laundering and lobbying scheme. *The Guardian*, 4 September 2017.

[14] Often data have to be 'scraped' together from neglected databases (Van Duyne *et al.*, 2009). Lack of proper statistical data is also a regularly mentioned criticism in the Mutual Evaluation Reports.

lations. For example, if each year a chunk of the supposed one trillion of crime money is laundered (or 'available'), starting from 1990 when the FATF rolled out its standards, then by 2015, we would have a global mass of $25 trillion of crime money. But this represents only a linear accumulation which may be misleading, because the rule "money makes money" also applies to crime money which then has to be augmented with an unknown multiplier because of annual interest and investment. Hence, to the roughly trillion dollars earned per year one must add an annual interest and dividend of the previous years, which further accumulates every year: the fruits of crime-money are also crime-money. And all this is 'available' for laundering. Or actually laundered? This may be a fundamental confusion we will discuss later in Chapter 7.

The next question is what has happened (and is happening) with this continuously accumulating financial 'criminal chunk'? In the literature we could not identify studies or data addressing this accumulation theme of the annual linear inflow + non-linear interest + dividend. As remarked above, if this is a plausible model then it implies an annually increasing, undifferentiated threat. It looks like a thick cloud that has failed to be dissected into differentiating statistics. There are a few 'bright sunbeams' through that cloud, but these do not address this question of criminal wealth accumulation (Savona and Riccardi, 2015; Van Duyne, 2003). Also, Alldridge (2003) justifiably sighs that thus far he has not seen the corresponding statistics of a global financial disaster due to laundering. As will be discussed later in Chapters 3 and 7, the early IMF inspired literature (Tanzi, 1996; Quirk, 1996) with its global financial risk list has now largely given way (with the exception of some of the European economists) to models addressing the relationship between regulation and laundering activity (see, for example, Masciandaro 1998, 1999; Araujo, 2008, 2010; Takáts, 2011; and Johannesen and Zucman, 2014).

Equally lacking are studies on global financial disruption due to laundering despite the many statements made by the World Bank or the IMF (Reuter, 2013). Nevertheless, a number of papers have reproduced these 'concerns' about crime-monies 'undermining the integrity of the financial system' and their negative impact on real economic variables (see for example: Arnone and Borlini, 2010; Quirk, 1996, 1997; Tanzi, 1996; Masciandaro *et al.*, 2007; and Unger *et al.*, 2006).[15] Actually, reproducing concerns must not be equated with furthering a pool of specific knowledge or a proper data management and analysis. Of course, there are occasional findings from research,

---

[15] The IMF has to admit that there are hardly any data on the relationship between laundering and banking crises. The IMF 2011 mentions the Latvia banking crisis of 1995, which was rather due to mismanagement, 'connected lending' and other forms of internal mismanagement (IMF/Hagen, 2011, p. 87).

but these appear to be fragmented and local. We will survey these later in Chapters 3 and 8.

Despite this relatively long history of the anti-laundering policy we cannot but conclude that the policy makers and legislators had no pool of systematic empirical evidence from which they could draw. Nor are there indications that around the time the new policy was put forward the most important stakeholders, the founder countries, showed any interest in data management to empirically underline their statements.[16] Even the IMF has to content itself with statistical proxies instead of proper statistics (IMF/Hagen, 2011, p. 63).

As we will see in our later elaboration of legislation, many of the statements contained within officially crafted documentation on laundering are circular: the FATF borrowed 'data' from the UN (UNODC) for its report in 1990, which was later again reused by the UN to be multiplied several times (Keh, 1996). This contributed to a repetition of wild guesses concerning the amount of laundering and the seriousness of the problem: apparently, big was (and is) beautiful.

This recycling developed as follows. The FATF 1990 report used the figure produced by the United Nations in 1987. This mentioned $300 billion as the estimated proceeds for drug trafficking (although qualified by the FATF in their report as: "*remains very uncertain*" (p. 4)) In fact, for the US and Europe the FATF arrived at estimated drug sales (heroin, cocaine and cannabis) of $ 122 billion per year of which "*50 to 70% or as much as $85bn per year could be available for laundering and investment.*" We observe that of the multiplier range of 50-70% only the higher end was used. Indeed, a remarkable piece of estimation (Van Duyne, 1994).[17] This number was again adopted by the UNODC (United Nations Office on Drugs and Crime). In a later report, the UNODC estimated the amount of crime-money (proceeds) at $ 2.6 trillion yearly of which $ 1.6 trillion would be 'available' for laundering (UNODC, 2011).[18] Meanwhile, the question of "where does all that money go" has thus far not been systematically addressed. Van Duyne (2003) and Savona and Riccardi (2015) made attempts to answer this question. They found much

[16] The recommendation to maintain comprehensive statistics was adopted in the 40 Recommendations 2004. Our study of the Mutual Evaluation Reports (Van Duyne *et al.*, 2016a, b) showed that this requirement was meagrely fulfilled: with a couple of crude statistics this recommendation was already considered complied. The presentation and layout of the quantitative material in the Mutual Evaluation Reports display a fair level of amateurism at the side of the FATF which has improved little over time.

[17] The FATF mentioned in the 1990 report one deviating opinion of one Task Force member who "estimated global profits at the main dealer level, which might be most subject to international laundering, to be about $ 30 billion per year" (p. 4). This perhaps more realistic observation disappeared silently from the public discourse.

[18] The two words 'proceeds' and profits have been defined in footnote 1 of the FATF report. Roughly proceeds denoted the turnover or gross sales and profits are the net gain, all business costs subtracted. Although this should have consequences for estimations, one does not find this differentiation systematically considered.

traditional economic investments taking place and little of the presumed sophistication.

Nevertheless, at the time of presenting the new global 'AML' policy, the FATF's wild guesses were common and generally shared (Pieth, 1999). In the absence of a critical debate, that did not matter: they counted politically.[19]

Pushing such far-reaching policy making, based on only slim data, is remarkable but not exceptional. As observed by Van Duyne and Levi (2005) and Bruun *et al.* (1975), it stands on a comparable level of manipulation and deception as the policy making in similar, closely related fields: transnational organised crime (Van Duyne and Nelemans, 2011) and international drug trafficking (Bewley-Taylor, 1999). Irrespective of a 'slim data methodology', the stakeholders exerted a political weight and momentum to maintain the threat picture: big organised crime, enormous drug revenues and related laundering. This may be cemented by a human factor: the small club of policy makers. The number of policy makers and other experts involved who meet each other regularly in related international fora is rather limited (Van Duyne, 2004).[20] This may contribute to the gap between the highly prioritised cluster of (transnational, organised) profit oriented (drug) crime, crime-money and laundering, on the one hand, and the meagre research findings, on the other hand. There was not much interest in or stimulus for empirical knowledge. Where there are voids, they appeared to be filled by anecdotal evidence. Or, as in the drafting of the Transnational Organised Crime Convention, by reference to just *one* article in *Forbes Magazine* in 1980 (Van Duyne and Nelemans, 2011, p. 45). Otherwise invalid statistics (Van Duyne and Levi, 2005) were relied upon, at least to the satisfaction of most policy makers: if they agree on the shape of the globe, round or flat, research is not required.

Outside this mainstream of policy makers and politicians we find thinly spread basic research by Levi and Osofsky (1995), Van Duyne and De Miranda (1999) and Reuter and Greenfield (2001). Their findings called for caution concerning the official estimates and the related evoked threat images. Nevertheless, these findings were neglected by the political mainstream that followed the IMF in its estimates. Since 1996, after a speech of the Managing Director, this estimate was called the 'IMF consensus'. This consensus was the foundation for Walker's (1995) and Unger's (2007) attempts at quantification, floating the estimates to further undreamed-of heights.

---

[19] See Enesto U. Savona and Michael A. Defoe. (1994) Proceedings of the international conference on 'Preventing and controlling money laundering and the use of the proceed of crime: a global approach', Courmayeur, Mont Blanc, Aosta Valley, Italy, 18th–20th June 1994.

[20] Bruun *et al.* (1975) observed a similar situation in the field of international drug policy: a small group of (usually) co-opted men (the 'gentlemen's club') heavily influenced the terms of the global anti-drug policy from the late 1920s onwards. See also Bewley-Taylor (1999) on the social cohesion achieved in the UN Narcotic Drugs Commission.

Altogether we are not short of literature. Since the first report of the Financial Action Task Force on money laundering (FATF, 1990), a never-ending flow of articles and books has been published though with little attention to basic facts and figures (Van Duyne, 2003, 2007). Many of the publications are either explanatory (laws and regulations) or confirmative. The confirmative publications just endorse or recycle official views and provide various justifications for the global anti-money laundering policy. The explanatory publications spell out what is meant by the various concepts and the anti-money laundering regime in terms of laws and regulations. If there are any empirical references, they most often concern 'facts' drawn from FATF reports or United Nations publications. As noted above, often times these are 'recycled facts' from earlier reports. Of course, such publications can be useful, but whether they should be considered as a pool of knowledge has to be determined. From this mainstream, critical scholars are not likely to be drawn into the discourse; see for example Alldridge (2003); Van Duyne and de Miranda (1999); Sharman (2008); Pieth (1999); Harvey (2005) and Hulsse (2008).

By its nature a pool of knowledge is never 'completed': new material is added while so-called 'loose ends' of previous research can provide a lead to new insights. However, lack of integration may lead to fragmentation, as is apparent in the volume edited by Unger and van der Linde (2013). This is a well-ordered and useful collection of separate contributions, each written for its own reason. But it does not represent an *integrated* stock taking: a heap of knowledge is not an accumulation of knowledge. Therefore, as mentioned before, there are clear gaps between the 'books on the shelves' that we trust our contribution will reveal. The aim of this book is to contribute to such an integrated stock taking which also implies analytical and methodological evaluations and not merely a 'lining up' of findings and publications. Stock taking and integration may also bring to light new 'knowledge holes' and loose ends. These can be important and must also be brought to attention as a kind of 'black fact'. The result, with or without holes, should enlighten us about the 'true story' of money laundering.

1.4 Conclusion

The history of anti-money laundering that has been mapped out over the preceding 25 or so years is one that has been more supported by righteousness than by empirical facts. We observe a tendency to recycle data without proper testing or searching for original sources. To move knowledge in this area forward there is clearly a need for a critical assessment or stocktaking of the current state of knowledge. A stocktaking requires an assessment of what has been contributed to our accumulated knowledge and understanding of money laundering within two domains. Firstly, from the official guidance handbooks and manuals that have been published by the authorities and, secondly, from the academic literature within its various disciplines. The methods by which we undertook our searches are set out in the next chapter.

2

Methodology

2.1 Introduction

We commented in Chapter 1 that despite over 25 years of academic study there is little in the way of accumulated knowledge or a pool of systematic empirical evidence on our subject. As a result, instead of following a fact-based policy, policy makers appeared to move around in a kind of 'socio-political aquarium': one swimming behind the other, quoting and re-quoting what is convenient and in making use of very narrow literature bases, only considering or placing greater emphasis on those statements that support their own stand. Thereby they created an interpretation of the world that has become a self-confirming reality (see Van Duyne, 1998; Levi, 2002; Gelemerova, 2011) wherein, money laundering has been and continues to be seen as a phenomenon that "*ultimately threatens the integrity of the financial system*"[1] and that "*shakes the very foundations of our society*".[2] With hindsight, society has proved resilient in the face of far bigger financial disasters, such as the 2007/2008 credit crisis, in which suspect bankers and dubious financial products proved to have a bigger potential for shaking financial and social foundations, though this is not properly studied in the money laundering literature.

---

1 US Department of the Treasury, available at: https://www.treasury.gov/resource-center/terrorist-illicit-finance/Pages/Money-Laundering.aspx. Accessed 4 March 2016.

2 Directive 2005/60/EC 26 October 2005 (page 1) on 'the prevention of the use of the financial system for the purpose of money laundering and terrorist financing', available from http://eur-lex.europa.eu/legal-content/EN/TXT/?uri=celex:32005L0060. Accessed 19 October 2015.

P.C. van Duyne, J.H. Harvey and L.Y. Gelemerova, *The Critical Handbook of Money Laundering*, https://doi.org/10.1057/978-1-137-52398-3_2

We do not discard these statements as merely 'opinions': whatever their validity, they are part of the literary discourse which must be included in our analysis. For this reason, it is important to carry out this literary search systematically through the discourse of both the official and academic literature.

2.2 The meaning and limitations of probing FATF reports

Our research into the 'official' documentation was approached much as one might complete a jigsaw puzzle in the absence of the picture on the box lid. Where some pieces were already locked together our task was made easier. But many others were randomly scattered in front of us without indication whether they even belonged to this set. Thus we had to 'wade' through many hundreds of documents and interrogate a wide number of websites in order to understand how the different documents related to each other, piecing together the jigsaw of rules, requirements and reports.

During the first reconnaissance we tried to keep the analysis of the official policy discourse separated from the outcomes of research. However, there is an inevitable cross-over between the two: laws, 'soft law' recommendations and regulations, all these are as much subject to academic interrogation and debate as any other topics (see for example, Baldwin and Cave, 1999; Kirkpatrick, 2006; Harvey, 2015).

Our predesigned methodology for the 'official' literature was one of documentary analysis[3] and by necessity was restricted to interrogating only what was available within the public domain. This prevents a more thorough probing and poking into the discussions that sat behind the 'public faces' of various institutions. And there are many public faces: the Reports of the FATF, the Statements of Plenary Meetings, the Mutual Evaluation Reports and other published documents on the anti-money laundering (AML) regime from the International Monetary Fund (IMF), World Bank (IBRD), United Nations (UN) and the Bank for International Settlements (BIS). Is there any documentation of how these reports and documents came about? For example, in the course of this project we made attempts to uncover the costs associated with maintaining the anti-money laundering regime. To that end we needed to operationalise the functioning of the relevant institutions (see Chapters 3, 5 and 8), in particular if specified in their annual financial statements. Through direct e-mails we asked for details, but the requests remained unanswered apart from one from the Caribbean FATF (CFATF) that merely pointed out

---

[3] Focused on an analysis of the written word, documentary analysis is a social science research method often used as a technique of triangulation. At a simple level it is a means of understanding the content of a document through deconstructing its meaning – both through what is written and how it is presented. Formally, the extraction of meaning from documents (Gardin, 1973).

that such information was confidential.[4] Much other interesting information remains likewise hidden behind the public face shrouded in silence. The FATF puts onto its website its annual reports, mutual evaluations alongside press reports summarising the outcome of its plenary meetings, but it is not possible to read about the discussions underlying the decision making as the recorded minutes are not in the public sphere. This implies that large stretches of information are not covered by our literature stock taking and analysis. So, we have to rely on official documents to which our primary question is: are these reliable and valid knowledge sources given that they are 'socially produced' (Ball, 2011)?

2.3 Official sources and their validity

Given the sheer volume of documents we had to draw a boundary around our enquiry for the sake of manageability. It made sense to focus, therefore, on those international institutions that were early promoters of the AML regime (principally the IMF, World Bank, OECD and the UN in addition to the FATF) and that also contributed to the flow of publications. Therefore, commencing with the FATF, declared by the G-7 Heads of State as an intergovernmental policy making body,[5] our documentary search followed something of an iterative process. We traced citations back to earlier publications (where correct referencing had been followed and enabled us to do this which was not always the case) and then moved onward through the documented processes and procedures by which the FATF enforces adherence to its rules and regulations, in particular the Mutual Evaluation Reports (MERs) which we discuss next. What kind of knowledge sources are these?

2.3.1 The Mutual Evaluation Reports

Despite the reservations expressed in the previous section, the FATF (the functioning of which is described in Chapters 3, 5 and 9) and its FATF-Style Regional Bodies (FSRBs, about which later) are profuse information disseminators. The FATF website has a long publication list concerning 'typologies' (an undefined concept) and 'specials' in which particular forms of laundering or risks are described: *e.g.* trade based laundering; the risks of new payment forms; the gold sector *etc.* These subjects are often picked up in the academic discourse and commented upon in scientific and professional publications.

---

4 The FATF, APG and GIABA have a financial statement in their annual report.

5 FATF 'who we are' available at: http://www.fatf-gafi.org/about/. Accessed 4 March 2016.

Of particular interest are the Mutual Evaluation Reports (MERs) concerning the state of compliance with the FATF Recommendations by countries across the world. These reports are the products of evaluation teams composed of, on average, five to six experts from different countries to the one being evaluated, the FATF office; and experts from the IMF, World Bank or Council of Europe. There are no fixed teams: for each evaluation of a country a team is composed anew. Based on documents and direct interviews the team gives an opinion – actually a judgment – on the state of compliance with the FATF Recommendations by the authorities and 'obliged institutions'[6] of the reviewed country. That opinion can be adopted by the Plenary of the FATF, which can lead to a 'Public Statement': severe warning (a kind of 'pillory' of non-co-operative countries with an appeal to other institutions to take measures against a deficient country); or a call for "Improving Global AML/CFT Compliance". For example: a compliment because of the "significant progress" made and a warning to correct the remaining deficiencies (which implies homework).

Clearly, a MER and FATF statements about country compliance are supposed to be important knowledge instruments. So, we investigated whether that is the case: how reliable are their observations and valid their conclusions? In order to properly understand the process followed in the evaluation and why some jurisdictions apparently warranted much more attention than others, we engaged in an extensive analysis of the content of the third round of the FATF mutual evaluations alongside those completed as part of the fourth-round evaluation up until the summer of 2016[7] – this is covered in Chapter 5.3. Details of the sample of countries selected for the purposes of this study are attached to this Chapter in Appendices 1 and 2.

For the third round reports, we started by looking at countries in chronological order of review commencing with Norway in 2005 (see also Van Duyne *et al.*, 2018a). The idea had been to analyse all reports but it quickly became clear that this was unfeasible due to the voluminous reports the teams produced: on average 216 pages with extremes to over 600 pages. Not only the evaluation of large countries (France's report reached 660 pages) produced voluminous reports: tiny countries could yield enormous reports as well, such as San Marino's MER of 303 pages. Hence, we continued until we had a completed sample of 69 country evaluation reports. We noted the number of

---

6 The term 'obliged institutions' refers to all entities and professions that have to comply with the FATF Recommendation: *e.g.* banks, exchange offices, car dealers and other traders in valuable commodities, legal service providers.

7 Countries that are in the fourth round under the latest Recommendations as at the date of our research and Van Duyne *et al.* (2018b): Armenia, Australia, Austria, Bangladesh, Belgium, Canada, Costa Rica, Cuba, Ethiopia, Fiji, Guatemala, Hungary, Honduras, Italy, Jamaica, Malaysia, Norway, Samoa, Serbia, Singapore, Spain, Sri Lanka, Sweden, Switzerland, Trinidad & Tobago, Tunisia, Uganda, Vanuatu, Zimbabwe.

evaluators, the time span of the on site visit and number of pages as standard data of the procedure. As 'content variables' we took the number of Suspicious Transaction Reports (STRs),[8] investigations, prosecutions, convictions and assets recovered, international legal aid and the budget/staff of the Financial Intelligence Unit (FIU).

It soon became apparent that a cross-country valid comparison was virtually impossible. Some countries mention the number of investigations, others cases solved or prosecutions only. Even if the same terms are used, one can never be sure that they have the same content or meaning. We also looked at the nature of the statistics, as we deem these essential for any policy making or comparison. We concluded that the statistical management was in many countries seriously lacking. Even if the evaluation team gave a 'compliant' judgment to this element, we often observed little more than crude frequencies, which sheds doubt on the quantitative skills of the evaluators. Many reports had no proper table names or did not even use the word 'table' for the representation of quantitative findings, impeding the search process. The word 'table' was usually reserved for the presentation of the compliance scores at the end of the MER. Concerning the cost-effectiveness evaluation only 22 reports mentioned a budget sum. For others there was reference to the budget but no numbers were disclosed. The rest of the reports (23 from our sample) remain completely silent on the costs of running the domestic AML regime, with little or no disclosure of staff numbers or budgetary resources.

The only area where we could find a semblance of consistent reporting (in the evaluators' perception) was in the compliance rating scale. According to the 2003 Methodology there are four compliance scoring intervals: Compliant (C); Largely Compliant (LC); Partially Compliant (PC); Non-Compliant (NC). In exceptional cases 'NA' (not applicable) can be inserted. The reader should, however, be warned: this is not a tidy 'Likert' five-point scale. Otherwise, there is no literature on scoring methodology (apart from FATF guidelines), nor on statistical processing of data *etc*. It is a somewhat amateurish checklist likely to lead to subjective scaling. For example: for Australia the rating of "*money laundering offence*" (criminalisation) is "largely compliant", but this goes with the annotation of "lack of prosecutions" and "not being effectively implemented". This criticism does not apply to the criminalisation item itself, but to law enforcement because so little has happened in terms of prosecution. However, this may not be due to the level of compliance but to the nature and volume of the criminal case input of which nothing is revealed. These external criterion variables appear to be systematically missing, something that will be discussed in Chapter 9.

Another area open to subjectivity concerned the compliance with the *sanction* recommendations, stipulating that these must be "dissuasive and propor-

[8] Referred to as 'Suspicious Activity Reports' in some jurisdictions.

tional". The factual implication of this wording is that the penal regime should be more *repressive*. Consequently, sentencing, which in the eyes of the evaluators was not perceived as sufficiently severe, was criticised and in consequence, the country received a lower rating. In this way the MERs could be more informative of the evaluators' perceptions and biases than of the state of affairs in the evaluated country. This is further elaborated in Chapter 9.

For these reasons the MERs were less of a knowledge source of the evaluated country than they could have been. But they shed a glimpse of light on the functioning of the FATF.[9]

An initial evaluation can lead to follow-up reports when the evaluated country shows deficiencies in compliance: a cycle of improvement reports from the reviewed country until the Plenary allows it to exit this procedure. We studied 18 out of 25 of such procedures, which lasted from 2006 until 2014. The reports, drawn up by the countries themselves were not checked by means of a fact-finding onsite visit but by way of a desk review for their plausibility. In five cases the reviewers expressed uncertainty about the real progress, but used their discretion to propose an exit from the procedure nonetheless. One may wonder whether this was worth so much effort.

The follow-up procedure can be quite a burden: three countries had to hand in more than ten follow-up reports before the Plenary was satisfied. The Caribbean FATF (CFATF) showed itself to be most assiduous in the post evaluation follow-up requirements that are placed upon individual countries requiring twice yearly reports. Despite this strictness, the Caribbean Plenary also took the curious decision, at its El Salvador Plenary in May 2015, that all Members who had not yet exited the fourth round follow-up process should simply be allowed do so by November 2015 – a kind of tidying up of the cupboard in anticipation of the next round. This means that at the time of the new (fourth) evaluation round all reporting countries were allowed to exit, irrespective of their state of compliance.

The sample of countries reviewed as part of the fourth round mostly comprised those that were reviewed during 2014 and 2015. Reflective of the updated Recommendations that guided the assessors during this round, our review also considered the National Risk Assessment and corruption.

The MERs are intended as valid sources of knowledge. As follows from the sections above, in fact they reflect a subjective judgment of the state of compliance with the Recommendations.[10] The instruments to reach such a judgment are subjective: within each evaluation and between evaluations there are no external yardsticks for proper measurement, while the underlying 'reality'

---

9 Halliday *et al.* (2014) also expressed their doubts concerning the quality of the evaluation reports: the contents as well as their expenses, estimated at, on average, $300,000 per country.

10 The FATF stipulated that the word recommendation should be written with a capital **R** for reasons of distinction. Also otherwise we followed the FATF use of capitals.

can only be observed by means of some crude statistics and mainly juridical and organisational descriptions. That is they inform whether and to what extent laws and supervisory structures are in place, but not how they work. We do not say that 'reality' is completely hidden, but that it remains difficult to identify it unambiguously through the text of the MER. The metaphor of the Greek philosopher Plato seems to apply: the human being is kept in a cave in front of a fire and learns about reality through the shadows of statues carried around that fire while names of these shadows are cited. Therefore, we are of the opinion that the MERs are not suitable for valid comparisons, though they can be used to evaluate the functioning of the FATF and FSRBs themselves. Naturally, that has never been the intention of the FATF.

2.3.2 The annual reports and strategic documents

This section is not intended to provide abstracts of the FATF-Annual Reports (FATF-ARs) and 'strategic' documents since 1991. That would require a full chapter with as many abstracts as there are such documents. Instead, we rather point at specific aspects of these 'knowledge' documents which the FATF itself thought important enough to put forward and if necessary we will give a short (critical) comment. (The topic was previously discussed in Van Duyne *et al.*, 2018b.)

a. The FATF annual reports (FATF-ARs)

Beginning with the 1991 report, each FATF-AR was read for content and structure. It was noted that the reports evolved over the years towards a more professional layout and format. Naturally an organisation's annual report is in the first place about its task fulfilment and (successful) deeds. In this case much attention is focused on the compliance with the 40 Recommendations and the ways the FATF handled this task: the state of implementation and compliance.

In addition, the FATF-ARs describe the FATF's activities related to spreading its 'good message' globally in two ways. In the first place as a kind of global 'conquest': each time welcoming either a new country or FSRB and mentioning "significant progress". In the second place it reports on extending its external relations or network with all organisations and institutions which have some relevance for financial aspects of crime: international financial institutions (*e.g.* IMF, World Bank, BIS), Interpol and Europol, Customs Cooperation Council, Commonwealth Secretariat *etc.*; each of these contributing to the international role of the FATF and strengthening its position. From year to year the FATF would point at "significant progress" being made or similar self-extolling phrases of its triumphal progress.

The FATF-ARs also provide information about monitoring money laundering trends and techniques, though one may wonder what purpose this serves, when the FATF-AR 1992-1993 (p. 16) mentions that "*It is rare for a genuinely new technique to be developed - and none were discernible in the monitoring exercise carried out in FATF-IV.*" For knowledgeable persons this is not a revelation, given the research literature (see UNODC, 2011). However, in the following sentence we read a reference to "*more sophisticated methods*", a somewhat frequent police mantra phrase with no content but with an important social and political persuasive function: sophisticated crime implies more threat and the requirement for more resources. This way of reporting should alert the reader that the FATF-ARs have other purposes than reflecting reality. Notwithstanding this, more typologies on methods of laundering and vulnerabilities of economic sectors (underground banking, securities market, gold, precious stones *etc.*) are described or referred to in most FATF-ARs. The typologies are presented as demonstration models, but having been made anonymous by removal of country names, they lack the necessary depth and precision to provide substantive educational value. This will be discussed in Chapter 5.[11]

In addition to this monitoring of types, trends or methods of laundering, whether or not labeled as a 'typology', there is also the recorded ongoing monitoring of the *compliance* of the member states represented by summaries (until the third round). The FATF-AR 2000-2001 mentions that the first and second round of mutual evaluations have undergone a total "in-depth" evaluation, though it remains unclear what that means: the evaluated source documents are not public while the evaluation appears to have been carried out by the FATF itself. For such an important exercise one would expect an external, independent evaluation much as an external auditor is required to sign off a company's annual report as being 'a true and fair reflection' of its affairs at that date. It took a further five years, in the third and fourth round of mutual evaluations, for the MERs to be put as a full document on the FATF website allowing the reader some material with which to check the statements concerning the rate of compliance of the evaluated countries.

Related to the compliance issue is the recurring subject of *non-cooperative states* (Non-Cooperative Countries and Territories: NCCTs). These are presented as the serious sinners against the AML regime, for example, by failing to have criminalised laundering, or having other serious shortcomings in legislation or implementation. These countries were, until 2006-2007, placed on a NCCT list with the implication that other compliant countries should be extra cautious in engaging in transactions or other relationships with them. As

---

[11] Reuter and Truman (2004) *Chasing Dirty Money: The Fight Against Money Laundering.* Chapter 3 provides a clear and accessible review of money laundering methods and markets.

a matter of fact, this is an international *sanction* of which the legal aspects have not been analysed and discussed, apart from by, for example, Goldbarsht and Michaelsen (2017) and Wechsler (2001). This subject returned in every FATF-AR until in 2007, the Plenary determined that all the NCCTs were 'delisted': mission completed (2006-2007 FATF-AR). Nevertheless, the Finance Ministers represented in the G20 were convinced that there were many more countries with "strategic deficiencies" and urged the FATF to continue its search of serious compliance weaknesses. At present these countries are mentioned in 'public statements' together with a serious warning about their 'deficiencies'. But essentially, this warning is an extension of the *sanction*s regime. What is of interest is that the documentation relating to these serious 'sinners' is not fully disclosed: whether the 'pillory' is deserved and based on a fair assessment and judgment (as the FATF claims) cannot, therefore, be independently determined. As a matter of fact, the FATF is investigator, judge and executioner at the same time, ignoring the basic rule of division of power (Goldbarsht and Michaelsen, 2017).

The FATF-ARs can also be informative about the uses of the *mandate* bestowed on the FATF, but such an openness is not a natural characteristic of the FATF. It is remarkable to observe that while only general references to the mandate are made in the FATF-ARs 1997-1998, the text of the 2004 mandate (extended for another eight years) was discussed within the text of the 2003-4 AR[12] and should have been fully presented in annex A of the FATF-AR. That was not the case: the mentioned annex appears not to exist or is not readily available. No link or other references were given. Only in 2012 was the full text of the G-20 mandate made public as a separate document.[13]

The FATF-AR 2003-2004 also demonstrates that it is important to "read between the lines": page 5, B. ("Review of the organisation of the work") and 'better understanding of problems' points at probable frictions between the FATF (Plenary), the preparation of documents, the organisation of working groups and the FSRBs. However, no content is disclosed. The same silence surrounds the interaction with the FSRBs in later annual reports: there are references to frictions (also observed by the IMF, 2011), but the reader is left to guess what it is all about. It does not evoke a very transparent impression.

From the FATF-AR 2004-2005 onward the annual reports are prefaced by a short introduction from the FATF President and the Executive Secretary. Naturally, these are encouraging texts. More important are the section on the *support services*, basically the secretariat, and a financial statement concerning the overall budget figures. At that time these amounted to 1,899,700: cur-

---

[12] FATF Annual report, 2003-4, 2 July, page 4, footnote 4 states: The full text of the mandate for the future of FATF can be found at Annex A. A copy of this Report is located on the FATF website at http://www.fatf-gafi.org/media/fatf/documents/reports/2003%202004%20ENG.pdf. Accessed 12 December 2017.

[13] Financial Action Task Force Mandate (2012-2020), 12 April 2012, Washington DC.

rency not indicated before the AR 2014-15 (sic). It allows the reader (guessing correctly whether he must calculate euros) to follow the (increasing) budget development of the FATF-office at the OECD premises across the years.[14]

As mentioned before, the FATF-ARs require reading between the lines as well as monitoring vanishing promises. For example, in the FATF-AR 2007-2008 (p. 20) we read: "*The FATF will also examine the available data to measure the impact of AML/CFT regimes on underlying criminal and terrorist activity, encouraging research into the effectiveness of its regime. It will examine the feasibility of implementing cost-benefit analysis across the field of AML/CFT policy.*" A firm and badly needed proposal of which subsequently nothing was heard. We may call it a 'strategic deficiency', this time on the side of the FATF. Most interestingly, it was allowed to be dropped under the table while nobody raised a question or pointed at the fact that the FATF specifically requests evaluated countries to provide proper statistics of the main AML aspects, a task that it had itself failed to perform.

A similar opaqueness can be observed in relation to the many working groups which the last FATF-AR presents in its organogram. That looks rock solid. However, we do not find any clear account of their structure, budget, staff composition, supervision, accountability to other bodies or other written facets of their functioning. For example, how does the very important International Cooperation and Review Group (ICRG) function? We read a few lines about the latter in the FATF-AR, to realises that it is an important and potentially powerful body, but further precision is absent. What about the other working groups? We return to these questions later in Chapter 5: this is a sufficient indication for the reader to interpret the FATF-ARs with caution realising that few questions will be answered.

While it is undeniable that the FATF-ARs are important knowledge source documents, they are basically 'accountability documents' to the Heads of States and the FATF ministers. As such, the annual reports may partly inform the public, but lack real transparency, one of the aims the FATF claims to have. It does not provide the information one needs or asks for, but just so much as the FATF deems sufficient to provide.

b. Strategic documents

Naturally the FATF does not only communicate through its annual reports and the annual series of typologies. There are also 'strategic issues' determining the AML-policy and which must be made public, if only because so many institutions are involved. However, there is no (digital) box with documents

---

[14] Since 1991, the OECD has provided office space and staff to the FATF in its Paris office building. Nevertheless, the FATF claims emphatically that it is independent of the OECD. However, its public documents are under the OECD shared copy rights.

with the name "strategic" on its lid. Searching with the word 'strategic' proved to be unfruitful: it produced only documents concerning 'strategic *deficiencies*' of countries, which we were not looking for. Hence, we combed through the whole FATF digital publication box and took out the documents that appeared to herald a change or the onset of a new policy.

The first strategic document, also the most debatable one, is the 'birth document' of the FATF: the first report on money laundering published in 1990. One may consider it outdated by now, but the basic tenets have not changed and are still accepted by all authorities, whether national or international, such as the United Nations, the IMF or the World Bank. Whether the content of the document had any intellectual level, proved to be irrelevant for its status: in the pre-twitter age it was the top 'followers' raising document. Indeed, the initiators were mighty and rich and attracted an audience of law enforcement and financial agencies eager to follow. Critical reflections on its content and methodology were few and far between (See for example, Van Duyne, 1994; Pieth, 1999), which did not seem to matter.

It is remarkable that on the basis of such a thin and superficial document, the FATF could expand the circumference of its power, without really issuing any new documents to discuss its course. Given the importance of this issue, the lack of underpinning documentation looks strange. Few have commented on this shortcoming: for instance, Van Duyne (1994); Pieth (1999); Levi and Osofsky (1995). For example, the FATF's fundamental decision in 1995-1996 'to go global' and arrogate the authority of a 'world inspectorate' would have been worthy of a separate document and discussion.

> In the FATF AR, 1995-1996, the FATF claimed that "*the FATF should develop a formal policy with regard to its relationship with non-members, a policy that assesses the progress being made in fighting money laundering by non-member countries.*" But then to enforce compliance the FATF should also be allowed to use sanctions against non-member and non-complying states: "*the FATF could decide to apply the procedures laid down in Recommendation 21 on a case-by-case basis, if there is evidence that a non-member has seriously failed to meet the international anti-money laundering standards*".

One could call this a quite fundamental issue: sovereignty and the claimed competence to sanction carried out by an informal body, this is an issue which is worthy of deep debate. That is not something the FATF waited for but instead applied Recommendation 21 (the 'blacklist' sanction) directly to the tiny island state of Seychelles (92,000 inhabitants). This act only received a short mention in the annual report and without raising questions, resistance or critical publications, it became a 'strategic fact'. This reminds the reader that important strategic decisions do not need a strategic document or facts and figures and also, that not all strategic documents lead to a strategic decision.

In fact, the publication of further strategic documents had to wait until 2007, when the FATF issued its first guidance on the *risk based approach.*[15] This was following the 2005 EU Directive that highlighted that resource allocation should be commensurate to risk. This was as such not an innovation: it was an approach borrowed from the insurance industry and widely followed within the banking industry. While there is nothing wrong about that, the reader will soon notice that the FATF-authors admit that they cannot provide a definition of risk for their approach. The FATF (2013a, pp. 7–8) attempted clarification by defining risk as 'a function of threat, vulnerability and consequences' without proper precision of these components.

These failures to define a core concept may be forgivable as risk has a statistical as well as a behavioural facet. However, neither were properly elaborated from the first document onward. For example we find no formal definition of 'likelihood', for any risk approach an essential concept. Of course, the basic perspective is clear: apply the resources against money laundering proportionally, with greatest emphasis on 'serious risk' getting the highest resources allocation, and 'low risk' situations getting fewer resources. That is not a revelation. However, the corollary is that with the extensive set of low risk cases, which cannot all be handled, one has to agree on a quota of 'slipping through': *e.g.* cash transactions below the median criminal proceeds (€ 5,000; Van Duyne and Soudijn, 2010).[16] Devoting expenses for chasing the many small fry must be weighed against the potential harm done to the international financial system by the large flow of small sums. The same thinking can be applied to countries as a whole: what is the meaning of the concept of a 'high risk country' when it is applied to economie like São Tomé and Príncipe (188,000 inhabitants; mainly agriculture focussed) or Vanuatu (272,000)? What are the saved costs by deprioritisation compared to the potential harm to the integrity of the global financial system of such territo-

[15] Following a meeting in December 2005 between the FATF and representatives of the banking and securities sectors, the FATF agreed to establish an Electronic Advisory Group (EAG) on the risk-based approach as part of its outreach to the private sector. The EAG, which is a subgroup of the FATF Working Group on Evaluations and Implementation (WGEI) was set up in March 2006. The work of the EAG followed a number of steps: responses to a questionnaire on risk-based approach were obtained, then the high level elements of a risk-based approach were identified and an outline of the EAG report was agreed. There then followed extensive consultation with both public and private sector members of the EAG, and a final report of the EAG to WGEI setting out draft guidance on the implementation of a risk based approach was provided in April 2007. After further international consultation with both public and private sectors, this Guidance Paper was adopted by the FATF at its June 2007 Plenary. This was the first time the FATF developed guidance using a public-private sector partnership approach. (See Guidance on the risk-based approach to combating money laundering and terrorist financing, FATF, 2007.)

[16] Median is the midpoint of a frequency distribution and differs from the arithmetic mean which easily influences by a few extreme values. *E.g.*, the 10% highest earners may pull the average significantly upwards.

ries? We think these questions are of material interest and should be addressed to give the risk concept a shape and profile before launching a risk-based project with a lot of noise.

The development of the risk-based strategy did not go that way. In the strategic documents hardly any attention is paid to these formal aspects of risk. The documents are the following:

a. *Guidance on the risk-based approach to combating money laundering and terrorist financing; High level principles and procedures* (2007);
b. *Money laundering & terrorist financing; Risk assessment strategies* (2008); and
c. the *FATF guidance; National money laundering and terrorist financing risk assessment* (2013).

However, the last document provides summarised examples of risk approaches in Austria, Switzerland and the USA that show a *qualitative* risk based approach. The examples look well thought through and worthy of following. However, no 'zero situation' and no outcomes were provided, nor a potential balancing of costs and harm causally attributable to money laundering. It does not look helpful to produce impressive matrices of a variety of threat factors without outcomes and results: this is not a substitute for the absent presentation of a real-life working system. Neither does a list of six pages of 'threat factors' bring any clarity.[17] For a risk-based approach the missing specification of realised harm (frequency and specified content) remains *the* essential flaw which is not compensated by again invoking the mantra-like drone of 'undermining the integrity of the financial system'.

Nevertheless, the documents of the risk-based approach were followed by a flow of additional documents giving guidance to national authorities, financial institutions and the non-financial sector. More important, these strategic documents found their partial translation in Recommendation 1, requiring countries to "identify, assess, and *understand* the money laundering *etc.* risks", adding a 'mental' element, with all the attached subjectivity, to the already uncertain content of these documents (Italic added by the authors).

In the summer of 2017, the European Commission issued a strategic document on the risk-based approach.[18] As a matter of fact, the Commission did

[17] The report's 'empirical' foundation consists of the research of Unger (2006). Notably, in that research we observe inconsistencies in regard to the ML definition and its application. It also appears to have relied on flawed statistics and lack of solid evidence as was challenged by Reuter (2013) and Van Duyne *et al.*, 2018a.

[18] Report from the Commission to the European Parliament and the Council: on the assessment of the risks of money laundering and terrorist financing affecting the internal market and relating to cross-border activities. Brussels, 26 July 2017.

not reveal any new insights but simply went ahead and did it all over again. It confirmed that many regulations did not work satisfactorily.

The last document to which we attribute strategic importance concerns the place of the FATF in its global network: *The High-level principles and objectives for FATF and FATF-style regional bodies,* October 2012. This is an important document because it makes clear that the FATF "*is the only standard-setting body and the guardian and arbiter of the application of its standard*", with which the relationship to the FSRBs is determined. The FSRBs are "free standing organisations" with no hierarchical relationship to the FATF. However, it is only the FATF which recognises an FSRB as such. Ergo, that can only occur of those FSRBs which have endorsed the FATF's work, Recommendations, tenets and principles. Both FATF and FSRBs are "*part of a larger whole*" and both protect the "*FATF brand*". Though this sounds very reassuring, the fact remains that the decision making power of the FATF rests with the Plenary, the ultimate summit of power. Summarised: "There is no FATF but the FATF and the Plenary is its voice". For further elaboration see Chapter 5.

2.4 The academic literature and the march of the economists

Review of the official, policy making literature was but one area of knowledge collection and one that we considered lacking in objectivity. Official publications by their nature are socially and politically constructed by their authors. To truly understand the subject, it was necessary to execute an integrated stock taking: One that provides an accumulation of knowledge capturing the 'mental history' of money laundering and not simply create a heap of texts without a narrative thread of enquiry.

We have ourselves researched and contributed to the literature and thus come to our enquiry equipped with considerable collective knowledge but inevitably with in-built biases and our own 'gaps' of knowledge. For this book, however, it was necessary to cast our net far wider than we had previously done in order to understand how academics had written about the topic since its appearance in the 1980s, and what the focus of their work had been. This concerns the major themes that were being explored, by what methods, whether they were responding to the evolving regulation and whether articles were making theoretical or empirical contributions. Hence, our initial decision to follow a structured review of the literature was later enhanced by a much wider interrogation of the academic literature base.

The final scope of the search described below produced an extracted database of 364 references. As noted in Chapter 1, most of the publications are either explanatory (laws and regulations) or 'confirmative' of the policy making positions. The confirmative publications (see for example Savona, 1997b;

Tanzi, 1996; Arnone and Borlini, 2010) rather uncritically endorse or recycle official views and provide various justifications for the global anti-laundering policy. Economists have applied both macro and micro approaches to money laundering, contributing studies aimed as measurements of the size and scale as well as models designed to explain and predict the overall level of laundering activity. The economists' models, which provide potentially powerful means to prove or disprove the scale of the threat, are discussed in Chapter 7. The reader is invited to ponder on the extent to which they truly illuminate dark financial corners through providing data that are intended to withstand rigorous scrutiny, or merely provide retrospective rationalisations leaving these corners in the dark.

The explanatory publications spell out what is meant by the various concepts and the anti-money laundering regime in terms of laws and regulations. If there are any empirical references, they most often concern recycled 'facts' drawn from the FATF reports, the UN or other governmental publications. Of course, such publications can be useful, but whether they should be rated as a 'pool of knowledge' has yet to be determined. At least they tell us something about the mainstream insights.

Regulatory economists have considered the costs and benefits to the regulated sector with a particular focus on compliance. A similar impact approach emerges from the field of legal studies where scholars have provided analyses of normative legal frameworks. Thus, we can organise the literature as arising from law, criminology, economics and regulation while acknowledging that a number of researchers in the field stray beyond their disciplinary bounds drawing on literature from multiple disciplines. Outside this mainstream and challenging its discourse emerge several scholars aligned to what can be labelled the 'critical school' (see for example: Van Duyne, 1994; Van Duyne and De Miranda, 1999; Pieth, 1999; Alldridge, 2003; Harvey, 2005; Sharman, 2008; Hulsse, 2008; Levi and Reuter, 2006; Verhage, 2009; Gelemerova, 2009 and 2011).

2.5 The nature of enquiry: Review and protocol development

Traditional literature reviews are referred to as being 'narrative' to distinguish them from structured or systematic reviews.[19] Our approach incorporated both as set out below. Steps 1 to 3 were followed for the *structured* review and for the *narrative* review these steps were repeated and added to with steps 4 and 5. The systematic enquiry focused on answering the question "how is

[19] Systematic reviews are common in science disciplines and provide a way in which to provide a comprehensive review of existing literature in relation to a specific question.

money laundering theorised within the literature?" This produced a narrow set of papers (discussed below). These were subsequently interrogated and the themes that emerged provided the organisational structure to the second stage, the broader narrative literature search that resulted in our final data base of peer reviewed publications. We covered published work contained in academic journals; academic papers published on the web in open access sources; and books and book chapters (where accessible either via the library or held in our possession). We considered work produced globally but largely published in English.[20] In total, our study utilised the following sources:

1. Data bases accessed through Northumbria University library: Emerald Insight; Scopus (Elsevier); Science Direct (Elsevier); the British Humanities Index (ProQuest); Web of Science (Thomson Reuters); Ebscohost; IEEE Xplore; JISC Journal Archives; JSTOR Collections; Oxford Journals Archive; Westlaw UK; Wiley Online; and Zetoc. In addition, one open access base was searched: the Social Science Research Network;
2. Searches of on-line library catalogues: Northumbria University;
3. Searches of any prior published reviews of the literature;[21]
4. Searches of bibliographies contained in all sourced documents selected as eligible for review;
5. Searches of our own hard copy holdings of journals, published manuscripts and books.

Results from this are presented later in the chapter.

2.6 The initial systematic scoping of relevant literature

In general, studies within the field of money laundering tended to use *ad hoc* narrative literature reviews, whereby the selection of content is largely determined by the discretion and interests of the individual author. Given our earlier declared experience-induced bias, our systematic review was undertaken as a means to minimise our own influence over the selection and interrogation of academic outputs (Hidalgo Lander *et al.*, 2011). Such a protocol driven approach to literature enables a disciplined line of enquiry (Armitage and Keeble-Allen, 2008), that often challenges the established view (Briner and Denyer, 2012) and facilitates a mapping out of the various quantitative and qualitative contributions from a range of disciplines and methodologies. A final advantage of a structured approach is that it has been widely

[20] Two of the authors were able to review and include for the narrative part papers published in other European languages.

[21] Using search strings: 'money laundering' OR 'anti-money laundering' AND 'systematic review' OR 'structured review' (in the article title, abstract and key words).

recognised as a means of providing a reliable research evidence-driven base for policy decision making (Briner and Denyer, 2012; Armitage and Keeble-Allen, 2008; and Tranfield *et al.*, 2003).

2.6.1 Searching for existing reviews of money laundering literature

Searching the five major databases[22] for systematic literature reviews in money laundering produced no results. It was thus inferred that either no prior structured reviews have been undertaken at the time of enquiry, or that the title, abstract and/or key words did not include refer to this method of systematic review. However, we did locate some items of relevance.

Firstly, a paper by Kruisbergen *et al.* (2015a) organises empirical literature on money laundering into three categories: one looking at measurement;[23] the second focusing on response to laundering[24] and the third on how offenders spend their money to conceal its origin.[25] It was only papers in this final category (15 in total) that formed the basis of their review, although there was no explanation on how they had been selected in any methodical manner other than to note it to be non-exhaustive.

Secondly, and held in the possession of one of the authors was a report that references a systematic literature report on "*the effects of money laundering*".[26] This was informative although the authors of this chapter did not describe in detail the search protocol followed: just the sources they consulted which were very much wider than purely academic literature. Frustratingly it is still not precisely clear which articles comprised their final list (one imagines duplicates had to be removed *etc.*) as they merely state that the 'useful' articles appear in the bibliography. They stated (pp. 81–82) that they examined the following resources:

1. The literature in a 'pre-study' carried out by the Ministry of Finance (not clear of what this comprised).
2. The websites of 'international organisations involved in the topic: the IMF, the World Bank, the OECD' and the FATF.

[22] Emerald insight, Scopus, Science Direct, British Humanities Index ProQuest and IEEE Xplore.

[23] Citing: Schneider, 2010; Barone and Masciandaro, 2011; Malm and Bichler, 2013.

[24] Referring to a review contained in Levi and Reuter 2006, p. 359 in support.

[25] Referring to the following sources: Malm and Bichler, 2013; Van Duyne and Levi, 2005; Levi and Reuter, 2006, p. 359; Suendorf, 2001, p. 9; Verhage, 2011, p. 172; Van Duyne, 2003, pp. 68–69; Fernández Steinko, 2012, p. 909; and Levi, 2012.

[26] Reported as chapter 4 in B. Unger, M. Siegel, J. Ferwerda, W. de Kruijf, M. Busuioic, K. Wokke, and G. Rawlings, G (2006) *The Amounts and the Effects of Money Laundering*, Report for the Ministry of Finance, Utrecht School of Economics, 16 February 2006; Fernández Steinko, 2012.

3. Econlit, an electronic bibliography hosted with EbscoHost but not one that we had access to – they employed the search term 'money laundering' returning 56 hits.
4. The library of Utrecht University, to search for books about the effects of money laundering where their search produced 30 hits when searching for the term 'witwassen' ('white-washing') and 23 hits for searching for the term 'money laundering'.
5. The Dutch central catalogue (NNC) which covers a wider range of Dutch libraries, using their terms 'witwassen' (119 hits) and 'money laundering' (82 hits)
6. The emerald published Journal of Money Laundering Control and Journal of Financial Crime for 'relevant articles dealing with economic effects', the number located was not disclosed.

2.6.2 Scoping search across the money laundering landscape

As commented already, we had in our possession a large number of books, articles and papers that we had collected over the course of our own writing. It was important, therefore, to see what was, in addition, published beyond these self-determined boundaries. We commenced our study in September 2014 with a full search using the high-level search terms 'money laundering' and 'anti-money laundering' across 13 identified subscriber databases (all accessed from the University of Northumbria NORA system)[27] plus one open access site.[28] In addition, a further search took place of the Northumbria University electronic catalogue (for books). The results of this review are included in Appendix 1 to this chapter. It was possible to carry out some initial sorting within the databases themselves and from this it was apparent that there are only a very limited number of publications on the subject prior to 1990.

Given the number of citations that were returned (6,756), we needed a more managed investigation of the sources. Inevitably a great deal of time was invested in simply looking through the citations and refining the filters that could be used. This allowed for the exclusion of articles without full text access and (at this stage), inclusion of those written in English and inclusion only of articles from scholarly publication, e-books, books and book chapters. Those selected were exported into the bibliographic software package EndNote X7.[29]

---

[27] NORA is the search engine accessed via the Library that uses new 'web-scale discovery' technology and is powered by the Serials Solutions Summon software.

[28] We had initially included Google Scholar as an open access database and this returned 2,500 citations. A decision was made at an early stage not to include this source as there was limited access to full versions of papers as well as overlap with the other databases where we had full access.

[29] Endnote X7 is a commercial package from Thompson Reuters used for managing references.

One of the benefits of using Endnote was that it enables the creation of 'smart groups' whereby the database can automatically return citations held within it against pre-specified criteria (see discussion below on themes).

The literature reviewed in Chapters 6, 7 and 8 present a reconnaissance of academic writing over the period from the 1980s to 2014. We acknowledge that while trying to include works from as wide a range as possible, for pure manageability it proved necessary to be selective. For example, a number of papers from the *American Criminal Law Review* published in the 1990s provided guidance for interpretations of the money laundering offences set out in the US criminal legal code. These papers followed a standard structure with similar content, discussion and conclusions. It was decided to include only a randomly selected sample of these papers. This sampling approach was also employed where a number of papers dealt with country specific issues or particular subject studies: for example, it was used for papers focused on particular methods of laundering such as the gaming sector; or particular criminal activities, for example cybercrime; or that dealt with the computing algorithms used to develop transaction monitoring software. Finally, there were papers that met our search terms but proved not to be relevant. An example was an article 'green money laundering' (Glaser, 2014[30]) dealing with sustainable methods of cleaning bank notes to increase their time in circulation and reduce replacement costs. Once citations had been exported to Endnote we removed duplications and those without full-text access.

We followed the reference sections of the included articles to pick up any missing literature and to improve the effectiveness of our search strategy by including references considered important by our peers. We included our own work when relevant to the identified themes. We also reviewed bibliographic lists obtained from books and papers in our possession and from official World Bank/IMF reports that included money laundering 'literature reviews'. By the end of the process which was concluded in the summer of 2015, we had a database of 364 outputs.[31]

2.6.3 Search terms definition for the structured review

A structured review of the literature is designed to answer a specific question. Employing the simple approach set out in Hidalgo Landa *et al.* (2011), we wanted to answer the question "*how is money laundering theorised within the literature?*" We started with how it was defined.

---

[30] J. Glaser (2014) 'Green money laundering' *Clean Technologies and Environment* Policy Vol 16 Iss 4 pp. 675–680.

[31] This collection included the outputs of the search described below in the structured review.

As will be discussed in some detail in Chapter 4, the legal definitions largely agree that laundering encompasses "*the conversion or transfer of property, knowing that such property is proceeds, for the purpose of concealing or disguising the illicit origin etc.*" A review of the language of the legal definitions produced a search string appropriate for further enquiry to see how others had approached the topic. We also consulted the semantic analysis of 18 definitions of (money) laundering by Unger *et al.*, (2006; ch. 1) and by Busuioc (in Unger, 2007, ch. 2). This enabled us to identify key words usually associated with the activity of laundering.

A subgroup of theoretical papers returned from all the search databases was established within EndNote. We utilised a Boolean-operator[32] query format to combine search strings that could be used in conjunction with the basic root string "money laundering" whereby the article title had to contain all of '*money laundering*' AND '*theory*' OR '*Definition*'. To this we added a second review whereby the *title* contained '*money laundering*' AND '*theory*' OR '*definition*' appeared in the article abstract and/or content. This gave us a total of 167 citations that had a main label 'money laundering' and a sub-label 'theory' or 'definition'.[33] A review of the abstracts enabled us to remove a significant number of duplicates (the same paper on multiple databases), those that were non-accessible and those that despite inclusion of the word 'theory' in the title, abstract or content, proved (as discussed below) to be focused on matters other than money laundering. This left us with a far smaller list of 21 useable papers as listed in Table 2.1 below.

2.7 Structured review output and theme development

We make no comment on whether these were the 'right' papers to interrogate for the themes: they were the ones that emerged having matched our search criteria and thus were the ones read in detail at this stage. They allowed us to interrogate what is and has been of concern to these writers and to identify the broad themes that were used to interrogate and organise our larger database.

As can be seen from the titles of the articles in the table above, these papers do not provide a theoretical explanation of money laundering. Rather, the authors apply theories and theoretical frameworks that had been developed in the 'root disciplines' of legal studies, economics, criminology, and regulatory theory. These have been used to explain, measure or model the phenomenon of money laundering or to suggest ways in which money laundering could be

[32] Boolean Searching is a technique that combines concepts/key words by using the operators AND, OR or NOT to provide more focused results.

[33] The searches produced the following citations: Emerald 8; Scopus 8; Science Direct 0; Ebscohost 9; Oxford Journals Archive 1; Zetoc 7; Westlaw 4; JISC 130.

Table 2.1 The 21 papers that were interrogated to generate further research themes

Author (year)	Title	Journal	Key Words (where supplied)
Alldridge, P. (2002)	"Moral Limits of the Crime of Money Laundering."	Buff. Crim. L. Rev	N/A
Araujo, R. (2008).	"Assessing the efficiency of the anti-money laundering regulation: an incentive-based approach."	Journal of Money Laundering Control	Money Laundering Regulation
Araujo, R. (2010).	"An evolutionary game theory approach to combat money laundering."	Journal of Money Laundering Control	Game theory, money laundering
Argentiero, A., M. Bagella, and F. Busato (2008)	"Money laundering in a two-sector model: using theory for measurement"	European Journal of Law and Economics	Money laundering, Two-sector dynamic general equilibrium model Illegal economy
Arnone, M. and L. Borlini (2010)*	"International anti-money laundering programs. Empirical assessment and issues in criminal regulation"	Journal of Money Laundering Control	Money laundering, Crimes, Regulation
Barone R. and D. Masciandaro (2011)	"Organized crime, money laundering and legal economy: theory and simulations"	European Journal of Law and Economics	Organized crime Money laundering Shadow economy
Coleman, J. (1992)	"Crime and Money: Motivation and Opportunity in a Monetarized Economy"	American Behavioural Scientist	N/A
Gordon, J. (1995)	"Prosecutors Who Seize Too Much and the Theories They Love: Money Laundering, Facilitation, and Forfeiture Notes"	Duke Law Journal	N/A
Otusanya, O. *et al.* (2011)	"The role of financial intermediaries in elite money laundering practices."	Journal of Money Laundering Control	Nigeria, Money laundering, Intermediaries, Financial intermediaries, Lawyers, Local banks,
Otusanya, O and Lauwo, S (2012)	"The role of offshore financial centres in elite money laundering practices: evidence from Nigeria"	Journal of Money Laundering Control	Nigeria, Money laundering, Developing countries, Globalization, Offshore financial centre, Elite
McCarthy, K., *et al.* (2015)	"Modelling the money launderer: Micro theoretical arguments on anti-money laundering policy."	International Review of Law and Economics	Money laundering Bargaining Deterrence

(*continued*)

Table 2.1 (continued)

Author (year)	Title	Journal	Key Words (where supplied)
Nardo, M. (2008)	"Building synergies between theory and practice"	Journal of Financial Crime	Finance, Crimes, Modelling, Money laundering
Naylor, R. (2003).	"Towards a general theory of profit-driven crimes."	British Journal of Criminology	N/A
Nichols, L. (1997)	"Social problems as landmark narratives: Bank of Boston, mass media and 'money laundering'"	Social Problems	N/A
Pellegrina, L., and D. Masciandaro (2008).	"The Risk Based Approach in the New European Anti-Money Laundering Legislation: A Law and Economics View."	Paolo Baffi Centre Research Paper	Money Laundering, Regulation, Risk Based Approach, EU Third Money Laundering
Walker J and B. Unger (2009)	Measuring Global Money Laundering: The Walker Gravity Model.	Review of Law & Economics	N/A
Schneider, F. and U. Windischbauer (2008).	"Money laundering: some facts."	European Journal of Law and Economics	Money laundering Quantification Estimation
Takáts, E. (2011)	"A theory of 'crying wolf': the economics of money laundering enforcement."	The journal of law, economics, & organization	N/A
Taylor, I. (1992)	"The international drug trade and money-laundering: Border controls and other issues."	European Sociological Review	N/A
Waris, A. and L. Abdul Latif (2014).	"The effect of tax amnesty on anti-money laundering in Bangladesh."	Journal of Money Laundering Control	Bangladesh, Money laundering, Tax amnesty, Tax
Young, M. (2013).	"The exploitation of offshore financial centres: Banking confidentiality and money laundering."	Journal of Money Laundering Control	Money laundering, Banking confidentiality, Banking secrecy, Offshore financial centres, Confiscation, Money, Banking

Source: the authors.

*This paper was included as although it included the word 'empirical' in the title, the content reviewed theoretical contributions from an extensive range of papers.

controlled, managed or reduced. It might be concluded that despite extensive academic interest in the subject (evident from our initial broad literature sweep) we have yet to witness the advances to knowledge in terms of theory building in which a proper operationalisation and hypothesis testing have a place.

This finding may be due to the fact that academics writing on the subject do so very much from the perspectives of their existing disciplines. So, for example, studies from legal scholars have, amongst others, contributed ideas about the scope and reach of the law, differences in jurisdictional approaches and proportionality. Macro-economists have written about ways of measuring and hence modelling the volume of laundering with the aim of determining the effectiveness of countermeasures or their effects on the economy. Micro-economists have focused on ways of ensuring compliance by the regulated sector. Finally, criminologists have considered how to ensure the criminal framework can be used as a deterrent. We rather reluctantly conclude that, essentially, there is no single narrative thread, let alone a theory.

2.7.1 Emergent themes and the narrative in literature review

In the absence of a theory of money laundering, the examined papers cover a range of topics pertinent to the subject of money laundering. Therefore, we undertook a principal subject analysis of their content. Each paper was read and the most obvious topics were identified. We do not claim this produced an exhaustive list of all their content, as we were simply identifying areas in our database. We further recognised the influence of our prior knowledge and interest so that, when scanning through an article, certain words or phrases could have been accorded greater significance. The specific topics were then combined into the broader and more general themes labelled below. Inevitably, we followed an iterative process whereby earlier papers were revisited for cross-referencing as new terms emerged from later papers, employing where possible the 'find' functionality within PDF files (Table 2.2).

2.7.2 Sorting our database

These eleven areas were then used to create smart groups within the Endnote Database with which to organise that literature (364 references) for discussion later in the book. Table 2.3 shows the number of references classified by making use of the wider search terms taken from Appendix 2. By way of example: 'Attractiveness of countries to criminals' combined *'money laundering' AND corrupt* OR lax OR conflict OR secrecy;* Macroeconomic combined *'money laundering' AND macro OR gravity OR dynamic OR equilibrium OR multiplier OR measure.*

Table 2.2 The 'themes' covered in the 21 papers

Theme	Author
Definitions	Arnone and Borlini (2010); Gordon (1995); McCarthy *et al.* (2015); Naylor (2003)*; Schneider and Windischbauer (2008); Waris and Abdul Latif (2014).
International standards	Arnone and Borlini (2010); Schneider and Windischbauer (2008).
Impact on economy	Alldridge (2002); Arnone and Borlini (2010); Araujo (2010); Coleman (1992); McCarthy *et al.* (2015); Otusanya *et al.* (2011); Schneider and Windischbauer (2008).
Impact of globalisation	Alldridge (2002); Arnone and Borlini (2010); Gordon (1995); Nardo (2008); Otusanya *et al.* (2011); Waris and Abdul Latif (2014); Young (2013).
Attractiveness of countries to criminals	Alldridge (2002); Arnone and Borlini (2010); Araujo (2008); Araujo (2010); Barone and Masciandaro (2011); Otusanya *et al.* (2011); Otusanya and Lauwo (2012); Young (2013).
Predicate Offences	Alldridge (2002); Arnone and Borlini (2010); Coleman (1992); Naylor (2003); Pellegrina and Masciandaro (2008); Taylor (1992).
Deterrent effect of increasing costs of money laundering	Arnone and Borlini (2010); McCarthy *et al.* (2015); Nardo (2008).
Microeconomic models	Alldridge (2002); Araujo (2008); Araujo (2010); Arnone and Borlini (2010); McCarthy *et al.* (2015); Pellegrina and Masciandaro (2008); Takáts (2011)
Macroeconomic models	Argentiero, Bagella, and Busato (2008); Arnone and Borlini (2010); Barone and Masciandaro (2011); McCarthey *et al.* (2014); Pellegrina and Masciandaro (2008); Schneider and Windischbauer (2008); Walker and Unger (2009).
Efficiency of regulation and impact on regulated sector	Arnone and Borlini (2010); Araujo (2008); Araujo (2010); McCarthey *et al.* (2014); Nardo (2008); Pellegrina and Masciandaro (2008); Takáts (2011).
Moral perspective	Alldridge (2002); Nichols (1997); Otusanya *et al.* (2011); Otusanya and Lauwo (2012); Taylor (1992).

Source: the authors.

*Naylor's definition is with regard to the classification of money laundering as a secondary offence. Refer to Appendix 4 for the list broken down by topics. Note that each paper can appear multiple times where they addressed multiple themes.

As these groupings contained quite high numbers of papers, especially in relation to regulation, a decision was taken to split the search terms down into more specific areas. By way of example: we wanted to understand more about the 143 references to "*efficiency of regulation and impact on the regulated sector*". Given that regulations are rules which have to be adhered to, we searched specifically for those dealing with compliance as a separate issue, thereby refining the search.

The broad phrase "*international standards*" was enhanced by the addition of 'effectiveness' of AML. Similarly, rather than looking at either micro or macroeconomic models it was useful to be able to see what had been written on 'measurement', as well as being able to investigate the precise content of papers purporting to contain 'models'. At this stage three final themes emerged. The

Table 2.3 Proportion of themes within papers*

Theme	Number of references containing search term	Proportion %
Definition	21	3.9
International standards	37	6.9
Impact on economy	33	6.1
Impact of globalisation	56	10.4
Attractiveness of countries to criminals	48	8.9
Predicate Offences	38	7.1
Deterrent effect of increasing costs of money laundering	35	6.5
Microeconomic models	57	10.6
Macroeconomic models	60	11.2
Efficiency of regulation and impact on regulated sector	143	26.6
Moral perspective	9	1.7

Source: the authors.

*As described above, smart groups were created through combination of search terms, *e.g.* 'money laundering AND macro', so references can appear in more than one category.

Table 2.4 Smart groups*

Money Laundering Smart Group Title	Number of articles containing search term
Corruption	23
Compliance	45
Effectiveness	71
Measurement	41
Models	45
Regulation	129
Risk	44
Terrorism	51
Information systems	34
Theory	9
Typologies	5
Western countries	31

Source: the authors.

*Smart groups were created through combination of search terms, such as 'money laundering AND model', references can deal with more than one theme and thus appear multiple times.

first of these, corruption, came from "*attractiveness to criminals*". Risk and terrorism were distinct areas covered in relation to international standards (Table 2.4).

At the end of this process, none of our total of 364 references remained 'unallocated' to one of these 'smart groups'. It is interesting to note that the majority of papers fell into the field of regulation. Given the impact of the FATF on individual countries, many academics have focused their research on the rules and procedures that were to be followed. The group 'Western countries' picked up papers written from the view point of the USA or Europe. We gleaned very little on the subject of theory underpinning money laundering.

Table 2.5 References by year of publication

Year	Number of articles	Percentage of total
Pre 1980	0	
1980–1989	21	5.8
1990–1995	14	3.8
1996–2000	42	11.5
2001–2005	85	23.3
2006–2010	122	33.5
2010–2014	80	22.0
Total	364	

Source: the authors.

We were also interested in the time distribution of publication. Having noted that we found nothing published by academics on the subject of money laundering prior to 1980, it is interesting to note the jump in outputs during the second half of the 1990s and the next decade. Our database was constructed at the end of 2014 with this analysis concluded by the summer of the following year but if one went through the exercise again today there would be further outputs during 2015 and 2016 that might suggest a continuation of the trend in publishing in the field (Table 2.5).[34]

2.8 Conclusion

Surveying our search, we have put together much material on which we will draw in the coming chapters. This does not imply that we will not deviate from this 'literature lining up': as with money laundering, many literary fishes (and not only the small ones) may have slipped through the net because they just did not have the right search terms. Nor will we feel impelled to use all the material we fished up: we want to let the money laundering narrative evolve and speak for itself. In this process the literature helps but does not determine the story. Naturally, that story is multi-dimensional and many past and present-day researchers are part of it. Nevertheless, it is the laundering narrative which in the end must come to the fore. We will remove, as much as possible, the 'silt' and deposits from the alarmist and 'world improvement' authors. Since the 2008 credit crisis (never viewed from a laundering perspective) or Libor scandal, we know that one needs more than a collection of bad guys dragging around sacks of crime-money to make the financial system shake. For such an effect one needs dishonest bankers and failing systems and inadequate controls. That sounds like a proper moderation, but it will not be the substance of our story. We will unfold the story as a policy making devel-

[34] It should be noted that as our writing has evolved and earlier drafts of the book have been revisited we have added to the main points of discussion using more recent publications and outputs.

opment, a legal or criminal law subject, a criminal control matter and in the end, the economy with the shadowy 'general victim' being brought to the fore as a kind of all-purpose but unprovable default argument. We believe we offer a unique stocktaking on the subject in a single tome. We are not certain whether we can clear all the fog, but will proceed until we have a clear outlook ourselves.

3

Historical overview

3.1 Introduction

The fight against crime-money as we know it today has a history of nearly half a Century, or even longer if we include the cases against the pre-World War II American gangsters, who were also tackled financially, such as Al Capone. We will only lightly touch on this 'pre-history'. The fight against crime money obtained a more recognisable contour after the first relevant legislation in 1970 – the US Bank Secrecy Act – after which the policy needed another 15 years to unfold and subsequently to 'ripen'. To appreciate the present 'fruits' of policy making and legislation we think it appropriate to look back in history.

3.2 The first steps of the crime money approach

The 'follow the money' adage has a modern sound, but its origin has long roots. Our short tour back in history enables the reader to realise that many facets of the anti-laundering policy are not revolutionary. Either they were already present in the 50 years prior to the onset of the anti-money laundering policy or they developed along gradual lines.

In this context it is customary to refer to the conviction of the Chicago gangster boss Al Capone in 1931, who could only be convicted of tax fraud.[1] This

---

[1] CRIME: Who Wouldn't Be Worried? Monday, 19 October 1931, Time magazine archives, available at: http://content.time.com/time/subscriber/article/0,33009,742429,00.html. Accessed 6 February 2016.

P.C. van Duyne, J.H. Harvey and L.Y. Gelemerova, *The Critical Handbook of Money Laundering*, https://doi.org/10.1057/978-1-137-52398-3_3

reference is correct, though it was not so much a follow-the-money-investigation which brought this infamous lawbreaker down. It was the comparison between the expenses for his lavish lifestyle and the simple observation that he never submitted any tax returns which brought his downfall, though he was 'linked' to gambling operations. This approach had its precedent: the US Supreme Court ruled in 1927 (*US vs. Sulivan*), that illegal earnings should be subject to taxation. Four years later, Capone became the first well-known wealthy criminal who was convicted of tax evasion because of his proven illegal earnings for which he paid no tax. Other fellow criminals followed (Abadinsky, 1994; pp. 188–190; 442) by being investigated on the basis of the same net-worth method.

Although this approach was fruitful, there are no indications from the literature that it was elaborated, extended or systematised before or after the Second World War. In contrast to this lack of attention there was much interest in organised crime in the 1950s and during the decades that followed. Beginning with the Kefauver Crime Committee (1950), the US witnessed an array of Committees and Commissions on organised crime, but we find little focus on addressing high-level (organised) 'criminal earners' from a financial perspective. That does not mean that there was no interest in 'shady finances'. As a matter of fact, in a piecemeal way the US administration and courts extended the legal instruments against criminal earnings. Stessens (2000, p. 96) calls these the "first generation anti-laundering instruments". A powerful legal concept was the "conspiracy to defraud the IRS". This legal construction was successfully applied in a complicated tax fraud case (the 'Klein conspiracy') in 1957.[2]

Of course, the legal instrument of conspiracy is by its nature limited in its effectiveness because of a shared intent. This is difficult to prove when the handling of crime-money is silently condoned (there were 'no questions asked') by financial service providers, such as the banks. Such condoning appeared to be more or less the daily financial practice in the 1950s and 1960s: the outflow of (hot) money to the tax havens surrounding the USA continued unabated. This financial mobility had various sources. There was a steady flow of (cash) money leaving the country bound for tax havens, such as the Bahamas and Panama. This was not only dirty money from crime, but also from legal sources, though not reported to the Inland Revenue Service (the USA had for most of the time, from 1960 through to 1982, a net capital outflow; see Hakkio and Higgins, 1985; further Walter, 1989, pp. 55–62). In addition, the existing crime markets of psychotropic substances had expanded rapidly

[2] This instrument was not rendered obsolete by later anti-money laundering legislation, but, in 1992, became part of it: conspiring to launder money became a criminal offence with a maximum penalty of 20 years.

in the wake of the Vietnam War and, with it, the flow of crime-money into and out of the USA (Van Duyne and Levi, 2005). This on-going drain of untaxed money raised serious concerns with the Inland Revenue Service. Naturally, the law enforcement agencies fighting drugs were equally as worried about the increasing out-flow of drug money. For this reason, a legal instrument was designed that would enable the authorities to monitor (suspicious) cash flows: The Financial Record-Keeping and Reporting of Currency and Foreign Transactions Act, also known as the *Bank Secrecy Act* of 1970.[3]

This Act was one of the 'second generation' anti-laundering instruments from 1970 to 1986, to which Stessens (2000) refers. It essentially laid the foundation of the current AML regulatory and law enforcement framework, domestically within the USA as well as internationally. It was the beginning of the transformation of financial institutions into tools of financial intelligence. This enabled law enforcement and regulatory authorities to track financial transactions in criminal, fiscal or regulatory investigations. This was achieved by creating the requirement for the financial industry to maintain records and file reports on financial activity:

(i) *Currency Transactions Reports* (CTRs) for transactions that exceed $10,000;
(ii) *Suspicious Activity Reports* (SARs) for suspicious, unusual transaction or account activity, transaction or activity inconsistent with the customer's profile. This was added in 1992.[4]

The BSA required the filing of CTRs by financial institutions on their customers. But it also required persons (subject to US jurisdictions) to report on their own activities. More specifically, persons (including banks) having a broadly defined financial interest of at least $5,000 abroad (whether bank account or other assets) had to file annually with the Treasury Department a Report of Foreign Bank and Financial Accounts (FBAR). Anyone (including banks) moving currency and monetary instruments of $5,000 into and out of

---

[3] As the website of the IRS indicates: "On October 26, 1970, in response to increasing reports of people bringing bags full of currency of doubtful origin into banks for deposit, Congress passed Public Law 91-508. This law is often cited as the BSA because Part I, codified mostly in Title 12 of the United States Code (USC), was intended to address a concern by Congress that U.S. citizens may have been using the bank secrecy laws of other countries to conceal illegal activities. Part II of the law is cited as the Currency and Foreign Transactions Reporting Act." See https://www.irs.gov/irm/part4/irm_04-026-005#idm139674432055184. Accessed 13 December 2017.

[4] The requirement to file a SAR was introduced by the Annunzio-Wylie Anti-Money Laundering Act (part of the Housing and Community Development Act of 1992, Pub.L. 102–550, 106 Stat. 3762, 4060).

the USA was required to file a Currency and Monetary Instruments Report (CMIR).[5]

Given that the Treasury Department took the leading role in implementing the BSA, it is likely that the focus was mainly on combating tax evasion. As discussed in the next sections, the IRS took an active interest in driving AML developments. It is also noteworthy that the BSA placed a particular focus on identifying the source and amount of cross-border transactions (whether with currency or other monetary instruments), *i.e.* funds flowing into and out of the USA rather than purely domestic transactions.[6] The BSA was also considered as an impediment to the handling of crime money from other sources such as drug trafficking. Another purpose of imposing CTRs was that it made it easier to obtain a court conviction for the concealment of funds, than to prove a person's criminal activities (Walter, 1989, p. 242).

The record-keeping and reporting requirements of the BSA meant that financial institutions had to introduce mandatory procedures for customer identification and process documenting. These customer identification procedures would later come to be known as Know-Your-Customer (KYC) rules. This concept was not new as stock brokers and other financial services companies already had to make sure that they knew their customers and were selling them the products best suited to them. They also had to establish that customers were able to understand the product risks and were willing to accept them. This requirement to serve the customer was now reversed: it should not serve the customer but the *supervisor*.

Retrospectively we would say that the BSA was an anti-money laundering law, but at that time the phrase 'money laundering' had not yet been adopted in the (legal) literature. That would come in 1972, in publications about the Watergate Affair (Gelemerova, 2011, ch. 1).

The introduction of the BSA did not imply that serious crime-for-profit was left unattended.[7] In the same year, 1970, the so-called RICO-act came into force: The Racketeer Influenced and Corrupt Organisations statute,

---

[5] Initially, the requirements for these reports and records were challenged as an unconstitutional infringement of privacy rights. Judicial decisions established BSA's constitutionality. See IRS' website, https://www.irs.gov/irm/part4/irm_04-026-005#idm139674432055184. Accessed 13 December 2017.

[6] In 1983, in US v. Deak Perera, 566 F. Supp. 1398 (DDC 1983), the revenue agent gathered information for tax examination purposes under the pretence of gathering the information for a BSA examination. But the court held that the IRS could not gather information by the use of false or misleading representations during the course of an examination. (See IRS' website, https://www.irs.gov/irm/part4/irm_04-026-005#idm139674432055184. Accessed 13 December 2017.)

[7] As discussed elsewhere in this book, the money laundering concept targets not only crime profit but, more generally, criminal revenues as well as criminal savings (*i.e.* from tax evasion) and any other benefit from crime. We have used the terms 'crime-for-profit' and 'acquisitive crime' interchangeably to include all of these nuances.

being the best-known part of the Organised Crime Control Act. The Act was intended to prevent high-level criminals from elbowing themselves into the 'upperworld', either through force or by their illegal wealth. Of course, that required legislation that facilitated a targeted financial approach. RICO proved to be as powerful as it was imprecise. Rather, it was powerful because it is so imprecise. Its core concepts, such as *racketeering* and *organised crime* remain undefined, allowing a wide range of application. Though RICO was designed as a tool against 'organised crime' (as an undefined you-know-it-when-you-see-it phenomenon), it is also successful in addressing the upper-world in two ways. In the first place, in thwarting 'organised crime' in getting a foothold in the public administration, trade and industry (Jacobs, 2006). In the second place, in attacking *corporate* crime, the commitment of which mostly requires a continuity and a pattern. Taken continuity and pattern together, they constitute an organisation which is literally a 'given' consequence of committing corporate crime. RICO fitted this form of crime perfectly. The RICO statute also has a *civil* application, either by the prosecution in the form of civil forfeiture provisions or private plaintiffs, aiming at a triple damage recovery.

Was RICO effective? Yes and no. On the one hand, success stories abound: RICO has been used to bring down the Colombo Family, to remove the leadership of corrupt unions (Jacobs, 2006). But it also tackled small criminal fry (Abadinsky, 1994, p. 456) that could not by the farthest stretch of the imagination be connected to 'organised crime'. Private plaintiffs for compensation filed so many cases that a special journal on the statute –*RICO Law Reporter*– became a commercially viable enterprise. On the other hand, as time passed by, the criminal markets, mainly of controlled psychotropic substances, expanded unstoppably. One can say that RICO could bring down criminal families, also financially, and clean up labour unions, but it could not stem the growth of crime markets and the related criminal finances. Additional legal tools were, therefore, required.

3.3 Next step: the criminalisation of money laundering in the USA

Did the BSA fulfil its objectives and thwart criminal finances? Hardly: from the beginning compliance by financial institutions proved to be low, while the intended intelligence function remained insufficiently effective (Stessens, 2000; Levi, 1991). Unrecorded money kept flowing to offshore centres increasing from about eight billion in 1970 to 165 billion dollars in 1985. Most of this money went to the Bahamas and Caymans Islands (Walter, 1989, p. 160). The efficiency of the BSA was also reduced because there were too many institutions involved in its oversight, while the punishment for failing to report was low ($1,000 per violation, unless a pattern of violations could be demonstrated involving transactions exceeding $100,000 in any twelve-month period[8]).

The project was not abandoned, however. Instead, more was to come when the President's Commission on Organized Crime, established in July 1983 by executive order was assigned "*to make a full and complete national and region-by-region analysis of organized crime* [. . .] *and the sources and amounts of organized crime's income, and the uses to which organized crime puts its income.*"[9] Apparently this issue had not been addressed by the previous organised crime committees.

The Commission submitted an interim report in October 1984: *The Cash Connection: Organised Crime, Financial Institutions and Money Laundering*. In accordance with the Commission's task, the report contains data and fact-based observations, though these were of very mixed quality. At the 'soft' end of the information gathering there were interviews with officials and employees of financial institutions, sworn depositions, also by convicts in prison, federal law enforcement and bank supervisory officials. Many of those statements were politically correct utterances or 'belief-statements'. At the 'hard data' end we find some crude statistics generated by the Department of Treasury (Ministry of Finance) concerning Currency Transaction Reports and money flows into and out of the country, sometimes combined with statistics about the flow of narcotics. In between there is the presentation of various evidence of which the validity is difficult to determine independently. For example, Congressional Committees' reports on specific aspects of money laundering, such as casinos, offshore banks or the oversight of the BSA, but they contain little precision. Much remained shrouded in clouds, as it still is today. However, 'anecdotal evidence' lends support to the description of a serious problem. The case of Chemical Bank is such an example.

The 'hard' data about laundering can be found in the chapter "*The scope of the problem*". Without the slightest hint of irony, the chapter opens (p. 8) with the statement: "*Sindona has stated to the Commission that one can launder a 'hundred thousand dollars (or) a hundred million dollars' in even a single transaction. This statement suggests that the scope of the problem is enormous.*"

---

8 See The Cash Connection: Organised Crime, Financial Institutions and Money Laundering, issued by the President's Commission on Organized Crime in October 1984 (discussed further below).

9 Executive Order 12435 – President's Commission on Organized Crime, 28 July 1983, available at https://www.reagan.utexas.edu/archives/speeches/1983/72883b.htm. Accessed 6 February 2016.

In 1977, Chemical Bank, one of the largest commercial banks in the USA (predecessor to JP Morgan Chase), became the first financial institution to be indicted under the BSA. The bank and several of its officers were charged for their failure to report more than $8.5 million in more than 500 cash transactions, some of which included individual cash exchanges ranging from $10,000 to $250,000. The transactions were undertaken on behalf of drug dealers, including Frank Lucas, a La Cosa Nostra associate. Bank officials knowingly facilitated the transactions, which included transfers abroad and the exchange of smaller denomination bills for larger ones. In a deposition taken by the Commission on 28 August 1984, Thomas Spinelli, one of the convicted Chemical Bank officers, described the delivery of cash from drug traffickers in paper bags, suitcases, and attaché cases. He had ensured cooperation from 15 bank officers under the pretext that he was helping his cousin, a bookmaster, to "wash" money. Spinelli apparently said, his "associates viewed the government's reporting requirements as an infringement on the people who were known members of the community and who may have to make a large transaction from time to time" (p. 48). The fact that officials of one of the USA's largest banks took Spinelli's statement as a valid argument – ***an infringement on the people*** – is indicative of the attitude at that time towards the emerging compliance burden.

Who is Sindona to whom so much authority is bestowed that his statements are considered sufficiently credible to conclude in the next sentence to an enormous problem? Michele Sindona was a tax and corporate attorney, handling money for the Mafia as well as the Vatican. He was convicted in the USA for causing the collapse of the Franklin National Bank (among others), and was extradited to Italy because of having murdered the attorney who had to liquidate his collapsed Italian banks.[10] So Sindona was supposed to be 'in the know'. That was correct: he was a first-hand witness of the abuse of offshore banks to disguise the source or application of funds, about which he provided useful information to the Commission. Concerning the scope of the problem he was no better informed than any layman. Nevertheless, the Commission regarded him as an authority on the subject.

The data presented in the report are partly systematically ordered: ten examples of implicated banks and corporations; ten case studies as illustrations, with some overlap and mainly concerning the role of the banks and its (complicit) staff. The

[10] This does not do justice to the varied life of the banker of the Gambino Mafia family as well as Pope Paul VI, to both of whom he rendered money services via the Vatican Bank to Swiss banks. Due to a stock market crash his banks became insolvent. Serving a 25 years prison sentence he was poisoned in his cell with cyanide in his coffee in March 1986.

descriptions focus, in particular, on the ways the bank managers dodged the reporting obligations of the CTR and the CMIR.[11] The Commission's report recounts that such non-reporting was usually because of the lack of awareness among obliged entities' staff or, more often, their reluctance to report suspicious activity to the authorities. This included, according to the report, "deliberate indifference" and "insider collusion". Often management and executive staff allowed themselves to be amply rewarded for non-reporting. In addition, the report notes that some bankers advised their customers about the reporting or were even active in devising better schemes to avoid detection. Only one of the case studies concerned a bank that was really unaware of the BSA requirements. According to the report, some banks felt uneasy and disrupted their relationship with clients after the first boxes or sports bag filled with cash were carried in. However, severing the relationship with a suspicious client did not motivate them later to submit a CTR.

Such testimonies pointed at a lack of integrity – or at least a low compliance awareness – concerning the banks' reporting obligations. Therefore, the case descriptions are as much about corruption in the financial institutions as about laundering. As far as the latter is concerned: there is only one reference to the *legitimation of* criminal revenues, which is the 'end product' of laundering. Other cases are about *disguising the movement* of (cash) money, which was allegedly regularly delivered in bags and boxes filled with bills of small denominations ($5 and $10). In most cases the disguising consisted of little more than not filling in the CTR or CMIR form or not sending the completed form to the Treasury Department. Other simple methods were knowingly accepting false names, identities or shell companies as account holders. Virtually all (or most) staff avoiding the BSA requirements were fully aware that they dealt with criminal money or criminals, but still did not ask questions. To their regret, some of the depositing businessmen proved to be undercover agents. Finally, commonly shared circumstances were: the mal-functioning of the BSA, the fragmentation of the oversight and the restrictive legal instruments for investigating cases of criminal money management.

The illegal money flows are presented as the core of the threat to be combated: basic is the criminal *cash* connection. In the presentation of these cash flows one finds some incongruence which remained unelaborated. The direction of the cocaine money (cash) flow was mostly described as outbound to Colombia and Panama.[12] The Central Bank of Panama was mentioned as the clearing point from where the surplus of dollars were sent back to the USA. In contrast, heroin money from Southeast Asia went mainly to the USA, reportedly, paralleling the increased heroin importation, but without a corresponding USA cash outflow to the exporting heroin organisations in Hong Kong. The report did not

---

[11] The CMIR stands for Currency and Monetary Instrument Report for financial interest of $5,000 abroad.

[12] Walter (1989), figure 6.1. mentions in order of magnitude: Bahamas, Caymans Islands, Mexico and Venezuela. Colombia is mixed with 'others' Source: US Federal Reserve.

raise further questions and the 'analysis' stops at this counter-intuitive observation. These are the main references to the connection between drugs and money.

The criminal, economic and financial implications of all these observations remain unclear. Crime-money is leaving the USA, but also returning to it and all that money mobility is subsumed under the new concept of money laundering.

Sometimes the reality was much more banal, reflecting bad management rather than a money laundering threat. In 1981, the US Custom Service carried out a search of Currency Transaction Forms (CTR) filled by departing and arriving passengers. Fewer departing passengers bothered to fill the CTR forms than the arriving passengers. The difference was that the CTR requirement is listed on the mandatory customs form, which was not the case with departing travellers (Walter, 1989, p. 243).

However, the Commission's report does not inform us of the laundering of the crime-money that remains *within* the US borders: the reporting and analysis appear to have largely focused on the cross-border element. However, the crude statistics of five years CTRs and CMIRs (1979-1983) are not very revealing either. Apart from that, the data analysis of the Treasury Department is such that the report has to conclude that "*These filings constitute a vast and constantly growing haystack of information, in which criminal investigators are expected to find the needles that represent criminal proceeds or unreported income being laundered.*" (p. 10) By implication the last part of the sentence about unreported income refers to tax evasion, a sensitive issue that would intermittently resurface during the next three decades.[13]

This survey, a 'haystack' plus 'illustrative cases', was roughly the empirical *national* basis for the next generation of USA legislation (and by hindsight of the present AML regime). The US authorities introduced the Money Laundering Control Act of 1986 to criminalise the evasion of the BSA-requirements and criminalise money laundering itself.

The lack of more methodical research did not hinder the Commission from inserting statements implying the need for the launch of a *global* policy. In the report there are unambiguous statements that this new national anti-laundering policy is bound to get an international sequel. For example: after indicating the value of a BSA-based analysis of money flows (concerning the dollar currents between Hong Kong and the USA) for strategic planning and decision making, the report stresses its importance also for "*the conduct of*

[13] It came again to the fore in the latest FATF recommendations and the EU directive on money laundering: the Directive (EU) 2015/849 of the European Parliament and of the Council of 20 May 2015 on the prevention of the use of the financial system for the purposes of money laundering or terrorist financing. This is discussed later.

foreign policy in a manner that complements such law enforcement planning" (p. 17). As has been the case with the USA drug policy, the USA solution to the money laundering problem was soon to be exported (Van Duyne and Levi, 2005; Bewley-Taylor, 1999).

3.4 With the BSA strengthening, the taxman was always near

With some liberty one can rephrase the adage "there is no smoke without fire" as "there is no money without taxes": eventually the tax administration always shows up. We have already mentioned the handling of the Al Capone case and how, thereafter, the Inland Revenue Service approach of comparing wealth and income became important in a combined fiscal and criminal law tackling of acquisitive crime. Unsurprisingly the US Treasury was actively interested in the BSA as a tool for uncovering hidden income, whether derived from crime or legal sources.

The BSA was introduced at a time when money was increasingly leaving the USA for financial 'havens', such as the Bahamas and Switzerland. Indeed, the IRS found evidence that organised crime figures were sending money overseas, in particular to Switzerland. Among them was Meyer Lansky, a major organised crime figure who was targeted in the 1960s. According to his biographer Lacey, Lansky regarded his numbered Swiss account as "an elaborate version of cash under the bed" (Lacey, 1991, p. 305).

The US tax authorities were a key advocate of the BSA as it would allow them to scrutinise accounts and money transfers (Wechsler, 2001, p. 42). It appears that, as the BSA focused on tax evasion in the main, the definitional net of what was later called 'money laundering', was deliberately cast quite broadly (Gelemerova, 2011). As a result, when money laundering was criminalised with the Money Laundering Control Act 1986, this act reflected the BSA's all-encompassing spirit: it defined money laundering broadly to include the mere transfer of illegal proceeds and the structuring of transactions into smaller amounts aimed at avoiding attention.

As elaborated in the previous section, the BSA did not meet expectations (see Gelemerova, 2011, pp. 46–47). While the underlying rationale was considered correct, the authorities needed greater powers to enforce it. The Money Laundering Control Act was aimed at achieving exactly that. In 1993, a senior official of the US Department of Justice admitted to a congressional committee that: "*The Bank Secrecy Act was not enough, standing alone, to combat money laundering. Rather, it was necessary to make the handling of dirty money a crime in itself*" (Hoekje *et al.*, 1993, p. 3). During a 1993 public hearing on money laundering in the State of New Jersey, Mary Medina, Chief of the Examination Division for the IRS in Newark, made the following statement: "*[T]he IRS views money laundering very broadly. Any activity or practice used to conceal or disguise the existence and origin of profits or money generated, whether from legal sources or illegal sources, is a money laundering concern for us*" (Hoekje *et al.*, 1993, p. 7).

Prompted by the Money Laundering Control Act of 1986, since January 1987, the Office of the Comptroller of the Currency (OCC)[14] has required banks under its supervision to establish and maintain a BSA compliance programme that, at a minimum:

a. provides for a system of internal controls to ensure ongoing compliance;
b. provides for independent testing for compliance conducted by bank personnel or an outside party;
c. designates an individual or individuals responsible for coordinating and monitoring day-to-day compliance; and
d. provides training for appropriate personnel (see FinCEN, 2004).

At the time the problem of money laundering was brought to the fore as a major law enforcement impediment, this fiscal angle remained in the background. For good reasons: the taxman does not win 'hearts and minds'. However, fear of drugs and organised crime does: in 1986 as well as during the subsequent triumphal global introduction process.

3.5 Globalisation by exportation of US legislation

The Commission's interim report of October 1984 had already stated that the discussed anti-money laundering policy should have an international counterpart: "*the conduct of foreign policy in a manner that complements such law enforcement planning*" (p. 17). This proved to be no idle statement. After the enactment of the US Money Laundering Control Act, it was time for foreign policy initiatives to internationalise the issue. The USA did not break fresh ground. The key principles of the US BSA were well known in Europe, naturally the most important region for a 'conversion mission'. To have the UK, France, Germany, Belgium, the Netherlands, follow suit meant potentially that many other countries would then follow. The Council of Europe had already promulgated its "Measures against the transfer and safeguarding of

[14] The OCC is an independent bureau within the US Department of the Treasury which regulates all US national banks and thrift institutions together with the federal branches and agencies of foreign banks in the USA. FinCEN has delegated its authority to examine financial institutions for BSA compliance to the primary federal regulators of those financial institutions: the Board of Governors of the Federal Reserve System, the Office of the Comptroller of the Currency, the Federal Deposit Insurance Corporation, the Office of Thrift Supervision, the National Credit Union Administration, Securities and Exchange Commission, the Commodity Futures Trading Commission, and the Internal Revenue Service (Small Business/Self-Employed Division). (See Appendix A, FinCEN, 2006.)

funds of criminal origin. Recommendation. No. R (80)10", adopted by the Committee of Ministers of the Council of Europe on 27 June 1980. However, this recommendation met the same fate as the original BSA: it proved ineffective. Nevertheless, its principles had been formulated and accepted by the Committee of Ministers and would ten years later with the introduction of the FATF be forcefully overhauled. However, first the ground had to be prepared at a global level: The United Nations.

The Reagan administration had many reasons for this move towards the UN. Not only because of the many cross-border facets of money laundering which could be dealt with bi- or multi-laterally. The most important reason was that the main platform through which to launch an international approach, the UN, was heading into a more liberal policy direction. This was contrary to the policy pursued by the US administration at that time (Van Duyne and Nelemans, 2011). The USA was advocating a more repressive criminal policy (Wechsler, 2001). This contrasted with the unwanted liberal and social political developments in the UN as promoted by the previous US president, Jimmy Carter. What were these unwanted developments?

From 1975 onwards, the Secretariat and the Congress of the UN had developed the concept of 'transnational crime', not signifying the Mafia, drug barons and their like, but denoting *corporate* cross-border wrongdoing (criminal or civil): crime as business, victimising (among others) developing countries. For example, committing environmental violations while exploiting the mineral wealth of developing countries, enabled by high-level corruption. Contrary to the common belief, the UN considered such wrongdoing to be more serious than 'traditional' criminality. The resolution of the 6th UN Congress, 1980, was even sharper in its formulation, referring to "*offenders and offences beyond the reach of the law*", by which it did not point at sinister drug barons, but at 'white-collar' abusers of power, corrupters, consumer fraudsters and marketers of "dangerously unsafe products" (Section 159).

Obviously, this did not reflect the repressive USA's 'war on drugs' policy and their view on 'traditional' organised crime and related money laundering. Neither did the UN Congress' stand against corporate crime win the support of the then leaders of the US and other industrialised nations. When Reagan came to power, in 1981, we can observe an interesting change in the sense that 'new dimensions' were gradually introduced to the UN's view on crime. These dimensions soon became clear, though they were not really new: they were a reflection of the 'war against' attitude to crime. The tone became correspondingly sharper and no longer only concerned 'abuse of power' but also embraced drugs, organised crime and criminal money.

The 'old' opinions expressed in previous resolutions were not deleted. Once an international resolution has been adopted, it is difficult to change it. The best tactic for undoing it is to dilute its significance and have it 'overgrown' by new resolutions: hence, the corresponding sentences still lingered on, but were diluted into subordinate sections. The new, but still debatable topics were smartly placed in less conspicuous sections or paragraphs. For example, in the 1986 resolution, one finds in the beginning sections a 'messenger statement' against drugs: "It is imperative . . ." and 60 pages later, under "other resolutions and decisions" we find first a long resolution on organised crime, then on drugs and wrapped within this resolution the 'financial tail': forfeiture of illicit profits and a recommendation that Member States adopt laws related to "taxation, the bank secrecy and gaming houses [. . .] to assist in the fight against organised crime and the transfer of proceeds across national boundaries." A masterpiece of 'resolution wrapping'. With the acceptance of this package of resolutions, irrespective of its modest place in the whole document, the opening for unfolding an active international anti-money laundering policy was created.

Once the ground was prepared, the USA then needed to induce the UN to formally implement the anti-money laundering agenda: the international criminalisation of the laundering of drug money. This was achieved through a UN convention: *The United Nations Convention Against Illicit Traffic in Narcotic Drugs and Psychotropic Substances*, signed in Vienna, 1988 (hence the "Vienna Convention"). Politically this was an uncontroversial issue: drugs are bad and, therefore, by association, the handling of drug money is also bad. Naturally, there is more than drug money to be laundered, but drugs provide the best socio-political 'crowbar' to achieve this first opening: and which country would dare to oppose this? Once the door was opened, the scope could be broadened to crime-money from other offences.

As discussed previously, in December 1988, the Basel Committee on Banking Supervision issued a number of principles to prevent the abuse of the financial system for laundering purposes: the *Basel Statement of Principles* "which encourages banks' management to put in place effective procedures to ensure that all persons conducting business with their institutions are properly identified; that transactions that do not appear legitimate are discouraged; and that cooperation with law enforcement agencies is achieved."[15] Compared with these broad principles, the G-7 focus on drugs and related revenues, during the meeting in Paris 1989, can be considered as a – temporary – narrowing of scope.

In section 1.3 we discussed the scarcity of empirical material related to money laundering. We have also seen that this evidence and knowledge gap did not impede far reaching policy making despite the rhetoric of 'evidence-based policy making'. This encompassed the development of international

---

[15] Basel Committee on Banking Supervision. Prevention of criminal use of the banking system for the purpose of money-laundering (December 1988).

conventions as well as the establishment of an institution, albeit an informal one, the Financial Action Task Force on money laundering (FATF). Once the FATF was established, it became the 'global standard setter', which it employed its leverage sometimes in a coercive manner. Its 40 'Recommendations' are anything but voluntary. They are the outlines of an intended global control policy over states and financial institutions, maintained by what is erroneously called 'soft law' (Stessens, 2000). As will be discussed in the next section 3.5 there is no law under which the FATF falls, allowing it nevertheless to exert a coercive power by means of Recommendation 21: "Financial institutions should give special attention to business relationships and transactions with persons, including companies and financial institutions, from countries which do not or insufficiently apply the FATF Recommendations". This could entail harsh consequences in terms of the speed of processing international financial transactions and direct foreign investment.[16]

Judged by its outcome, the policy, which started in the USA with the not very successful BSA, was pursued step-by-step from 1984 onwards and, within a time span of five to ten years, successfully laid the basis of a global anti-money laundering regime. As we have already observed, what made this success the more remarkable, was that it was achieved with very little underlining evidence and barely any valid statistics. Empirically, the FATF started in the semi-darkness in which it continued and unfolded as an informal organisation not covered by any law; a development that exactly matched the desire of the USA (Wechsler, 2001).

3.6 The FATF and its extending reach

The FATF is one of the international organisations that everybody in the field of finances knows by its acronym without the need of writing it in full. Of course, this feeling of acquaintance is no guarantee of a proper understanding of the 'task force'. What is a 'task force'? According to the Webster on-line dictionary, a task force is "a temporary grouping under one leader for the purpose of accomplishing a definite objective", which clarifies the meaning of the FATF: it has the definite and 'temporary' policy making task of fighting against money laundering globally. As mentioned in Chapter 1.2., it received its 'birth certificate' from an informal gathering of the heads of seven industrialised states of which it inherited its informality: the FATF is an *informal* club established by another informal club, the seven Heads of State, who in Paris in 1989 gave it a mandate for five years to fight money laundering. This infor-

[16] Anti-Money Laundering and Combating the Financing of Terrorism (AML/CFT). Report on the Review of the Effectiveness of the Program. IMF, 11 May 2011, pp. 82–83.

mality matters as one of its consequences is that European laws on public information access do not apply to it. The Task Force has no public information duty and can release just as much to the public domain as it pleases. One cannot sue the FATF if it refuses access, because it is not a legal entity: legally it does not exist.[17] This means that for a description of the functioning of the FATF we are entirely dependant on its publications.

At first the FATF only published annual reports, mainly extolling its "significant progress". Later a growing number of topic-related publications and 'public statements' were displayed on its website. However, it provides no access to the underlying documentation for this information, for example about the discussion and subsequent decision making within this informal and diverse club. The Plenary is presented as the highest organ coming to decisions and opinions "by consensus" which are then only shared if deemed useful.[18] Hence, we only know the publicly available outcomes of the Plenary, if they are presented in the FATF's annual reports, public statements, or other working group reports. Some highlights of its history are summarised in a booklet *FATF 25 years and beyond* published in 2014: a kind of 'silver jubilee-history' with a high degree of somewhat predictable self-congratulation.

For research this is a serious impediment: as a global 'standard setter' the FATF is only accountable to the informal G-7 (now G-20) statesmen which leaves us and the wider public with many 'documentary evidence gaps' of its activity which can only be filled by interpretation.

3.6.1 The development of the informal anti-money laundering club

a. The first years

As remarked before, the FATF was put into place as a task force and not as an organisation with a head and the accompanying bureaucratic machinery. It was (and still is) an international group of 'experts' with attendees comprising representatives from the members Ministries of Finance or other competent authorities. As we will see, in so many words it expressed its intention to maintain informality and to avoid bureaucracy (FATF AR, 1990-1991, p. 17). It began with an annually rotating presidency.

---

[17] An informed source did indicate to the authors in the autumn of 2017 that the topic of legal incorporation was to be discussed at the November Plenary, however, there is no mention of this in the 'Outcomes Joint FATF/GAFILAT Plenary, 1-3 November 2017 or otherwise in the public domain. http://www.fatf-gafi.org/publications/fatfgeneral/documents/outcomes-plenary-november-2017.html. Accessed 14 December 2017.

[18] High-level principles and objectives for FATF and FATF-style regional bodies. FATF, Paris, 2012.

Starting with the seven participants from the G-7 summit, plus the European Commission it was soon joined by seven more countries all of whom had endorsed the 40 Recommendations (FATF-Annual Report 1990-1991, p. 13), further discussed in Chapter 5. These countries were already members of the OECD.[19] In addition, the FATF invited the three most important off-shore banking centres and areas: Hong-Kong, Singapore and the Gulf Cooperation Council (composed of Saudi Arabia, Bahrain, the United Arab Emirates, Oman, Qatar and Kuwait) to participate. Subsequently, the FATF launched a global campaign to disseminate its 40 Recommendations and secure as much endorsement as possible.

In the third year, the FATF reached the 28 members. Would the FATF become a kind of mega-task force? No: having reached this number, the FATF decided that no more members should be allowed. For an organisation that "*prides itself on its informality of procedure and ready ability to achieve consensus*", it considered this the maximum membership (FATF-AR, 1991-1992, p. 18). This would remain the case for almost the next ten years before the Plenary decided to further expand its membership (FATF-AR, 1998-1999).

By 2000, most OECD countries and major financial centres had become FATF members. The FATF was supplied with office space and a secretariat from the OECD. Despite these facilities, the FATF claimed full independence from the OECD even if there appears to be a an overlap of personnel: the ministers or Heads of State of the then G-7 to whom the FATF is responsible, are also dominant in the OECD.

The restriction of membership did not imply that the FATF locked itself away: it held frequent meetings all over the world that were attended by, among others, 150 experts from international financial institutions, the UN, and international policy making and law enforcement institutions. The FATF was active in ensuring that no continent or potentially relevant institution was missed in its mission to further the endorsement of the 40 Recommendations. It announced this mission loudly and clearly that it would continue "*spreading the FATF message to those parts of the world where even awareness [. . .] remains at a very low level*" (FATF-AR, 1992-1993, p. 24). It reads like a programme of evangelisation (Levi, 2003).

Meanwhile the FATF created three working groups for (1) legal (2) financial and (3) international matters. Apart from the small OECD-provided secretariat, the FATF operates through such working groups, reporting to the Plenary. These working groups were essential in forging international ties, compensating for the restricted FATF membership. This implied a worldwide spreading of activities. Van Duyne *et al.* (2016, p. 174) observed that "There are 93 institutions visiting the organisational events of the FATF" and for that

[19] Denmark, Finland, Ireland, New-Zealand, Norway, Portugal and Turkey.

reason spoke of the *Monty Python Flying Circus*. There was an ongoing mutual attendance at each countries' seminars, symposiums and other events, "*as the world-wide mobilisation against money laundering is the ultimate goal of the FATF, its external relations work will be given a high priority in the forthcoming years*" (FATF-AR, 1993-94, p. 24). In this and the following years one can observe an on-going strengthening of ties (FATF-AR 1994-95, p. 19). To further this worldwide dissemination the FATF obtained an extended five-year mandate, which would be renewed after each term. While it again decided not to expand its membership, it allowed stakeholders in the fight against money laundering to take part as observers in its events (Plenary, seminars, work group meetings), which was reciprocated. It also created followers: the FATF Style Regional Bodies discussed in the next section.

b. The FATF Style Regional Bodies

While this proselytisation programme did not result in an enlargement of the FATF organisation (which officially did not exist), the FATF helped with the establishment of separate regional FATF-like organisations. The first to emerge was the *Caribbean FATF*, established in 1990 in Aruba when the ink of the FATF's recommendations was hardly dry.[20] It consisted of the countries of the Caribbean basin. We found no documents explaining why this happened so soon: the CFATF website archive does not display documents older than 2001. It is apparent that establishing regional FATF-like bodies appears to have been the model by which the FATF extended its influence.[21]

In 1994/1995, the *Asian secretariat* of the FATF was established (funded through confiscated crime-money), followed a year later by the proposal to create an Asia/Pacific Steering Group on Money Laundering. This Steering Group resulting in a regional anti-money laundering group in the Asia/Pacific region, which was considered very significant (FATF-AR, 1996-97, p. 5) and an example for others to follow. This they did: at a Southern and Eastern African Money Laundering Conference the participants agreed to form a regional FATF. This meant that in addition to the Caribbean regional FATF two new regional FATFs were established.

---

[20] Documents about why and how this first FSBR came into being are lacking or are not readily available.

[21] At that time: Anguilla, Antigua and Barbuda, Aruba, the Bahamas, Barbados, Belize, Bermuda, the British Virgin Islands, the Cayman Islands, Costa Rica, Dominica, Dominican Republic, Grenada, Jamaica, Montserrat, the Netherlands Antilles, Nicaragua, Panama, St. Kitts and Nevis, St. Lucia, St. Vincent and the Grenadines, Suriname, Turks and Caicos Islands, Trinidad and Tobago and Venezuela.

In October 1996, thirteen southern and eastern African countries attended the first Southern and Eastern African Money Laundering Conference in Cape Town. The Conference agreed on a proposal to set up a regional mechanism which would later become the *Eastern and Southern African Financial Action Task Force*. But its implementation took some time with the first gathering of the ESAAMLG task force taking place in April 2000.

The *Asia/Pacific Group on Money Laundering* was established a few months after the fourth Asia/Pacific Money Laundering Symposium (February 1997), followed by a ministerial statement from the Finance Ministers of the Asia Pacific Economic Cooperation (APEC) in April 1997. It would host its first annual meeting in Tokyo, March 1998. At that time the group consisted of sixteen countries.[22]

Since its anti-laundering convention of 1990, the *Council of Europe* (CoE) has also remained a stakeholder in this field and decided in September 1997 to establish a Select Committee (PC-R-EV, later called MONEYVAL) to conduct compliance evaluations (self- and mutual evaluations) for those CoE member states which were not members of the FATF (mainly countries of the previous 'Eastern Block').[23]

Preparatory actions were also taken in Latin America and Central and Eastern Europe. In Latin America a *Group of Experts on money laundering* was to convene twice a year. In Eastern Europe the Baltic States issued the Riga Declaration on the fight against money laundering (November 1996). These were to bear fruit later.

As this short survey shows, there were a lot of anti-money laundering activities in all parts of the world, often 'ignited' by the FATF. For the future course of the FATF it was important that the then G-7 Heads of States would agree on a mandate renewal in 1998. But who was the decision maker? The G-7, the OECD, or some kind of consensus encompassing both? According to the account of the FATF-AR (1997-1998, p. 9), the Ministers of the OECD made the first move and issued, in April 1998, a Communiqué in which it "welcomed the decision of the FATF to extend its work for another five years and the new strategy it has adopted". Apparently the FATF itself had already made a (preliminary) decision. On 8 May 1998 the G-7 Finance Ministers commended the FATF's work and endorsed its decision to continue its mandate and its new strategy. It also stressed the problem of offshore financial

[22] At that time: Australia; Bangladesh; Chinese Taipei; Fiji; Hong Kong, China; India; Japan; New Zealand; the People's Republic of China; Republic of Korea; Republic of the Philippines; Singapore; Sri Lanka; Thailand; United States of America and Vanuatu.

[23] Albania, Andorra, Bulgaria, Croatia, Cyprus, Czech Republic, Estonia, Georgia, Hungary, Latvia, Liechtenstein, Lithuania, Moldova, Malta, Poland, Romania, Russian Federation, San Marino, Slovakia, Slovenia, Macedonia and the Ukraine. Since January 2001, Armenia and Azerbaijan have also become members of the Committee PC-R-EV when these countries joined the Council of Europe.

centres (OFCs). This statement was repeated by the G-7 Heads of State on 17 May 1998, welcoming the FATF decision to continue, together with its partnership with regional groupings. It also pointed to the financial offshore problem. This statement meant that the FATF could continue with its regional partnership building while it was left free in the way to shape them. The difficulty in locating the real decision making in this process can be considered a consequence of the chosen informality: it did not matter.

During this first phase of development not much attention was paid to what these bodies were actually supposed to do, except that they must endorse the FATF programme and would be instrumental in spreading the 'message'. Only after 1998-99, were these regional bodies called "FATF-*style* regional bodies" (FSRBs), indicating their similarity to the FATF based on the original 40 Recommendations. Although, purportedly, they are 'stand-alone', their mutual evaluation procedures must be endorsed by the FATF (according to the agreement of the FATF Plenary meeting in 1998, see Koh, 2006). We will discuss the position of the FSRBs in sections 3.7 and 3.8.

After the ministerial endorsement and the further preparatory work discussed in the previous sections, new FSRBs were established or preparations for new ones were carried out. The *Eastern and Southern African Anti-Money Laundering Group* (ESAAMLG), discussed above, was finally established at a meeting in Arusha (Tanzania) in August 1999.[24] In April 2000, the ESAAMLG held its first meeting of task force officials in Tanzania. In December 1999, the Heads of State of the Economic Community of West African States (ECOWAS) decided to establish an inter-governmental group against money laundering.

Initiatives were also taken by states in South America to form a task force, which was launched on 8 December 2000, as the South American Financial Action Task Force on Money Laundering (GAFISUD, later changed into GAFILAT) at a meeting of Ministers held in Cartagena (Colombia). A Memorandum of Understanding was signed by the nine members of the group (Argentina, Bolivia, Brazil, Colombia, Chile, Ecuador, Peru, Paraguay and Uruguay): it accepted the Recommendations and agreed to operationalise the new task force. This was effected at the second plenary meeting in June 2001 in Montevideo (Uruguay). A permanent secretariat, located in Buenos Aires, was established in the same year.

Preparations in *West Africa* also continued. At an Inter-Ministerial meeting it was decided to establish an Inter-Governmental Action Group against Money Laundering (GIABA: *Groupe Inter-gouvernemental d'Action contre le Blanchiment en Afrique*).[25] Statutes were submitted for approval in December

[24] Its members are: Botswana, Kenya, Lesotho, Malawi, Mauritius, Mozambique, Namibia, Seychelles, South Africa, Swaziland, Tanzania, Uganda, Zambia and Zimbabwe.

[25] Members: Benin, Cape Verde, Gambia, Guinea-Bissau, Mali, Nigeria, Senegal, Togo, Burkina Faso, Guinea, Liberia, Niger, São Tomé and Príncipe, Ghana.

2001. However, no agreement was reached on the location of the Secretariat or for the funding of this FSRB. Eventually, a secretariat was established in Dakar (Senegal). As far as *Central Africa* is concerned, the Heads of State of the Economic and Monetary Community (CEMAC: Communauté Economique et Monétaire d'Afrique Centrale) decided in December 2000 to create an Action Group against Money Laundering (GABAC: Groupe d'Action contre le blanchiment d'Argent en Afrique Centrale), which would be elaborated the following year.[26]

2004 saw the creation of the final FATF-Style Regional Bodies with the '*Eurasian Group*' and the *Middle-East and North-Africa* group joining the ranks. The Eurasian Group on Combating Money Laundering and Financing of Terrorism was established at the initiative of the Russian Federation on 6 October 2004.[27]

In the North Africa/Middle East group Tunisia took the initiative. The Middle East and North Africa Financial Action Task Force (MENAFATF) was established by signing the administrative Memorandum of Understanding on 30 November 2004. This FSRB consists of 18 countries.[28]

By furthering the establishment of FSRBs in every continent, by 2004, the FATF had realised a global reach. With the exception of Iran and North Korea, even the smallest territories such as the Faroes, were covered by its Recommendations. As had been its original intention, a global network had been created through an additional mutual observership. Given this had been achieved by the establishment of the last FSRBs on the one hand (see Table 3.1), and the still informal character of the FATF and the FSRBs on the other hand, one may wonder whether more attention should have been paid to structure and organisation. Indeed, we are not the first to question the lack of formal constitution.[29] What is the opinion of the FATF on this matter?

c. High-level principles for the FATF and the FSRBs

Measured by public documents, it has taken a number of years before the FATF formulated its opinion on its position *vis a vis* these regional bodies. It

---

[26] Member countries: Cameroon, Central African Republic, Chad, Republic of the Congo, Equatorial Guinea, Gabon.

[27] 'Founding states': Belarus, Kazakhstan, China, Kyrgyzstan, Russia and Tajikistan. They were later joined by Uzbekistan, India and China, the latter two changing their observer status into that of membership in 2010.

[28] Tunisia, Jordan, United Arab Emirates, Bahrain, Algeria, Saudi Arabia, Syria, Oman, Qatar, Kuwait, Lebanon, Egypt, Morocco, Yemen, Sudan, Iraq, Mauritania and Libya.

[29] Evidence supplied by Prof. Peter Alldridge to the UK House of Lords and referred to on pp. 3–8 of chapter 2: 'The fora for international cooperation', House of Lords, Money laundering and the financing of terrorism – European Union Committee available at http://www.publications.parliament.uk/pa/ld200809/ldselect/ldeucom/132/13205.htm. Accessed 11 August 2016.

Table 3.1 The FATF and the FATF-Style Regional Bodies (FSRBs)

Organisation	Members	Remit
Asia/Pacific Group on Money Laundering (APGML)	Afghanistan, Australia, Bangladesh, Kingdom of Bhutan, Brunei Darussalam, Cambodia, Canada, People's Republic of China, Cook Islands, Fiji, Hong Kong (China), India, Indonesia, Japan, Republic of Korea, Lao People's Democratic Republic, Macao (China), Malaysia, Maldives, Marshall Islands, Mongolia, Myanmar, Nauru, Nepal, New Zealand, Niue, Pakistan, Palau, Papua New Guinea, Philippines, Samoa, Singapore, Solomon Islands, Sri Lanka, Chinese Taipei, Thailand, Timor-Leste, Tonga, United States of America, Vanuatu, Vietnam.	An inter-governmental organisation focused on ensuring that its members effectively implement the international standards against money laundering, terrorist financing and proliferation financing related to weapons of mass destruction.
Caribbean Financial Action Task Force (CFATF)	Anguilla, Antigua and Barbuda, Aruba, Bahamas, Barbados, Belize, Bermuda, BVI, Cayman Islands, Curaçao, Dominica, El Salvador, Grenada, Guyana, Haiti, Jamaica, Montserrat, Saint Kitts and Nevis, Saint Lucia, St. Maarten, Saint Vincent and the Grenadines, Suriname, Trinidad and Tobago, Turks and Caicos Islands, Venezuela	An organisation of states of the Caribbean Basin, which have agreed to implement common countermeasures against money laundering.
Eastern and Southern Africa Anti-Money Laundering Group (ESAAMLG)	Angola, Botswana, Ethiopia, Kenya, Lesotho, Madagascar, Malawi, Mauritius, Mozambique, Namibia, Rwanda, Seychelles, South Africa, Swaziland, Tanzania, Uganda, Zambia, Zimbabwe.	An FATF Style Regional Body committed to eradicating money laundering and terrorist financing in the Eastern and Southern African region.
Eurasian Group (EAG)	Republic of Belarus, People's Republic of China, Republic of India, Republic of Kazakhstan, Kyrgyz Republic, Republic of Tajikistan, Russian Federation, Turkmenistan, Republic of Uzbekistan.	The Eurasian Group supports countries in the region to create an appropriate legal and institutional framework combating money laundering and terrorist financing in line with FATF standards.
Financial Action Task Force of Latin America, GAFILAT, (formerly known as Financial Action Task Force of South America (GAFISUD))	Argentina, Bolivia, Brasil, Chile, Colombia, Costa Rica, Cuba, Ecuador, Guatemala, Honduras, Mexico, Nicaragua, Panama, Paraguay, Peru, Dominican Republic, Uruguay.	A regional inter-governmental organisation which brings together the countries of South America in order to combat money-laundering and terrorism financing by means of the continuous improvement of national policies and the strengthening of different methods of co-operation between Member States.

(***continued***)

Table 3.1 (continued)

Organisation	Members	Remit
Inter-Governmental Action Group against Money Laundering in West Africa (GIABA)	Republic of Benin, Burkina Faso, Republic of Cape Verde, Republic of Côte d'Ivoire, Republic of The Gambia, Republic of Ghana, Republic of Guinea, Guinea Bissau, Republic of Liberia, Republic of Mali, Republic of Niger, Federal Republic of Nigeria, São Tomé and Príncipe, Republic of Senegal, Republic of Sierra Leone, Togolese Republic.	Established by the Economic Community of West African States (ECOWAS) as one of its major responses and contributions to the fight against money laundering. GIABA is a specialised institution of ECOWAS that is responsible for the prevention and control of money laundering and terrorist financing in the region.
Middle East & North Africa Financial Action Task Force (MENAFATF)	Kingdom of Jordan, United Arab Emirates, Kingdom of Bahrain, Republic of Algeria, Republic of Tunisia, Kingdom of Saudi Arabia, Republic of Sudan, Syrian Arab Republic, Republic of Iraq, Sultanate of Oman, State of Qatar, State of Kuwait, Lebanese Republic, State of Libya, Arab Republic of Egypt, Kingdom of Morocco, The Islamic Republic of Mauritania, Republic of Yemen.	Member countries of the MENAFATF endeavour to adopt and implement the 40 Recommendations of the FATF. To implement the relevant UN treaties and agreements and United Nations Security Council Resolutions. To co-operate together to raise compliance with these standards and measures within the MENA. To work together to identify ML/TF issues of a regional nature. To take measures to combat ML/FT in a way consistent with cultural values, constitutional framework and legal systems in the member countries.
Council of Europe (Represented by its MONEYVAL Committee)	Albania, Andorra, Armenia, Azerbaijan, Bosnia and Herzegovina, Bulgaria, Croatia, Cyprus, Czech Republic, Estonia, Georgia, Hungary, Israel (active observer status), Latvia, Liechtenstein, Lithuania, Malta, Moldova, Monaco, Montenegro, Poland, Romania, Russian Federation, San Marino, Serbia, Slovak Republic, Slovenia, "The former Yugoslav Republic of Macedonia", Ukraine.	The aim of MONEYVAL is to ensure that its member states have in place effective systems to counter money laundering and terrorist financing and comply with the relevant international standards in these fields.

Source: the authors based on an earlier version compiled by one of the authors and included in ***CISI Combatting Financial Crime: the official learning and reference manual***. First edition October 2011 and using information from organisation websites.

was not until 2012, that it issued the "*High-level principles and objectives for the FATF and FATF-style regional bodies*". In this document the FATF is explicit on two points:

a. "the FATF is the only standard-setting body and the guardian and arbiter of the application". In that capacity it tables "consistency issues" while taking into account the fact that it depends on input from the FSRBs.
b. The relationship between the FATF and FSRBs is that of "*free-standing organisations*" (p. 1).

The FATF stipulates that there is no organisational *hierarchy* between it and the FSRBs, and that the latter can also pursue other, regional, purposes. However, in the same sentence it stresses that "recognition as an 'FATF-style body' is the *conditio sine qua non* for being considered an FSRB". Interestingly, it is left unsaid who offers that recognition (or withdraws it). Is it the FATF Plenary? If that is the case, the latter would by implication nevertheless claim a hierarchical power over the FSRBs. Alternatively is it the G-7 (at present the G-20) or the Finance Ministers of the G-7/ the OECD? Or a combination of these? As discussed above, the Plenary decided in 1998 that the FRSBs' mutual evaluation procedures had to be endorsed by the. Essentially the FATF extended its reach and influence into farther parts of the world but without incurring any corresponding liability.

While not answering this question, the FATF document continues by emphasising the shared common goals and partnership, in a somewhat metaphysical tone. Despite their 'autonomy' the FATF and FSRBs share common aims, culminating in "identifying and addressing threats to the financial system" which "makes them part of a larger whole, thus the success or failure of one organisation necessarily affects all of them."

This formulation reads like a compelling 'moral goal bonding': one for all and all for one, approaching a *belief* system to which all are bound. This bonding finds its expression in the aim of "the protection of the FATF brand [which] is therefore in the common interest of the FATF and FSRBs". What is this 'FATF brand'? That is not expressed in a formula, but it looks like a type of holistic collectiveness in the style of all outputs. It is "not limited to FATF output, but also extends to any FSRB output based on the FATF Recommendations, assessment methodology, best practices and guidance papers, mutual evaluations and follow-up." Clarification of the FATF brand is deferred to the end of that paper (pp. 8–9) and elaborated in seven sections. They concern mutual evaluations, risk and typologies and stipulate that such FSRB papers must be in accordance with the FATF *universal procedures* and other standards. If that is not the case, they cannot be published with the FATF cover page and are thus considered null and void. So, that is an FATF hierarchy after all.

The High-level Principle paper also imposes more detailed requirements for governance structures, such as for membership, observers, presidency and budget. Though these conditions do not imply a direct organisational hierarchy, they impose an organisational blueprint that comes close to subordinating the position of the FSRBs.

We are of the opinion that these sections must be read against the background of the meaning of the opening sentence of this document concerning the standard setting axiom: "the FATF is the only standard-setting body and the guardian and arbiter", which makes the FATF the High Protector of its own FATF brand with the FSRBs being free-standing organisations without a hierarchy, but only as long as they do not deviate from the FATF orthodoxy. Other aspects of the FATF task fulfilment are elaborated in Chapter 5.

3.7 Regulating the extension of the FATF

We have seen in section 3.6.1 that in 1992, the FATF stopped inviting more countries to become members beyond the 28 members it already had. We have also seen that this restriction was not at odds with a strong drive to spread the anti-money laundering message through regional bodies and close cooperation with international financial institutions and the private sectors. Nevertheless, in April 1998 the 'FATF Ministers' urged the FATF to foster the establishment of a world-wide anti-money laundering network based on an adequate expansion of the FATF membership. This was to be accomplished in the subsequent years, but it would be limited by a number of strategic conditions. To be invited, the candidate countries should have strategic importance in their region and already play an important role in the fight against money laundering. The Annual Report of 1998-1999 mentions the following criteria (p. 34) as "the minimum and *sine qua non* criteria for admission":

1. to be fully committed at the political level: (i) to implement the 1996 Recommendations within a reasonable timeframe (three years), and (ii) to undergo annual self-assessment exercises and two rounds of mutual evaluations;
2. to be a full and active member of the relevant FATF-style regional body (where one exists), or be prepared to work with the FATF or even to take the lead, to establish such a body (where none exists);
3. to be a strategically important country;
4. to have already made the laundering of the proceeds of drug trafficking and other serious crimes a criminal offence; and
5. to have already made it mandatory for financial institutions to identify their customers and to report unusual or suspicious transactions.

This looks already like a formalisation of procedure and a sharpening of criteria.

As the FATF was bound to act and did not want to wait for applications, it decided to be pro-active and invite those countries believed to be of strategic importance. Given their existing political commitment to this policy, in June 1999, the FATF invited Mexico, Brazil and Argentina to become members and to attend the next Plenary in September of the same year as *observers*. Not as full members because the countries first had to undergo two mutual evaluations each, the first held in the reporting year 1999-2000. Their content apparently justified the conclusion that the three countries met the criteria for membership. While candidate members were already granted full membership, the second evaluation still had to be carried out. Unfortunately, the FATF-AR 2003-2004 mentioned the evaluations as being contained in the annex, but that was missing in the on-line document, nor could the evaluations be retrieved from the FATF website. What could these evaluations reveal? We thought this a relevant question as the summaries of the first evaluations look somewhat 'sugared': no word about the endemic corruption in these countries, no figures of the thriving drug trade or of prosecutions or any other tangible facts being mentioned.

In order to get some approximation of what the second evaluations could display, we checked the website for any other evaluation report of these countries and searched for figures of prosecution and conviction. We found the Third Round Evaluation Reports of Mexico 2008, Argentina 2010 and Brazil 2010 that were carried out by between eight and nine assessors. The law enforcement statistics on laundering for the nearest year were as follows: in 2004 Mexico had 17 prosecutions and 15 convictions (p. 19); Brazil in 2006, had 462 indictments and 14 convictions (first instance; two final convictions; p. 36); in 2010 Argentina mentioned four cases of prosecution and no conviction (pp. 36–37 and 59).

As these figures represent the nearest known performance after accession as new members, one may wonder what their performance was in 2000. Notwithstanding such (unknown) facts, and despite the missing second evaluation, the FATF membership was extended with the inclusion of these three countries.

South Africa and the Russian Federation were the next two countries to be invited to become FATF members after they committed themselves in 2002 to endorse the 40 Recommendations, undergo a mutual evaluation and play an active role in their region. The evaluation took place in 2003 and both countries complied with the preconditions of extended criminalisation, customer identification and reporting. However, despite this generally satisfactory compliance, law enforcement effectiveness proves to be limited: South Africa counted five convictions from 1997 onwards (p. 13) and Russia only one prosecution (p. 16).[30] Nevertheless, they were welcomed as members

[30] Though the membership should be given after two MERs, we could not find the second evaluation. It appears to have been silently dropped as a condition.

bringing the total number of FATF member states to 31 to which the regional organisations of the European Union and the Gulf Cooperation Council (Gulf States) should be added.[31]

The new eight years mandate of 2004, stipulated for the coming years that the FATF should increase its membership and so: "the FATF should continue to work actively towards the membership of China and India" (FATF, 2003-2004, p. 4). India and China were already long-standing Asia Pacific Group members. To open the dialogue, the FATF organised a workshop with China in March 2003 (FATF-AR, 2003-2004), while India was visited by a 'high-level mission' led by the FATF President. The new criteria would be applied, though with an important change: the requirement of a double mutual evaluation is no longer mentioned. We do not know if this was silently dropped as being too cumbersome As it is not the FATF's habit to give explanations. In January 2005, China was given observer status and after the mutual evaluation it became the 33rd full FATF member in 2007. An ongoing dialogue with India was opened and in 2006 it was granted observer status. In the same year South Korea was also granted observer status.

These developments look like a genuine 'growth-spurt'. Could the FATF cope with this extension? In 2008 the FATF Ministers approved a mid-term review for the 2004-2012 mandate. One of the outcomes of this review was a tightening of the membership criteria, which look more specific and bureaucratic than before. We present them here in full.

FATF MEMBERSHIP CRITERIA 2007-2008

February 2008 p. 29

Step 1 - Fundamental criteria of membership

a. The jurisdiction should be strategically important:

   Indicators

   - Size of gross domestic product (GDP).
   - Size of the banking sector.
   - Impact on the global financial system, including the degree of openness of the financial sector and its interaction with international markets.
   - Regional prominence in AML/CFT efforts.
   - Level of commitment to AML/CFT efforts.

[31] Argentina; Australia; Austria; Belgium; Brazil; Canada; Denmark; Finland; France; Germany; Greece; Hong Kong, China; Iceland; Ireland; Italy; Japan; Luxembourg; Mexico; the Netherlands; New Zealand; Norway; Portugal; Russian Federation; Singapore; South Africa; Spain; Sweden; Switzerland; Turkey; the United Kingdom and the United States.

Additional considerations

- Level of adherence to financial sector standards.
- Participation in other relevant international organisations.
- Level of AML/CFT risks faced and efforts to combat those risks.

b. If the jurisdiction was to become a member, the FATF's geographic balance should be enhanced.

Step 2 - Technical and other criteria

a. The country should provide a written commitment at the political level:

(i) Endorsing and supporting the FATF Forty Recommendations 2003, the Nine Special Recommendations 2001 (together referred to as the FATF Recommendations) and the FATF AML/CFT Methodology 2004 (as amended from time to time).
(ii) Agreeing to implement all the FATF Recommendations within a reasonable timeframe (three years).
(iii) Agreeing to undergo a mutual evaluation during the membership process for the purposes of assessing compliance with FATF membership criteria, using the AML/CFT Methodology applicable at the time of the evaluation, as well as agreeing to undergo subsequent periodic mutual evaluations following admission as a full member.
(iv) Agreeing to participate actively in the FATF and to meet all the other commitments of FATF membership, including supporting the role and work of the FATF in all relevant fora.

b. The country should be a full and active member of a relevant FATF-style regional body.
c. The overall mutual evaluation needs to be regarded as satisfactory, and in particular the level of compliance for the Recommendations dealing with the money laundering and terrorist financing offences (R.1 & SR.II), freezing and confiscation (R.3 & SR.III), customer due diligence (R.5), record-keeping (R.10), suspicious transaction reporting (R.13 & SR.IV), financial sector supervision (R.23), and international co-operation (R.35, R.36, R.40, SR.I & SR.V) need to be acceptable.

- In determining whether the overall level of compliance is satisfactory, some flexibility may be allowed with respect to Recommendation 5 due to its complexity and multi-faceted requirements. The assessed country is, however, expected to demonstrate significant progress toward full compliance with the components of Recommendation 5.
- It is expected that a country should obtain ratings of fully or largely compliant for all FATF Recommendations listed above in para-

graph c). If that is not achieved however, then the country must at a minimum achieve ratings of LC or C for a large majority of these Recommendations, and for the remainder, should demonstrate substantial progress toward full implementation and provide a clear commitment at Ministerial level to come into compliance within a reasonable timeframe and a detailed action plan setting out the steps to be taken and the timeframe for taking them.

The new policy of observer status at the FATF looks equally detailed.

How are these criteria applied? The annual reports do not provide a summary of how the findings of the mutual evaluation reports (MERs) are compared to the requirements of the new criteria. However, comparing the ratings of Table 1 of the MER of China, we see that only Recommendations 36, 40 and SR V[32] respectively are largely or fully complied with. Perhaps China mended these flaws in the eight subsequent follow-up reports, but these occurred *after* its accession: the last follow-up report was submitted in February 2012 (FATF-AR 2010-2011, p. 22). The ratings of the Indian evaluation were not much different, with the exception of SR III. India was accepted but also had to submit eight follow-up reports and a progress report on an Action Plan (FATF-AR 2011-2012, p. 42). One may wonder to what degree the new accession criteria form just a dead-weight bureaucracy, dressing up decisions which had politically already been made. As the decision process is not public, this question cannot be answered.

The process of extending the FATF continued. Two more countries were subsequently invited to become members: Malaysia and Saudi Arabia. In October 2014, the FATF invited Malaysia as an observer, but at its June 2015 meeting the FATF Plenary still encouraged Malaysia to "address its shortcoming to a satisfactory level" and to report its progress (FATF 2014-2015; pp. 13; 24). In June 2015, Saudi Arabia was also welcomed as an observer country to the FATF.

The FATF's extension to 35-member jurisdictions and two regional organisations[33] as well as the evermore detailed conditions reveal a development from a club, fostering its informality as was the case in the early 1990s, to a more rule-oriented organisation in relation to member accession. What about the functioning of the FATF itself: has that still retained its loose, informal nature?

---

[32] R. 36: "Countries should rapidly, constructively and effectively provide the widest possible range of mutual legal assistance in relation to money laundering and terrorist financing investigations, prosecutions, and related proceedings." + four additional specific requirements.

R. 40: "Countries should ensure that their competent authorities provide the widest possible range of international co-operation to their foreign counterparts." [. . .] "Exchanges should be permitted without unduly restrictive conditions." + 3 specific requirements.

SR V: Special Recommendation in terrorism matters.

[33] The steps of extension were from 17 members in 1990, to 26 members in 1992 and 31 members in 2000.

3.8 Organising the FATF: the unfolding shape and structure

We have thus far not devoted much attention to the question how the FATF could expand and exert so much power, while so little attention is paid to its own 'institutional arrangement' or: 'organisational structuring'? This seems to be a consequence of the FATF being set up as an *ad hoc* body, not as an organisation. In the annual report for 1993-1994, in the very short section on "*institutional arrangements*" (p. 7), it was repeated that "the FATF intends to continue to function as a *free-standing ad hoc group* . . ." What is meant by 'free standing'? Apparently not so free, because in the same sentence it is stipulated that the FATF *reports to the Finance Ministers* (or another authority) of the member governments. It then concludes that "It will also continue to send its reports to the OECD Ministerial Meeting and the G7 Summit." It is right to investigate whether the same Finance Ministers who also take part in the OECD are present in the G-7 delegation as well. Indeed, this arrangement looks very *ad hoc*, and very closed: a small club.

Concerning the internal organisation, the report only expresses the opinion that the "*plenary will therefore play a greater role in FATF meetings*". What does that mean? 'Plenary' means fully attended meeting which turns this recommendation into a kind of pleonasm. Due to the impersonal formulation we do not know what authority is advising here or who is advised: the G-7, the Finance Ministers or the President of the FATF? We remind the reader that this is the 'institutional arrangement' with which the integrity of the global financial system is guarded and which could make or break the financial reputation and welfare of entire countries.

This arrangement remained in place and was silently re-affirmed in 1998 and 2004 when the G-7, expanded to the G-20 (but still remaining informal), gave the FATF a mandate for eight more years.[34] This is a long time span which made a mid-term review in 2008 desirable. This was announced a year earlier "because of significant changes that have occurred in the FATF, as well as in the international landscape . . ." However, the Annual Report 2007-2008 does not reveal what this actually implied or whether the 'FATF ministers' or the FATF itself took the initiative for such a review. The review also implied a revised mandate for the time span of 2008-2012:

- Revise and clarify the global standards and measures for combating money laundering and
- Terrorist financing;
- Promote global implementation of the standards;
- Identify and respond to new money laundering and terrorist financing threats;
- Engage with stakeholders and partners throughout the world.

---

[34] An Ad Hoc Group chaired by Italy introduced various procedural efficiency changes, particularly concerning the structure of the Plenary meetings, the preparation of documents and the organisation of the working groups. However, the annual report does not specify these proposals (2003-2004, p. 5).

The text of the revisions (pp. 19–22) consists mainly of an explicit description and confirmation of on-going activities: "the FATF will continue . . ." or "will intensify". One assignment looks really new: a *cost-benefit analysis across the field of AML/CFT policy.* A wise proposal, essential to any responsible undertaking, but to our knowledge this has never been carried out and has never been heard of again: it was silently dropped from the follow-up mandate revision of 2012.[35] At the same time, the new criteria for membership (see elaboration above) and observer status were drafted.

As it stands, the FATF currently comprises 35 member jurisdictions and two regional organisations (after the expansion in 2000 to 31 member countries). As part of the adoption of the revised recommendation in 2012, its mandate was renewed under the Italian presidency for a period of eight years to 2020.

Regarding the FATF structure and organisation, the flexibility with which to face future threats is emphasised. It is interesting to observe the mentioning of the *Steering Group*: it looks like the dusting down of an old institution, introduced at the inception of the FATF in 1990, but after 1992 no longer heard of up until the annual report 2006-2007; p. 12. No reasons are given for this long absence. This Steering Group consists of seven members and will have an advisory task for the Presidency (the present President, the immediate past Presidency, and the Presidency-designate.) We have the impression that the FATF did not know where to place this Steering Group within its organogram: it is inserted a year later, in 2009-2010, located under the President – doing justice to the statement that the FATF is still an *ad hoc* group in its functioning and flexible in its structure.

The 2008 revision ends with a last but by no means least statement which makes clear where in the view of the ministers the centre of accountability is located.

"*Ministerial Accountability*:

> The FATF is accountable to the Ministers of its membership. To strengthen this accountability, the FATF President will report annually to Ministers on key aspects of FATF work, including on global threats. Given the potentially destabilising effects of criminal and terrorist action against the international financial architecture, occasional ministerial meetings will provide an ongoing accountability mechanism whereby Ministers can shape the strategic direction of FATF policy-making" (p. 22).

---

[35] The full text of this section is: "The FATF will also examine the available data to measure the impact of AML/CFT regimes on underlying criminal and terrorist activity, encouraging research into the effectiveness of its regime. It will examine the feasibility of implementing cost-benefit analysis across the field of AML/CFT policy."

This is not an expression of a democratic principle or a striving for transparent accountability, which is most unlikely given the variation of the democratic character and quality of the member states (Chapter 5). It rather re-affirms the conditions of its birth: an *ad hoc* body still in the hands of its political creators from the most powerful states who may have thought it time to re-affirm who was in charge by tightening the reins and calling for firm action.[36]

Meanwhile the FATF established three working groups to assist the Plenary:

- Working Group on Terrorist financing and Money laundering (WGTM) is among others tasked with interpretations and guidance of standards, typologies or methodology;
- Working Group on Evaluations and Implementation (WGEI), which assists among others the Plenary with the mutual evaluation process, guarding the quality, consistency and transparency of the MERs and serves as a contact point for international financial institutions and private sectors and advises on risk based approach.
- Working Group on Typology which gathers and studies information on money laundering and trends.

To this is added later (FATF-AR 2008-2009; pp. 8–9) the:

- International Co-operation Review Group, among others preparing statements regarding high-risk jurisdictions, counter measures, identifying high-risk jurisdictions for a review.[37]

Demonstrating the lack of transparency in the FATF reporting, the last-mentioned working group was already referred to in the 2007 annual report as having been established in 2006. In any case, it has an important task: spotting weak states that are failing to implement effective AML/CFT systems. Help can be provided, but if the country chooses not to be helped, "firm action" will be taken (FATF-AR 2007-2008; p. 20) in line with the US policy of 'convincing' countries (see Wechsler, 2001). It does not matter whether such a country is a member of the FATF, FSRB or neither. The reach of the group does not stop at its own perimeter of FATF members: it operates globally and (mostly) uninvited.

It is interesting to observe that the report does not mention staffing and other operational details. This omission also concerns provisions such as '*associate membership*' for the FSRBs in order to cement a close working

---

[36] The leaders of the Group of 20 asked for more action also because of the credit crisis of 2008. Actually, that originated from their countries. (2009 AR. pp. 14 and 28).

[37] There are four regional review groups, covering: the Africa/Middle East, the Americas, the Asia/Pacific, and the Europe/Eurasia regions (FATF 2010-2011; p. 20).

relationship with the FATF by allowing mutual access to each other's (Plenary) meetings and documents. It is a reciprocal arrangement, already mentioned in 2005-2006, but '*ad hoc*', without elaboration of 'rights and obligations'. The required regulation came a few years later: the FATF-AR 2009-2010 enumerates in 14 articles the Rights and Obligations of Associative Members in Annex I (pp. 35–36). It looks like: "we make an organisational provision first and think of regulating it later (if it works)". Or: *ad hoc* action followed by *post hoc* structuring or bureaucratisation.

Irrespective of the interpretation of these developments – structuring or bureaucratisation – the steady expansion of the FATF, its regional bodies and working groups, some of them institutionalised, others still *ad hoc*, all this requires a clerical professional support by a secretariat. How did this aspect of the organisation develop? Naturally in parallel to the FATF itself. It started in 1991 within the OECD in which the small secretariat was located. We find no mention of the number of staff or expenses except that it was a "small specialised unit" (FATF AR 1991-1992, p. 4). We do not know how the secretariat developed, as an FATF or OECD organisation, but the annual reports regularly mention the many tasks it fulfilled. These were not only of an administrative nature: the secretariat appeared to have taken part in many international meetings and discussions, almost as the 'right hand' of the President. With the introduction of the Executive Secretary, Mr Alain Damais, this was narrowed to clerical tasks in 2004. The new Executive Secretary also wrote a foreword (a novelty). There is no mention of the Executive Secretary in previous Annual Reports or why he was introduced in that year. The staff is still housed in the office of the OECD, Paris.

There are no indications of how the work or the secretariat changed, but from 2004 onwards we get a more precise picture of its work and expenses. The earlier references to the activities of the secretariat were strewn all over the annual reports displaying its broad involvement in tasks. From 2004, only its supporting task is neatly mentioned in a small section of the chapter "Support Services and Financial Statements". Also, for the first time, the composition of the staff and a financial statement is presented. From the financial statements 2004-2015 we have extracted the following budget figures as shown in Table 3.2.

The summary of the FATF's budget development shows a linear increase more than doubling in ten years. We also included the travelling expenses as a measure of the increased travel arising from the expanded international network obligations, which in 2017 shows an increase of 75% compared to 2016. These figures show that the FATF has grown into a sizeable organisation that does not stand alone. Around it are the bureaux of the regional organisations: the FSRBs with their own budgets. Unfortunately, most FSRBs do not publish a financial statement. The Asian/Pacific Group (APG) mentioned for the fiscal year 2013-2014 AU$3,212,530 expenses; Middle East and North Africa (MENAFATF) a "statement of comprehensive income" $1,149,428. Requests

Table 3.2 FATF budget 2004 – 2015: Staff, total and travel expenses

Year	Staff	Total €	Travel €
2004	n.a.	1,636,300	148,200
2005	10	1,740,100	220,000
2006	12	1,899,700	225,000
2007	12	2,064,252	250,000
2008	15	2,583,200	275,000
2009	18	2,797,200	294,300
2010	20	3,108,421	313,800
2011	21	3,305,445	295,000
2012	22	3,273,639	210,045
2013	22	3,447,404	250,000
2014	22	3,511,280	296,958
2015	26	4,044,692	289,872
2016	30	4,093,700	346,093
2017	31	4,839,992	606,220

Source: The authors based on FATF Annual Reports 2004-2017.

for budget information sent to other FSRBs remained unanswered. As standard-setting bodies demanding transparency in the financial sector, the FSRBs, which are endorsed by the FATF, should be transparent themselves by publishing the finances of anti-money laundering activities.

3.9 The rise of the compliance industry and compliance costs

a. The pre-history

The many new tasks and refined requirements imposed on the financial institutions and other obliged commercial and professional sectors arising from the Recommendations from 1990 onwards, all this implied far-reaching changes in the supervision landscape. They are all intended to fend off the threat of money laundering, which is a different security risk than the regulated sectors are used to, in particular the financial one. The normal risk financial institutions face is that criminals take money away, either by violence or fraud. Now they have to face the challenge of criminals bringing money into the institution to disguise or legitimate its origin. This implies an entirely different security system to keep suspicious money and customers out, either by preventing their entry or by declining their custom. This is a task for every client relationship manager, but also something more specialised, entailing modern software tools and technology, going beyond the 'naked eye'. Given the general weighing of operational costs to determine an in-house or outsourced solution, it was inevitable that a specialised compliance industry would develop to service this activity.

This industry did not emerge overnight: it grew gradually over several decades. In the early 1990s, it was still very much at the grassroots level. Now it is a multi-million (or perhaps, rather, a multi-billion) industry, as will be elaborated in this section. The phases of development are barely mentioned in the literature such that a particular development from a point in history can be followed.

For as long as financial institutions have been regulated, there has a always been a compliance function. It was the crime-money (and laundering) issue which stimulated the development towards AML compliance specialisation. Also, this has its pre-history, at any rate dating from 1970, when the US BSA came into force. As we have seen in the first sections of this chapter, in essence, this law laid the foundations of the current AML regulatory and law enforcement framework internationally. Although it did not explicitly contain the term 'money laundering' (a term that was not yet in circulation), it began transforming financial institutions into a global financial intelligence tool that enables law enforcement and regulatory authorities to track financial transactions in criminal, fiscal or regulatory investigations. Although this desired outcome was far from the reality of the first 15 years after the introduction of the BSA, as can be deduced from the critical evaluations made during the preparation of the Money Laundering Control Act 1986.

In section 3.2. we have described how the BSA required that the financial institutions maintain records and file reports on financial activity, including: (i) Currency Transactions Reports (CTRs) for transactions that exceed $10,000 (as required by the original BSA of 1970); (ii) Suspicious Activity Reports (SARs) for suspicious or unusual transactions, or account activities, transactions or activities inconsistent with the customer's profile (as required by the Annunzio-Wylie Anti-Money Laundering Act of 1992).[38] These reports have to be sent to a specially designated authority: in the USA this was first the Treasury Department's Office of Financial Enforcement (OFE) which administered the BSA but then it became FinCEN.[39] Such bodies, called Financial Intelligence Units (FIUs), gradually emerged in other countries too (see Gelemerova, 2009, 2011). The presence of an FIU became also an FATF requirement.

The record-keeping and reporting requirements created by the BSA meant that financial institutions had to introduce procedures on customer identification, verification and on process documenting (*i.e.* evidencing every step of the AML process for audit trail purposes). Customer identification procedures would later come to be known as Know-Your-Customer (KYC) rules. As already mentioned in section 3.2, the KYC concept was not new as stock

---

[38] As discussed previously, the BSA requires also that persons subject to US jurisdiction, including banks, file CMIRs and FBARs. Banks also file a Designation of Exempt Person form to designate an exempt customer for the purpose of CTR reporting under the BSA.

[39] FinCEN, also part of US treasury, was established in 1990. In 1994 it merged with the OFE (see posting by Pike on the website of FAS, 1998; see Gelemerova, 2009 and 2011).

brokers and other financial services companies had to make sure that they knew their customers. However, prior to the BSA, this concept focused on fair trading (*i.e.* selling a product best suited to the customer) and on fraud prevention. The BSA expanded the concept to include collecting financial intelligence (*e.g.* on customer's backgrounds and sources of funding) for regulators and law enforcement authorities.

As has been described in the previous sections, the BSA enforcement was originally weak: many banks were either ignorant of the BSA requirements or were deliberately circumventing them (Walter, 1989, ch. 9). A substantial study of examples of banks failing to comply with the BSA and organised crime taking advantage of this was published in 1984.[40] An example of this laxity is the indictment in 1977 of Chemical Bank already discussed.

In the first decade after the introduction of the BSA, exposure to laundering across the various sectors of the financial system was still largely unexplored. The general idea was that laundering was a feature of organised crime and drug trafficking, although among regulators and law enforcement there was the recognition that evading tax on legitimate income was to be chased through the same channels, as was illustrated by a report in the *New York Times* published in 1981.

> The article noted that "the municipal bond market's use as a laundering machine was unexplored. The municipal bond market is where the debt securities of city and state governments were (tax-exempt) bought and sold", in 'bearer form' (anonymous). According to the authorities "the illicit money being invested in municipal securities might be coming from organised crime, [while] the bond market was used also as a vehicle for tax evasion by otherwise law-abiding citizens."

We observe two justifying elements: (organised) crime for profit, and tax evasion. Depending on the political audience, both could be brought to the fore, though for the time being organised crime and drug trafficking (or their combination) would dominate the agenda and the political discourse. This did not imply that the US tax authority (IRS) was not taking an active interest in the means of hiding income. As we have seen (section 3.3), the taxman is always near. The US tax authorities were a key advocate of the BSA as it was to allow them to scrutinise accounts and money transfers. Later, they would purposefully label this law-breaking broadly as a means of laundering money and to use the AML tools to curtail tax evasion. We will discuss that later.

[40] *The President's Commission on Organized Crime, The cash connection: organized crime, financial institutions and money laundering. Interim Report to the President and the Attorney General.* Washington, October 1984 (see p. 44).

First, we observe that the reported violations of the BSA by major financial institutions and, more importantly, the resulting sanctions against them, did not go unnoticed by the financial sector. Banks had started paying attention to customers' risk profiles (from an AML perspective), refusing to on-board undesirable clients.

b. The unfolding of the compliance industry

As with many temporal developments, we cannot point at a specific moment in time from where the compliance industry took-off. As a matter of fact, it was always there as a shadow of the growing extension of regulations. However, political developments, such as the introduction of the Money Laundering Control Act (1986), the Vienna Convention (1988), which prohibited the laundering of drug money, the establishment of the FATF (1989) and its subsequent introduction of its 'Recommendations', contributed to imposing new requirements on financial institutions. New requirements implied new tasks, which eventually raised the question of who is going to carry them out That is: doing things oneself and/or outsourcing the execution of tasks.

Naturally there is no dichotomy but a gradual scale of in-door or outdoor execution of the compliance function: developing and executing all in one institution may be just as expensive as a full outsourcing. In the first variation there is always need for some hard- or software servicing (unless one chooses for full autarky). In the second version, one always needs extra staff for monitoring the outsourcing. Indeed, there has always been a compliance industry around the regulated institutions, gradually unfolding over several decades. In the early 1990s it was still very much unfolding, now it is a multi-million or possibly multi-billion dollar industry (see Levi, 2007). One may reach such figures if one would collate all in-house and out-of-house activities encompassing all income generating compliance costs. For a full assessment one should also consider whether the 'public' compliance sector should be included: for example, the staff of regulatory and supervisory institutions, the FIUs and law enforcement efforts. And what about the FATF and FSRBs? They are very much part of the compliance industry: they are the '*momentum keepers*' for which they are also remunerated. Before we move on to unexplored quarters of the compass, let us first look at what happened 'in-house' within the financial institutions.

b.1. The in-house units

Following the practical order of financial transactions, we start with the interactions between customers and the customer relationship managers. Here the KYC rule has to be applied: the relationship manager must investigate whether the customer may present a financial crime and reputational risk. This applies to opening an account (or offering another product/ service) and all further transactions. This is represented as a *first line of* defence in what became known as the 'three-lines-of-defence risk governance model' (see Institute of Internal Auditors, 2013; Verhage, 2009, 2011; Sandulescu, 2014, 2016). The first line of defence are the revenue generating employees. They are usually supported by a team of KYC specialists. The KYC specialists are typically also a part of the first line of defence (but as a back- or middle-office) and advise relation managers on what KYC documentation is required. They will collect, verify and analyse the KYC data.

In cases where (potential) customers pose a risk (either by their backgrounds or transactions) a report goes to the *second line of defence*: the specialist unit of money laundering reporting officers (MLRO or a 'nominated' officer) within the institution. This unit is established to investigate (potential) money laundering and submit reports to the authorities. In bigger organisations the MLRO or another senior officer typically heads a financial crime team comprising specialists in AML/CTF measures, including enhanced due diligence, sanctions (although some institutions prefer to have a separate team dedicated to sanctions), and transactions monitoring.[41] The KYC and financial crime specialists are *in-house units* that form part of the broader AML/ CTF compliance industry.

Audit, which is the third line of defence, pertains to the more general concept of risk governance which includes check and balances on all types of processes, not only AML/CTF.

b.2. The out-of-house services: forums and associations

While KYC and financial crime specialists are not necessarily required to have specific qualifications – although an inquisitive mind is a must – keeping up with changes in relevant legislation and industry practices helps develop and strengthen the specialist knowledge that is needed to perform the job.

A whole industry of specialist conferences, seminars, courses, qualifications or diplomas providers, bulletins and publications, blogs and professional networking groups has emerged to service that front and offer a forum in which to speak and share knowledge (see Verhage, 2009, and Tsingou, 2017). These,

---

[41] The second line of defence may be structured in different ways. Sanctions can be the responsibility of a separate team; the same applies to terrorist financing. Surveillance over transactions and corporate chatrooms for signs of insider trading is typically undertaken by another part of the compliance department. Fraud may also be dealt with by yet a separate team. In any event, the separate parts of the second line of defence cannot and should not work in silos.

aside from the professional networking groups which use networking media such as LinkedIn, are typically available for a fee.

An important role is played by industry associations. While some of these associations and societies were not originally established to service the compliance industry, they have started to represent it. To that end, they have dedicated substantial resources to the compliance industry. In addition to offering a platform for shared knowledge, as well as a forum for voicing concerns, they engage in lobbying the regulators and policy makers on behalf of the compliance industry.[42]

b.3. Professional investigative consultancies

Other enterprises show an interest in servicing the compliance needs of the financial sector. This is borne out by the growing industry of *independent* investigative and due diligence companies, *i.e.* third-party due diligence vendors, such as US-headquartered international firm *Kroll.*[43] To be a private investigator is no longer just about commercial espionage or detective work in suspected affairs or nasty divorce matters. The investigative business, often through synergies with security and executive protection, has developed into a multi-billion industry.[44] Companies willing to know more about their potential partners, new markets, other industry players' agendas or litigation adversaries can hire an investigative firm. In the 1990s, the industry actively expanded into adjacent fields. For example, it developed a specialised service focused on background checks to provide information to the regulated institutions and facilitate their AML compliance task.

The level of due diligence carried out by vendors of compliance services varies. It can focus, for instance, on developing an understanding of a particular aspect of money laundering or identifying red-flag issues; or it can be all-encompassing. The cost of a due diligence report on a company or individual varies widely (for instance, in the UK, from as little as £500 to over £30,000). Cost depends on a number of factors, such as the level of due diligence and

---

[42] This section reflects the authors' first-hand observations of the industry and insight gained through informal interviews with compliance specialists.

[43] Information about Kroll is available www.Kroll.com/en-us/compliance. Accessed 4 April 2017.

[44] See Bloomberg (2017), and The Economist (2013). The Bloomberg article notes that corporate intelligence's "going rate can run as high as $1,200 an hour", According to the Economist, "[Kroll's] zenith was its sale in 2004 to Marsh & McLennan, an insurance broker, for a tidy $1.9 billion." The company's value at that point can be seen as a clear indicator of the industry's growth and revenue streams: Stephanie Baker and Tariq Panja, *For Spies Inc., $1,200 an Hour Buys Dirt on the Likes of Trump,* Bloomberg, 13 January 2017, https://www.bloomberg.com/news/articles/2017-01-13/for-spies-inc-1-200-an-hour-buys-dirt-on-the-likes-of-trump. Accessed 5 November 2017 and The Economist, *The bloodhounds of capitalism*, 5 January 2013, http://www.economist.com/node/21569028. Accessed 5 November 2017.

what it entails (for example, what records need to be searched; whether it includes human intelligence enquiries in addition to public records research), the complexity of the subject's profile, and the business sector and jurisdictions of the subject's operations.

It is not mandatory for financial institutions to hire third-party vendors for due diligence. Some institutions, however, feel that they are in a more defendable position to the supervisors if they obtain an external, 'independent' assessment of a subject's reputation and source of wealth/capital. However, hiring a vendor also means that if the vendor provides an assessment that rests on bias and unsubstantiated allegations, the vendor's due diligence report will potentially create more problems than it resolves: irrespective of the work of the vendor, the principal retains accountability.

Poor quality due diligence can easily break a deal. This particularly applies to due diligence on subjects in challenging environments where contextual analysis is critical to avoid seeing things in black and white. Without such contextual analysis – as the definition of money laundering has been cast in such broad terms – it would be virtually impossible to deal with customers from jurisdictions where business and politics (and/or government) are closely intertwined. China, the Russian Federation, some of the former Soviet republics and the Middle East, where half of the rich are Politically Exposed Persons (PEPs), provide good examples.[45]

In addition to due diligence and business intelligence, third-party vendors can provide a range of KYC- and AML-related services: these range from KYC-outsourcing to advice on how to develop KYC- and AML-compliance programmes; or how to improve existing programmes; advice on how to prepare for a visit by a regulator or to respond to a regulator's inquiry.

b.4. Monitoring sinners: imposed shopping in the compliance sector

Often consultants are deployed as 'monitors' of institutions, as a result of a criminal or regulatory investigation or inquiry. Typically, in the USA, a monitorship is imposed by an authority as part of a settlement agreement, in particular deferred prosecution agreements and non-prosecution agreements, to ensure adherence to improvement measures.[46]

---

[45] http://www.scmp.com/news/china/policies-politics/article/1890470/dead-detained-or-missing-new-normal-chinas-business. Accessed 30 January 2017.

[46] DPAs and NPAs allow companies to avoid prosecution if companies comply with the agreement. The key difference is that under a DPA, the government files criminal charges with the court which it then waives if the company meets the terms of the agreement, while under an NPA no charges are filed. A monitorship can also be imposed as a result of a corporate guilty plea. The use of monitors by the DOJ was recognised in the early 1990s but monitors were used as early as the late 1970s by the Securities and Exchange Commission (SEC) when in SEC v. Page Airways, Inc.; the defendant agreed to 'retain a Review Person to evaluate the methods and procedures followed in this investigation' (see Lissack *et al.*, 2017, and SEC News Digest, 1980). Also see SFO '*Deferred Prosecution Agreements*'. https://www.sfo.gov.uk/publications/guidance-policy-and-protocols/deferred-prosecution-agreements/. Accessed 14 December 2017.

The practice of imposing monitors was been introduced by US authorities and was shared with other countries (for example, the UK). A monitorship can be quite intrusive as companies must provide their monitor with access to all relevant data and aspects of their business. It is also expensive (see below).

The organisation that has been imposed with a monitorship is free to propose its potential monitor from a pool of candidates with the proposed monitor subject to approval by the competent authority.[47] But if that authority is in the USA, it is to be expected that the monitor would also be from the USA. One could argue that if an international bank breaches US legislation in its USA-based branch, then the USA should have judicial authority over it. But, in reality, firstly, programmes imposed under monitorship are never limited to a US branch only – they span across the bank's global operations. Secondly, the USA can exercise judicial powers even in non-US branches if there is a connection to the USA. For example, the transaction includes a US dollar component. Monitoring is then frequently carried out by former US prosecutors or CIA agents. These monitors' firms may also sell compliance tools, software and services.

Installing a US monitor enables the USA to police international organisations, at no cost, as monitors are paid by the monitored organisations. For instance, after *Standard Chartered* paid about $700 million in penalties for money-laundering violations, it later had to pay another $300 million as a result of its hired monitor, who found that the bank was apparently failing to correct its behaviour (see further details below).[48] These are considerable amounts having a significant impact on an organisation's balance sheet. HSBC had to pay $1.92 billion as part of its settlement agreement.[49]

If being fined is not hurtful enough, imposed monitorships can also be costly as illustrated above. They are usually imposed for five years and if the

---

[47] The subject of selecting a monitor received considerable attention in 2007, when then US District of New Jersey Attorney Chris Christie approved, reportedly, without a bidding process, a contract for a consulting firm founded by the former Attorney General and Christie's boss John Ashcroft, to serve as the monitor for medical device company Zimmer Holdings under a contract, apparently, worth between $28 million and $52 million. As a result, conflicts of interest and cronyism concerns prompted the US Congress to hold an investigative hearing to better understand the process (see Lissack *et al.*, 2017; Walsh, 2015). It is, of course a direct conflict for a monitor to sell compliance services to the monitored organisation. However, in practice, there is seemingly nothing to prevent a company that acts as a monitor to one organisation from offering compliance services to another organisation.

[48] Standard Chartered's settlements with US authorities cover the period between 2001 and 2007 when it improperly handled transactions with customers from Iran, in breach of sanctions. Standard Chartered has a settlement with the Department of Justice and another settlement with the New York State Department of Financial Services, after the head of that body Benjamin Lawsky called the bank a "rogue institution" for its lapses in surveillance of transactions at its New York branch. (Lawrence White and Suzanne Barlyn, "StanChart faces extension of U.S. money-laundering vigilance", Reuters, 2 September 2016, http://uk.reuters.com/article/uk-hsbc-stanchart-compliance-idUKKCN118223. Accessed 12 February 2017.)

[49] Lawrence White and Suzanne Barlyn, "StanChart faces extension of U.S. money-laundering vigilance", Reuters, 2 September 2016. http://uk.reuters.com/article/uk-hsbc-stanchart-compliance-idUKKCN118223. Accessed 12 February 2017.

monitor reports in four years that the pace of reform is too slow, as was the case with HSBC,[50] the monitorship is likely to be extended. With that, the bill is also increased. As an article in the *Evening Standard* estimates, "*monitors charge $1,200 an hour to hunt down further wrongdoing*".[51] It also notes that "*so many of these deals have been cut that there's now a booming industry of specialist monitoring firms making a killing from these miscreant institutions.*" The article further highlights, investigative companies are "*flogging private consultancy work direct to misbehaving banks. One of the main services? Helping banks control their monitors.*"[52] This looks like a pervertive twist of 360 degrees.

Interestingly, in some cases monitorships are introduced under the umbrella of AML-weaknesses even if the key reason for the investigation came down to *sanctions breaches* in the first place, which is more a part of US foreign policy rather than anti-money laundering policy. Sanctions compliance and the

> For instance, in 2012, US prosecutors accused HSBC of failing to recognise suspicious activities related to Mexican and Colombian drug cartels. They also accused the bank of handling transactions for customers in countries subject to US sanctions (such as Myanmar, Cuba and Iran).
>
> In the USA, Standard Chartered reached a deferred prosecution agreement in 2012 in relation to an investigation into Iran-related sanctions violations. In 2014, it agreed for the monitorship to be extended until the end of 2017. As part of the agreement with the Department of Justice, the bank established in 2013 a financial crime risk mitigation programme to improve its money laundering prevention and sanctions compliance worldwide. Upgrading the bank's technology to meet US standards is part of the programme but, as the media has noted, it is "***proving a daunting task and it could face years more of investment***" (White and Barlyn, ***Reuters***, 2016).[53] Standard Chartered's monitor tested the software used by the bank and found that the bank's processes missed millions of possible violations.

---

[50] HSBC's monitor, Michael Cherkasky, was installed in 2012. In 2016 the bank told the media that the monitor had "*expressed significant concerns about the pace of that progress, instances of potential financial crime and systems and controls deficiencies, whether HSBC is on track to meet its goal to the monitor's satisfaction within the five-year period of the US deferred prosecution agreement and, pending further review and discussion with HSBC, did not certify as to HSBC's implementation of and adherence to remedial measures specified in the US DPA*" (Treanor, Jill, "HSBC 'taking too long to tackle financial crime'", *The Guardian*, 22 February 2016, https://www.theguardian.com/business/2016/feb/22/hsbc-full-year-profits-edge-up-to-132bn-as-chief-stuart-gulliver-takes-pay-cut. Accessed 11 February 2017.

[51] See also Ensign and Colchester (2015), *Wall Street Journal.*

[52] Jim Armitage, "Double dealing means these bank monitors need watching", *Evening Standard*, 1 September 2015, http://www.standard.co.uk/business/jim-armitage-double-dealing-means-these-bank-monitors-need-watching-a2924996.html. Accessed 12 February 2017.

[53] Lawrence White and Suzanne Barlyn, "StanChart faces extension of U.S. money-laundering vigilance", Reuters, 2 September 2016, http://uk.reuters.com/article/uk-hsbc-stanchart-compliance-idUKKCN118223. Accessed 12 February 2017.

related regulatory and law enforcement actions have been another driving force behind the development of the compliance industry in the USA, the UK and elsewhere. It is also notable that it is not uncommon for US regulators to require improvements that also include expensive investment in software and technology. This too is a significant driver behind the development of the compliance industry with all its ancillary services.

Both Standard Chartered and HSBC began, as part of their settlements, to invest hundreds of millions of dollars in overhauling technology and hiring new staff. Standard Chartered said in its annual report that it increased compliance spending to over a billion dollars in 2015, up 40 % on the previous year. In 2015, HSBC spent more than $680 million and hired 2,584 compliance staff. Since 2004, US authorities have imposed more than $16 billion in fines on banks worldwide for breaching sanctions related to Cuba, Iran, Libya, Myanmar and Sudan, all part of the financial crime/ AML complex. Whatever one thinks of the money laundering relevance or the otherwise political use of sanctions, these fines appear extortive.

Another piece of the regulatory puzzle is the Skilled Person monitoring regime in the UK, a concept not dissimilar to the US monitor. Under the UK Financial Services and Markets Act 2000, as amended by the 2012 Act, the UK's financial watchdog, the Financial Conduct Authority (FCA), has the authority to obtain a view from a third party – a 'skilled person' – about aspects of a regulated firm's activities in cases where the FCA has concerns or requires further analysis. The regulated entity pays the bill.[54] Among the firms the FCA has hired since 2012, to act as a skilled person we recognise some well-known compliance industry players, *e.g.* Deloitte, KPMG, EY, PWC, BDO, as well as law firms, for example Clifford Chance, DLA Piper, but also some less known firms.

A regulated firm in the UK may easily end up having a US monitor and a UK skilled person at the same time and, of course, pay for both. It would be an interesting dilemma if the US monitor and the UK skilled person were to make conflicting recommendations.

It is also notable that the FATF 2016 MER of the USA identified a number of material deficiencies in the US anti-money laundering system, including inadequate beneficial ownership requirements. What is of interest is that these gaps were also identified in FATF's earlier report. Putting aside the question of why the USA was not branded as non-compliant and/ or non-cooperative, what do these gaps speak of the credibility of the US authorities in seeking to police the international banking community through monitorships?

It is not clear how the US and UK authorities assess the relevant financial crime experience of the individual members of the firms acting as monitors or

[54] https://www.fca.org.uk/about/supervision/skilled-persons-reviews. Accessed 12 October 2017.

skilled persons, especially given that these later assess the experience of the supervised entities' compliance staff. It is equally unclear how potential conflicts of interest are handled. Firstly, once a private consultancy firm is through the door, it will naturally have a vested interest in perpetuating the image of a regulated firm as non-compliant – the longer the perceived problems within a regulated firm exist, the longer the consultant will generate revenue. Secondly, compliance industry firms tend to provide the whole spectrum of financial crime compliance-ancillary services, from due diligence, audit, assessment of processes, assisting with remediation exercises to being a monitor/ skilled person and so on. Many of these firms also offer technology/ software/ artificial intelligence solutions for resolving KYC backlogs, undertaking monitoring and on the like. While a Chinese wall can be created between two different departments of a consultancy firm, a complete segregation of duties is not possible. Why? Because all departments of a consultancy firm will benefit from industry scaremongering, irrespective of source. For instance, if a consultancy firm is acting as a monitor or a skilled person, they will have a scope for interpreting the law to their advantage and can claim that a regulated firm is being non-compliant. They will propose a solution, for instance, automated transaction monitoring tools or artificial intelligence systems. Meanwhile, the regulated firm will be fined and have remediation measures imposed, including taking onboard the bitter pill of the skilled person's suggested solution. While this solution will not necessarily be offered by the same skilled person firm – this would be a direct conflict of interest – the media will do its job in spreading the message across the industry. Regulated firms will want to implement the same solution in order to avoid the fate of the firm next door that had just been probed, criticised by the skilled person (while footing the skilled person's bill) and potentially even fined. This means that the skilled person firm or, likewise, a monitor, will be able to offer their solution to numerous other anxious regulated firms that want to stay 'safe'.

Consultancy firms produce surveys, white papers and other similar PR tools that they can successfully use for scaremongering purposes. And scaremongering is easy in the absence of clear guidance from regulators or of a clear picture of the money laundering threat. True, regulators have issued some guidance over the years but that is far from sufficient to address the multiple complex issues regulated firms are facing.

Whether and to what extent it is appropriate for regulators and law enforcement to outsource reviews of regulated firms to private companies remains a pertinent question and one that has not been the subject of an extensive debate.

Furthermore, when the industry lobbied for a risk-based approach to attune efforts to risk priorities, they did not realise that this would turn into the regulators' and consultancy firms' advantage. The problem is that regulators and firms acting as their monitors/skilled persons appear to be process-focused rather than outcome-focused. Even if a regulated firm has the best and most efficient staff who would never let crime proceeds go through the firm's accounts, that will not matter to a regulator if the firm cannot demonstrate that it has documented a process that fits the regulator's concept of the right process. As there are no clear definitions of what a right process is, it becomes a 'human factor' variable or, a matter of arbitrariness.

For instance, most firms categorise clients as low-, medium- or high-risk. What defines these categories can vary. There may be clients on the border. If a client is on the border between medium and high risk, but rated medium risk, a regulator/ monitor/ skilled person can argue that the client should have been placed in the high-risk category and that the regulated firm's process is not clear enough. The fact that this client is not a criminal, has never committed a crime and is unlikely to commit a crime will not matter to the regulator.

Furthermore, regulators, monitors and skilled persons can also always argue that a regulated firm has failed to ensure sufficient mitigation. In the absence of guidance from regulators as to what constitutes sufficient mitigation, firms learn through a trial and error, if possible at all (Gelemerova *et al.*, 2018).

Another common issue is that regulated firms are typically cautious not to challenge a regulator or a law enforcement authority, or their representatives. This means that regulators, monitors and skilled persons remain unaccountable. This perpetuates the threat imagery they promulgate. In the end, the application of the risk-based approach defeats its purpose.

3.10 Cost estimations and the compliance market

Thus far we have not talked about the issue of everybody's concern: the revenues or expenses, depending on whose angle one takes. We remarked earlier that the compliance business is a multi-million or (more plausibly, given the cases described above) a multi-billion dollar industry. That is an intuitive judgment but academics who have studied the expenses of the financial institutions report that the industry perceives these costs as ever-increasing (Harvey, 2008; Levi, 2007; Alldridge, 2008).

It is sufficient to observe that compliance costs have been rising steadily since the 1970s. For example, in the early 1990s, the cost in the USA, where it all began, was already considered high, partly due to the massive flow of currency transaction reports. According to a 1994 congressional hearing in the USA,[55] legislation amendments at the time required Treasury to "*weed out*

[55] https://archive.org/stream/antimoneylaunder00unit/antimoneylaunder00unit_djvu.txt. Accessed 22 March 2015.

categories of Currency Transaction Reports, referred to as CTR's, that have no useful law enforcement purposes and have, in fact, over the years, been counterproductive in the effect that it clogs up the system so much that law enforcement doesn't have the time to properly scrutinize those transactions singled out as suspicious." The Treasury was required to achieve a 30 % reduction in CTRs, which, as was heard in Congress, would not only make it easier for law enforcement to examine their files, but it "*also should have a major benefit for businesses by reducing unnecessary paper work*" (*op. cit*). It was noted that estimated costs to businesses were around $3 to $4 to file each CTR (presumably the cost for filing SARs was within a similar range[56]). With businesses filing nine million CTRs annually, this was seen as an "enormous cost" of the reporting requirement and a "burden" imposed on the economy. This concern expressed at that time, however, did not drive major changes towards decreasing regulation and pressure on the regulated sector in the USA or globally. To the contrary, the compliance industry continued growing with new players emerging and generating profit on the back of the regulated sector's AML obligations. Some exemptions from filing CTRs were introduced, as a result of the increasing cost and volume of non-relevant CTRs. But as focus shifted towards identifying suspicious activity, that simply meant that regulated entities had to do more to analyse data and identify red-flags, with the 'ought to have known' principle leaving limited scope for defence.[57]

The actors in the compliance industry are on the one hand, not very forthcoming with data about costs (for the financial institutions) or revenues (for the actors on the compliance market). Big financial institutions that have a separate compliance department are likely to have a specified budget for at least a part of the compliance costs. However, such budgets are usually not made public being 'corporate sensitive information'. On the other hand, the same institutions want to keep the costs down and are, therefore, interested in initiating studies to get some idea of the compliance expenses if only as a signal to the legislator and supervisors to mitigate the compliance burden. This does not go unnoticed and therefore the authorities also address specialist consultancy firms for cost estimates. However, these firms are not disinterested as they are themselves part of the compliance industry. It is therefore of interest to shed light on their outcomes and methodology (this subject was previously discussed by the authors. See Van Duyne *et al.*, 2018b).

---

[56] As mentioned previously, the requirement to file suspicious activity reports was introduced with the Annunzio-Wylie Anti-Money Laundering Act in 1992.

[57] The Money Laundering Suppression Act of 1994 prescribed a number of mandatory and discretionary exemptions which were broadened throughout the 1990s (exempting, for instance, banks from filing CTRs on US government entities, listed companies and payroll customers).

One of the reports on compliance costs was commissioned by the City of London and carried out in 2005 by *Z/Yen*.[58] Apart from data from open sources, the findings in the report derive from interviews with 386 employees from the financial service sector of which 105 are from the international sector. The methodology and reasoning can be challenged as their diverse and unexplained "best estimates" comprise a simple midpoint between two subjective estimates of a range. This is little more than collecting opinions, presenting them in tables and declaring them as "best estimates" (Van Duyne *et al.*, 2018a,b).

The New Zealand Ministry of Justice (Ministry of Justice, 2008) commissioned *Deloitte* to assess the AML compliance costs.[59] The report provides details per financial industry branch and remains fairly independent in judging the plausibility of respondents' estimates by adding its own adjustments. Thus, the provided estimates of start-up costs and on-going costs of NZ$ 227.6 million and NZ$128.2 million per year were scaled down to a more plausible: NZ$ 111.8 million and NZ$ 42.7 million per year respectively. Though not indicated as such, it looks like an admission of the weakness of subjective estimates in interviews. Apart from that, the empirical basis is too small for extrapolations: there were only 32 interviewees spread over 15 targeted sectors.[60] Again, another debatable "best estimate".

A report by consultants of *Europe Economics*[61] in 2009, on behalf of the European Commission, aimed to study the effects of five measures of the Financial Services Action Plan. For the study 78 firms were interviewed from across the EU. Also in this report the 'best estimate' methodology is put forward, based on "*quantifying the impact of the Directives into a series of steps and thought experiments . . . which we hoped to be, in large part, intuitive*" (p. 124). It is difficult to see how it is possible to quantify through intuitive 'thought experiments'. Otherwise it remains a mystery where the numbers come from "*since in many cases the numerators and denominators would not be exactly comparable*" (p. 50). So, we find tables with averages and medians but without the required 100%. Indeed, the report may be the best (paid) 'intuitive thought experiment' ever presented in this field.

---

[58] M. Yeandle, M. Mainelli, A. Berendt and B. Heal (2005) *Anti Laundering Requirements: costs, benefits and perception.* City Research Series (no. 6). The countries compared were: the UK and the USA mainly, and Germany, Italy and France occasionally added.

[59] *New Zealand: Assessment of business compliance costs of the indicative anti-money laundering regulatory requirements.* Ministry of Justice, July 2008.

[60] Deloitte gave a stiff disclaimer at the end of the introduction (p. 4) of which the last sentence reads: "*We provide no assurances that the cost estimates will remain relevant beyond the date of this report and accept no accountability or responsibility for any changes to these estimates which might be occasioned when the final anti money laundering regulatory requirements become available.*"

[61] *Study on the Cost of Compliance with Selected FSAP Measures. Final report by Europe Economics.* London, 5 January 2009.

KPMG – "*named Global AML firm of the year 2014*" – issued a report in 2014 on the global costs of compliance.[62] It is based on a questionnaire to which 317 persons responded, all in knowledgeable positions within the financial industry worldwide. Among other things, they were asked to give an estimate of the increase in compliance costs: "*How much has total investment in AML activity increased compared to three years ago?*" Methodologically this is a difficult question: it supposes knowledge of two points in time plus a judgment about increase across three years: knowledge of the present AML-specific expenses and those of three years earlier (which is the 100%). From this cognition (if present) a comparative estimate must be made in percentages with broad and unequal intervals (p. 13: 25-50%; 50-100% and > 100% increase). No specific numbers were asked about identifiable compliance actions that are not interwoven with ongoing compliance activities ("sunk costs"). For example, the acquisition of new monitoring tools or the outsourcing of certain tasks. These should be identifiable costs as they must be budgeted. If they cannot be disclosed because of being 'business sensitive', then that should have been mentioned as part of the methodological accountability. Naturally, this study was also presented as a 'best estimate'.

Regarding this output, two questions should be raised. The first concerns the reception of these and similar works: are they being accepted with their methodology unchallenged? The second concerns what these studies tell us and what purpose do they serve? While the 1994 cost study in the USA, arguably, resulted in some exemptions from the CTR regime (as discussed above), subsequent studies of compliance cost internationally do not appear to have been consistently conclusive, or have led to any major constructive legislative adjustments.

Another, related question concerns the independence of these studies or rather, the authors. The companies who carry out such research are part of the professional compliance sector and may be sensitive to remain within the boundaries of prevalent opinions and what is considered as prudent and socially acceptable by this sector. That does not easily go hand-in-hand with a rigorous methodology which may result in other outcomes than are welcomed in the compliance market place.

This state of affairs is also reflected in the work carried out by Verhage (2011), which gives a description of what she calls the "anti-money laundering complex". This is broader than the compliance industry as elaborated in this section: it also encompasses the public authorities (supervisory authori-

---

62 *Global Anti-Money Laundering Survey*. KPMG, 2014.

ties, police, prosecution) tasked with anti-money laundering functions. Within that complex the compliance industry market reacts on demand and supply (Verhage, 2011; ch. 7). One of the product categories are the reports on compliance costs as discussed in this section, to which should be added that the revenues of these products are not mentioned. From this market perspective it is surprising that the reporting firms do not downplay these expenses. One would expect sellers of tools and seminars to present a picture of high risks versus moderate compliance product prices: "With us safe and at a bargain". Instead, risks and costs are both presented as unbearable threats and burdens. Is there a shared interest in keeping both costs and threats high?

There are grounds for having a closer look at this market conduct of which we do not find much in the literature. There is a host of compliance product sellers,[63] but we do not find any meaningful description of competition between them, which is the essence of a free capitalist market. Looking at this contradiction we should consider threat and fear as market drivers, or rather polluters, as they may be considered as interfering with free will. Financial institutions are afraid of reputation damage, from the side of the regulators and fellow banks, not from their customers (some of whom may be eager to hide their savings from the tax administration). Threats may come from the competition which may make the financial institutions overzealous in demonstrating their good behaviour. That makes them willing to avoid censure and brow beating, "whatever it takes" (Moorman, 2005).

That is not a very rational conduct, one would otherwise expect from the institutions guarding our financial life-arteries. But who claims that the anti-money laundering field is operated rationally?

3.11 Conclusion

In the course of the journey from the US BSA to the current international AML framework, the money laundering concept became a powerful tool of scrutiny in the hands of authorities internationally. The reader might reasonably at this stage halt to breathe in and reflect upon how easily the interests of one country became the preoccupation of the rest of the world; and how readily countries that apparently had little to gain were prepared to invest in the infrastructure required to support the global AML regime. Further, that they were open to the poking and prodding by groups of international 'experts' who can at the end of their visit pronounce their judgement. An interesting contemplation that will be further discussed in later chapters.

[63] Just to mention a few drawn from Verhage (2011, ch. 7): CCL Compliance Consultants, Brunia Compliance Consultancy, Eurogroup Consultancy, Uniskill, KPMG, EY, Deloitte, Norkom, Mantas or SAS.

It may be argued that the bringing together of representatives of the international community for the Plenaries, provides a valuable opportunity for members to exchange information and, generally, catch up with each other through the all important 'networking'. In recognising this perceived benefit, we should not lose sight of the significant cost and effort required to support the FATF and its approach. Any commercial organisation would closely inspect these costs and benefits (as we ourselves do later) asking if there is a better and easier way to achieve the desired outcomes.

The regime also became an invaluable marketing pitch for consultants in the compliance industry. By driving the benchmark higher and higher through increasing penalties and costly monitorships and skilled persons' reviews and without providing guidance on how to mitigate risk. The key risk, after all, became not the risk of money laundering, but of being fined for the same purported failures over and over again. In the end, organisations may take the easier path of not dealing with those clients that require more mitigation, such as charities, money transmitting businesses, third party payment processors, virtual currency providers and PEPs. This could entail that a whole range of law-abiding, albeit considered high-risk, customers will remain without a financial service provider. And this is certainly not what the AML regime was meant to achieve.

4

Concepts, assumptions and consequences

4.1 Introduction

"What's in a name?" This is a badly understood quotation from Shakespeare, with the implication of "what does it matter how you name a thing as long as it has a name". Such indifference was not intended in the play Romeo and Juliet, where the family name mattered very much. In our field it also matters and the quote should not be used to justify the avoidance of the dry and unexciting labour of concept analysis. As we will show, concepts in this policy field are as important as the family names or that of 'pint' and 'yard' for the British or the 'camembert' for the French. Everyone involved with these products would take their naming anything but light-heartedly. We think the precise concept of 'laundering' as important as the concepts of 'pint' or 'camembert' for respectively the English and the French for which reason we devote this chapter to concept analysis.

4.2 The need for precision

In the first chapter we discussed the gap between the firmness of the anti-money laundering policy making and its enforcement on the one hand, and the lack of an underlying accumulation of precise knowledge on the other hand. Precise knowledge presupposes *conceptual clarity*. This brings us to the question about a clear and unambiguous meaning of the phrase 'money laundering'. Here we soon run into problems. There are almost as many *legal* descriptions of the concept of money laundering as there are national criminal

P.C. van Duyne, J.H. Harvey and L.Y. Gelemerova, *The Critical Handbook of Money Laundering*, https://doi.org/10.1057/978-1-137-52398-3_4

codes. In addition, there are international conventions with different wordings. Apart from this legal diversity, there are also economic and behavioural definitions. It is reasonable to assume that they all have a common semantic stem, but that may be overgrown by additional connotations that are only functional in the specific field of application. To the extent that these meanings are divergent, the delineated phenomenon may be different as well. We will see whether such divergent meanings of this kind of crime do lead to different legal and law enforcement 'realities'.

By conceptual clarity we mean more than a basic precise definition. In our view conceptual clarity also implies bringing underlying, often implicit, assumptions to the surface. For example, we can formulate a definition of laundering, without specifying but assuming that it concerns 'real' money; or we can assume that it also covers *non*-monetary assets and advantages. Such assumptions can narrow or broaden the circle of application. For instance, illegally excavated archaeological finds can be 'laundered' by means of producing forged provenance documents about the exact location of the discovery. The object has thereby become 'whitened', even if it is not sold and is instead put on the mantelpiece (Charney, 2009). If one excludes this by choosing instead a monetary ('real' money) definition, one will have a smaller circle of application than when it includes any illegally obtained object as 'launderable'. But why should it be assumed that laundering is only about objects and money? Laundering can be about any criminally obtained *advantage*: fraud in science (*e.g.* presenting invented data) may also result in laundering. Indeed, the act of properly defining the phenomenon is not just playing with words, but is also about determining interests and consequences. What laundering is in real terms, as intended to be carried out by criminals may be different from what it constitutes in legal terms. The difference between the two may have a serious impact on the outcome of any research into the matter, potentially skewing the results and blurring the line between evidence and the 'best estimates' or guesstimates we described in chapter 3.

Before we proceed with discussing definitions, we first have to set the standards for what we think a definition must do. Its essential function is simply given in its original meaning: a definition determines the *finis* or boundary of a piece of land. Figuratively, it means delineating or determining the circumference of a concept. A suggested definition that does not fulfil this task is not a definition. Setting a boundary means *excluding*: a definition that does not exclude is not a definition. There are standards for a proper formulation. One standard is: each component is itself unambiguous in its meaning. That entails: no *value* terms and no open '*such as*' sentence parts. For example, defining 'organised crime' with reference to 'serious' crimes is not a definition, unless one sets a boundary for this term such as: serious = a criminal offence with a maximum penalty of five years imprisonment. The inclusion of a 'such as' element implies an open list, potentially to be supplemented when opportune. Metaphorically, the concept becomes a 'walking dune' intermittently reshaped by the prevalent (political) wind.

Another standard is the principle of non-overlap of the constituent components as this can result in parts being made redundant. Violation of this standard does not 'kill' an intended definition, but it can make it clumsy. For example, the 'structured' nature of activities and 'task distribution' as distinctive features of organised crime, where the latter concept already implies some type of structure.

In the end, the definition must act as a *decision rule* such that it can determine unambiguously whether to include or exclude each new object or phenomenon. This has practical implications for policy making as well as law enforcement where decisions must be made: does this or that activity belong to the set of laundering or not? As we will see, this has implications for the economic approach of laundering: if the economic formula implies no underlying decision rule, the formula is void and the economic consequences of money laundering remain undeterminate.

4.3 Defining laundering: observation or conclusion?

We first have to address the question of the basic *observation* of the phenomenon: we can observe the action of bread baking, drug selling or, in extreme, a suicide bombing. But can we observe the act of laundering? And if we think so, what do we really see? We can observe that people transport hidden banknotes in luggage or on their body; we can observe people buying things with cash while refusing invoices or conversely asking for an inflated invoice; we can observe the conduct of people depositing money in the bank ("client is nervous and has sweaty hands") and later a transfer to another bank. We can observe much more, but all we actually see are various forms of handling or managing of assets, money or valuables. We observe 'asset management' as a form of (usually financial) conduct, but still we do not observe money laundering. However, we have learned to believe that we can observe money laundering if the conditions of a criminal law context are satisfied. This implies that we come to a *conclusion* which is not a pure observation but one based on a *legal construction*.

This *positivist* approach has consequences for denotation: instead of the phrase 'money laundering' we think it more appropriate to use the phrase '*criminal asset management*'. This is for scientific as well as for legal reasons, as it is fundamentally wrong (a 'mortal sin') to start with a conclusion: money laundering as the construction of a criminalised conduct that has yet to be proven.

In the previous section we juxtaposed 'money' and 'assets' as subjects of criminal management. At this point we have to make a choice in wording: 'money' or 'asset' management. This is not an invitation to engage in hair-splitting subtleties, as the choice determines the field of application. We think 'asset' is the correct term: it indicates a possession, acquisition and, possibly, use of a measurable advantage obtained by means of criminal law-breaking. Therefore, handling such assets can be considered as managing them which encompasses a range of conducts, from mere possession to sophisticated accountancy fraud, from stripping a stolen car to hiding profits from environmental crime by fraudulent paper work, such as illegal waste dumping (saved expenses) or selling wood from unlicensed logging as ecologically 'certified'.

In whatever way one handles criminal assets, there remains one flaw: the criminal origin has not been replaced by a pretended licit one. Smuggling money, burying it in the garden or buying high value assets, is still mere handling or managing of assets which remain tainted if not covered by a specific action, namely the *false* justification of their origin. This false justification is strictly laundering in the meaning of pretending a licit origin of the acquired assets ('white washing'). In this sense it is also a form of managing, but a *subset*: all laundering is criminal asset management, but not all such management is laundering through a false justification.

Given these considerations, we propose to restrict the phrase (money) laundering to the following conduct:

- **a justifying activity intended to falsely legitimise or 'whiten' (an) unlawfully obtained asset(s) or advantage(s).**

Summarised: all handling of criminal assets is criminal asset management. That part of the management that aims to falsely *justify* the acquisition of these assets is, strictly speaking, criminal asset laundering. In addition, we have the daily household subsistence or lifestyle spending that requires its source to remain hidden. For a subset of the financial conduct one can conclude that it is necessary to justify the acquired assets. That justification may range from a simple lie[1] to elaborate constructions behind fraudulent corporate (off-shore) bookkeeping. Whether and what forms of criminal asset management (CAM) are punishable is a matter of criminal legislation and prosecutorial construction, which does not change the nature of the conduct itself. Such constructions may have surprising (or embarrassing) consequence. For example, the case of a unknowing widow whose late husband had lived on social benefit his whole life, had never worked, but left a fortune in his bank.

[1] If this would be qualified as laundering we have a tension with the principle of non-self-incrimination: not lying about the proceeds means getting caught.

The execution of his estate was successfully constructed and prosecuted as money laundering.

Meanwhile we have reached a simple model, consisting of two circles of application: the specific laundering one within the general management one. As the phrase 'money laundering' is an established expression we will use that mainly, occasionally interchanging it with CAM, as we see appropriate.

4.4 Defining in legislative and policy making settings

In the preceding section we put forward a simple definition of laundering, although we acknowledge an abundance of existing definitions. In its report to the Dutch Ministry of Finance, the Utrecht School of Economics (Netherlands) provided an elaborate semantic analysis of 18 definitions of (money) laundering (Unger *et al.*, 2006; ch. 1; see also Busuioc in Unger, 2007, ch. 2). We put the term 'money' in parentheses on purpose as not all the definitions contain that word. This indicates that there is little agreement on the wording of the concept. Regarding the variety of criminal law definitions this is a logical consequence of the given national legal systems in which the formulation of the penalty clause of money laundering must technically fit. Moreover, the criterion in a criminal law context is primarily not the linguistic strictness of a defining formula, but whether it enables the prosecution to obtain convictions. In criminal law practice there is also the flexibility that an initially partially defined criminal conduct can later be specified by jurisprudence and complementary case law.

Naturally, criminal law policy making institutions (Parliaments, Ministries) have other, broader interests than heeding the formal requirements of a definition intended to draw a sharp line around a phenomenon. Policy makers, economists and economic institutions also have other objectives. Policy makers must see to a supportive constituency. Economists present political and economic issues by estimating the volume of money laundering and its potential effect on the economy. In addition, as Gelemerova (2011) has elaborated, the concept of money laundering has evolved, broadening as time passed and institutional and legislators' interest increased.

The elaboration and linguistic analysis of such a range of definitions by Unger and Busuioc (see references above and in Chapter 2) is of interest as it straddles legal, economic and policy making formulations. It makes a proper differentiation between the distinctive dimensions of the 18 selected definitions:

- Subject of laundering: 'stock' (such as property); flow or both;
- Source of subject: a criminal offence and
- The goal: hiding the (criminal) source or making it appear legal.

Leaving the wording aside, the most important difference between definitions concern (a) the 'source' (criminal) and (b) the objective of the behaviour (hiding the source or pretending a licit origin). Point (b) has already been elaborated above: general CAM or specific laundering.

Thus far the point of obtaining illegal or criminal gains, or as is often called 'proceeds', has not been touched on in this chapter. Yet this distinction is decisive for the scope of the phenomenon as the meaning of 'criminal' is more restrictive than that of 'illegal': the latter may not be criminal. For example, in many jurisdictions cartel building is illegal as a regulatory (or 'administrative') transgression. Hence, the gains from prohibited cartel building are 'illegal, but not criminal', a defence put forward in a massive price fixing conspiracy in the US (Conklin, 1977, p. 1). Managing these proceeds would not constitute money laundering. In other jurisdictions cartel building may be a criminal offence and handling its proceeds would be laundering. Consequently, jurisdictions in which cartel building is a criminal offence will have a larger money laundering problem than the jurisdictions where this activity is only an administrative offence.[2] This distinction gains significance in the context of a global anti-money laundering enforcement which also encompasses environmental crime. For example, the IMF mentions illegal logging specifically as a predicate offence. If this were to be adopted globally, it would have consequences for wood importers, who, if caught importing uncertified wood, cannot defend themselves with the excuse that their conduct is "illegal but not criminal".

4.4.1 Criminal law formulations

The title of this section does not contain the word 'definition' but 'formulation' for the simple reason that many penalty clauses are not definitions in form nor in content. Some contain just a string of verbs in a long sentence, others a list of sub-paragraphs; many have additional stipulations relating to their applicability but not to the content of the elements that constitute the criminal offence. As mentioned in the previous section, in the practice of prosecution and sentencing this is not a problem: contested interpretations

[2] To this we should add two remarks. The first is that one does not so easily escape the commission of laundering if it is only a regulatory offence: the ways of disguising the cartel can be a criminal offence, such as forgery of documents (Van Duyne, 2007). Then, as a consequence of that forgery the gained assets are the proceeds and their handling is laundering. The second question is more difficult to solve: the commission of an illegal act by cooperating perpetrators in different jurisdiction. What will be the outcome if the act committed in one jurisdiction is a criminal offence but an administrative offence in the other jurisdiction? In one country, the same behaviour can lead to a laundering charge and in the other country to just an administrative offence. How are international financial institutions that process cross-border transfers supposed to handle such situations?

use to be solved by the jurisprudence of the appeal courts or the Court of Cassation.

There is one concept that is rarely explicated in these formulations: the pretence of *justification* or '*white* washing', the ultimate completion of the laundering act as discussed in the previous sections. Nevertheless, we find the recurring use of the verb 'to disguise' juxtaposed to 'hiding' and followed by the purpose of the activity, be it hiding the origin or the rightful claimant (victim). Is this equivalent to laundering in its narrow meaning? The dictionary description of the verb to 'disguise' is according to the Oxford Dictionary is:

1. a. conceal the identity of oneself, person or thing as someone or something else.
   b. misrepresent, show in false colours.
2. Noun: artificial manner, deception

This meaning of disguise can be the same as laundering. Indeed, it is just to disguise the unlawful acquisition of something by misrepresenting it through a pretended legal origin. One can try to blur or erase the original criminal source through a series of off-shore companies, but one still has an unaccountable possession if it is not supplied with a licit origin. And at present unaccountable possessions are quickly associated with criminal sources, for example tax evasion as is recommended by the FATF Recommendations, 2012 as a predicate offence.

Having the main elements of Criminal Asset Management in place, we will survey its formulation in legal texts: two conventions and four anti-laundering legislations.

We will first look at the 'starting-definition' of the US Money Laundering Control Act of 1986. Subsequently we will follow the further evolvement of the defining process from the Vienna Convention (1988) to the Council of Europe Convention of 1990 (changed in 2005), the EU Directives, and a selection of national laws. We will not analyse the full text of the laws and conventions, but instead search for the meaning and implication of those distinctive features that were adopted to delineate the criminalised conduct. Shared elements which we do not quote for every formulation are: (a) "proceeds" as any asset derived from *crime*; (b) "with the intent", "knowing that" or "should have known"; and (c) attempt is punishable.

1. The US Money Laundering Control Act of 1986

The lengthy eight-page formulation of this law concerning financial transactions is very broad and various sections go beyond what may be qualified as specific laundering activities. For example, we find in the first subparagraph

(A) transactions with "proceeds with the intent to promote specified unlawful activity" (Sec. 1956 (a)(1)(A)(i)) and in the following subparagraph (ii) violation of certain tax laws (specifically sections 7201 or 7206 of the Internal Revenue Code). Such unlawful acts can be promoted by specific laundering conduct, namely:

> "(i) to conceal or disguise the nature, the location, the source, the ownership, or the control of the proceeds of specified unlawful activity" (Sec. 1956 (a)(1)(B)(i)).

The sentence part after (i) consists of a concatenation of concealing (hiding) and disguising (strictly laundering) with a string of badly sorted aims as the object.[3]

Subparagraph (ii) concerns the purpose of avoiding a "transaction reporting requirement under State or Federal law" (the BSA requirements).

The next section (2)(B)(i) deals with money (monetary instruments or funds) and "the transportation, transmission, or transfer" in and out of the country and knowing that these activities are designed "to conceal or disguise the nature, the location, the source, the ownership, or the control". This can be referred to as the "*conceal/disguise money laundering* dimension". The next section (ii) criminalises again the avoidance of reporting.

It should be noted that the law is focused on the "laundering of monetary instruments", though in subparagraph (c)(3) an elaborate summary of transactions is given.

Since the introduction of the Money Laundering Control Act of 1986, almost every newly designed formulation of money laundering in international legislation has reflected parts of the 1986 Act, in particular by adopting the elements of 'concealment' and 'disguise'.

2. The Vienna Convention 1988

The first of the conventions is the *UN Convention against Illicit Traffic in Narcotic Drugs and Psychotropic Substances*, 1988. Naturally the legal scope is restricted to proceeds from illicit drug trafficking as the predicate offence. In subparagraph (3)(b) we find (i) the "conversion or transfer of property [. . .] for the purpose of concealing or disguising the illicit origin of the property . . ." and (ii) "The concealment or disguise of the true nature, source, location, disposition, movement, rights with respect to, or ownership of property", which seems to be partly copy-pasted from the US Money Laundering Control

---

[3] Initially the US focused on cash proceeds in particular, which in the time of the cash-based cocaine boom is understandable. This had its effects on the policy orientation of the FATF, where cash remained important. Attention to wire transfers developed later.

Act. The term 'property' can be considered as equivalent to the term 'proceeds' used in the US Money Laundering Control Act.

The Vienna Convention also adds new components to the definition which appear in successor definitions found within national legislations, EU Directives and the Council of Europe Convention. These components are described in subparagraph (b)(i) ("conversion or transfer of property, knowing that . . ." *etc.*) and (c)(i) ("The acquisition, possession or use of property, knowing that . . ." *etc.*).

It is notable that the summing-up of relevant 'laundering' components is spread over a number of (sub)paragraphs without actually containing the word 'laundering'. This does not really contribute to the cohesion of the content, though the intention of the text is clear.

3. The Strasbourg Convention

All elements mentioned above come together in the Council of Europe *Convention on Laundering, Search, Seizure and Confiscation of the Proceeds from Crime* of 1990. As this convention had a leading role in the drafting of national laws in Europe (in both the EU and in other member states) we present the relevant article 9 in full. In that article all actions under the title of 'laundering offences' are summed up in the first paragraph, sections a-d. These concern:

a. the *conversion* or *transfer* of property, knowing that such property is proceeds, for the purpose of *concealing* or *disguising* the illicit origin of the property or of assisting any person who is involved in the commission of the predicate offence to evade the legal consequences of his actions;
b. the *concealment* or *disguise* of the true nature, source, location, disposition, movement, rights with respect to, or ownership of property, knowing that such property is proceeds;[4]

and, subject to its constitutional principles and the basic concepts of its legal system;

c. the *acquisition*, *possession* or *use* of property, knowing, at the time of receipt, that such property was proceeds;
d. participation in, association or conspiracy to commit, attempts to commit and aiding, abetting, facilitating and counselling the commission of any of the offences established in accordance with this article.

---

4 For interpretative clarification: the disjunction "or" must be read as inclusive "and/or". Both elements can be true.

Though the title "laundering offences" clearly denotes the general subject, it cannot be considered as a strict definition of laundering. Apart from subparagraph (d) these are all forms of handling criminal assets which in (a) and (b) are listed together with the strict laundering element 'disguise': the 'illicit origin', respectively the 'true nature' (*etc.*). Subparagraph (d) points at co-offending by participation in or conspiracy to facilitate all offences in (a) – (c).

For the purpose of this Convention the central elements of the definition are the verbs 'concealing' and 'disguising'. Otherwise it draws much from the UN and US predecessors: section (b) of article 9 looks to have been copy-pasted from the Vienna Convention. In addition, we find in (c) the components of acquisition, possession or use, also mentioned in the Vienna Convention, without disguise or concealment and lastly, "participation, association or conspiracy" in the commission of the crimes mentioned in a-c, which rather points at perpetrators and accomplices. Subparagraph (a) contains a sentence part: "assisting to evade [. . .] the legal consequences" of the offender of the predicate offence which deserves further explication as this is not concealing or disguising and may in this formulation apply to any defence lawyer who by the nature of his profession will try to support his client in evading 'legal consequences' by striving for acquittal. The problem of defence lawyers legally receiving fees from criminals with no other income than the proceeds for which they are prosecuted caused a debate amongst legal scholars.

<u>The Convention on self-laundering, or not</u>

An important addition at the end of Chapter 2 of the Strasbourg Convention is to be found in article 6 section 2(b): "*it may be provided that the offences set forth in that paragraph do not apply to the persons who committed the predicate offence*". This concerns the important issue of '*self-laundering*', which is automatically fulfilled with the possession of the proceeds (paragraph c). This entails that if self-laundering is also punishable, we have a 'wall-to-wall coverage' which makes even an attempt to commit a predicate crime an attempt of money laundering. Laundering is consequently a built-in element of any profit-oriented crime, without requiring independent added value.

There are various acts following or overlapping with the predicate offence that by their nature are unavoidable. For example, the act of 'possession' does not only imply a physical act of having a stolen object in one's hands, but also variations of disposition, such as a bank account, fed by proceeds from fraud or criminal deception in an investment scheme. In the same clause we also find the word 'use' which may be an addition to the possession, though that is not a necessary outcome. Having a stolen Picasso painting on the wall is possessing just as with having a stolen car in the garage, and this is, therefore, laundering but not 'using' in any conceivable meaning, unless one qualifies aesthetically enjoying stolen artwork as a form of using. Of course, a painting can be used in a barter trade with other criminals (Tijhuis, 2006, 2009;

Charney, 2009; Duyne and Vorm, 2015; Balcells, 2015) and the car can suitably be used for a Sunday drive or as a get-away car in a bank robbery: this usage can be qualified as laundering.

Of interest is the theft of intellectual property in relation to the elements of laundering: possessing and using. Plagiarism is theft of creations, ideas or concepts which is only materialised when they are *used*: having someone's idea, concept or formula in your head is not intellectual theft. But *using* that idea, concept or creation *is* a crime that also falls under the definition of (self)-laundering. This is not a petty, overly refined differentiation when one compares the maximum penalty: in the USA depending on the nature of the property theft, the punishment is three to ten years imprisonment compared to twenty years for laundering and fourteen years in the UK. Naturally, benefitting from intellectual property theft is also self-laundering.

Criminalising self-laundering has not slipped into the legislation by accident. In the Strasbourg Convention the option of leaving this modality out of the penalty clause has been explicitly mentioned. Most Member States have not made use of this clause. The Belgian laundering penalty clause stipulates explicitly that the acts of laundering also apply "*if the perpetrator of those acts is also the perpetrator or accomplice of the crime*". The UK law does not rule out self-laundering as a crime. The original penalty clause in the Dutch Criminal Code criminalised money laundering by broadening the offence of receiving stolen property. This met with serious criticism from practitioners as well as the FATF because the act of receiving does not apply to the thief himself, which impeded the prosecution of self-laundering. After criticism from the Public Prosecution Office a new section, 420bis, was added to the Criminal Code enabling the prosecution of self-laundering.

Countries choosing not to criminalise self-laundering have been systematically and severely criticised by the FATF. As a result, various countries, for example, Sweden, Norway and Italy have criminalised self-laundering which has produced an increased flow of small cases. Germany originally chose not to criminalise self-laundering. However, it appears that the pressure by the FATF was effective and Germany amended its legislation. According to the IMF (2016), "Germany notably strengthened its ML offense by criminalizing self-laundering in 2015. The offense appears to cover the conversion, transfer, concealment, disguise and acquisition of property with the knowledge that they are proceeds of crime. It does not cover possession and some aspects of the use of the proceeds of crime." Germany added the exception of bringing the proceeds from law breaking into circulation by disguising its origin (par. 261 StGB). Hence, the mere act of keeping the proceeds to oneself and using it is not punishable as laundering (the underlying offence is punishable for what it is) but transferring it and pretending it is legally obtained, is laundering. If, in order to keep the proceeds to oneself, a third party is engaged to ensure the proceeds look legitimate, that third party will be committing money laundering.

The act of laundering becomes a real built-in aspect where the predicate offence is (tax) fraud. In fact, the instrument of fraud, the forged document or false tax return, at the same time serves as an instrument of laundering, pretending a licit origin of the illegal gains. Van Duyne (2003, p. 72) calls this "*canned laundering*": the element of laundering (the approved forged document) is by the nature of the predicate crime (committing fraud) already in the same 'can'.

We must conclude that all profit-oriented crime entails laundering, including the attempted offences. This has consequences for prosecution as well as determining the scope of the phenomenon. The prosecution can always mention money laundering as a second count in the indictment, where the volume of laundering coincides in principle with the total of assets from crime, whether or not some act of laundering act has been carried out, or assets have got lost, damaged or fully recovered.

4. Four European legislations: Germany, UK, the Netherlands and Belgium.

Given the zealous lobbying by the US it is not surprising that following the Strasbourg Convention, the European Community published its first Directive issued in 1991 (91/308/EEC). Given the competence of the EC, which does not cover criminal law, it is a binding assignment to the Member States to put an anti-money laundering structure in place. As far as the formulation of the laundering offences is concerned there is little innovation in this document: it just copied the Strasbourg Convention. This means that we find in the national laws derived from this document roughly the same elements consisting of hiding, concealing or disguising property from crime or their acquisition, possession, transfer and/or use.

In the next sections we give a short exposé of four national laws criminalising CAM.

- *The UK formulation*

This is quite simple and straightforward in its wording: under the title "Money Laundering" of Part 7 of the Proceeds of Crime Act (POCA) 2002, it states in article 327 under the title "*Concealing etc.*" that a "person commits an offence if he" (a) conceals, (b) disguises, (c) converts, (d) transfers or removes criminal property from England and Wales or from Scotland or from Northern Ireland. In the next article 328 it criminalises involvement in "arrangements" that, the offender knows or suspects, facilitates (by whatever means) the acquisition, retention, use or control of criminal property by or on behalf of a third person. Finally, article 329 makes the acquisition, use and possession of criminal property an offence. Failure to report and tipping off are also laundering offences.

- *The Belgium Criminal Code*

Article 505 has no heading mentioning 'laundering', but starts in section 1, which criminalises *receiving* property that has been stolen, embezzled or obtained through other offences. This is not strange because there is an overlap between receiving and what is stipulated in paragraph 2 of this article, namely: knowingly buying, exchanging, receiving for free, possessing, keeping or managing property derived from crime. This aligns with the corresponding section (c) of the Strasbourg Convention, though the components of 'keeping' and 'managing' the proceeds are additions in the Belgium law. The components of conversion and transferring are found in paragraph 3, but there must be the *intention* to obscure (or disguise) the illegal origin or of "helping" the perpetrator of the predicate offence to "escape the legal consequences" *etc.* The fourth paragraph stipulates the concealment (or "keeping secret") or disguising of the "nature, origin, location, alienation, removal of property", all under the assumption of "knowing or should have known".

- *The Dutch money laundering article 420bis Criminal Code*

This article has only two sections. The first section specifies "guilty of laundering will be punished [. . .] (a) he who hides or disguises the real nature, origin, location" *etc.* or the "rightful claimant" of an object or who has it at his disposal and (b) "he who acquires, has at his disposal, transfers or converts . . ." *etc.* The second section determines that objects are "all assets and property rights".

There are two additional variations to the main article. (a) The aggravate form: article 420ter of the Criminal Code stipulates that a perpetrator who is guilty of habitual laundering will be punished with at most six years imprisonment. (b) The culpa form of article 420quater states that those who should have reasonably suspected the elements of 420bis will be punished with at most one-year's imprisonment.

- *The German paragraph 261 StGB (Geldwäsche; Verschleierung unrechtmäßig erlangter Vermögenswerte).*[5]

[5] Money laundering: veiling unlawfully obtained assets. § 261 CC.

The essential components of hiding and disguising the criminal origin recurs as in the other legislations: "He who hides an object from crime, disguises its origin . . ." which is in the same sentence immediately followed by another element, namely "or obstructs or endangers the investigation of its origin, its being found, its confiscation, its deprivation or its being officially secured". Section 2 stipulates that "likewise will be punished he who 1. procures an object indicated in subsection (1) above for himself or a third person; or 2. keeps an object indicated in subsection (1) above in his custody or uses it for himself or a third person" *etc.*, which covers paragraph (c) of the Strasbourg Convention.[6]

While the wording and structure of the articles in the four laws differ due to their place in the national criminal law system, the common components are the acts of hiding/concealing, disguising the objects from crime or their origin and the disposing of such objects (possessing oneself or by another). Can we consider the wording of these penalty clauses as formal definitions? What we observe is that the broad circle of application, namely *hiding*, is mentioned alongside the strict meaning of laundering by way of *disguising* the criminal origin. From a strict definitional angle this implies that the element 'laundering by disguise' is actually redundant when it comes to applying these penalty clauses: hiding and concealing would be sufficient with disguising as a specific variety. The elements '*acquisition*, *possession* or *use* of property' can be considered as forms of *receiving*, as is the case in the Belgian Criminal Code.[7]

What is the relevance of this comparison? Essentially, drawing up penal clauses is not a matter of formal operationalisation by a logical analysis of concepts but of stipulating which conduct can be prosecuted and convicted as a criminal offence. To this end it is sufficient to mention the subject only in the heading while enumerating the criminalised acts, as is the case in UK's POCA or the German article 261 StGB. But the Belgian Criminal Code shows that even such a heading is not necessary: the laundering clause is included in Part IV "*Receiving and other acts concerning objects obtained from crime*" without the mention of the phrase 'money laundering' itself. One can also choose to impose a lengthy sentence as is the case in the Dutch law starting with "guilty of laundering is . . ." followed by a formula that approaches a formal definition. However, from a criminal law perspective, a full formalised definition of the criminalised phenomenon is of secondary importance. The question is not about what laundering *is* – but, rather, which forms of conduct related to profits from crime should be punishable. In this regard, the discussed formulations are successful: they have a broad coverage. Some have a

6 Par. 261 StGB has recently been amended, as discussed above in the section on "The Convention on self-laundering or not".

7 Strictly speaking, 'receiving' overlaps with 'acquisition' and 'possession', but not necessarily 'use'; 'acquisition' can also mean obtaining by the criminal, whereas 'receiving' is usually by a third party.

real 'wall-to-wall coverage', others have 'fringes' of exceptions which we will elaborate in the next sections.

4.4.2 Defining from the perspective of policy making

If formulating a penalty clause leads to a useful legal instrument but not necessarily to a precise formula intended to delineate a phenomenon, how is the task of delineation fulfilled at the level of policy makers or their institutions? Their task is to bring a particular phenomenon to the fore, such that it raises political attention and, ultimately, brings about political action in the form of legislation and increased budgets for law enforcement. Drawing up a precise definition is of secondary importance.

Policy making bodies can be part of a ministry, such as Justice or Finance, but there are also policy making bodies operating outside national government institutions, often as inter-governmental bodies: technically independent but still government-oriented or government-linked. Examples of such bodies are the FATF, the OECD, the IMF, World Bank or the UNODC.

a. The FATF

The FATF uses a rather truncated definition of money laundering, which is described on its website as "*the processing of criminal proceeds to disguise their illegal origin.*" A further elaboration, conceptual analysis or definition of concepts is not provided. Instead it provides in a free-floating text some illustrative reasons for criminals to "*enjoy these profits without jeopardising their source.*"[8] It then enumerates the various forms of ['traditional'] crime that can generate "huge amounts of proceeds." In contrast to the first FATF report over time, white collar crime was also included in the later documents: "Embezzlement, insider trading, bribery and computer fraud schemes can also produce large profits and create the incentive to '*legitimise*' (our emphasis) the ill-gotten gains through money laundering." It is a strange formulation, as there is no other way of legitimising but through laundering (unless there is an amnesty): concealing and disguising. It may be accidental that this phrase is used in connection with white collar crime and not with 'traditional' or the 'usual suspect' acquisitive crimes in the 'underworld economy'.

It should be noted, that the terms 'proceeds' and 'profits' seem to be used interchangeably; the reason for which is not clear from FATF's reports. In the first FATF report in 1990, the two terms were clearly differentiated: "proceeds

[8] The FATF may mean 'disclose' or 'reveal a criminal origin'. The official 'carved-in-stone' wording of the FATF does not always lead to clarity or linguistic usage.

means the value of the sale of illegal drugs, without deduction of costs . . ."; "profits means the value of the drug sales less costs incurred . . ." (p. 3) For the act of laundering this distinction is of little relevance. However, for estimating the financial volume of money laundering this distinction is methodologically very important: criminal business costs do not always need to be laundered, though that depends on how one interprets the business transactions. For example, bribes paid in criminal businesses are at the same time business costs (for the briber), while obviously the same amount of money is criminal income for the corrupt official (with the follow-up laundering if required). These corruption costs may still need to be covered up, for example by inserting false expense invoices to balance the books. Is this also laundering? The answer is 'yes' if this is instrumental to hiding or veiling the unlawful advantages derived from corruption. In the end bribery entails the act of laundering, while the same bribe can be laundered twice: by the bribe giver and receiver.

Hence, not taking account of these differentiations may lead to double counting and inflated outcomes. In Van Duyne *et al.* (2005, p. 137) an example is presented of the multiple laundering outcomes starting from a hypothetical VAT fraud figure of €500,000 as basic proceeds: by inserting various business transactions and actors the accumulated laundered sum of money ranged from € 110,250 to € 860,500. In general, taking gross 'proceeds' as the basis of monetary estimations will lead to higher numbers and possibly to double counting. Indeed, conceptual precision matters.

b. IMF and World Bank

The IMF has long considered itself to occupy a unique position in relation to money laundering and terrorist financing through its oversight of the financial systems of its member countries. It incorporates assessment (by being part of many of the review panels of experts on the MERs) supported by provisions of technical assistance aimed at improving regime compliance with the FATF largely through strengthening their legal, regulatory, institutional and financial supervisory frameworks. AML/CFT assessments are a mandatory part of every Financial Sector Assessment Programme (FSAP) and Offshore Finance Centre (OFC) assessment. In matters of money laundering the IMF cooperates with the World Bank and, therefore, they both use the same definition: "Money laundering is a process by which the illicit source of assets obtained or generated by criminal activity is concealed to obscure the link between the funds and the original criminal activity."[9]

---

[9] 'The IMF and the Fight Against Money Laundering and the Financing of Terrorism Factsheet, 21 March 2016. Available at: www.imf.org/external/np/exr/facts/aml.htm. Accessed 15 August 2016.

This definition in the text of the factsheet is apparently not intended for further precision: there is no elaboration or clarification. It is striking that the verb 'to disguise' is not used in the definition, where otherwise one always finds the phrase 'conceal or disguise'.

The World Bank views its programmes on AML and CFT as comprising an integral part of its development mandate for financial sector integrity, reinforcing and supporting its complementary work on governance and legal framework issues, in a way that is similar to that of the IMF.

c. UNODC and IMF model legislation of IMF 2005 and Commonwealth 2009

The United Nations Office on Drugs and Crime (UNODC) worked together with the IMF to elaborate a model legislation on money laundering and terrorist financing. Four years later the exercise was repeated in cooperation with the Commonwealth Secretariat in the sense that the 2005 proposal was extended and adapted to the common law legal systems. In both papers the definition is similar in that they have the same components that are considered the minimum requirements that should appear in every anti-money laundering legislation. Besides these minimum components both texts insert variations or options.

We select from the UNODC-IMF (2005, p. 34) document the following:[10]

"Article 5.2.1 Criminal offence of money laundering

(1) For the purposes of this law, money laundering shall be defined as follows:

a) The conversion or transfer of property,
   Variant 1: by any person who knows or should have known
   Variant 2: by any person who knows or suspects
   Variant 3: by any person who knows, should have known or suspects that such property is the proceeds of crime, for the purpose of concealing or disguising the illicit origin of such property or of assisting any person who is involved in the commission of the predicate offence to evade the legal consequences of his or her actions;
b) The concealment or disguise of the true nature, source, location, disposition, movement or ownership of or rights with respect to property
   [*Variant 1*: by any person who knows or should have known
   Variant 2: by any person who knows or suspects

[10] UNODC and IMF (2005) 'Model legislation on money laundering and financing of Terrorism'. Available at https://www.imf.org/external/np/leg/amlcft/eng/pdf/amlml05.pdf. Accessed 15 August 2016.

Variant 3: by any person who knows, should have known or suspects that such property is the proceeds of crime];

c) The acquisition, possession or use of property
[*Variant 1*: by any person who knows or should have known
Variant 2: by any person who knows or suspects
Variant 3: by any person who knows, should have known or suspects]
[Option: at the time of receipt] that such property is the proceeds of crime.

d) Participation in, association with or conspiracy to commit, attempts to commit and aiding, abetting, facilitating and counselling the commission of any of the elements of the offence mentioned in the foregoing subsections."

This is not intended as a formal definition but as an ordered alignment of building blocks with options available for national legislators. The 2009 Commonwealth document[11] is shorter in the way it mentions the building blocks but is more elaborate in its clarifying annotations. Under the heading "kinds of offences" the relevant section mentions:

"As the UN's Legislative Guide [. . .] make clear, there are four general kinds of conduct that should be criminalized.

The minimum requirements for each are:

1. Conversion or transfer of proceeds of crime.
2. Concealment or disguise of proceeds of crime.
3. Acquisition, possession or use of proceeds.
4. Participation in, association with or conspiracy to commit, attempts to commit and aiding, abetting, facilitating and counselling."

This brevity is compensated by elaborate annotations attached to each of these minimum requirements. It should be observed that compared to the 2005 document one element taken from the Strasbourg Convention is now missing: "*or of assisting any person who is involved in the commission of the predicate offence to evade the legal consequences of his or her actions.*" No reasons are given for the deletion of this least clear element of the Strasbourg Convention definition: maybe the UN and Commonwealth authors could not handle this phrase. But it seems that a wide group of law-abiding legal professionals would have been caught by this clause for simply representing a client who is a criminal and charging them fees.

[11] Commonwealth Secretariat (2009-updated 2016) 'Common Law Legal Systems Model Legislative Provisions on Money Laundering, Terrorism Financing, Preventive Measures and Proceeds of Crime'. Available at http://thecommonwealth.org/sites/default/files/key_reform_pdfs/Common%20Law%20Legal%20Systems%20Model%20Legislative%20Provisions%20EB_0.pdf. Accessed 24 July 2018.

In the 2005 UNODC and IMF document on model legislation as well as in the IMF *Fact Sheet* of September 2014 (current version March 2016), we find another definition, though it is not at odds with the "minimum requirements" of the 2005 and 2009 documents above.

The reason for such different descriptions of laundering by the same institution is a matter of speculation. One could claim that the Fact Sheet is only meant to inform a broader audience and, therefore, a looser wording has been adopted. If this is the case, we do not agree with this intention: a broader audience must be served with an accurate description that should not deviate from the one used in other documents. We observe that even after 25 years there is still little effort to come to an unambiguous well-worded definition of money laundering.

4.5 'All crime' or a catalogue of offences and national criminal law

The observation in the previous section of a widespread indifference to a proper definition, goes strangely hand in hand with worries about differences in penal clauses between jurisdictions. Some legislative 'loophole' might allow criminals to get away with their proceeds, particularly in multi-country cases. (One would suggest: "repair your definitions first.") Unger *et al.* (2006, p. 25) express this concern strongly: "*Given such differences among jurisdictions, in a situation in which the predicate crime [. . .] took place in one country but the proceeds thereof were laundered in another country serious problems concerning investigation and prosecution could arise.*" This point has been taken up by Busuioc (2007) pointing at the 'all-crime' versus the 'predicate offence list' formulations and the inclusion or not of self-laundering in the penal clause of laundering. Do we have a real problem here or one only existing in the mind of purist jurists?

We are of the opinion, that there is a problem, though it is not certain whether it is a serious one, being a problem inherited from the 1990 Strasbourg Convention. As we have seen (p. 110) article 6 section 2b allows the exception of self-laundering while Chapter II, article 6, section 4 also allows the listing of a selection of criminal offences to which the penal clause of laundering will apply. If this is considered a defect, even if based on a political compromise, it has not been mended by later refinements or proposals such as in the 2009 Commonwealth Secretariat Model Provisions document. Indeed, the potential for variation seems to be consolidated by suggesting variants from which the national legislator may choose. This diversity can be overcome by adopting the 'all crime' formula.

The 'all crime' variant seems to be the simplest or most 'elegant' in terms of formulation, for example, as it has been formulated in the Dutch law on money laundering: that speaks of handling (concealing or disguising) proceeds "derived from *any* crime". This includes all the offences of Book 2 of the Criminal Code and criminal offences mentioned in the Law on Economic Offences, the Opium Law, the Law on Weapons and Ammunition and the General Law on Taxation. As a result, tax crimes or other economic crimes are brought within the circumference of money laundering. Misdemeanours and regulatory (administrative) offences are excluded.

Other legislations use a threshold of seriousness which also gives rise to diversity. The 2009 Commonwealth Secretariat Model Provisions proposes that where countries apply a threshold approach, the predicate offences should at least comprise "serious offences under their national law" or should include offences punishable with a maximum of more than one year's imprisonment. In legal systems with minimum punishments the threshold should be at least six months' imprisonment. Whether these suggested thresholds are demarcation lines for what may be qualified as a 'serious crime' is a matter of appreciation, but one may wonder whether any crime-for-profit will be under this threshold of a maximum one-year imprisonment.

One can have a combination of threshold and list of specifically mentioned criminal offences. For example, Austria has set a general threshold of one year imprisonment and, in addition, a list of criminal offences is mentioned in the same section of which the handling of proceeds also constitutes laundering: documentary fraud, participation in a criminal organisation, perjury, tampering with exhibits, bribery and smuggling.[12]

As mentioned in the beginning of this section, and as follows from the Austrian example, apart from the threshold approach the legislator may determine that the application of the laundering clause applies only to a list of designated categories of crime. This allows also some variation between jurisdictions, despite the list in the 2009 UNODC Model Provisions (13-14), adopted from the Glossary of the FATF-40. The proposed list in this document comprises 20 offence categories, ranging from murder (obviously for profit only) to insider trading. Because under national laws each category may encompass more specific crimes the number of listed specific predicate offences can differ between jurisdiction while still adhering to the proposed 20 offence categories. For example, Greece has a list of 20 predicate offences, Canada 45 and the US more than 130 (Unger *et al.* 2006; p. 25). As we have seen with the case of Austria, the threshold approach can be combined with a list approach. In our opinion, this does not add to clarity.

Having taken stock of the main approaches to delineate the field of application of the penal clause of money-laundering, there remain two questions.

[12] §§ 223 StGB (forgery official document), 224 (forgery protected documents), 225 (accreditation fraud), 229 (document destruction or theft), 230 (illegal border replacement), 269 (threat against authorities), 278 (criminal organisation), 288 (perjury in court), 289 (perjury in administrative procedures), 293 (false exhibit), 295 (tampering with evidence) or 304 (public service corruption) 309 (private corruption: accepting bribes).

The first is: do these differences matter? The second concerns again the point of definition.

The first question is a legal as well as a practical issue. The legal issue concerns double criminality and mutual legal aid. When countries have different lists of predicate crimes, then those they do not share do not meet the condition of double criminality. That is a correct observation, as put forward among others by Stessens (2000), Unger *et al.* (2006) and Busuioc (2007). Whether this also hampers the fight against money laundering is uncertain. When we look at the list of categories as suggested by the UNODC 2009 documents there are hardly any crimes for profit that are left out. From legal practice there is no mention of examples of failed investigations or prosecutions due to differences between lists of predicate offences or thresholds. This does not imply that it has never happened, but more probably, if it has happened, it was of insufficient importance for recording.

The issue of the legal circle of application should not lead to neglecting political diversity in prioritising national legislative developments, for example, due to changes in criminal policy related to specific predicate offences. The recent changes in soft drug policy may illustrate this point: if Uruguay decriminalises the soft drug market one can no longer speak of related proceeds in that country. But what about the proceeds of soft drugs from Argentina that are transferred to Uruguay?[13] In that case Argentina's fight against laundering for this specific national offence could be thwarted by its neighbouring country. Is that bad when it is a consequence of deliberate national policy differences between countries? A similar example can be presented concerning differences between abortion regimes: abortion related revenues are proceeds in a strict restrictive regime, such as in Poland, but (under national legal conditions) not in the neighbouring country of Germany. Why should Germany or other countries that are more liberal on this issue bother about supporting the search or confiscation of proceeds of a crime not recognised in their own criminal law?[14] This is not a rhetorical question. According to Recommendation 37, "Countries should render mutual legal assistance, notwithstanding the absence of dual criminality, if the assistance does not involve coercive actions." In cases of the specific requirement of double criminality, that should be deemed fulfilled if "both countries criminalise the conduct underlying the offence." But if countries de-prioritise requests for mutual

[13] The interstate consequences of the decriminalisation of the cannabis market in California, Washington and Colorado for money laundering in the USA are not clear yet. Perhaps the double criminality discussion is just a reflexion of a 'western-bias' in the drug related laundering policy. We do not find this argument in discussions concerning the proceeds from illegal alcohol trade in Muslim countries or the proceeds from illegal ivory trade in Africa and its main consumer country, China.

[14] Within the UK this conundrum is referred to as the 'hypothetical Spanish bull fighter', allowed in Spain but prohibited in the UK.

legal aid for offences which they have de-criminalised, that may put a strain on international relationships. This issue is revisited in Chapter 7.2.1.

We think the concerns of double criminality should be weighed critically: harmonisation of the lists of predicate offences to further the fight against money laundering is rational but should remain subordinate to national criminal policy and should not be used as a disguised tool to impose a kind of universal criminal law policy on otherwise sovereign states.

In the threshold and predicate list issues we are again haunted by the definition question. And not only that, we are also haunted in the wrong direction. Though it is said that thresholds and lists of predicate offences define laundering, they actually fail to do so. While leaving the core of the 'definition' in the law intact, they only delineate the *field of application* of the penal clause. As we have seen, the law may broaden or narrow this field without changing the legal essence of laundering itself: that is CAM in general and/or disguising their criminal origin of assets in particular.

4.6 Assumptions and threats of laundering (in a behavioural approach)

In Chapter 4.3 and 4.4 we discussed CAM ranging from simple to sophisticated. This behavioural approach contains only one assumption: there is a profit orientation. It refers to the actions of people if assets derive from a criminal offence. This may include punishable violations of regulatory and administrative laws, depending on political choices. CAM contains no moral or economic assumptions. Naturally, we are not oblivious to the potential moral or economic harm that may be related to CAM. But that is a consequence (not in the centre) of the basic empirical CAM approach. In that section, we argued for a narrow description of laundering as a disguise of criminal origins to make criminal assets 'white' as a pretended licit income or acquisition. That does not imply that all other forms of handling proceeds that do not result in 'whitening' are *a priori* relegated to a lower level of importance: 'unlaundered' criminal assets may be of equal importance as far as their effects are concerned. Or not?

a. Assumptions: threat

The most widespread assumption is that criminal assets pose a threat to society and the more so when they are laundered, because that would allow them to flow into our non-criminal upperworld economy. It is difficult to deny the almost self-evident validity of this assumption. As if the supposed self-evident nature of this assumption is not enough, we find it spelled out in detail by the

IMF: by its managing director (from 1997 to 2000) Michel Camdessus and by authors in the IMF. All drew on the original statements of the FATF followed by a UNDCC report authored by Keh (1996) with even higher estimates than the FATF (one trillion US dollar laundered annually). While the methodological foundations of such statements were highly debatable, giving rise to the qualification of '(gu)estimate', Camdessus, was undeterred by this serious uncertainty and went one step further. He announced at the IMF's Interim Committee in October 1996, which was repeated at the FATF Plenary meeting, February 1998[15], that "*2 to 5 percent of global GDP would probably be a consensus range.*" No underlining references were given nor was it clear what 'a consensus range' meant, nor who were included in this consensus. Consensus within the IMF? The follow-up IMF working documents of Tanzi (1996) and Quirk (1996) do not contain this figure (despite the assertion of UNODC, 2011; p. 19).[16] Notwithstanding, the '2-5% GDP consensus range' went into the 'quotation mill': This same estimate was repeated in the World Bank's *Reference Guide to Anti-Money Laundering and Combating Financing of Terrorism* (pI-6) which they converted to between $950 billion and $ 1.5 trillion (1996 prices) (sourcing Tanzi, 1996). This became subsequently a standard article of faith within the mainstream laundering expert community.

The assumptions of this huge volume slipped unchecked into the subsequent introductory remarks and preambles of important policy papers. A good example can be found in the Preamble to the Third Money Laundering Directive of the EU 2005: "(1) *Massive flows of dirty money can damage the stability and reputation of the financial sector and threaten the single market* [. . .] (2) *the soundness, integrity and stability of credit and financial institution and confidence in the financial system as a whole could be seriously jeopardised by the efforts of criminals* [. . .] to *disguise the origin of criminal proceeds* [. . .]." This is a clear political statement, of which content and empirical correlates are lacking, ten years ago as well as at present.

In order to assess the validity of this threat claim, we must do some detailed conceptual analysis to avoid getting stuck in a kind of indiscriminate 'conceptual porridge'.

---

[15] M. Camdessus, ML – the importance of international countermeasures' 10 February 1998. Available at: http://www.imf.org/external/np/speeches/1998/021098.htm. Accessed 11 August 2016.

[16] UNODC (2011) *Estimating illicit Financial flows resulting from drug trafficking and other transnational organised crime. Research report.* Vienna. This report included an estimate of the amount of crime-money (proceeds) at $2.6 trillion yearly of which $1.6 trillion would be 'available' for laundering (UNODC, 2011 p 6). This report also references the IMF 'consensus range' of 2%-5%.

First, there is the alleged threat to society by the 'dirty money': what does that term encompass? Using the term 'dirty' opens the door to the informal tax evading economy in which many shades of black and white can be identified. We will return to that in Chapter 6.4. In the second place, a distinction should be made between laundered and *un*laundered money, or what the FATF vaguely calls money "available for laundering" but without specifying its meaning (Van Duyne, 2013; Van Duyne *et al.*, 2016). As the mainstream of experts and scholars never questioned the FATF authority, we may assume that they also accepted this dichotomy of laundered and *un*laundered money. Returning to the commonly shared threat image, we should equally determine whether we must differentiate between the menace stemming from both categories of crime-monies. It is far from certain that they are the same.

Given the valuation of laundering as a serious offence, we assume that the main threat is posed by the completion of the offence: the launder*ed* money. Unger *et al.* (2006; Ch. 4) and Unger (2007; ch.7) have neatly listed all the possible negative effects that are commonly mentioned in the literature and that can be attributed to money laundering. That 'threat list' looks impressive,[17] though while applying the broad definition of money laundering ('crime-money flowing into the licit economy') these alleged effects become puzzling: has laundered money not become licit, or at least, has its *criminal origin* not successfully been concealed? As that is a direct implication of the definition, the next question to be addressed is: what is the difference between rightfully licit and pretended licit crime-money in their effects (aside from the moral ramifications) given their identical legal appearance? The consequence of this legal appearance is that the crime money has become part of the upperworld economy: it has become part of the GDP and is from its successful final laundering act onwards normal taxable wealth. Is that financially harmful? If that is the case, it would be worthwhile carrying out a back-testing: can we identify the criminal origin of monetary assets from differences, as mentioned in the literature, in the ways they are being used after laundering. This implies looking at the nature of investments, their management or the spending of funds only and based on that, identifying their origin. For example, 'sub-optimal' investing in real estate or objects of art or a luxurious lifestyle, instead of 'optimal' investment in shares and bonds, and then hypothesise from only this information the origin of the funds. This methodology would constitute a proper 'blind testing' similar to recognition experiments of beers or wines. Similar to this suggestion, Ferwerda *et al.* (2007) carried out an exploratory study on real estate in four Dutch cities. The investigation had a broader scope than just laundering and revealed various patterns of abuse in the real estate sector, concerning rental as well as buying transactions and price manipula-

---

[17] The threats on this list have meanwhile be refuted by Ferwerda (2013).

tion. However, inferior management in this sector could not necessarily be connected to potentially prior criminal money management.

Money laundering could allegedly lead to 'sub-optimal' investments because 'launderers' have other considerations than the best return on their investments, a point made by Keh (1996) as well as Tanzi (1996). Therefore, the funds of launderers would flow to countries with fewer controls, but also with lower profit rates on the investment. This again could have a depressing effect on the world growth rate (Tanzi, 1996; pp. 6–7). But do we observe such destabilising money flows attributable to laundered monies, again in a blind origin test? Tanzi's and Keh's concerns may be genuine, but hilarious against the background of the 2008 financial crisis ten years later. That was not caused by laundering criminals but by irresponsible bankers tasked with guarding the integrity of the financial system.[18] It is interesting to observe that this event, followed by the failure of the Greek financial system, due to alleged fraud and corruption facilitated by bankers, or the corrupt 'clientelistic' banking system in Italy and Spain, did not get a place in the mainstream money-laundering discourse (see Keršmanc and Ahtik, 2013).

Many of these and similar mainstream statements (further elaborated in Savona, 1997a) are, to a great extent, based on speculation and conceptual analysis that can be challenged. First, they do not differentiate between unlaundered and laundered money. To convert the dirty money into a laundered, justified status may indeed be costly (cheaper for the numerous self-launderers), but once the assets are properly laundered there are no sound reasons to argue that criminals would invest their money in low-productive economic sectors because of fear of law enforcement (unless the laundering technique was defective). Instead, their spending is rather driven by the psychology of the 'new-rich man' (Van Duyne and Kabki, 2016; Van Duyne, 2003). Against the background of the Mason and Stanford mega 'investment' fraud schemes in which normal Americans invested, this IMF's hypothesis of low-productive asset investment by criminals is amazingly biased. If criminal investors tend to avoid the promising schemes of these high-level crooks and choose for a lower and safer return, they act more rationally than millions of deceived 'licit' investors craving for the highest return.

In the second place, aggregate empirical data show repeatedly that the criminal income distribution is (and has always been) very skewed. Most criminal earners are in the lower income category (median value of recovery orders in the Netherlands 1995-2011 = € 3,300. Van Duyne *et al.*, 2013; Table 2). Older Dutch FIU data (1994-1996: Van Duyne and De Miranda, 1999) also reveal this skewed distribution: a small sample of 179 suspected

---

[18] *The Observer,* 13 December 2009: 'Drug money saved banks in global crisis, claims UN advisor' available at: www.theguardian.com/global/2009/dec/13/drug-money-banks-saved-un-cfief-claims. Accessed 15 August 2016.

persons/enterprises (7%, clustered in 87 cases) handled 674 million Euros, which was 89% of the total volume of suspicious 754 million Euros during this time span.[19] Van Duyne and De Miranda concluded: "*Few move much and many move only few*" (Van Duyne and De Miranda, 1999; p. 257). In fact, there is much 'criminal Lumpenproletariat' that only formally (self-) launders money but otherwise "are hardly able to meet their consumption requirements" (UNODC, 2011, p. 79). These skewed wealth distributions are at odds with the general assumptions or speculation about the effects of crime money on economies. This is rather a sub-theme within the general discussion of new riches and their economic effects. Against this background Van Duyne and Levi (2005; Ch. 7) wondered whether there is a difference in economic effects between windfalls from the drug trade and the extraction industry such as oil.

In the third place, it still remains to be seen whether laundered money flows to or remains in badly regulated jurisdictions with a lower profit rate. It is one thing to have an off-shore company in a tax-haven or off-shore jurisdiction and another to keep the deposited crime-money in a bank account in the same jurisdiction. According to data from the Bank for International Settlements (BIS), there are no indications that offshore centres are also the place where the big accounts are kept. In reality these offshore centres have substantial deposits in on-shore bank accounts elsewhere: the 35 recognised offshore countries in the BIS system ('BIS-countries') reported onshore claims to the amount of $5,440 billion in 2014 (van Duyne and van Koningsveld, 2017; Table 3).[20] In addition, if we assume that part of the tainted wealth (together with other licit assets) is managed professionally, it is not plausible that such monies are bound to flee to questionable banks in offshore centres and remain there.

We can come to an intermediary conclusion: there are insufficient empirical data to substantiate the claims that 'launderers' (whoever they are) divert their ill-gotten gains preferably to disreputable financial centres (See Van Koningsveld, 2015; ch. 6), or prefer investments with a low return because of laundering. Van Koningsveld (2015) presented data showing that most 'off-shore' assets were held in Europe. This shows clearly that this is a European problem which is not cured by 'finger wagging' at remote and small islands (Unger, 2017). In short, the observations put forward by the IMF from 1996 onwards have no proper basis: unless better substantiated they are to be con-

[19] This skewness is also mentioned in the UNODC 2011 report of financial flows. However, their median of criminal income is little more than speculation. The authors come to "assuming that the threshold level for money-laundering is the average or median income of a normal employee."

[20] Source: Bank of International Settlement, Table 7A Quarterly data 2002 to end 2014. This concerns only bank deposits and not other assets such as shares, bonds, real estate and other registered assets (boats).

sidered speculation which by repetition became part of the stock of laundering legends.

Fortunately, there is more between heaven and earth than IMF consensus models. What matters in the end is that the outcomes of a model are tested against 'data on the ground': assumption against refutation. To this end Ferwerda (2013) has listed the presumed effects of money laundering on the economy, of which he found 25 in the literature (the 'consensus'), and tried to find empirical evidence for each of them. Using a large variety of (open) sources, the author had to admit that for most alleged effects independent evidence was lacking, an observation that had also been made by Reuter (2013). Worse, for many of the stated effects pretences of evidence had been made without any trace to sources. Ferwerda quotes Barlett (2002) who stated: "*It is clear from available evidence*", though without any reference to that apparent evidence. Nevertheless, without a thread of evidence Barlett discussed the effects of laundering such as: distortion of consumption, investment, savings, imports and exports, income and employment, demand for money, interest and exchange rates, corruption, reputation and increase in crime. Apparently he got away with these unsubstantiated statements and was (and still is) widely quoted. Reality shaping by legend quotation.

A final important assumption concerns the heart of the issue: a precise delineation of crime-money. From an empirical point of view, one expects a clear delineation. Contrasting with this requirement, one finds rather unclear outlines as if drawn by a shaky hand. The IMF working paper by Quirk (1996) is a good example. This paper took the FATF definition of laundering as its point of departure and summarised various purported effects and consequences of money laundering for the economic welfare of countries. It also adopted the figures of the FATF first report on laundering (1990). But then the author went his own course, though without explanation. He went beyond the FATF laundering definition by assuming that all forms of unaccounted economic activities entail laundering. "*It seems reasonable to expect that virtually all income from criminal and illegal activities must be laundered. An exception might be the theft of unidentified banknotes*". This implicit 'all crime' perspective was not stated in the main text, but in a footnote later in the paper (p. 16). By doing so the proceeds from tax evasion are silently slipped into the set of predicate offences. On various occasions the author also included *insider trading* as a predicate offence into the discussion.[21] There is nothing against the 'all crime' perspective of anti-laundering that the author advocates, if he had explained this beforehand: science is not the art of juggling perspectives

---

[21] What type of conduct is considered criminal varies across jurisdictions, as discussed elsewhere in this book. Insider trading was prohibited in the USA as early as the 1930s. Later, in the FATF 2012 Recommendations, insider trading would be recommended to be globally adopted as a predicate offence.

but of transparency. So while writing he broadens the scope without warning and without explaining what is meant by laundering of the proceeds of tax fraud and insider trading. It is interesting to observe what happened to these points so silently slipped into an influential working paper. It looks like an early invitation to qualify these offences as predicate crimes. In the end, though it took some time, insider trading and tax fraud did indeed became predicate offences. The latter in the Annex to the 2012 adopted Recommendations as well as in the proposed new directive by the European Parliament and Council. To get all the sheep in the barn the IMF displayed a remarkable patience!

If this is the way in which the money laundering threat is represented, first by the FATF, then fuzzily elaborated by the IMF, which is very prominent in the 'Consensus', and subsequently almost endorsed by acclamation, then this must have consequences for the perceived size of the problem and subsequent measures to fight it.

b. Consequences: the size and threat of the problem

The implication of this way of addressing the money laundering threat issue is that in essence the whole field of anti-laundering encompasses the *hidden economy*. Given the IMF research background of the author (Quirk) and his reliance on older macro-economic research on the hidden (or informal) economy, his paper is indeed a kind of importation of old economic data, concepts and research outcomes of the informal markets into the FATF circumference.

This is borne out by the way the author tried to single out the effects of money laundering, despite the fact that this concept as a statistical variable is nowhere properly defined. Hence, Quirk formulated a "proxy variable" in the form of 'all crimes' as published by Interpol and the United Nations. Using such databases in this context should have been accompanied with a serious suspicion concerning their reliability. They should certainly have been taken with more than a pinch of salt. However, Quirk only mentions some authors who commented on the unreliability of these data and then without further comment simply continues using them for assessing the effects of laundering on the welfare of nations. This is done by using an older study on the influence of human capital and private investment-to-GDP ratios (Barro, 1991) *and* inserting the Interpol/UN all-crime laundering proxy-variable into its outcomes. The author then carried out a regression analysis and came to the conclusion of a "*0,1 percentage point reduction in industrial country annual GDP growth rate for each 10 percent rise in money laundering associated with crime.*" (p. 20). No further methodological considerations were given. This paper is considered in Chapter 7.5.

Apart from these consequences for the growth rate, the author points at the negative influence of crime and underground activities and associated money laundering. Because policy makers would not be able to take these underground economic and financial activities into account they would be led to "*misdiagnosis and incorrect policy-setting.*" Further, he argues that unanticipated cross-border transfers of funds could lead to volatility in exchange rates and interest rates; an unstable liability base of financial institutions; effects on tax collection (if money has *not* been laundered) and public expenditure and other misallocation of resources are mentioned. These consequences, routinely mentioned in older research on underground or informal economy, are not money laundering specific.

A specific laundering question that is not addressed concerns the volume and role of the launder*ed* money or the 'after-laundering' finances. While it is true that the underground economy can have a distorting effect on national statistics and economic policy making, as remarked before, the successfully laundered monies ('whitened') are by definition assimilated into the upperworld economy and thus have become a part of the official national accounts and are taxed (by property or wealth tax). This applies directly to the formally laundered (tax) proceeds (by approved false income tax return) as well as indirectly to the unnoticed spending on life style and daily maintenance by buying taxed legal objects and services (indirect taxes). This is laundering in its broadest meaning: 'using' proceeds in the regulated upperworld economy. This leaves the question open how these upperworld finances are victimised at the same time.

A good example of laundering by assimilation of proceeds is the frequently mentioned *insider trading*, although usually within the context of financial crime. Proceeds of this category of crime are laundered as a consequence or rather, as an element of the deal, right in the financial upperworld.

Another relevant observation concerns the earlier mentioned skewed criminal income distribution: a sizeable part of the proceeds are in the hands of a host of small criminal earners, who just spend their ill-gotten income to supplement their household maintenance. If this happens on a major scale there may be a distortion of the national economic statistics because there is more consumer spending than can be accounted for by net (after tax) income plus borrowing (*e.g.* for Serbia: Van Duyne and Donati, 2009) But that is a 'positive distortion': spending in the economy. However, there is uncertainty in interpretation. Should all this spending be attributed to *criminal* underground activity and therefore to laundering in the broad meaning presented by Quirk and the IMF (illegal earnings flowing into the upperworld. (See also Greenfield, 1993). We think the literature is rather inconsistent in what is to be qualified as laundering and how this is related to the various depicted threats.

The consequences of the chosen assumptions can be far reaching in terms of the alleged size of the 'threat' as well as the accompanying uncertainty. These are not only academic questions. Addressing the question of what should be included within this circle of the 'laundering threat' becomes highly political as soon as one applies the definition as a *decision rule*. Should the profits made by carmakers be considered crime proceeds, with all the ensuing consequences, because they cheated government emissions tests?[22] The same applies to the proceeds from the LIBOR manipulations and the questionable bonuses earned by bankers. Conceptually there is nothing wrong with following the logical consequences and including defrauding bankers and cheating and stealing captains of the industry into the circle of money laundering application. And if that would taint parts of our industry and financial system as a black pit of money laundering, so be it. Though it remains a question whether applying the money laundering definition to this type of conduct – canned laundering – is helpful in all instances. For example, at an individual level it may be appropriate to speak of laundering. But at an organisational level? Should banks involved in the LIBOR scandal or similar rate-rigging schemes be avoided as clients or counterparties? If not, how are regulated institutions expected to treat such customers?

4.7 Conclusion

This chapter has made clear that answering the question 'what's in the name?' should be taken seriously. Defining the meaning of the concept 'money laundering' has political and law enforcement consequences. It determines the categories of conduct which are to be included and, thereby, their criminal law consequences. This chapter shows that there is much conceptual diversity covered by the phrase 'money laundering'. Not all these varieties have been properly discussed as the discourse is very much focused on money derived from crime. Non-monetary advantages have received little attention. We have also pointed at the fact that money laundering is a legal construction and that the relevant observable conduct consists of the management of criminal assets, for which reason we introduced the concept of 'criminal asset management'. Observing such activities, hiding or disguising, has largely led to the *conclusion* of laundering. However, one should not start a narrative with the conclusion.

It appears that in the discourse of money laundering such methodological 'mortal sins' are common. Surveying the numerous attempts to define money

[22] In April 2017, a US federal judge ordered Volkswagen "to pay a $2.8 billion criminal fine for rigging diesel-powered vehicles to cheat on government emissions tests" in an "unprecedented" plea deal Volkswagen agreed to earlier in 2017. The sentence includes independent monitor to audit the auto maker's regulatory-compliance practices for at least three years (see *Wall Street Journal*, 2017).

laundering one does not get the impression of a very disciplined analytical approach. The criminal law specifications can be long, eight pages for the USA, or just one long formula sentence, as in the Dutch Criminal Code, or, as in Belgium, they can be written without the title "Money Laundering". It does not seem to matter very much: Politicians must convince their political audience and constituencies. These do not ask for precision but rather for an impressive threat and the ways to combat it. Law enforcement does not need much precision either, as long as they get the required powers and budget.

We have also seen that what matters is not conceptual precision and clarity but to span the net so broadly that every 'laundering fish' is caught. This explains the pressure to criminalise self-laundering, despite the contrary option mentioned in the Strasbourg Convention. The circumstance that this criminalisation results in a simultaneity of predicate offence and laundering does not seem to bother policy makers. Their priority appears to be that of wall-to-wall coverage. That the net gets clogged with a flow of small fry is not mentioned as a burden, or anticipated.

Given this 'nail them all' attitude it is surprising that the FATF has not exerted more pressure for an 'all crime' criminalisation. Working with catalogues of predicate offences or thresholds seems a less efficient approach. Notwithstanding, in the daily practice of law enforcement there does not seem to be any problem: the predicate lists are so long and the thresholds for applying the criminal law are so low that hardly any crime-for-profit category remains outside the laundering circumference. This will certainly be the case when tax crime is also covered by the laundering clause universally.

We observed that the methodological basis for the variously estimated volumes of money laundering are highly debatable, particularly when the applied concepts change during the elaborations like 'walking dunes' in the wind. The literature also shows examples of speculation which by repetition became 'real' and included into the stock of mainstream laundering legends. In one aspect the stakeholders in the laundering community proved to be consistent: they remained throughout its history virtually immune to refutations, that use to be ignored.

An aspect of that intellectual immunity is that thorny questions seem to be avoided. One of the questions avoided is at the heart of the subject: what to do with the following subsets of money: *un*laundered money, that is 'available' for laundering and the *successfully* laundered money? The latter should be unproblematic: due to their 'whitened' status they are part of the GDP, though we may not like it morally. The *un*laundered monies 'under the mattresses' are as safe and immobile as the silver hoards of the Vikings buried on the shores of the Volga. That may change if they are intended to enter into the upperworld economy. Is this the category mentioned as 'available for laundering' in virtually all FATF, UNODC and IMF documents? With so much references, this must be important, though we are still not told exactly what it is. That does not matter; what matters financially is: when and how will the money leave the mattress for further criminal asset management. Whether this is an important impact must be related to the skewness of the criminal income distribution: *Few move much and many move only few* (Van Duyne and De Miranda, 1999). This remains a matter of speculation which should be researched.

We returned to the role of definition as decision rule. We related the decision rule to the recent financial scandals and proposed to draw the logical consequences and include the law breaking economic elite. So be it.

5

Learning more about the FATF: Knowing the tree by its fruits

5.1 Introduction

The FATF prides itself on being the authority that sets global standards for combating money laundering, the financing of terrorism and the proliferation of weapons of mass destruction. It is an inter-governmental organisation and in that capacity a "policy making body". It does not present itself as a public organisation falling under some other super-ordinate public organisation or authority. It is funded with public money: all members contribute to its operations, roughly in proportion to the size of their economy (GDP). This also applies to the 'FATF style regional bodies': the FSRBs. As the whole undertaking is funded from the public purse these bodies should be publicly accountable. Given the inter-governmental status of the FATF, this accountability is assumed to work through the G-20 Heads of State and/or the "FATF-ministers": the real principals of the FATF who decide on determining and prolonging its mandate. Naturally, the ministers and Heads of State are politically responsible in their own countries. Analogue to this, the FSRBs are responsible to their participating governments: ministers or other designated authorities. Does this imply democratic accountability? The answer is uncertain and depends on the extent of political appreciation. We find no mention of participating countries having different 'degrees of democracy', which they do have, ranging from full democracies to one-party states or thinly veiled autocracies. Apparently, this does not hamper the FATF in its functioning (see 3.5.).

The question is: are 'we', the public at large, aware of the way in which this ministerial responsibility works? This is far from being a rhetorical question. Apart from new AML legislation and amendments to existing laws, that

P.C. van Duyne, J.H. Harvey and L.Y. Gelemerova, *The Critical Handbook of Money Laundering*, https://doi.org/10.1057/978-1-137-52398-3_5

require parliamentary consent, the competent ministers can formally be held accountable for the FATF's deeds under its mandate. Does that happen? In the UK, a select Committee of the House of Lords looked in detail at the existing arrangements for international cooperation with respect to money laundering and the financing of terrorism. As part of its work the Committee heard evidence on the operations of the FATF and FSRBs with respect to both transparency and accountability.[1] We are not aware of similar political attention and responsibility in other member states. Nor can we find any systematic evaluation or debate related to or preceding a continuation of the FATF's mandate. As we have seen, the FATF arrogates the authority of a global evaluator of every country (member state or not), while there is no public and independent evaluation of its own functioning. Who evaluates the Evaluator?

Naturally, we do not have the authority to carry out such an evaluation, though we share the reader's interest to know more about the FATF's functioning than is contained in the Annual Reports. To that end we will attempt to deduct (and interpret) as much as possible from the FATF public documents. Lacking yardsticks, this is not an evaluation, though evaluative remarks cannot be avoided.

Learning about how an organisation functions through its own publications has serious methodological limitations: one can identify a tree by its fruits, but when the gardener presents only his own selection, one gets a biased 'basket of shining apples'. This implies that whenever we suspect a 'missing apple', we will raise questions, though without much hope of locating the missing fruit: open communication with the FATF proved well-nigh impossible. Apart from that, we are not only interested in the fruits falling from the FATF tree, but also in all costs of maintaining such a global tree, covering all countries and financial institutions. After all, it uses public money and under the principle of transparency that the FATF claims to embrace, the public has a right to know and authorities the duty to inform. A first instalment of meagre information on costs was presented in Table 3.2.

5.2 FATF tasks and its fulfilment

The task of the FATF is clearly described on its website page "About"[2] as being: "*to set standards and promote effective implementation of legal, regulatory and operational measures for combating money laundering, terrorist financing and other related threats to the integrity of the international financial system.*"

---

1 House of Lords, European Union Committee 19th Report of Session 2008–09 'Money laundering and the financing of Terrorism' Volume I: Report Ordered to be printed 14 July 2009 and published 22 July 2009, London : The Stationery Office Limited available at: http://www.parliament.uk/documents/lords-committees/eu-sub-com-f/MoneyLaunderingReportfinal.pdf. Accessed 15 August 2016.

2 See http://www.fatf-gafi.org/about/.

This is a broad task, in particular because of the clause "other related threats" which seems to make it boundless. However, this should not be the case: if certain financial practices do not pose a threat, they should be considered as outside the duties of the FATF.

As observed, the FATF claims to be a *policy making* body: it is not an *advisory* body. Of course, it may consult or advise international stakeholders and regulated sectors as well as national authorities, but in the end the FATF determines the AML policy for all countries without exception. Not even headstrong North Korea can escape from its reach. The statement that it "works to generate the necessary political will to bring about [relevant] reforms" is a sheer understatement (though one may wonder who would want to launder funds in North Korea). As we will see, the FATF rules through its Recommendations and, as discussed in Chapter 3, these "are intended to be of *universal application*" (italics added), whether or not there is a political will to implement them. Therefore, we will first discuss aspects of the Recommendations while in a later section we will see what happens when a state has no political will to comply with what the FATF tells it to do.

The FATF Recommendations can be considered as the most important product of its policy making role. They contain standards to be globally imposed on states as well as financial and non-financial institutions. At the same time, they are a tool to *enforce* their compliance. The word 'recommendation' and the often-used verb 'should' are misleading: the verb 'should' has the meaning of '*must*'. So, this is a serious matter for which reason the word 'recommendation' must be written with capital R. Hereby the FATF has gone further than its assigned policy making role: it is *enforcing* policy at the same time. It is the first informal global policy enforcing body in history. The FATF has also assumed a further more wide-reaching task: it also makes Recommendations in matters of procedural criminal law that do not appear to have any direct relationship with the integrity of the (global) financial system. For example, the Recommendations concerning the criminal liability of legal persons (Recommendation 7) and the seizure and confiscation of property derived from crime (Recommendations 8 and 38) as well as the international coordination of prosecution actions (Recommendation 39).

This is not the only border crossed. The FATF also ventures into the field of criminal justice policy and law enforcement, strictly beyond the financial institutional boundary, although often adjacent to it. The FATF displays little restraint in judging the work of the constitutionally independent judicial institutions (judiciary and Public Prosecution Office) that are called upon to heed the recommendations and judged by their compliance. Thus, as an example, in the Mutual Evaluation Report of Spain (2014; p. 17) we read that:

> "*the main reason for lowering the* [effectiveness] *rating is that the terms of imprisonment being applied in practice appear to be low. The term of imprisonment applied in recent cases is 3 to 10 years.*"

And under the heading of Key Findings (p. 43) we read:

> "*Criminal sanctions may not be dissuasive. The majority of natural persons convicted for ML are sentenced in the lower range of six months to two years of imprisonment. Penalties of six or more years imprisonment are rarely imposed, even in cases where there was a professional money launderer involved.*"

It goes without saying that sentencing practice is always open to discussion and development. However, it is another matter entirely to exert pressure on a sovereign state and reproach its independent judiciary as not sufficiently 'dissuasive', with the meaning of not 'severe' enough. And if a jurisdiction defends the independence of its judiciary, it gets a lower rating. At the same time, when assessing a country's effectiveness in fighting money laundering, the FATF fails to factor in the level of its judiciary's independence. So, whether or not this is all legitimate, Recommendations matter as they are a real command. This will be further elaborated in Chapter 10.4.

A reason for this relative lack of sensitivity for constitutional and criminal law principles may be the professional composition of the G-7/20 and the FATF: these are not criminal law experts, but financial policy makers and senior staff from tax authorities. Over time this has not changed. For example, the composition of the 2012 Plenary was as follows: 21 delegates from the Departments/Ministries of Finance or Central Banks; five Ministries of Justice; two Ministry of Interior; and four FIUs in addition to other disciplines.

a. The Recommendations and its addressees

This chapter is not intended to open the debate on the contents of the Recommendations. Apart from being laborious, Recommendations may be changed or updated depending on new findings or insights elsewhere. For this reason, we look at them more or less from the outside as an output that can inform us about the FATF.

The FATF says that the list of Recommendations evolves with the changing financial landscape to which they must be applied. This means that from time to time revisions have to be considered and, where appropriate, introduced. We have at present the fifth edition of the 40 Recommendations. The first list was issued in 1990, followed by revisions in 1996, 2001, 2003 and most recently in 2012. The most important revisions occurred in 2001 and 2012. The 2001 revision was a response to the 9/11 terrorist attacks in the USA. It led to the extension of the FATF mandate with the inclusion of fighting terrorist financing. As a consequence, Special Recommendations directed at financing of terrorism were added to the list of 40 Recommendations: SR I-IX.[3]

A second almost equally important change was related to the introduction of the *risk based approach* to laundering. Countries "*should identify, assess, and understand*" money laundering and terrorist financing risks and attune their efforts: enhanced efforts for high risks and less effort for low risks. This sounds self-evident, but not, apparently, for the FATF. The FATF needed three full pages of "interpretive notes", for the countries as well as obliged institutions, summed up in five paragraphs for each of them, to make sure it was properly understood and to elaborate all the implications of this approach that was intended to lead to greater efficiency. In addition, countries should have nationally relevant policies and "*have effective mechanisms in place which enable them to cooperate, and, where appropriate, coordinate domestically.*" This implies that countries are ordered to establish a formal organisation unless the phrase "mechanism" means something informal. As can be deduced from later mutual evaluations, these are not meant to be just informal gatherings. In addition, the risk assessments evolved to become formal National Risk Assessments (NRA) which each country is supposed (= must) to have drawn up: an international constitutional *novum*.

It is interesting to observe that while for some time the number of Recommendations (40) did not increase, the FATF's need to explain them certainly led to an increasing number of explanatory notes: the *exegesis* outgrew the basic Recommendations. The 1990 Recommendation had no explanatory notes – just seven pages that were supposed to speak for themselves; the second (1996) had five pages of Recommendations and three pages of interpretive notes; the 2003 and 2004 Recommendations of 12 pages were accompanied by a three-page glossary and six pages of interpretative notes; a somewhat more extensive *exegesis*, but still manageable. However, the 2012 Recommendations consist of a small pocket edition of 134 pages: 20 pages of Recommendations, 78 pages of interpretive notes, a 14-page glossary, with the rest comprising references to updates and guidance documents. This is quite an achievement, though the frontline compliance officer, FIU employee or anyone who is in the management or supervision of the compliance may justifiably feel burdened. They would be well advised to follow extra training to cope with this paper work!

An important question that has not been addressed thus far is the international legal status of the Recommendations. They are primarily directed at

[3] The 2012 version of the Recommendations reincorporates the additional special Recommendations to revert to a list of 40.

countries, *sovereign states* and *territories*, that are ordered in unambiguous terms by an *informal* body what to do. For example: "should, without further delay, take steps to fully implement the Vienna Convention, and proceed to ratify it." This is an interesting state of affairs: while the United Nation's Congress accepts a Convention by resolution and subsequently *invites* Member States for ratification, the FATF as an informal body of at present 37 states/organisations *orders* about 160 other states to ratify "without further delay", irrespective of being a member of its "global network". Does that mean that the FATF has become in its field a higher authority than the UN?[4] And if so, with what authority? We will return to this legal aspect in section 5.4. where we discuss the legitimacy of sanctioning.

b. The tools of the mutual evaluations

After the Recommendations come the evaluations of compliance. In the beginning, when the FATF was still a small club, the members also carried out self-evaluations parallel to mutual evaluations. We do not know much of their content as they are not readily available. We will see in section 5.3 that at the end of the 1990s the FATF had proclaimed its universal competence in judging the level of cooperation of all states, whether or not they were members of the FATF or the FSRBs. This had its consequence for the mutual evaluations, which had to be universal as well. It was also decided that after being approved by the plenary they would be published. The result was an enormous output of documents (methodologies, 'tools', and MERs) that spread across the world from 2005 onwards: first, the output of the third mutual evaluation round was published and, since 2014, that of the fourth and possibly most elaborate mutual evaluation round was published.

Naturally, such undertakings should not be taken lightly and indeed, the FATF engaged in a proper administrative setup and methodological preparation. For each round it issued a methodology and a set of 'tools'.

<u>1. The third round: evaluation tools</u>

For the third round evaluation the FATF made the following documents available:

a. a handbook for countries and assessors (April 2009; 99 pages) with a detailed questionnaire of 55 pages (twice amended in 2005 and 2006);
b. a hand-out on "Process and Procedures" (October 2009; 24 pages) and

[4] One may wish that the global climate change problem would be addressed in a similar way.

c. a methodology for assessing compliance (February 2004; updated February 2009; 79 pages).

Of course, the 40 Recommendations plus their interpretive notes are also part and parcel of the evaluation tools, to which should be added the relevant international conventions, UN resolutions as well as previous evaluation reports for a comparison of progress with earlier performance. For the teams of assessors (on average 5-6 members but often more) this must be a burdensome box of equipment with which to get to grips.

Without judging the validity of the tools of the assessors, it should be remarked that even at first sight they cannot guarantee unambiguous outcomes. The questions asked about the countries and their economies, the nature and development of money laundering, law enforcement actions, the state of law (corruption and ethical standards) *etc.*, addressing all these subjects in a valid way requires an almost utopian criminological and statistical sophistication and insight, not only from the assessors but also from experts within the evaluated country, who must produce internal documents evaluating the existing state of affairs. As a matter of fact, the documents rarely reflect a deeper knowledge, especially of reliable statistics and accessible databases as the first basic tool for an evaluation.

The third round of mutual evaluations led to an enormous output with an average report size of 215 pages, with France's evaluation of 664 pages proudly towering above all other evaluated countries (see Van Duyne *et al.*, 2016). The literature about the FATF's evaluations is not particularly rich or positive, despite the importance of the subject and their expenses (estimated at $300,000 per evaluation). Halliday, Levi and Reuter (2014) were invited by the IMF to review the third evaluation round (also refer to our Table 8.4). They conclude that the effort had brought little valid output and that for measuring the effectiveness of the FATF regime another instrument was required. Other approaches, such as suggested by Ferwerda (2009) and Johnson (2008) have not been tested. The authors (Van Duyne *et al.*, 2016) inspected a sizeable sample of the MERs and were struck by their diversity, inconsistency and mantra-like conclusions, such as the "undermining of the integrity of the global financial system", concluded in the evaluations of small island states of barely 200,000 inhabitants. Similarly, the authors observe comments such as this one in the Danish MER (Special Recommendation II p. 58):[5]

> "The criminalization of the financing of terrorism by Denmark is fully compliant, but Greenland and the Faroe Islands have not yet adequately criminalized the financing of terrorism, terrorists and terrorist organizations".

---

[5] MER available at: http://www.fatf-afi.org/media/fatf/documents/reports/mer/MER%20Denmark%20full.pdf. Accessed 25 September 2015.

Therefore the rating was reduced to 'Partly Compliant' irrespective of the extremely limited potential for criminal or terrorist infiltration of the small societies and economies of either Greenland (population 56,000) or of the Faroes (population 49,000). (Van Duyne *et al.*, 2016; p. 172).[6] There is no semblance of irony in all this.

Though the FATF presents this output as a 'significant' achievement – as it usually does – a real methodological investigation of this mutual evaluation is required to determine whether the large investment made is balanced by the validity of its output. Such an evaluation has never been carried out, despite the firmly expressed intention in 2003/2004 Annual Report, of carrying out a cost-benefit evaluation.

2. The fourth-round evaluation tools

Even if an evaluation at the end of the third round (in approximately 2014) had taken place ('lessons learned'), it would have no impact, as the FATF 'evaluation train' roared on with a new methodology: the *risk based approach* on which the new Recommendations are based. This is not really an innovative initiative as most of its elements were already present in the 2003 Recommendations, but the FATF did not consider this earlier version to be explicit and clear enough. Also, the risk based approach is common practice in the insurance and financial industry and, for this reason, was adopted in December 2005 by the FATF (following the introduction of the third EU directive) and by their advisory representatives of the banking and securities sectors. Subsequently, in order to elaborate the risk-based approach a working group, the Electronic Advisory Group, was established as a sub-group of the FATF Working Group on Evaluations and Implementation (WGEI). Altogether four documents were published to further and explain the 'new' approach:

a. FATF *guidance on the risk-based approach to combating money laundering and terrorist financing; High level principles and procedures*. Issued in 2007, the elaborated principles are outlined in 47 pages.
b. *Money laundering & Terrorist Financing risk assessment strategies*. Issued in 2008 it outlines the risk approach at national level (45 pages).
c. FATF *Guidance: Money laundering and terrorist financing risk assessment strategies*. Issued in 2013, it is a 60-page hand-out for practitioners with indications for conducting a national risk assessment.
d. A *methodology for assessing technical compliance with the FATF Recommendations and the effectiveness of AML/CFT systems*: a manual of 160 pages published in 2013 for the assessors of the fourth round.

[6] Denmark which, according to the ECOLEF report (p. 281) has the lowest 'threat level', is nevertheless reproached by the FATF for not having criminalised self-laundering.

Of course, to this output of 312 pages should be added the Recommendation booklet of 134 pages, bringing the total pages devoted to this approach to 446. This enormous output outshines the documentary tools for the previous round of evaluation. It is also evidence of the great diligence with which the risk-based approach was conducted. However, where Halliday *et al.* (2014) had already raised the question of available skills and knowledge with regards to the previous evaluation round, this question has to be repeated with even more emphasis for this fourth round. The reason for this doubt is provided by the content of the first two reports on the new approach. The first one (2007; p. 2) admits that "*there are no universally accepted methodologies that prescribe the nature and extent of a risk-based approach.*" The second 2008 report raised a question in footnote 5, which we quote in full:

> "*There are currently no standard definitions used internationally within the AML/CFT context for the terms risk, threat, and vulnerability. This project identifies concepts linked to these terms in order to promote a consistent approach by countries, but does not go so far as to suggest precise definitions for adoption by the international community. Having a clear understanding of what the concepts mean, however, will assist countries when establishing the terms of reference and scale of ambition when conducting a national ML/TF assessment.*"

This reads like a confused and contradictory 'agnostic' confession which should provide sufficient grounds for a responsible management to halt the undertaking, although we suspect evident 'sunk cost' bias[7]. While the 2013 National Money Laundering and Terrorist Risk Assessment mentions three elements in the threat approach – threat, vulnerability and consequence or harm – it also says "*it is accepted that incorporating consequence into risk assessments may not involve particularly sophisticated approaches [. . .] countries may instead opt to focus primarily on achieving a comprehensive understanding of their threats and vulnerabilities.*" (p. 8). Thus countries may skip the element 'consequences' and nevertheless still achieve 'comprehensive understanding', whatever that may mean if there is only a threat (not an event) and some vulnerability. The (unknown) consequences are actually the events that matter. In such situations the standard consequence that is resorted to is one of the FATF mantras, such as "undermining the integrity of the financial system".

Despite the significant effort already vested in this approach it could simply be set aside as not fit for an unambiguous output. Without a proper definition of the central terms the project itself does not "identify concepts" and does not have a "clear understanding of what the concepts mean" or how to deal

---

7 Sunk cost bias results in decision making that is determined by the accumulated investment that has taken place making such investment harder to abandon.

methodologically with consequences or harm, a basic component in the conceptual risk framework. This confession of indeterminability, as such, is frank and makes itself felt in all the relevant documents. For example, it is correct to point at the need to individualise the threat and risk per country and within each country per sector and to take account of the financial and economic contexts. If properly executed this suggested approach may result in a broad study per country differentiated by sector, which may produce an accumulation of divergent interpretations. The FATF-AR 2008 also displays an open mind stating that "*in the absence of data or case studies identifying these* [laundering] *methods, financial institutions and competent authorities must rely on creative intuition and a careful analysis of potential systemic weaknesses*", whereby the potential 'systemic' weaknesses refer to methods which neither financial institutions nor criminals have yet detected (p. 5). One could wonder where such a 'careful analysis' of something undetected must come from. Indeed, against the background of such consistently confusing threat conceptions 'creative intuition' is not likely to bring much clarity.

Given this assessors' 'toolbox', the foundations of the fourth-round evaluations do not appear to meet the criterion of solidity as should be expected in view of the serious consequences of shortcomings within the evaluated countries. What does it mean that a country has "not properly understood" the risks of money laundering, terrorist financing and proliferation of weapons of mass destruction? Does the assessors' toolbox contain the yardstick for the correct understanding of the threat of money laundering and its related crime? No, the FATF guidance and methodology documents are explicit about this: such a yardstick does not exist. But then neither is a 'creative intuition' the proper substitute.

An important aspect of the risk-based approach, which could have been operationalised for policy making as well as mutual evaluation is the recognition, contained in the first two reports, that one cannot detect all cases of money laundering. This implies that a risk based approach aiming at balancing efforts against threat must also accept a percentage loss of *missed cases*: 'fishes swimming through' the loopholes. How much will be considered as acceptable may be the outcome of a real risk analysis in which the 'no-loophole' interests (of policy makers or regulators) must be weighed against the financial costs of fully guarding them. For example, the proportion and money value of the set of 'self-laundering' cases should be offset against the estimated 'threat to the integrity of the financial system' and the latter assessed for various thresholds, such as: €50,000 or €100,000 with estimated enforcement expenses for each threshold. This is an extension of the present €15,000 cash reporting threshold or the €2,500 for money transfers (as per the EU directives). This way of statistical risk evaluation does not appear in the 'methodology' or guidance documents produced by the FATF. What we read in the interpretive notes (to Recommendation 1) is that there must be a "*proven low risk*" if countries decide not to apply some of the Recommendations (Methodology, 2012; p. 33). However, as risk is about statistical *uncertainty*, one may justifiably raise the question whether the authors (the FATF) of the *2012 Methodology* understand the very concept of risk itself.

We cannot conclude this discussion of the (fourth round) 2012 evaluation without commenting on the first Recommendation, in particular the opening sentence: "*Countries should identify, assess, and understand the money laundering and terrorist financing risks for the country*". At first sight this looks self-explanatory. But how should one determine this understanding? This assumes an assessor with a superior knowledge of the country on the basis of which the national actors' level of 'correct' understanding is assessed. And this would go from the central government actors right down to the non-financial sectors and professions. Last but not least: how is the assumed assessor's 'superior' knowledge assessed? This approach, with so many unanswered questions, sets the door wide open to subjectivity and arbitrariness.

5.3 Herding the Member States and enforcing compliance

It was not the intention of the Task Force to issue its 40 Recommendations and then to wait for their adoption and implementation: the political arena of finances is not like that of environmental policy. The new money laundering policy was the new message that had to be spread, adopted and carried out as a new global financial orthodoxy. Naturally in 1990, the Task Force could not immediately start imposing the implementation of its 40 Recommendation worldwide. The FATF first had to see to it that the countries that had joined the Task Force implemented the Recommendations themselves. This was not a foregone conclusion. As a matter of fact, many member states were still groping with uncertainties concerning national legislation, the interaction with the financial industry and law enforcement. An important socio-political mechanism to further compliance was *group pressure*: the '*anti-straggler's psychology*' according to which nobody wants to be seen to lag behind. The instruments to exert such group pressure were the self- and mutual evaluations. These documents would lay open their achievements or arrears to all FATF members. Would that work?

The straggler's psychology worked fairly well, but according to the FATF, it was still not good enough. The FATF soon showed its adherence to orthodoxy and went for the 'full hundred percent' – a partial achievement was *no* success. Yet some uncomfortable situations had to be faced. For example, the FATF had to concede that a number of member states did not have much profit generating crime, because of which they could not share the urgency felt by the more zealous member states: for example, Ireland, Uruguay or Denmark were hardly laundering 'hotspots'. There were also national interests that were at odds with the FATF's stand. This was the case with the *anonymous accounts* in Austria and Turkey, to which must be added that the latter country was lagging behind in virtually all aspects of legislation and implementation (FATF, 1994-1995; p. 11). Later Turkey would for a while be placed in the 'dock' for non-compliance.[8]

In its Annual Report 1994-1995 the FATF observed that in Turkey money laundering policy was not a high priority, despite the willingness expressed by the Turkish authorities. Turkey only introduced the required Bill in Parliament four years after joining the FATF. With so little achievement, Turkey's evaluation had to be postponed. However, the lack of further compliance remained a matter for concern and was consequently put onto the agenda: this non-compliance "was clearly damaging to the FATF and its mission" (p. 15). Hence, a stepwise pressure was exerted. First the former President of the FATF wrote a stiff letter to the relevant Turkish ministers about this lack of progress. Apparently, there was no satisfactory answer, because in April 1996 the FATF sent a "high-level mission" to Turkey to warn that it could only avoid more serious steps from the FATF Plenary by passing the requested legislation by September 1996 (FATF 1995-1996; p. 15). That was a strong statement, or rather an ultimatum, and a forewarning of the FATF non-compliant policy that from 2000 onwards was to refer to "non-cooperative countries and territories". There was also the application of the dreaded *Recommendation 21*: the order to all countries (whether members or not) and their financial institutions to apply extra screening to transactions from or to a non-cooperative country. This would have the effect of slowing down or raising the costs (or both) of international financial interactions by the recalcitrant country.[9] In the end Turkey gave way.

The *anonymous accounts* remained an issue for some time in Austria. In Austria this was a matter of internal policy, not concerning the integrity of international finance, as the country had already restricted the use of anonymous passbooks to their own residents. But it violated the principle of customer

8 Turkey was threatened with suspension unless it enacted Counter-terrorism legislation. It dutifully complied and the threat was lifted. (http://www.fatf-gafi.org/publications/fatfgeneral/documents/outcomesoftheplenarymeetingofthefatfparis17-19october2012.html) (http://www.fatf-gafi.org/publications/fatfgeneral/documents/outcomesofthefatfplenary20-22february2013.html).

9 Recommendation 21. "Financial institutions should give special attention to business relationships and transactions with persons, including companies and financial institutions, from countries which do not or insufficiently apply the FATF Recommendations. Whenever these transactions have no apparent economic or visible lawful purpose, their background and purpose should, as far as possible, be examined, the findings established in writing, and be available to help competent authorities. Where such a country continues not to apply or insufficiently applies the FATF Recommendations, countries should be able to apply appropriate countermeasures."

identification and, therefore, had to be banned. This point remained on the Plenary agenda until it was 'solved' to the satisfaction of the FATF, of course. To achieve this solution, a non-compliance procedure had to be set in motion in 1997, after Austria appeared to cling to its anonymous passbooks. First the FATF formulated as a principle its claim to demand global compliance:

> "*Being aware that it could not expect others to do what certain of its members fail to do, FATF defined in 1996, a policy for dealing with its members which are not in compliance with the initial forty Recommendations. The measures contained in this policy represent a graduated approach aimed at enhancing peer pressure.*" (FATF, 1997-1998, p. 24)

Then came the application of gradual pressure beginning, as with Turkey, with a stiff letter to the Austrian government expressing the FATF's concern. When Austria did not give way, a 'high-level mission' was sent to Vienna in mid-September 1998 to reinforce the concern. Meanwhile Austria had improved its anti-money laundering approach, except for the contested anonymous passbook on which it appeared to remain stubborn. Thereupon, in 1999, the FATF issued a 'public statement' and called on Austria "*to remove anonymous passbook accounts, and warned financial institutions of the risks that are associated with such accounts.*" What these risks were remained unclear, as these passbooks concerned only saving accounts. These were highly popular and were a living refutation of the hypothesised laundering scare among the public: this bit of secrecy certainly did not damage the reputation of the banks. In advance of the general elections the government did not dare to give in to such an unpopular measure as abolishing the passbook. After the elections the Austrian interim government hinted that it would meet the FATF's requirements. The FATF did not think this a sufficiently firm commitment and ran out of patience: it threatened Austria with suspension of its membership unless it gave in, whereupon the Austrian government backed down and consented to introduce the relevant Banking Act (FATF, 1999-2000, p. 21). The erring sheep was brought back into the fold.

This handling of Austria and Turkey not only illustrates the outlines of the non-compliance procedure, it also implicitly posed the principle of FATF's *global competence* in money laundering matters. The hidden crowbar in the formulation is the implication of the first line: "*expect others to do* . . ." Once the "others" as non-members are brought into the circle of FATF's tasks, its reach has become global. From then on, the verb "expect" is to be replaced by "should" in the strong meaning of "must" (also stressed by the IMF; see Van Duyne *et al.*, 2016).

This process of extending the FATF circle of influence continued in the following years when the FATF announced its intention to target jurisdictions (including offshore) that "offer excessive banking secrecy and allow shell companies to be used for illegal purposes" (FATF 1998-1999, p. 35). This was a long-standing aim of the OECD. For this aim an *Ad Hoc* Group was established with a broad task: the "*scope of the group's work covers all significant financial centres, both inside and outside FATF membership.*"

This expansion can also be read in the Annex within the next annual report 1999-2000: this devoted a separate chapter to "non-cooperative countries and territories". Apart from an *Ad Hoc* Group, for this subject, four regional 'review groups' (Americas; Asia/Pacific; Europe; Africa and Middle East) were established in February 2000. With this explicit formulation, the circle of compliance inspection and enforcement finally includes non-FATF members: actually it comprises the whole world.

The Ad Hoc Group drew up 25 criteria defining the non-cooperative state, which were clustered as follows (FATF-AR, 1999-2000, p. 19):

- Loopholes in the financial regulations causing inadequate supervision;
- Lack of suspicious transaction reporting;
- Weaknesses in commercial regulations: beneficial ownership and registration;
- Obstacles to international criminal and administrative law cooperation;
- Inadequate resources for the implementation of tasks.[10]

Subsequently 27 countries and jurisdictions were inspected. However, within the Ad Hoc Group assignment, most of them could not be considered a "significant financial centre". Fifteen of the screened jurisdictions were reported as having serious systemic shortcomings (Annex A, p. 12).[11] Encouraged by the first exercise, the FATF repeated the examination with another sample of thirteen countries of which six were qualified as non-cooperative.[12]

These countries were urged to improve their indicated deficiencies and thereby get off the Non-Cooperative Countries and Territories (NCCT) list. Meanwhile, the FATF advised financial institutions to screen transactions with these countries and to take extra precautions in relation to them as these might be related to laundering in which they could of course be implicated. Naturally, the FATF and its members offered help such as technical assistance,

---

[10] Later the FATF formed another cluster and considered as particular important (1) the relevant aspects of criminal law, (2) financial supervision, (3) customer identification, (4) suspicious transactions reporting and (5) international co-operation. (FATF, 2001-2002; p. 15).

[11] Bahamas, Cayman Islands, Cook Islands, Dominica, Israel, Lebanon, Liechtenstein, the Marshall Islands, Nauru, Niue, Panama, the Philippines, Russia, St. Kitts and Nevis, St. Vincent and the Grenadines. (FATF, 1999-2000; p, 41). According to a later report, only Nauru, the Philippines and Russia remained non-cooperative, but are mentioned as working on their deficiencies. (*Review to identify non-cooperative countries or territories: increasing the worldwide effectiveness of anti-money laundering measures*. FATF June 2001).

[12] Egypt, Guatemala, Hungary, Indonesia, Myanmar, Nigeria. Again, no significant financial centres.

but if the non-cooperative countries maintained their "detrimental rules and practices", counter-measures would be considered. Some identified jurisdictions did not wait for that to happen and showed commitment to improve their shortcomings; other non-cooperative states were less responsive and stayed on the list for years.

The FATF deemed its vetting of non-cooperation a success, because many targeted countries took measures to improve their AML legislation and supervisory system. However, the FATF's drive caused some strains in its relationships with the FSRBs who were also responsible for evaluating 'their' members. By way of a consolation prize, the FATF proposed giving greater weight to their evaluations, provided the 25 non-cooperation criteria were adopted. Though it was not explicitly expressed, it was the FATF and *not* the FSRBs that determined the NCCT policy and passed judgements on non-cooperativeness and related listing (FATF, 2000-2001, p. 11). The FSRBs were only mentioned in passing, making it difficult to deny a hierarchy in this important subject.

In the following years there was a coming and going of countries being placed on the non-cooperative-list and subsequently delisted when they succeeded in mending their 'strategic deficiencies'. Some narrowly escaped a public statement for countermeasures, such as Russia and the Philippines, whereas little Nauru was less lucky. So, we observe that the NCCT-list, mainly consisting of smaller economies, grew and shrank over the years. Some hurried to obey, others like Myanmar, Nigeria or Nauru needed more time or more 'growls' before returning to the fold.

The FATF could congratulate itself: all 23 identified non-cooperative states were delisted in October 2006 and the procedure was closed (FATF-AR, 2006-2007, p. 10). Despite this success the FATF had to remain vigilant. In the following years new countries with deficiencies were identified: Iran, Uzbekistan, Pakistan, Turkmenistan, São Tomé and Principe, and the northern part of Cyprus. With the exception of Iran (and later North Korea), who proved defiant, all the deficient countries were pressured into compliance. Or, in the language of the annual reports: "The FATF welcomed their progress . . . *etc.*" But the FATF remained "*vigilant on international co-operation issues and responds, as necessary, to jurisdictions that pose a threat to the international financial system . . .*" (FATF, 2008-2009, p. 17).

The above-mentioned call to remain vigilant must be seen against the background of the summit of the G-20, in London in 2009. In its "Leaders' statement" of 2 April 2009, the world leaders of the G-20 devoted one section to non-cooperative jurisdictions, including tax havens, and stated threateningly: "*The era of bank secrecy is over*". The FATF took this statement as a call for further action against non-cooperative jurisdictions, though this statement was actually addressed to the OECD, as a call for that organisation to take action. In the follow-up summit in September 2009 in Pittsburgh the G-20 now called on the FATF to issue a list of high-risk jurisdictions by February of the following year. As February is the usual month for public statements about non-cooperative countries, the FATF could easily produce the requested list (it already had one on its shelves) with the following classification of its reactions: (1) a Public Statement mentioning the countries with *strategic deficiencies* and (2) mentioning countries that were "*Improving Global AML/CFT compliance: on-going progress*", which we call the 'improving list'. By way of short hand, we call this procedure the *Public Statement procedure* including the 'Improving list'.

The **Public Statement** is a Black List in two degrees:

1. Jurisdictions which remained obstinate and against which *countermeasures* are recommended. At that time that was:
   Iran;
2. Jurisdictions with strategic deficiencies and without an action plan: *financial institutions were warned to consider related risks.*[13] These were:
   Angola
   North Korea
   Ecuador
   Ethiopia

In the Public Statement of February 2011, only Iran and North Korea (moved to category 1) remained defiant.

In the follow-up summits (Toronto, June 2010; Seoul, November 2010; Paris, February 2011) the leaders of the G-20 repeated their call on the FATF to update its list of non-cooperative countries. This stimulated the FATF to introduce and renew its review procedure for which the *International Cooperation Review Group* (ICRG) was identified as the responsible body within the FATF. When the ICRG receives negative information of money laundering or terrorist financing in a jurisdiction, for example from the Mutual Evaluation Reports, it can defer the case to one of the four *regional review groups* (Africa/Middle East, North and South America, Asia/the Pacific, and Europe /Eurasia)[14] to carry out a preliminary investigation and report its findings to the FATF. The FATF then decides whether a deeper investigation should be carried out. This will be done by the relevant regional review group which can invite the competent authorities for a face-to-face meeting. It is uncertain whether the old criteria for determining a non-cooperative country

[13] A third category: *Jurisdictions previously publicly identified by the FATF as having strategic AML/CFT deficiencies, which remained to be addressed as of February 2010* (mentioning Pakistan, Turkmenistan and São Tomé and Príncipe) was dropped in the October 2010 Public Statement.

[14] A more specific indication or demarcation is not available.

from the 2006 closed procedure were still being used at this point in time. The concept-report is discussed and an opportunity for drafting an action plan is provided. The condition for further cooperation is a high-level political commitment from the government itself. Then, depending on its findings, the Plenary can issue a Public Statement: Degree 1 or 2 of the Black List2. In June 2011 the Public Statement degree 1 recommended countermeasures against Iran and North Korea. Public Statement degree 2 gave a warning concerning Bolivia, Cuba, Ethiopia, Kenya, Myanmar, Sri Lanka, Syria, and Turkey (as discussed, the latter had already collided with the FATF).

In the following year the public document *Improving Global AML/CFT compliance: on-going progress* (June 2011) mentioned 33 countries.[15] In this 'improving list' the FATF encourages all 'good' members (the cooperative states) to consider the strategic deficiencies of the identified countries when doing business. This implies screening of transactions with the listed states and extra precautions, which may hamper their international business activities.

The FATF claimed that, since the start of the latest non-cooperation project, it had reviewed over 80 jurisdictions and identified 58 as non-cooperative of which 41 made the required reforms (FATF, 2014-2015; p. 18). Not all of them were on the severe Public Statement degree 1 or 2 list: most were on the 'Improving list', though that is also a document of public shaming: the 'soft pillory'.

While the FATF congratulates itself with its successful outcomes, this proved to be a far from smooth or speedy process. Surveying the procedures from 2011 onwards it appears that of the 19 jurisdictions on the Public Statement 2 (strategic deficiencies) list, three of them were listed for only one term; a listing for two to three terms was the most common and one jurisdiction remained on the list for four years. Of the '*improving list*' 18 states were listed for only one term, but nineteen for two to three terms and eight for four terms. So, either the reviews were a real overload for the FATF, causing a backlog, or the relevant jurisdictions did not rush to implement the imposed reforms. The documents do not inform us about the reasons for delay. The time span for implementing reform appears to have no relation to the size of a country's economy: Turkey and Indonesia were on the Public Statement 2 list three times and so were the smaller countries like Ecuador or São Tomé and Príncipe; Argentina (big) and Cambodia (small) were both on the 'improvement list' for four terms.

---

[15] Angola, Antigua and Barbuda, Argentina, Bangladesh, Brunei Darussalam, Cambodia, Ecuador, Ghana, Honduras, Indonesia, Mongolia, Morocco, Namibia, Nepal, Nicaragua, Nigeria, Pakistan, Paraguay, the Philippines, São Tomé and Príncipe, Sudan, Tajikistan, Tanzania, Thailand, Trinidad & Tobago, Turkmenistan, Ukraine, Venezuela, Vietnam, Ukraine, and Zimbabwe.

This raises some more detailed questions about the functioning of the ICRG and the four regional review groups that are considered as a part of the FATF organisation. They vet the jurisdictions for 'strategic deficiencies', based on all kinds of information, including the MERs, and compare these with the 25 criteria for non-cooperation. Despite all these described activities we do not know anything about their staffing, location and working conditions.

The relationship between the Public Statement procedure and the mutual evaluation is also difficult to determine. When the MERs, the product of six to nine assessors and months or years of work and procedures culminating in the acceptance by the Plenary and thus are considered as a valid source of information for the review group, so why should the compliance investigation not be carried out by the assessment teams themselves? This double investigation does not look very efficient. It is equally unclear what the relationship is between on the one hand, the follow-up procedure after an evaluation report for mending a number of identified shortcomings and on the other hand, the monitoring within the Public Statement procedure. For example, Nigeria was listed as a non-cooperative state from 2001 until 2006 when it was finally delisted. In 2011 it emerged again on the 'improving list', then one degree higher on the Public Statement 2 list. It seems that the first delisting was a wrong decision because its MER of 2008 showed a rating one would not expect from a delisted state: on 18 Recommendations it scored *non-compliant*, on 22 partially compliant, seven *largely compliant* and only two times *compliant*. The MER proposed 31 points of improvement. No surprise that Nigeria went on the list again.

A closer look at the case of Nigeria is illustrative. After years of stagnation the FATF Plenary observed in 2007 with satisfaction that "As of June 2006, the NFIU (Nigerian FIU) had a staff of 58 (up from 27 in June 2005), and received approximately 1,500 STRs in 2005. The NFIU had referred 42 STRs to investigative agencies. The EFCC [Economic and Financial Crime Commission] prosecuted 29 money laundering cases in 2005, resulting in 12 convictions. For 2006, there were 8 additional convictions and 96 ongoing investigations as of May. In addition, in 2005, the NDLEA (Drug Prosecution) prosecuted 30 money laundering cases, resulting in 22 convictions. On the basis of this progress, in June 2006 the FATF removed Nigeria from the NCCTs list."[16]

However, a year later the seven assessors for the mutual evaluation could hardly find any statistics and whatever limited statistics they could retrieve did not match with that of the FATF report on the NCCT procedure. Lack of statistics was one of the recurring deficiencies the assessors observed with all aspects of AML output.

[16] *Annual Review of Non-Cooperative Countries and Territories, 2006-2007*: eighth annual review. p. 11.

This discrepancy points at the need for more comparisons of the MERs with the Public Statement procedures. Likewise, the evaluations should be compared with the inspections, the follow-up procedures (for the MERs) or the monitoring procedure. The role and functioning of the non-described regional review groups and ICRG also requires clarity. These entities can harm or heal a country, but they are shrouded in fog. Is this transparency?

Despite this observation, the FATF claims that the Public Statement procedure is transparent and fair which may or may not be true, but there is no documentary evidence to support this claim, which should not be taken for granted. Apparently non-cooperative countries are carpeted ('*vis-a-vis*'), but we do not hear their voice. What were their arguments for not complying with important Recommendations? As a matter of fact, throughout all the FATF reporting we only hear one voice – and that is of the Plenary which invariably praises itself for its "important work" and the "significant progress" achieved. We are of the opinion that such self-justifying and self-congratulating judgments deserve evaluation too. Otherwise the reach of the FATF rises above accountability.

5.4 The legitimacy of sanctioning

Against this background of self-congratulation and insufficient accountability, it is important to consider this ongoing 'global financial herding' from the angle of *legitimacy*: the application of Damocles' Sword or Recommendation 19 (previously 21) which is more a *sanction* than a protective measure. The IMF 2011 report by Hagen (IMF, 2011, pp. 82, 83) drew attention to the negative impact on GDP growth of countermeasures against affected countries. Has this sanctioning been legally settled in a correct manner? This is far from certain.

To find out, we first look at the addressee of Recommendation 19: "Financial institutions *should be required* to apply enhanced due diligence" *etc.* Is this an order to countries and states to oblige their financial institutions to apply enhanced due diligence measures to their counterparts in countries that "do not or insufficiently apply the FATF Recommendations"? This seems to be the most plausible interpretation, especially in view of the next sentence that informs the states that they must be "*able* to apply appropriate countermeasures when *called upon to do so* by the FATF." This is clearly not an 'invitation', but a command, that is also ambiguous. What is meant by to be 'able'? States can be able without doing anything.

The next question is whether the measures suggested are *sanctions* or just '*measures of conviction*' to further the desired conduct. This is not a legal subtlety: sanctions are purposefully harmful responses or punishments, meted out after a transgression. 'Measures of conviction' can be applied as an accompanying support or with preventive intentions. In their intended effect of eliciting compliant behaviour, the two overlap. But punishments are in essence intended to hurt and are, therefore, in any legal system regulated by safeguards. So, should the countermeasures be considered sanctions because they are harmful to the non-compliant countries? Without engaging in an exposé of international law (which would not be a luxury), we state that the countermeasures hurt and are to that effect real punishments.

If one looks at the interpretive note to Recommendation 19[17] plus the reference to the interpretive note to Recommendation 10,[18] one gets a good impression of the harassing effect to a country being considered a 'strategic risk' or worse. Once a country lands on the FATF's list of non-cooperative 'sinners', reporting institutions may well deem clients from those countries as being outside their acceptable boundaries of risk. So indeed, it is appropriate to speak of sanctions. As mentioned above, this is borne out by the IMF/Hagen paper (2011; pp. 82–83) which estimated that public statements (the 'pillory') and countermeasures led to a drop in foreign investment and revenues. This applied to small offshore centres as well as to larger economies such as Egypt, Israel, Lebanon and Russia (Kurdrle, 2008). So, the IMF speaks plainly of a sanction imposed by the FATF.

Given this conclusion, there should be an authority with the appropriate powers to hand out punishments. According to the formulation of Recommendation 19, as set out above, it is the FATF which is assumed to be the competent authority. However, the very nature of the FATF should exclude this: it is an unofficial policy *making* body serving a group of mutually co-opted Heads of States under a mandate that has no foundation in international law. All claims to the contrary should be considered an arrogation of power. After all, the FATF and all its regional bodies have no formal authority under which to impose sanctions and countries are sovereign in implementing recommendations. They may have legitimate and rational grounds to be selective in their compliance. For example, when the whole machinery of the imposed AML system is disproportional to the states' wealth, the size of their economy and financial sector or the actual threat to the global financial system (for example, Faroe Islands, Greenland or some other small island states).

[17] Recommendation 19 Higher risk countries: Financial institutions should be required to apply enhanced due diligence measures to business relationships and transactions with natural and legal persons, and financial institutions, from countries for which this is called for by the FATF. Countries should be able to apply appropriate countermeasures also independently. Interpretative notes to Recommendation 19 on p. 83.

[18] Recommendation 10 Customer due diligence: Financial institutions should be prohibited from keeping anonymous accounts or accounts in obviously fictitious names. Financial institutions should be required to undertake customer due diligence (CDD) measures when (among others) establishing business relations; and carrying out occasional transaction above $15,000. Interpretative notes to Recommendation 10 on p. 62. Available at: http://www.fatf-gafi.org/media/fatf/documents/recommendations/pdfs/FATF_Recommendations.pdf. Accessed 5 April 2017.

It seems that the FATF is well aware of its lack of legitimacy. Therefore, it seeks justification of its policy by claiming that "the work which FATF has undertaken on non-co-operative jurisdictions is *fully in line with measures elaborated by the international community* to protect the global financial system *etc.*" (FATF-AR, 2001-2002, p. 15, italics added). What is this 'international community' that is protecting the global financial system? The IMF? If that is the case, it should be an IMF task with no need of an informal body like the FATF. Ten years after this claim, the FATF still appeared to be seeking legitimacy in its dealing with non-cooperative states. In his foreword to the 2009-10 Annual report the then President of the FATF, Paul Vlaanderen, remarked (p. 4) that "*Since September 2009, G20 has referred to the activities of the FATF* [related to NCCTs] *in all its communiqués, further adding to the legitimacy of this world-leading body in its field of expertise*". Such a self-praising formulation is easily overlooked or its validity is taken for granted. Nevertheless, it is misleading: the G-20 is as informal as the G-9 or the FATF itself and cannot lend a legitimacy it does not itself have to another institution of its own making.

In a way, similar to the statements about the volume and threat of money laundering, there is repetition and a 'time delusion' effect: by the mere passage of time the repeatedly pretended legitimacy slips into a perception of validity. But that perception is deceptive.

5.5 Approximating the identity of the FATF

The discussion in the previous section is not at odds with the repeated claim by the FATF that it is the "global standard setter" on measures against money laundering. But being proclaimed as such even by the IMF, World Bank and the United Nations still does not solve the problem of the FATF's identity and authority.

Not only in the general terms as formulated in the previous sections, but also more technically, the FATF is not a legal person registered at the Paris Chamber of Commerce; it has no separate address as it is resident at the OECD, which supplies and pays its staff. The FATF cannot be summoned to appear in court, because of a contested decision: for example, if a country feels prejudiced having received a bad rating or thinks the issued 'warning' by the Plenary is unjustified and a tort. Is there an authority above the Plenary? According to the FATF High Level Principles and Objectives (2012), "*The FATF is the only standard-setting body and the guardian and arbiter of the application of its standard*". This looks like a threefold task within one body (see also Goldbarsht and Michaelsen, 2017). And when it comes to decision making: the FATF *is* the Plenary where all decisions are taken by consensus, according to article 19 of the 2012 mandate. Nevertheless, as befits a non-legal non-person, according to article 48 of the same mandate: "*This mandate is not intended to create any legal rights or obligations.*" What does this remarkable demarcation of accountability imply or entail? Irrespective of how long one reflects on this proposition, the answer is simply "nothing": there is no legal person and no legal accountability and no redress if anything goes wrong. This is a serious international risk, given the fact that a lot of things with far-reaching, harmful consequences for dozens of states are enacted by the FATF that can prove wrong. What is known of the FATF and what remains hidden?

What is known is presented on the FATF's website and can be learned from its annual reports and the 20th and 25th Anniversary booklets. There is no need to describe here what the reader can learn from this open source for themselves. But the website content does not reveal all of the FATF's functioning which as we have seen goes farther than just policy making: the FATF actually *rules* over the anti-money laundering policies of its members and all other states worldwide. It demands entry into and inspection of every jurisdiction, orders assessments of the state's implementation of its Recommendations, evaluates them and judges further steps to be taken if it deems these to be required. This is a serious neglect of any separation of powers (Goldbarsht and Michaelsen, 2017). These further steps matter if we want to speak of 'ruling' in the sense of governing because these steps are intended as enforceable decisions by states against other states: they are inherently coercive. However, apart from authority, the FATF does not have an executive enforcement apparatus.

5.6 FATF's 'indirect rule'

This is an extra ordinary situation that to our knowledge has no precedent. If we look for a historical model, we may try to make a comparison with the indirect rule of the British and French empires of the 19th and first half of 20th Century. According to the mandate, the real principals are the G- States' meetings: starting in 1989 as the then G-7, now the G-20 Heads of States. At the level of delegated ministers of Finance there may be an overlap with the OECD: some FATF texts hint at this situation. Given the informal nature of the G-7/20, this could happen. More importantly: this circle of Heads of States and ministers present a power nucleus determining the FATF mandate and its final accountability. They are represented in the Plenary, the ultimate consensual decision-making body. But there is no information about how consensus is achieved: are all 37-member states equal? That would be an unprecedented political miracle. Is there no accompanying power play or a power politics involving clusters of states? Is there no voting of which the outcome is presented as a 'consensus'? We are not informed about these aspects of decision making. But what we can observe is that some countries, for instance the USA, are more heavyweight than others and take part in more events and decision-making meetings.

Leaving aside the Plenary as it is presented on the website or what may happen behind the scenes, it remains unknown how it rules over so many countries from the outside. Is there a metaphor or analogue which may help us to understand this? As suggested above, looking into the history, perhaps the way the British Empire was ruled, may provide a useful analogue. Britain ruled large stretches of the earth, which together were far too large for a direct rule exercised from one power centre. So, the British (and also the French) ruled their colonies, protectorates and 'spheres of influence' largely through local authorities, such as the Indian princely states. Of course, there remained central tasks, such as foreign affairs, defence, legislation and its implementation, to which the local princelings had to consent: voluntarily, but if not, they knew that the 'British gunboat' was never far away. Admittedly, the analogue is not perfect: the Plenary is not like a Colonial Office, but it still makes 'local authorities' comply with its rule even in countries that are not full members. And all know: the 'FATF gun boat', announced by a 'stiff letter', then a 'high level visit' and finally Recommendation 19, is never far away.

The nature of this indirect rule is exemplified in the way the FATF dealt with NCCTs as described in sections 5.3 and 5.4 through its review organs: the *ICRG* and the four *regional review groups* established in February 2000. Does the functioning of these bodies fit into this colonial analogue? The comparison with the old British Colonial District Officer could be instructive.

The analogue ends here, because we know more about the historical District Officer than about the ICRG and the four regional review groups. The ICRG is mentioned in the organogram of the FATF, but as observed before, nothing is known in the public domain about its composition, working schedule or reporting. Nevertheless, it plays a role in the essential function of the global compliance enforcement policy. It 'sniffs around' to find indications of lack of zeal, deficiencies in the AML structures and defective implementation. In general, it looks for any lack of commitment evidenced by any signs of insufficient participation in the work of the FSRB to which a country belongs (no specification given). The Review Group then reports on suspected neglect or shortcomings. Based on this (not public) report, the FATF decides whether an in-depth investigation is warranted, beginning by looking the suspected foot dragger deep into the eyes: the face-to-face meeting. The FATF also demands a high-level political commitment to implement an action plan for mending the shortcomings.

This section of the annual report ends with a clear statement from which the imperial tone cannot be denied: "*The FATF continues identifying and reviewing potentially non-cooperative jurisdictions in this process*" (FATF-AR, 2011-2012, p. 31).

Given this commanding, proud statement, one can say that irrespective of the legal '*non-beingness*' of the FATF, its universal enforcement claims and

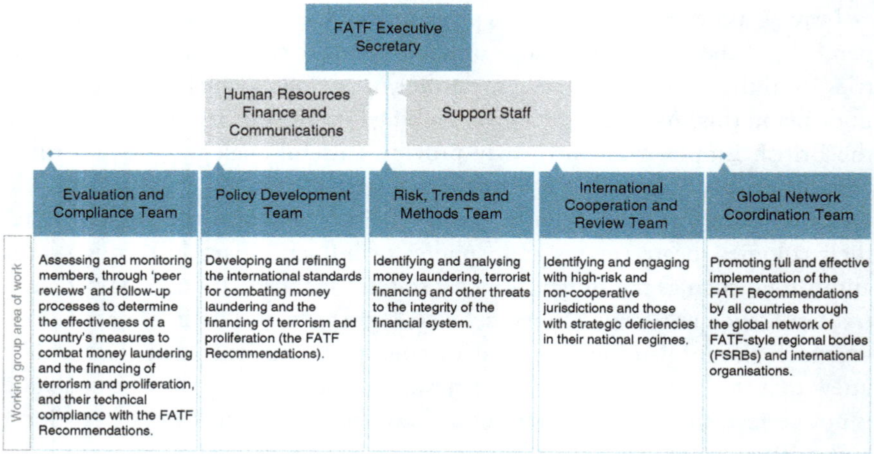

Fig. 5.1 Organisational structure of the FATF. Source: FATF website http://www.fatf-gafi.org/about/fatfsecretariat/#d.en.3198

posture lend it a certain imperial identity. But this is not the only facet of the FATF's identity. The *working groups* also contribute to its identity as a global standard bearer and network builder. This has been an ongoing, evolving process during which the number of working groups adopted within the FATF structure grew to five teams, though there are also working groups outside the structure presented in the following Figure. This represents the structure shown on the FATF website under 'Secretariat' (Fig. 5.1).

Apart from these summary task descriptions one does not find evidence of their actual functioning, with the exception of the ICRG of which the functioning is mentioned briefly in the Annual Reports, and of the Risk, Trends and Methods team, formerly the Typologies team. As stated before, there is no mention of staff, national composition, or accountability concerning working schedules for meetings, expenses or documentary output. As the FATF fosters its 'FATF-brand', as referred to in its "High Level Principles and Objectives" (2012), we assume that these teams are directly subordinate to the Plenary such that its documents are FATF Plenary output, whether published or not. This means that we have to look at the documented output to approximate the FATF's real identity.

5.7 Educational publications: typologies

The reports that the FATF publishes with the highest frequency are its 'typologies'. What are these typologies, considered so important that a special Working Group on Typologies (WGTYP) was established? The FATF does not give a clear definition of the term 'typology'. The Merriam-Webster dictionary gives two definitions: one is theology-related; the other is: "*study of or analysis or classification based on types or categories.*" The latter description indicates forming clusters based on common distinctive features. As the FATF uses the word in the plural (*e.g.* FATF-VII Report on money laundering typolog*ies*), it can be interpreted as 'studies based on types', though not necessarily in the sense of common features. It seems that the FATF means: subjects illustrated by examples or short case descriptions, from AML practice.

In its June 1996 report (p. 2) the FATF states that "*The purpose of the 1995/1996 'typologies exercise' was to provide a forum for law enforcement experts – those primarily tasked with combating money laundering – to discuss recent trends in the cleansing of criminal proceeds, emerging threats, and effective countermeasures.*" Then we see from all subsequent reports that "methods and trends" are a recurring theme. The FATF claims that these trends and methods are identified based on real examples of money laundering or terrorist financing, although the underlying statistics are not available. The 1997-1998 typology report (published February, 1998) was the first report, however, in which the FATF presented such examples as opposed to just giving abstract summaries of trends. These examples are, of course, redacted. They are presented as case studies to illustrate particular money laundering or terrorist financing trends or methods. Case studies can be a useful educational tool and so it is fair to say that the FATF launched an initiative with educational potential.

The first typology was mentioned in the FATF's first Annual Report of 1990-1991, though it was not published at the time. At present, the oldest typology report on the FATF's website dates from 2003 and all typologies reports since then have been made available in the section entitled "Methods and Trends". The FATF's previous reports are to be found on *Asia/Pacific Group*'s Methods and Trends webpage (the oldest available is from 1995-1996). It is unclear why the FATF has chosen not to make them available on its own Methods and Trends webpage.

Since the very beginning, the FATF's reports have tended to repeat and recycle material. The older reports were shorter in length. The oldest FATF report, available on the Asia/Pacific Group's website, from June 1996 (entitled 'FATF-VII Report on Money Laundering Typologies', which suggests there were other reports prior to this), was only 13 pages. Subsequent reports, up to 2001, ranged from 25 to 30 pages. Since 2001 the length of the reports has significantly varied, sometimes reaching around 150 pages but never under 33 (see Table 5.1). The frequency of publication has also varied. Prior to 2006, it was generally a typology report per year; since 2006 the FATF has been publishing reports several times a year.

a. Selecting subjects and their frequencies

Until 2003, the Typologies reports had no specific themes, but they typically highlighted that narcotics trafficking was estimated to be the largest source of

Table 5.1 Topics of typologies reports and frequencies

Type of Typology	Number
Corruption	3
Terrorist financing (including non-profit sector)	8
Proliferation financing	1
Insurance sector	3
Securities sector	2
Legal profession, corporate vehicles, trusts, company service providers	4
Commercial Websites and Internet Payment Systems	1
Wire transfers, remittance and Hawala, currency exchange, new payment methods	6
Virtual currency	1
Trade based laundering	2
Free trade zones	1
Casinos and gaming	1
Human trafficking	2
Transportation of cash	1
Tax fraud	1
Real estate	1
Tobacco	1
Maritime piracy and related kidnapping for ransom	1
Football	1
Afghan opiates	1
Diamonds and gold	3
Counterfeiting of currency	1
Total	**46**

crime proceeds. From 2003 onwards each Typologies report was dedicated to one topic, essentially becoming *phenomenon* reports. The majority of the reports or sections of reports discuss the money laundering conduit, such as the insurance sector or trade in diamonds; fewer focus on the criminal predicate activities.

The topics are decided upon by the FATF's Plenary during an annual meeting. The FATF's 'experts' – this is how the FATF describes them but it is unclear how they are selected and for what expert qualities – then get together for a workshop to brainstorm and elaborate case studies which are published the following year. These experts formed the Working Group on Typologies[19] until 2016, when it silently slipped into the working group Risks, Trends and

[19] It appears to have been established in 2004. The 2004 report explains: "Unlike previous years, the typologies exercise for FATF-XV used a slightly different formula for its experts meeting. For three of the topics – wire transfers, NPOs and insurance sector vulnerabilities – some work was done in small groups before the experts' meeting in order to bring some greater focus to discussions of the topics. Then during the experts' meeting, a smaller break out session (consisting of about 30 operational and policy making personnel) was held for each of the three topics to identify relevant trends and examine any policy implications raised by the identified typologies. The findings of the three workshops were then presented in the full meeting of experts where they were further debated along with presentations on PEPs and gatekeepers."

Methods Team (see Table 5.1). These experts represent various countries (in some instances organisations), some of which are contributors of case studies material.

It is not clear how countries are selected for a particular workshop and whether all countries (at least among the FATF's members) are being invited to contribute case studies, for instance, by circulating a consultation paper rather than having a representative attend a workshop. Neither is it always clear from a report which countries attended a workshop. For some of the reports it appears that the underlying material is derived from the completion of a questionnaire circulated among all of the FATF's members.[20] On several occasions the FATF had combined the answers from the questionnaire with material from specialised literature, the media and information provided directly from sections of the regulated sector (such as insurance companies, as will be discussed later).

According to the FATF's 2004 Typologies report (p. 2):[21] "*Each year, the FATF typologies exercise focuses on a series of topics or themes that were agreed to by the FATF Plenary*". The report further states: "*The Plenary attempts to select topics according to the current work of the body or to follow up on methods or trends identified in previous typologies exercises.*" (*ibid.*) If clear trends are identified, it remains a question why there is such a limited statistical analysis in the reports. FATF's 2003 Typology report (p. 1)[22] states that "*Written material produced by the FATF delegations and invited experts was collected and circulated [. . .] Also as part of the typologies exercise FATF members submitted money laundering statistics and information on other relevant trends, as well as examples of money laundering indicators*" Nevertheless, the statistics are restricted to a few crude frequencies tables, in this and subsequent reports: not quite the detailed material for a reasoned subject selection.

Indeed, it appears that the topics are not the result of a comprehensive analysis of the STRs, or crime statistics (for example, case studies based on the top five most commonly used money laundering methods), but are rather a reflection of the subjective view of the Plenary as to what might be topical. For instance, the 2003 and 2004 reports that resulted from meetings in 2002 and 2003 respectively, contained a substantial number of case studies devoted to terrorist financing, and many of the subsequent reports were either entirely devoted to terrorist financing or have sections devoted to this subject. The

---

20 The 2005 report, which has a section devoted to the insurance sector, states: "A project leader with relevant experience in examining ML and Insurance was appointed, who drew up a project plan which was agreed by the Working Group on Typologies.

21 FATF Report on Money Laundering Typologies 2003-2004, available at: http://www.fatf-gafi.org/media/fatf/documents/reports/2003_2004_ML_Typologies_ENG.pdf. Accessed 3 February 2017.

22 FATF Report on Money Laundering Typologies 2002-2003, 14 February 2003 available at: http://www.fatf-gafi.org/media/fatf/documents/reports/2002_2003_ML_Typologies_ENG.pdf Accessed 3 February 2017.

9/11 terrorist attacks indeed marked a change in the compliance landscape. Terrorist financing deservedly attracted policy-makers' attention. The FATF stated in its 2003 report (p. 25) that "*In the weeks immediately following the September 11th terrorist attacks, a significant increase in suspicious transaction reporting occurred in many jurisdictions. This sudden change in reporting patterns was already indicated during last year's typologies exercise. [. . .] FATF members were therefore asked to follow up on this change in reporting patterns after September 11th and through 2002.*" However, that is not to say that terrorist financing really began to dominate the financial crime scene overnight. To the contrary, the FATF itself admitted in its reports that terrorist financing does not necessarily occur on a large scale and transactions ordinarily entail small amounts of money.

The selection of subjects seems sometimes to be based on unstructured 'reasoning' lacking underlying facts and jumping to conclusions. An example of this remarkable reasoning in the selection of a topic is the *insurance industry*, which also looks rather counterfactual. What do we find? In two reports – 2003 and 2004 – there is a section devoted to money laundering through the insurance sector. This is despite the fact that the International Association of Insurance Supervisors itself does not regard the insurance sector's vulnerability to be as high as in other sectors of the financial industry (2004, p. 1). Nevertheless, the FATF's 2005 report[23] (Chapter II, p. 41) states that: "*FATF typologies research indicated that there was a low detection of ML within the insurance industry in comparison to the size of the industry and in comparison to other parts of the financial services industry.*" However, in order to know whether the detection rate is low, one must be sure that money laundering is indeed occurring: in what forms and to what extent. Stating that there should be more SARs/STRs because of the size of the industry, without further evidence is unfounded *a-priori* reasoning. There may be a limited 'detection' because there is a limited laundering activity – as simple as that. Nevertheless, the FATF stresses (Typologies Report, 2005, p. 44): "*In the experts' view, the generally low suspicious transaction reporting activity relating to insurers is remarkable in and of itself. However, it may not be entirely surprising given the differing characters of banking and insurance and when also considering that in many jurisdictions AML regulation in the insurance sector is relatively recent. Nevertheless, the small amount of reporting from the insurance sector is noteworthy for two reasons:*

[23] FATF money laundering & terrorist financing typologies 2004-2005, 10 June 2005, available at: http://www.fatf-gafi.org/media/fatf/documents/reports/2004_2005_ML_Typologies_ENG.pdf. Accessed 3 February 2017.

- *Firstly, the insurance sector's relative size within the financial services industry of each jurisdiction is such that one would expect it to be exposed to the risk of being infiltrated by money launderers and criminals in general to a much wider extent than the number of STRs would indicate.*
- *Secondly, the identified vulnerabilities [. . .] clearly show that the sector is exposed to reasonable degree of ML risk.*"

What is a reasonable degree? This is jumping to an unfounded conclusion along the reasoning: "if it is big there must be something more". Close reading of the second point shows a combination of vagueness ('reasonable degree') and semantic circularity of vulnerability with exposure to risk which remains rather empty without a specification of 'reasonable'.

Nevertheless, this kind of reasoning justified three typologies on this sector while it also sent a message to the banking sector that insurance companies are high-risk clients. It does not occur to the rapporteurs that the insurance sector may simply not be sufficiently known or attractive to those who seek to launder money and that the identified vulnerabilities are little more than theoretical truisms. Moreover, on what facts are the vulnerability judgements based? Expert intuition? Let us not forget that insurance companies typically have dedicated anti-fraud professionals on their teams who investigate every case of insurance payment, policy surrender or premium withdrawal. They also examine the source of funds so how likely is it that there is a regular presence of 'interested launderers' who will endeavour to subject their criminal activity to so much scrutiny?

b. Quality of the typologies

Naturally it is difficult to judge the quality of the typologies: there are no yardsticks for accuracy, depth and sharpness of analysis or composition, let alone something intangible such as style. Nevertheless, it cannot be denied that the typology reports are of a varying quality and level of detail. They are also detached from the practical side of due diligence and investigation. Very few case studies make reference to requirements and best practices in terms of due diligence. In general, a lack of analytical depth appears prevalent.

As already commented, until 2005, the reports did not stipulate which countries had contributed the case studies. This was probably because of the choice to keep countries and cases anonymous. However, this was not helpful as case studies are often intended to examine how trends develop across specific geographic areas. From 2005 onwards, however, the FATF started naming the countries in most (but not all) cases. There appears to be a consistent group of country contributors, with the top two being the USA and the UK, with Belgium, France, Canada and Australia being also among the more regular contributors. Most other countries appear to be 'shy' and only occasionally provide case studies material.

It is perhaps not surprising that the USA and UK have remained over the years the two main contributors. We say 'not surprising' because these two jurisdictions have had a leading position worldwide in terms of the (combined) volume of financial services and the amount of regulations. This could lead to a bias in the selection of cases and an uncertainty as to what these cases really represent given the unanswered questions: (i) are these two jurisdictions comparable, given the diversity between the various states within the US (London in the UK versus the various states of the USA, such as New York, Delaware, Nevada *etc.*); (ii) is the number of case studies indicative of anything, such as a trend? If that is the case, the time variable should be mentioned, but most cases have no such indication, thereby effectively excluding any possibility of observing trends.

Another observation is that many cases were as old as Methuselah; on a number of occasions we recognised case stories recycled from books on money laundering (for example, from Jeffrey Robinson) or other old literature.

Furthermore, as remarked, there is a distinctive lack of analytical depth and as noted in the previous section, there is 'jumping' to conclusions. We observe a lack of full-cycle case studies, for example, real-life cases, even if redacted, that show how a red-flag indicator of suspicious activity – 'a suspicion trigger' – evolves from a STR/SAR into a fully-scoped investigation, prosecution, trial and sentence. While it can be appreciated that at the stage of ideas gathering for a Typologies report, FIUs may only have the raw STR/SAR data for some of their cases, the following should be considered:

1. cases that are still at the stage of raw STR/SAR data can be presented from the perspective of the financial institution filing the STR/SAR, *i.e.* provided that the case studies are based on a STR/SAR, and if not, then the FIU should be able to present that perspective hypothetically so that the case study turns into an educational exercise for the regulated sector that describes the profile of the client and the nature of financial activity and, most importantly, *what triggered the suspicion?*
2. cases that have progressed beyond a STR/SAR can be presented in phases – from the point of filing a STR/SAR to whatever next stage is appropriate, with the FIU providing clues as to how STR/SAR information is converted into a criminal investigation and how the illegal scheme is being dismantled;
3. cases that are not based on a STR/SAR can also be presented from the perspective of a financial institution, *i.e.* how a regulated entity could have spotted the red-flags.

In all of the above points, it would help to know the suspected nature of the predicate offences: whether the crime proceeds are suspected to have been generated through human trafficking, drug trafficking, corruption, embezzlement, fraud, *etc*. The criminal financial management of the proceeds will often depend on the nature of the predicate offence (see Gelemerova, 2011). Naturally in the cases with direct laundering as a consequence of the *modus operandi* employed, the proceeds will already be within the financial system ('canned laundering', see Van Duyne, 2003; Van Duyne *et al.*, 2005). The level of sophistication will vary as well, according to the nature of the crime. A typology is valuable when it allows the reader to understand and appreciate the various elements of the laundering activity. And that starts with explaining the predicate offence and the corresponding criminal asset management.

Most importantly, case studies should be an illustration of how to identify suspicion triggers or red-flag indicators. At present, some examples have little in terms of red-flag indicators; others have red-flag indicators provided as a separate list that does not form part of the case studies. Very few have red-flag indicators incorporated into the actual case study.

c. Commensurate attention or just passing by

The typologies exercises are intended to raise awareness of important manifestations of laundering such that participants will take an intellectual message home or increase their skills in recognising forms of money laundering. As mentioned in the introductory section, the subjects are decided upon by the Plenary after which the FATF's expert group will elaborate cases. How this is carried out remains unclear: is the attention paid to the selected subjects commensurate with their importance? For example, the prevalence of types of STRs, investigations and prosecutions or other fact-based material. We find no indication for how the educational importance is determined. In fact, we find a mixture of subjects that do not reveal much ordering. Some get only one-off attention, others such as the insurance industry, are put on the agenda a number of times.

In view of its place in the research literature as well as the media, it would be a euphemism to call the real estate sector just 'vulnerable'. Van Duyne *et al.* (2009) as well as Unger (2007) and Ferwerda and Unger (2013) identify the real estate sector as a field with many red-flags and a popular destination of crime-money with the skewed distribution of wealth this usually entails: "*Few move much and many move only few*". In relation to really expensive real estate in the chic areas of a metropolis, such as London and New York, the media report (Guardian[24]) regularly about the very wealthy buyers from Russia, China or Nigeria with the implication of shady persons and connected shady payments. But there is little mention of these purchases by the FATF.

Despite all these public indications of a sector that is traditionally receptive of crime money, we find only one typologies report, June 2007: a stock taking project led by Spain and the Netherlands. Case examples were provided by Belgium (eight), the Netherlands (three), France and Spain (two each), Ukraine, Australia, Mexico and Canada (each provided one case): altogether not a really overwhelming collection. Notably, there are no case studies from the USA and the UK despite having a vast collection of STR/SAR records. And despite the fact that in its corruption-focused Typologies reports the FATF has included USA and UK case studies indicating that corruption money has flown into the real estate sector. Surely if such cases exist, it is worth looking into the technicalities of laundering through real estate.

The real-estate report mentions letting property and the practice of mixing rental income with crime money (a method similar to the one allegedly used by an English wholesale cocaine trafficker, Curtis Warren, currently serving time in the Netherlands). There is no observation of how such a system of laundering works: for example, whether the tenants must sign false tenancy agreements with a higher rent mentioned than is actually paid.

Though we think this report is an example of a better structured material (albeit it is not a very innovative typologies report), it has the defect of not connecting the case descriptions with the follow-up of investigations, prosecutions and, possibly, trial and finally the recovery of the ill-gotten assets. If these real estate cases are so clear and prevalent with many references to them present in other typologies reports, the outcome of investigations, prosecutions and trials should have been specified, or if not available, other cases for which the full law enforcement outcomes were known, should have been selected. Though the title of this report also mentioned 'terrorist financing' there were only two cases with a 'possible link' to that crime category. Otherwise one finds the meaningless ritual phrase of "money laundering and terrorist financing", a word string without further specification and, therefore, useless for a frequency search. Given the importance of real estate in the field of criminal finances, more of these typologies should have been carried out if only to find out whether there are developments in this area. With this

[24] See for example: *The Guardian* 'End London's role as a clearing-house for dirty money' Tristram Hunt; 20 November, 2016 available at https://www.theguardian.com/commentisfree/2016/nov/20/london-property-dirty-money-clearing-house-property-market. Accessed 3 February, 2017; *The Guardian*, 'Foreign criminals use London housing market to launder billions of pounds', Damien Gayle, 25 July 2015, available at https://www.theguardian.com/uk-news/2015/jul/25/london-housing-market-launder-offshore-tax-havens. Accessed 3 February 2017.

single report the attention paid to this subject is not commensurate to its importance.

Other subjects recurred regularly which leads us to question whether that can be justified by providing a gradually increasing insight into the specific phenomena. 'Terrorist financing' was the most frequent typology subject, though time and again the relevant reports (eight) admitted that few cases were brought to light, particularly in the security and insurance sectors. As mentioned before, in view of these sectors' economic size, the FATF considered these results implausible. Thus, this low prevalence was attributed to various causes, such as lack of awareness. As discussed previously, apparently, it did not dawn on the FATF that another plausible counter-hypothesis should be considered: namely that these sectors are simply not attractive to (terrorist) launderers as they may be completely alien to their skills and culture. By mentioning terrorist financing frequently in other reports on other subjects, one gets the impression that terrorist financing occurs everywhere. In fact most of the time there is mention only of an unspecified 'vulnerability', suggesting more than exists in reality. Most often we find the 'TF' reference as a dummy component in a sentence. If there were relevant cases mentioned, these "involved only small amounts". We found not much discussion of the management of terrorist funds.

We find a similar lack of precision in the tobacco and trade-based typologies: a few instances are highlighted, but little is disclosed about the management of the illegal funds, while that should be the essence for a typology: the criminal money management.

As far as 'trends and developments' are concerned, the reports mention the "emergence of . . .": a certain criminal or terrorist financing development. But does emergence imply a trend? Unfortunately, statistics are lacking while the cases presented by the participating members lack any representativeness: years are lacking and affected countries are unsystematically mentioned while the descriptions or analyses are superficial and usually defective where police investigations, prosecutions, trials and assets recovery are concerned.

As mentioned before, there is much jumping to conclusions, without serious underpinnings. This seems to be furthered by the use of the vague term 'vulnerable'. Vulnerability appears everywhere: when few cases are reported in a sector, it is described as just as vulnerable, as sectors where many cases are reported. For some manifestations of CAM the report attributes its low prevalence to stricter control and supervision in other chains of proceeds processing. Examples of this include the physical transportation of cash or conversely, trade based money laundering. While the hidden physical transportation of cash has been the norm over the decades, nothing is really mentioned about its numerical trend. No mention is made about the next and more important stage: the real laundering of the money in terms of 'whitening'. Conversely, the trade based laundering does not start with cash, but with tampering with the paper work and invoice forgery, next to regular wire transfers between seller and buyer. But what happens next to the over- and under-invoicing?

These questions can be qualified as 'no questions asked', this time by the FATF as rapporteur. Most strikingly no question is asked about the connection of all these typologies with the act of laundering, the CAM and its alleged consequence: the undermining of the integrity of the financial system. There are few cases with a more precise elaboration. Naturally, the FATF is dependent on the input of its member states, but this is not an excuse: the FATF is part of the group of 'experts' in the preparatory phase: perhaps even the key expert. This superficiality cannot be attributed to member states only.

The FATF as rapporteur also failed to ask other obvious questions. Earlier we mentioned the under-discussed real estate sector. While it is sufficient to type in the search terms 'real estate', 'London' or 'New York' and 'laundering' to get a full overview of newspaper articles about suspicious money flowing into the high priced West London and Manhattan real estate sector, one finds nothing of this information throughout the typologies when 'real estate' is casually mentioned. Were there no STRs or SARs filed relating to transactions with high-valued property in the USA and UK? Whether the legal instrument of Unexplained Wealth Order in the UK[25] will bring a change remains to be seen (also see Chapter 10).

The diamond and gold typologies also raise unanswered questions about how and where money laundering takes place and in what quantities. It is a small world, particularly the diamond sector, in which it takes time for diamond traders to become established and recognised among elite artisans. Does this imply that laundering is difficult or that it happens more often but is kept well concealed due to habitually 'looking away' in such a closed social climate?

A question of major importance that has arisen since the emergence of the risk-based approach is whether the typologies are being prepared from this risk perspective. This entails an additional question: to what degree are the presented typologies of laundering conducive to understanding those economic sectors that enable a particular volume of laundering such that it can jeopardise financial stability and integrity, or, conversely should some types of laundering merely be considered a 'financial nuisance'? Trying to address this question would force the participants of typologies sessions to think out some rank order of importance. However, thus far this question has not really been considered as food for thought.

---

[25] An Unexplained Wealth Order requires a person to explain and account for the source of his or her assets.

5.8 The FATF in its global network

One of the assignments of the FATF, following from its first mandate, is to create a network of institutions and countries that are of importance to the fight against money laundering and that endorse the 40 Recommendations. Naturally, this goes beyond the FATF consisting in 2018 of 37-member states and organisations, as this network is intended to span the earth so that one can speak of the *FATF Global Network*.

What does that mean?

> "*The FATF has grown out of a small group of like-minded countries in the early nineties, to a body where 34-member countries, 2-member organisations and eight associate members meet. These associate members are our eight so called FATF-style regional bodies (FSRBs). These regional bodies gained a stronger status in our new mandate and take part in all our activities, all our working groups they are active, they have rights and obligations. All in all, this is called the Global Network of FATF, with more than 180 countries who all have endorsed the FATF Standards.*"
>
> *FATF President Bjørn S. Aamo at the United Nations, New York, 20 November 2012*

This is not the only high-level speech in which the FATF Global Network is identified. The FATF Global Network today includes 198 jurisdictions: the 39 direct members, nine FSRBs, working in partnership with the UN, IMF, World Bank and others. It is a network based on consensus (there are no dissenters), which is considered highly flexible and adaptable, and suitable for working in an alleged changing landscape. However, a network is not a body or an organisation even if it requires much organisation to keep the network going.

How does the FATF see this global network? According to the 2012 *Mandate* and the *FATF High Level Principles and Objectives* 2012 (shortened to FATF High Principles), the 'central node' of this network is the FATF. As we have seen in section 3.5, the FATF determines and protects the 'FATF brand': anything not in accordance with this brand is not adopted in the network. This simplifies the picture of the network, beginning with the FSRBs: the regional bodies committed to the implementation of the FATF standards and principles.

The FSRBs can be considered as the first circle of nodes around the FATF, with which they have mutual connections in terms of reciprocal rights and obligations. According to the *2012 Mandate* (p. 4), the FSRBs are associate members of the FATF and are committed to take part in the work and objectives of the FATF. This applies not only to full access to documents but also to meetings and events, including the Plenary, working groups and sub-group meetings. Such attendance is supposed to be an active one: "providing input to each other's discussions and decision-making processes [or] submitting written comments and feedback under the name of their jurisdiction on any FSRB/FATF document and papers" (*FATF High Principles*, p. 4). The FATF and FSRBs should also provide secretariat assistance and participate in the peer review process (mutual evaluation).

In addition to this general mutual access, participation and support, these regional bodies have to comply with a number of requirements concerning governance structures: membership, mission, institutional set-up, financial procedures and budget in such a way that they are truly FATF *style* bodies. The *FATF High Level Principles* and the *2012 Mandate* do not specify what 'style' is supposed to mean, though the implication of these requirements make the FSRBs look like an FATF franchise chain: like *Burger King* or *McDonalds*. Independent but strictly tied to the brand-protecting formula of the parent.

Characterising the FSRBs as a ring of nodes around the FATF is, however, too static and incomplete a representation. Each FSRB is a node with its own network in which we find observers who also attend the FATF Plenary and other FSRBs meetings. Some FSRBs have more observers than they have members, for example, the Eurasian Group has 16 states and 17 international and regional organisations with observer status, which is more than the nine-member states. One may wonder why. Notably, this group's members include Russia, India and China, while its observers include the USA and the UK. Whereas individual member countries cannot be found among the FATF's observers; the latter comprise supranational organisations and inter-governmental bodies, *e.g.* the UNODC and the World Bank (as discussed below).

As the websites of most FSRBs do not have a list of participating observers or associated members in the plenaries, it is difficult to make an estimate of the 'observer density' in the global network.

A second ring of nodes consists of the organisations with *observer status* for which they are eligible if they endorse the FATF Recommendations, guidance and other relevant policy and otherwise contribute to the work of the FATF. There are 29 observer organisations ranging from international financial institutions to institutions with a law enforcement task to the Commonwealth Secretariat or World Customs Organisation. The UN has seven sub-organisations that are also observers to the FATF. The observer policy of the FATF knows seven criteria the most important being: underwriting the FATF aims, being 'inter-' (-national, governmental, regional) and generally adding value to the work of the FATF. Of particular interest are the IMF and the World Bank, which also participate in the execution of the mutual evaluation activities.

An important node in the network is the *Egmont Group* of Financial Intelligence Units (FIU). This consists of the Heads of the national FIUs who, with the Egmont Committee, the four Working Groups, the eight Regional Groups, the Egmont Secure Web communication network, and the secretariat performing the tasks of the Egmont Group. With its 151-member FIUs and 18 observer organisations the Egmont Groups is a global network of its own (Annual Report 2014-2015). The Egmont Group also has 18 international partner organisations, though the website does not mention what that partnership entails in terms of support or involvement. The international partners do not overlap with the observers, with the exception of the IMF. Many of the observer organisations in the Egmont Group are in their turn also observers to the FATF making the network more intensive.

The network is extensive and labour intensive to operate. Attendance at the events, such as the typologies seminars, looks occasionally overwhelmingly. Little is known of the expenses involved and likewise the added value. Of course, there is some socialising effect in this networking: the mutual sharing of opinions, attitudes, and principles. That is an undeniable benefit. However, when we look at the Global Network's *real* effectiveness in terms of investigations, prosecutions and convictions, as presented in the poor output statistics, it is difficult to maintain claims about added value compared to the total efforts put into it: the costs of this network mobility were dubbed by Van Duyne *et al.* (2016) 'the Monty Python Flying Circus of money laundering'.

5.9 Conclusion

We raised the question that a tree must be judged by the fruit falling from its branches. To that end we looked for evidence enabling us and the reader at large to reach a judgement. One obvious piece of evidence are the FATF Recommendations, of which the capital **R** is symbolic for what they are: imperial orders that must be complied with. As indicated by the IMF: all uses of "should" in these documents are to be read as "must". In this way, the FATF has become more than an advisory informal network. When it comes to assessing its functioning, the network representation is misleading: the working of its Recommendations is not restricted to its direct network but applies globally and overrides the sovereignty of states. This means that for the application of the Recommendations network membership is irrelevant.

In maintaining the Recommendations, the FATF has arrogated the three powers of investigation, judgment and sanctioning, the latter without any process of appeal. One of the tools of investigation is the mutual evaluation and reporting (MERs). The yardsticks to be used by the assessors (and the FATF Plenary) are anything but unambiguous. This applies particularly to the evaluation by the new Risk Based Approach, assuming that the assessors have a superior knowledge of the risk understanding of the authorities of the evaluated countries. In addition, it should be noted that according to the FATF itself there are no proper definitions of the key concepts of threat and risk. Despite this confession of agnosis, the fourth round evaluation went ahead with much "creative intuition" and "systemic weaknesses" setting the door wide open to subjectivity.

Despite this subjectivity, its informal position and its arrogation of the "three powers", the FATF developed a system of 'herding the sheep into line' by its Recommendations. To that end it uses a sliding system of blacklisting: from 'helping and guiding' to calling on states to take 'countermeasures'. In effect this is a sanction system for which there is no legitimate basis. If there is no such basis to hand out sanctions how should the ruling by the FATF be characterised? We made a comparison with the indirect colonial rule as used by the colonial powers Great Britain and France: ruling through local princes, who comply in the knowledge that the 'imperial gunboat' (the blacklist) is nearby.

The FATF is a prolific producer of guidance and reports on special subjects, many presented as typologies. The produced typologies, considered as an important output, raise many unaddressed questions: not only why certain subjects are put to the fore, but also why the underlying reasoning, more often than not exhibits a jumping to conclusions. While the typologies sessions, with attendants from all over the world, may have a socio-psychological function, their intellectual value-added remains uncertain.

The FATF prefers to present itself as a network in which it is the central node. Around it are the regional bodies, which are only recognised as 'FATF-style' if they contribute to the maintenance of the FATF brand. This may be characterised as a franchise organisation like a restaurant or burger chain: standing alone but maintaining the same principles and products. Around and overlapping there are other networks, such as the Egmont Group, all mutually associated and attending each other's meetings which gives solid reasons for an abundant mobility: the Monty Python Flying Circus of money laundering (Van Duyne *et al.*, 2016).

6

Legal studies literature

6.1 Introduction: legal foundations and legal laundering research

In this book we discuss the legislative framework for AML. However, we have not looked at principles and axioms which are the foundations of a rule of law and whether and how these emerged from our database presented in Chapter 2.

Much of the early literature written by legal scholars gave consideration to the legal ramifications of the content of the changing Acts of Congress in the United States but did not challenge their foundations. As we have seen in Chapter 3, there is consensus that the roots of money laundering as a legal concept were firmly planted in the US 1970 Bank Secrecy Act (see for example Levi and Reuter, 2006; Gelemerova, 2009). But it was referred to, by the authorities, more clearly as an existing phenomenon in the USA Commission on Organized Crime Report of 1984 (see for example, Buchanan, 2004; Comstock, 1994; Cuéllar, 2003; Boran, 2003; Newland, 2008; and Provost, 2009) that led to the Money Laundering Control Act, 1986. The latter criminalised money laundering. Some scholars note an earlier and a more informal reference to the term appearing in 1973 in connection with the Watergate Scandal (Schneider and Windischbauer, 2008; Gelemerova, 2009 and 2011). There is also a theory tracing laundering back to the Mafia in the USA in the 1920s (Unger, 2007; Mccarthy *et al.*, 2015).

P.C. van Duyne, J.H. Harvey and L.Y. Gelemerova, *The Critical Handbook of Money Laundering*, https://doi.org/10.1057/978-1-137-52398-3_6

Early studies of anti-money laundering legislation generally tended to accept the counter-drugs justification.[1] Gradually some scholars began raising questions. They noted that the 1986 Act and its subsequent amendments in 1988[2] were introduced in the run up to elections, in a manner that was hurried through without due care such that the legislation was "*seriously flawed*" (Strafer, 1989, p. 207; see also Pieth, 1999). At around the same time, the UK adopted a more cooperative stance in dealing with its financial institutions. Rider (1990) notes that the UK authorities encouraged voluntary reporting of suspicious activity not related to drug offences. Early legislation distinguished between the laundering of drug money under the Drug Trafficking Offences Act (1986), and non-drug offences captured in the Criminal Justice Act 1993 that amended the Criminal Justice Act, 1988 (Bell, 2003). The distinction was removed by the Proceeds of Crime Act 2002 (Ryder, 2008).

There are a number of foundations on which a 'legal structure' should be based. The list of such foundations is quite extensive, divided by substantive and procedural law. For our purposes we enumerate only those principles that we feel are of relevance for our research on laundering though they apply to other legal subjects as well. We do not exclude the existence of other legal foundations and if during our narrative they prove to be relevant, we will take them on-board. The following foundations are in our perception relevant for our study:

- Interest and harm
- Proportionality and subsidiarity
- Scope and *lex certis*
- Sanctions
- Recovery of 'ill-gotten' assets

These are basics which are to be found in text books on common law and European continental law systems. Obviously, these are not distinctive con-

[1] Although it must be noted that some scholars did challenge the 'war on drugs' concept (see, for instance, Hindes, 1977) but this was not necessarily in papers focusing on money laundering and / or management of crime proceeds.

[2] The key milestones in the history of US AML legislation are: Bank Secrecy Act (1970), Money Laundering Control Act (1986), Anti-Drug Abuse Act (1988), Annunzio-Wylie Anti-Money Laundering Act (1992), Money Laundering Suppression Act (1994), Money Laundering and Financial Crimes Strategy Act (1998), Uniting and Strengthening America by Providing Appropriate Tools Required to Intercept and Obstruct Terrorism Act/USA PATRIOT ACT (2001), Intelligence Reform & Terrorism Prevention Act of 2004 (see Fincen's website: https://www.fincen.gov/history-anti-money-laundering-laws). The 1988 amendment introduced with the Anti-Drug Abuse Act aimed at strengthening the anti-drug abuse enforcement regime by introducing stricter penalties but also by expanding the group of reporting entities (*e.g.* to include car dealers) and by requiring the verification of identity of purchasers of monetary instruments over $3,000.

cepts: they overlap and interact in their application. For example, proportionality and subsidiarity overlap or are adjacent to other legal areas. It is our objective to investigate how these have been used by legal scholars in their elaboration of the legal aspects of the phenomenon of money laundering: in a way we let the legal researchers speak.

6.2 Interest and harm

It is almost a platitude, or at least should be so, that there is no criminal law without an interest and related harm worth protecting in cases of law breaking. As discussed by the sociologist Vold (1958), laws are brought into being by the political majority, but they are also there to protect all of society's members without discrimination. Naturally, political majorities change and, as a result, the concept of criminality is fluid. It expands as more laws are brought onto the statute books, while at the same time more groups are identified who do not adhere to the values or culture of society. The criminal exhibits behaviour and engages in acts that can be seen as causing harm to others, whether snatching a handbag in the street or defrauding a company. It follows that the aim of criminal law is to prevent unjustified harm and/or to seek redress in the event of its occurrence.

As far as money laundering is concerned, these principles apply likewise. However, there is a difference because of the multi-layered nature of laundering. The harm caused by the handbag snatcher or the defrauding accountant is clear. But the harm of the subsequent management of the ill-gotten profits is much less clear. The thief steals an expensive iPad and sells it for 10% of its value while the accountant transfers his proceeds to an offshore haven from where it is repatriated later. This is (self-)laundering in both cases. But what harm does this additional law breaking add to the harm of the predicate offence? If money laundering is viewed as harmful in its own *moral* capacity ('crime should not pay'), moral harm to the financial system may be caused by this co-mingling of dirty and clean money, which seemingly underpins the arguments of policy makers discussed in earlier chapters. However, the certainty of this harm by co-mingling is indeterminate, at least unsupported by historical evidence: laundered and legitimate funds can be deposited into the same saving accounts and can subsequently be transferred to other accounts elsewhere (see Van Duyne, 2013; Harvey and Lau, 2008). Will these accounts be infected by the crime-money? As we will discuss in Chapter 9 this is important as it concerns a basic question: "What is all this good for?" For the moment we can determine that the earlier quoted Ferwerda (2013) could not find much evidence of financial or economic harm. As a matter of fact, his careful analysis resulted in the refutation of the list of harmful effects of money laundering composed by the IMF (Quirk, 1996) and adopted as valid by Unger (2007). Also, Reuter (2013) made clear that despite his vetting of the literature, he could not find much historical evidence of endangered sectors of the financial system because of money laundering.

Despite this criticism and these doubts we have the earlier identified a deep-rooted "IMF Consensus", as mentioned in the research report of the UNODC (2011; p. 42) and that stretches back as far as Camdessus' address in 1996. It has a wide following (Unger *et al.*, 2006; Walker, 1995 and follow-up publications) and as such lends authority to the harm statement and to the high prioritising of money laundering as a real global threat. It should be observed that the harm statement is many faceted. More specifically, laundering facilitates the continuation of crime with two effects: the Mr. Big can grow and thrive, while his increased proceeds (laundered or *un*laundered) continue to flow inside or outside the financial system (and remain 'available'). This implies that stemming the harm from Mr. Big and his like can be achieved by preventing their money laundering. In Chapter 3 we considered the desire and motivation by the US authorities to focus on the flows of illegal money (proceeds) as an approach to combat the threat from organised crime and drugs. Although as discussed, ultimately there were other benefits to the authorities, for example, tax proceeds.

The second effect concerns the facilitation of a nexus of crime and the upperworld. As previously discussed and noted by Pieth (2002), the criminal offence of money laundering emerged from the desire to cut off the funding for the drugs trade.

Official publications outline an illegal nexus that links together drugs, shadowy and high-level figures in organised crime and money launderers able to organise and execute complex financial transactions. Attacking money laundering would simply cut that off. It would also cut off access for rich criminals to the upperworld for their laundered funds. Van Duyne (2003; p. 76) pointed at "*corruptive permeation: crime money enters the veins and nerves of the 'control rooms' of the upperworld.*"

Rather than challenge the all-encompassing approach, a number of authors reproduced the justification that this very broad AML approach was an essential tool in the fight against organised crime as it allowed for an attack on the finances of these criminal groups (see for example, Newland, 2008, p. 741; Provost 2009, p. 837; Dombrink and Meeker, 1986). A distinct strand of literature dwelt on the concern amongst attorneys as to whether by acceptance of their criminal defence fees they might find themselves in receipt of laundered funds (see for example: Boylston, 1987; Wolfteich, 1988; and Weinstein, 1988). There is also a rather unquestioning acceptance in this literature of the scale and complexity of the criminal organisation of money laundering and the perception that there are substantial sums involved (McCarthy *et al.*,

2015, see also Chapter 7). We also note the distinctively challenging approach adopted by Alldridge (2003, 2002) and Cuéllar (2003).

Levi (2002) notes that the official rationale for the AML intervention is to stop (1) the expansion and financing of crime groups; (2) the corrosive impact on financial institutions ('corrosive' being a word also employed by Cuéllar (2003)); and (3) the somewhat nebulous 'harm' to legitimate capital.

This reasoning looks like a mental triple jump with institutional corrosion through which we inevitably arrive at the stated harm to 'legitimate capital' caused by laundering as an aggravation of harm already caused by the predicate offences. The causal connection between the three statements remains intuitive only. Admittedly, most writing in support of the requirement for the introduction of money laundering as a criminal offence does not even make such an acrobatic jump. The authors mainly pointed to their belief in the existence of a select group of third-party laundering professionals.

As a result, this legislation was considered the only means with which to reach those at the pinnacle of the criminal hierarchy: leading criminals who are sufficiently well removed from the predicate offence to be untouchable through more traditional means (McCarthy *et al.*, 2015; Nadelmann, 1986; Nichols, 1997; Cuéllar, 2003). The presumption within both official discourse and this academic literature is of the existence of a pyramidal structure with laundered proceeds passed back up the hierarchy (Alldridge, 2002). As Cuéllar (2003, p. 325) has remarked, the flow of money upwards requires more laundering than the handling of cash payments at the street level, an observation which does not require deep insight.

Formulated in this way the harm-justification seems to have drifted from a description of the harm to the financial system (corroding integrity) to that by organised crime with all the conceptual ramifications which that assumption allows. And because organised criminals are in need of financial institutions, one arrives with another jump back at the harm to the financial system. Most of the legal studies discussing the justification of the money laundering criminalisation does little to dissect these aspects and to recast these propositions into something more systematic. The very few attempts to dissect these aspects require a follow-up.

6.3 Proportionality and subsidiarity

The previous section juxtaposed the harm proposition and the scholarly legal theorising. Next, we look in the legal studies literature at the question of what would be a proportional response and the 'least adequate effort', denoted, respectively, as the proportionality and subsidiarity principles. These are essential concepts permeating all legal measures related to anti-money laundering policy. To clarify this proposition, we refer to the previous section about harm: regulatory and law enforcement responses must be proportional to or in balance with the harm caused by money laundering while the measures taken should be the minimum required: it is the proverbial "don't use a sledgehammer to crack a nut" (Van Duyne *et al.*, 2016; Gelemerova, 2011).

What does the literature on legal research say about this proportionality between offence and sanction? To say something meaningful about this dual subject, one would expect in the first place a juxtaposition of harm and the corresponding regulatory and criminal law measures. In the previous section and in Chapter 4 we reviewed the legal research on harm or threats, finding that while many authors mention some forms of harm, their identification is rarely precise. Related to this deficiency a proportionality match on the level of criminal law and sentencing is absent in the literature: there emerged no comparison between the level of the legally stipulated punishment and harm, or more generally, how to relate ideas of harm to particular law enforcement interventions.

Concerning the conversion of policy opinions into levels of penalties, there is no direct relationship to be observed across-countries if we only look at the maximum imposable punishments (Table 6.1.). The range of maximum imprisonment for what is considered the most serious form of laundering is broad: from five years (Austria, Belgium, and Switzerland) to 25 years in Australia.

Obviously, these differences do not reflect a linear conversion from perceived threat into levels of punishment. Maximum penalties for specific offences must be projected against the background of the average punishment level in the relevant jurisdictions. For example, Switzerland and the Netherlands may have a less punitive criminal law policy than Australia, the UK or the USA. These differences do not reflect a shared opinion of what is considered to be a dissuasive punishment. In addition to these differences it is interesting to note the differences in scaling 'seriousness' of offences and how they are connected to maximum imprisonments.

The principle of proportionality implies that the penalty applied must be related to an assessment of seriousness and be sufficient to ensure that '*crime does not pay*' McClean (1989, p. 334). However, Table 6.1 shows little harmony concerning the legislators' perception of proportionality. There are some general findings in the legal research which could be interpreted as referring to proportionality across the whole AML-regime, but not specifically concerning criminalisation and sanctioning. This is partly due to the fact that with the US 1970 Bank Secrecy Act most initial attention was devoted to information gathering as a consequence of the preventive facets of the anti-laundering package. Abramovsky (1986, p. 476) noted that the Money Laundering Control Act "was intended to enlarge the amount of financial information

Table 6.1 Maximum penalties for committing money laundering in selected jurisdictions: imprisonment only

Country	Maximum penalty
Australia (Criminal Code, Chapter 10, Part 10.2, div.400) scale of culpable conduct	
a: > Aus $ 1,000,000 + intent/recklessness/negligence	25 years / 12 years / 5 years
b: > Aus $ 100,000 + same scale of conduct	20 years / 10 years / 4 years
c: > Aus $ 50,000 + same scale of conduct	15 years / 7 years / 3 years
d: > Aus $ 10,000 + same scale of conduct	10 years / 5 years / 2 years
e: > Aus $ 1,000 + same scale of conduct	5 years / 3 years / 1 years
f: Any value	1 year / 6 months; 10 penalty units
g: Property reasonably suspected being proceeds:	
1: > 100,000	3 years
2: < 100,000	2 years
Austria (§ 165, 1 and 4 Strafgesetzbuch)	
a: > € 50,000 or participation in criminal organisation	10 years
b: otherwise	3 years
Belgium (art 506 Strafwetboek)	5 years
Canada (Criminal Code Canada 462.31 (1)(2), a and b)	
a: on summary conviction	6 months
b: on conviction on indictment	10 years
France (Code Pénal 324-1 and 324 1-1)	
a: simple	5 years
b: aggravated: professional and criminal organisation	10 years
Germany	
a: in general	3 months – 5 years
b: aggravated circumstances: professional and OC	10 years
Netherlands (420 bis and ter, Wetboek van Strafrecht)	
a: negligence ("should have known")	1 year
b: simple	4 years
c: "habitual"/regularly	6 years
Switzerland (Schweizerisches Strafgesetzbuch: 305 bis)	
a: simple	3 years (305 bis-1)
b: aggravated (participation CO; gang or professional)	5 years (305 bis-2)
UK (Proceeds of Crime Act; 334)	
a: summary conviction	6 months
b: conviction on indictment	14 years
USA (Money Laundering Control Act § 1956 (a))	
Any kind of stipulated offence	20 years

Source: the authors.

available to government law enforcement agencies in criminal, tax and regulatory prosecutions".

It is important to highlight the first part of this statement, the objective of information gathering, which seems at odds with normal criminal law enforcement and has clearly lost any connection with proportionality. In this case the objective is apparently not to pre-empt or deter criminal activity but to hoard financial information, just in case. This is an important interpretation also picked up by Naylor (1999), who draws attention to the huge difference between using financial information on a targeted basis to enhance a prosecution, and trawling through records on the off-chance of discovering criminality. In providing itself with such power to collect the financial data of its citizens, the Money Laundering Control Act would appear to fail the test of proportionality in the absence of a more precise formulation. Pragmatically digging up a threat such as Mr Big, organised crime group, or violation of financial integrity is no substitute for specifying proportionality.

No attention is paid to the requirement of balancing at least two facets of a policy of which 'threat of liberty' could be an element to put into the scales of the balance, as does Amann (2000). He explored the threat to liberty posed by the incursion into the affairs of citizens by such an information-collecting approach (see also Alvesalo and Tombs, 2005; Naylor, 2003; Van Duyne *et al.*, 2005), in particular the extra-jurisdictional powers taken by the authorities to roll back bank 'secrecy' (Harmon, 1988; Araujo, 2010; Young, 2013; Levi, 2002). So, his discussion relates to information gathering and citizen's rights. He concludes that in a more or less unspecified way, an imbalance in the proportionality is in the end to the disadvantage of citizen's rights.

Does legal research produce more detailed discussions about AML proportionality? Our survey does not give many hits. In an older study by Freiberg and Fox (1992), the authors provide a detailed description of forfeiture and confiscation in sentencing: should confiscation be such that it surpasses the ill-gotten gains themselves, as some practitioners argue? But then proportionality with the basic sentencing may be lost, in particular when asset recovery is executed as a revenue exercise separated from the primary trial. The accumulation of punishment and expropriation could then be 'heavier' than if both would have been handled in one trial. Following this course could have shed light on aspects such as the seriousness of the money laundering threat as reflected in maximum punishments and actual prosecution and sentencing. Unfortunately, a first initiative comparing asset recovery methods with sentencing and the opinions of the convicted criminals, carried out by Vruggink (2001), had no follow-up.

It is regrettable that the subject of proportionality within anti-money laundering measures has received such scant attention. For example, in the recent handbook of Unger and Van der Linden (2013) the concept receives only five mentions, all in a theoretical economic chapter, not related to a discussion on the balancing of interests versus measures taken in the AML policy.

This lack of attention is the more surprising if we realise that in the present FATF *risk-based approach* the concept of proportionality is built-in: risk is always a fraction of damaging events divided by all events, to which can be added the size of the reported damage. However, Ross and Hannan (2007, p. 107) notice that while this risk-based approach "has always been integral to thinking about money laundering", "the concept of risk remains elusive". And so is the concept of proportionality in their elaborations: the idea of low risks requiring less effort is overgrown by what Ross and Hannan see as the justified threefold requirements of a risk approach: (1) an agreement of what risk is; (2) an agreed model of relevant risk attribution and (3) feedback of results to those who handle a risk-based decision model. All this is correct but concerns only the reporting stage 'at the frontline' of compliance. Other dimensions of proportionality and risk taking remain untouched, such as the acceptance of a proportion of 'fishes slipping through the net' due to a lower due diligence approach for less risky transaction categories (see Chapter 5.3).

The authors (Van Duyne *et al.*, 2018a) analysed the relationship between risk and proportionality in depth. They investigated how the relevant FATF reports attempted to make this relationship practical for national policy makers and obliged institutions. We noticed the structural absence of an unambiguous definition of the concept of risk in these reports, the understanding of which was rather led by intuition than by sharp concept analysis. Worse, by first suggesting three elements of risk and subsequently cutting off one element ('consequences'), the FATF all but cripples its own approach.[3] Related to this vagueness is the persistent lack of proper statistics despite the FATF emphasis on Recommendation 33, which stipulates its importance. There is clearly not much professional understanding at the FATF of the intricate connection between proportionality and statistics.[4]

This search through the literature is mainly directed at the criminal law side and policy making. This is not the only angle of approach: there is also the question of proportionality of threat versus expenses incurred by the regulated sectors and society as a whole (such as law enforcement efforts). Are these in proportion to the threat and – from the subsidiarity perspective – is the whole heavy anti-laundering 'artillery' really a commensurate answer to an identified threat?

This cost side of the equation evoked more discussion, though with little legal theorising. This is not surprising: compliance expenses have to be borne by the financial institutions and other designated economic sectors, though Reuter and Truman (2004; p. 102) make the "*rough guess that private sector institutions are able to shift up to a third of their gross financial costs to consumers*". These sectors are well aware of the proportionality question, or rather, what they perceive to be *dis*proportional; especially against the 'black hole' concerning the balance between the industry's burden and AML-results (see

---

3 FATF: *Guidance National Money Laundering and Terrorist Financing Risk Assessment,* February 2013, p. 8.

4 This is also borne out by the FATF publication on statistics, containing many platitudes and generalities and few technical clarifications in support for the badly needed database building. *FATF Guidance AML/CFT data and statistics*. Paris 2015.

discussion in Session 3.9.c): "The mutual evaluations conducted by FATF do not consider the costs actually borne by the private sector [. . .]. The mutual evaluations also do not quantify the scale of the criminal economy [. . .] or the actual overall results in disturbing or preventing criminal activity achieved".[5] This is, in a nutshell, the (dis)proportionality problem as the industry sees it: we bear the costs and do not even know whether it has any relationship to the objectives and effects in the real world. This is correct, to which should be added that the industry itself does not contribute by shedding light on this darkness as elaborated in Chapter 3.9. Cost estimate studies carried out by big consultancy firms lack a robust methodological discipline. For example, percentage increases are mentioned without baselines; subjective estimates by interviewees; no mention of the sample size, or mysterious outcomes from an 'intuitive thought experiment' in which "*in many cases the numerators and denominators would not be exactly comparable*".[6] Naturally, the industry as the main bearer of the AML expenses has a point in bringing the financial facet of the proportionality question to the fore, while pointing at the non-quantified scale of the threat and the absence of overall results. But that should have been a stimulus to produce high-quality reports compensating these deficiencies. This did not happen: the proportionality issue was submerged in complaints about mounting compliance costs of the regulated institutions and professions (Van Duyne *et al.*, 2016).[7]

The subsidiarity question is briefly touched by Goldby (2013, pp. 367–368) who wonders whether the UK law was "achieving the aims behind the legislation efficiently and effectively or whether there is evidence that these aims could be achieved better through a reconsideration of the law". An opinion anticipated by Alldridge (2002). Unfortunately, this remark did not lead to any meaningful follow-up debate on the possibility of a simpler regime to attain similar results.

Surveying this part of legal theorising on the AML-regime we must conclude that while the legal concepts of proportionality and subsidiarity should in general be considered as essential in regulatory and law enforcement thinking, we find few traces of a serious debate or detailed studies to apply these concepts in a disciplined way to the field of money laundering.

---

5 The Law Society at the UK House of Lords hearing in 2008, published 2009.

6 *Study on the Cost of Compliance with Selected FSAP Measures. Final report by Europe Economics.* London, 5 January 2009.

7 M. Yeandle, M. Mainelli, A. Berendt and B. Heal *Anti Laundering Requirements: costs, benefits and perception.* City Research Series (no. 6); *New Zealand: Assessment of business compliance costs of the indicative anti-money laundering regulatory requirements.* Ministry of Justice, July 2008; *Global Anti-Money Laundering Survey.* KPMG, 2014.

6.4 Scope and *lex certis*

From a legal research perspective a major theme in anti-money laundering policy that is also connected to proportionality, is the scope or reach of the penalty clause. What did our literature sweep produce? In the first place the easy result: the extension of criminalisation beyond the Vienna Convention's set of drug offences. This shift was soon recognised by Reuter and Truman (2004) and Levi (1997, 2002) and has less to do with legal theory than with the drug issue (and later organised crime) providing a crowbar for further extension of the law. In the late 1980s one opened more legislative doors with the 'drug annex organised crime' crowbar than with fraud and economic crime, let alone tax offences. But what happened once doors were opened?

Unger *et al.* (2006) and Busuioc (2007) made a survey of the ways in which the circle of criminalisation was drawn within national legislation together with its legal consequences. Referring to Ping (2004), Unger *et al.* (2006, p. 25) made the following differentiation:

1. all acquisitive crimes (The Netherlands, the UK[8]), or those that might be tried in a higher court (*e.g.* Australia, Finland, Italy);
2. crimes with a specified minimum period of imprisonment *e.g.* Austria; (greater than three years), New Zealand (greater than five years), Switzerland (greater than one year);
3. a list of predicate offences, *e.g.* Canada (45 crimes), Greece (20 crimes), USA (130+ crimes).

The approach of treating those being tried in a higher court as predicate offences, filters out insignificant cases: it is a kind of built-in proportionality. The second category above achieves the same.

The authors Unger, Rawlings and Busuioc do not criticise the free choice of countries to coin their own legal definition of laundering and the connected scope of crimes falling under the applicable penal clause. Instead they point at the connected international uncertainty caused by the requirement of dual criminality. Except in the regime of 'all crimes', criminal money management may be punishable in a country where these acts are predicate offences, while the acts are committed in a country where that is not the case. For

---

[8] In the UK, in addition to filing a SAR, a regulated entity would need to obtain consent from the FIU before proceeding with any transaction which was suspected of involving criminal property. However, there is currently a £250 threshold under which deposit-taking bodies are allowed to continue to operate accounts without the need to seek consent in each case. This does not apply to the duty to make a disclosure in respect of the initial opening of an account or, as the case may be, at the time when the deposit taking body first suspects that the property is criminal property. See: https://www.cps.gov.uk/legal-guidance/proceeds-crime-act-2002-part-7-money-laundering-offences. Accessed 5 August 2018.

example, bull fighting is prohibited in the UK but not in Spain. How would investment of the profits from bull fighting in Spain be categorised if invested in real estate in London? Or the act of laundering the profits from secret London bull fighting in Spain? This 'Spanish bull fighting' provides a metaphor for differences in criminalisation of profit making conduct. It is the issue of a lack of dual criminality: being a crime in one country but not in a neighbouring country, where the profits are deposited, invested or wired elsewhere. Other examples are: the liberalisation of cannabis growing; toxic waste trade; illegal cartel building *etc*. As discussed in Chapter 4.4., Recommendation 37, concerns the mutual legal aid problem, which the FATF sought to solve by stipulating that: "Countries should render mutual legal assistance, notwithstanding the absence of dual criminality, if the assistance does not involve coercive actions."

Will this impediment be resolved by adopting the Dutch 'all crime' approach? That overlooks the fact that 'all crime' concerns only the domestic national criminal code. As long as bull fighting is not criminalised in Spain or abortion in the Netherlands or Germany the all crime approach is only convenient internally. According to Busuioc, neither is this dilemma solved by the formulation of the Council of Europe Convention 2005, art. 9(7), which states that "Each Party shall ensure that predicate offences for money laundering extend to conduct that occurred in another State, and which would have constituted a predicate offence had it occurred domestically". However, this is not mandatory and it is not to be expected that a legal abortion clinic in Germany or the Netherlands will be subjected to money laundering investigations if requested by Poland.

The scope of the money laundering regime is extended enormously by the inclusion of self-laundering. This extension is further broadened if connected to the element of 'possession'. Van Duyne *et al.* (2005) and Gelemerova (2011) analysed this concept in-depth, concluding that with crimes for profit it is difficult to escape a charge for laundering: committing the crime must result in illegal possession, which is a form of laundering. It is apparently easier to escape from Alcatraz than from laundering. In this book we have discussed on several occasions the criminalisation of self-laundering (and especially in section 4.4.1.). It should not be overlooked that this criminalisation is highly criticised by European scholars for reasons of double jeopardy (Stessens, 2000 being cited by both Levi, 2002 and Unger *et al.*, 2006 in this regard). Nevertheless, *not* criminalising self-laundering is considered by the FATF to be a regrettable exception. In almost every Annual Report the FATF has stressed the importance of criminalising this form of laundering, though it became evident in many Mutual Evaluations that prosecuting self-laundering is an easy way of increasing the numbers.

These are the practical aspects of the issue of self-laundering. Apart from by the authors mentioned above, self-laundering was taken for granted and a proper theoretical discussion has not emerged from our interrogation of the literature comprising 364 titles. Nevertheless, such a discussion would be valuable because of the requirement of *lex certis*. This also hinges on the attempt to commit a predicate crime: if the attempt of a predicate offence is punishable, why not the inherently connected but not realised follow-up conduct of CAM? We do not intend to engage in a legal discussion here, but observe that a theory regarding this point did not emerge from our literature database. Maybe the proposal for a directive of the European Parliament and Commission on ML (21 December 2016) may encourage such a discussion. The Commission proposes to limit the criminalisation of self-laundering to "conversion or transfer and concealment or disguise" and does not include possession or use (p. 4).[9] So it basically says: enjoy your stolen Vermeer painting silently but otherwise, don't conceal it. The same applies to your stolen bike: you can cycle on it, as long as you do not repaint it for the purpose of concealing. Possessing and using money requires a moment of reflection: having crime money merely in possession and paying your daily bills would not be laundering, as long as there is no follow-up CAM to conceal and disguise the possession.

There are still various legal aspects to this issue that remain undiscussed. An interesting one is the principle of non-self incrimination. Is it admissible that the self-launderer lies about the nature, location or origin of his illegally obtained asset, in order not to incriminate himself? But, is lying in that case laundering (concealing, hiding)? In that case every thief who lies would also be a launderer. To avoid that he must remain completely silent, unless that is also qualified as concealing. Then there is no escape from laundering. Thus far we have not found such questions properly debated in the literature.

Concerning the extension of the scope of the AML-regime it is also interesting to note the tax objective. The clear intent is that eventually laundering will apply equally to the managing of ill-gotten funds, as well as to *legally acquired* funds, by concealing them from the tax authorities. (Yaniv, 1999; Rider, 1996).[10] This is an important point which deserves a separate investigation. Does this imply that tax evasion is a predicate offence if the hidden funds are legally obtained? There are reasons for qualifying tax evasion as a predicate offence: though the income may be legal, hiding it all or part of it is a criminal offence if committed with intent. The laundered proceeds are the portion not paid as income or corporate tax (*i.e.* an illegal saving) and are further hidden or concealed from the tax administration by

[9] The newly proposed directive appears to be an acknowledgement that having all these types of conduct under one denominator blurs the picture.

[10] See further discussion in Chapter 9 also about the 'intent' of the legislation from cross-discipline objective.

means of a fraudulent tax form and, thereby, constitute laundering (Alldridge, 2002). In that case the forged tax form is the instrument used to defraud as well as to disguise the illegally acquired financial advantage, as earlier described by Van Duyne *et al.* (2005) as "canned laundering". The focus on tax evasion as a predicate offence is of older date but re-emerged in 2010 when the FATF proposed to lift 'the distinction between tax fraud and tax evasion' (Unger, 2013, p. 660). Levi (2002, p. 182) also touched on the difficult and disputed area of tax evasion. He indicated that most countries "began by criminalizing the laundering of the proceeds of drug trafficking before . . . broadening the scope to include all or most serious crimes (tax evasion being the key area of dispute)." While in the Netherlands and in the UK, tax evasion (with the component of criminal intent) is a criminal predicate offence, in many parts of Europe it remains a sensitive subject. The Directive 2005/60/EC of the European Parliament and of the Council did not solve the problem of tax evasion as this is still strongly considered as a subject under national sovereignty (Unger, 2013; p. 661).

This prevarication of a diversity of measures "inevitably gives rise to suspicion that behind the facade of combating organised crime and terrorism the reality is a target of minimising illegal tax evasion" (Haynes, 2008, p. 304). That suspicion is justified in view of FATF's revised recommendations in 2012 (formally expanding the scope of predicate offences to include tax crimes) and the EU 2015 amendment to the Directive on money laundering, section 11: "It is important expressly to highlight that 'tax crimes' relating to direct and indirect taxes are included in the broad definition of 'criminal activity' in this Directive, in line with the revised FATF Recommendations." The introduction of tax crimes passed below the radar into the field of laundering: with only one mention in the long list of "designated categories of offences" and no explanation of this change in the interpretive notes.

6.5 Imposing sanctions on countries

In section 6.3. on proportionality we reviewed what emerged from the legal literature about sanctioning in terms of sentencing. But as we have seen in Chapter 5, there is more sanctioning than sentencing culprits: states can be sanctioned because of a lack of compliance. If such states persist in non-compliance, the FATF will publish this fact (collectively in the public statements discussed earlier in the book) and can call upon its members to take countermeasures. These are in fact financial sanctions which impede smooth and fast business with the states placed on the 'black list', as was done in 2000. Countries are given explicit permission by the FATF to impose such financial sanctions through Recommendation 19 (previously R21) *High Risk Countries.*[11] This Recommendation states that countries should be able to apply appropriate countermeasures when called upon to do so by the FATF. As discussed previously, thus far there has been no meaningful formal discussion about the right of the FATF to impose sanctions on non-cooperative countries and the consequences of such sanctions.

Stessens (2001) compared the heavy-handed way in which the FATF treated these countries with the way the OECD addressed the same countries because of 'harmful tax practices'. He also pointed at the finding that all blacklisted countries were not members of the FATF, while the compliance of some of the FATF members was equally not beyond criticism (see also Gelemerova, 2011). This could have been a good occasion on which to theorise about the basis of sanctioning sovereign jurisdictions by an informal body, and the substantive and procedural safeguards which may be appropriate in cases of 'punishment'. Among the few scholars who have undertaken a more in-depth research into this question we particularly note the work of both Comstock and Gallant, below, that emerged from the legal studies research.

Concerning the legitimacy of punishing non-cooperative countries, Comstock (1994) took a slightly unusual line and looked for a constitutional basis for the sanctions approach to enforcing country compliance. He argues that implementation of trade sanctions on non-cooperative countries would be legally consistent with GATT and GATS and would prevent laundering (presumably he supports the global application rule).[12] This approach would force equal sharing of the cost of AML-enforcement, although he does not elaborate how this would be achieved. Comstock argued (*ibid*, p. 166) that the tariff could be shaped as denial of access to the markets of compliant countries which is almost exactly the approach adopted in 2000 by the FATF through an invocation of its NCCTs. It is uncertain whether this comparison with the trade treaties is valid.

Gallant (2010, pp. 180–182)[13] is critical of the United Nations Security Council arguing that the UN, via resolution 1373 on terrorist financing, stepped into assuming "the role of legislator of global laws", something that hitherto it had not undertaken. As such, she argued that it effectively compromised its own credibility and accepted a role on the international stage in that it "jeopardizes the legitimacy of its function as international arbiter of

---

[11] International Standards on Combating Money Laundering and the Financing of Terrorism & Proliferation, The FATF Recommendations, February 2012, p. 12.

[12] General Agreement on Tariffs and Trade and General Agreement on Trade in Services.

[13] Gallant cites Chesterman (2008) "The United Nations Security Council and the rule of law: The Role of the Security Council in Strengthening a Rules-based International System", Final Report and Recommendations from the Austrian Initiative, 2004-2008 New York University School of Law, Public Law & Legal Theory Research Paper Series Working Paper No. 08-57, available at: http://ssrn.com/abstract=1279849.

international peace and security". This is certainly something worthy of further consideration. Tracing the development from UN resolutions through to the FATF, Gallant helpfully informs the reader (p. 176) that the main basis for the international approach to AML "consist of four international conventions, 49 recommendations issued by the FATF and UNSC resolution 1373".[14] What is important is that she identifies an essential difference in procedure: "The UN conventions emerged from international negotiation and thus contain the minimum standard that all signatories could agree upon". In contrast Gallant observes that the FATF represents the collective specialist knowledge that provides detailed interpretation of the conventions. In addition, it issues Recommendations of global mandatory application, that are simply imposed but without negotiation. This entails a fundamental lack of legitimacy, which however, is disguised: "the recommendations assume, to a degree, the de facto status of international law. Although the FATF has no precise international legal authority over individual states, states tend to respond to its edicts" (p. 180). Does this response imply that such edicts are legitimised and with them, the FATF? Politically these questions seem to be suppressed. According to Wechsler (2001), the inspirers of the AML-policy (USA) wanted to move on without debate in the UN where "under-regulated financial regimes would outvote those with a commitment to strong international standards" (p. 49).

Though sanctions are essential as a final piece – the stick if the carrot does not produce the required compliance – they have not attracted the legal research attention one would expect, despite the fact that a number of authors argue that there is no evidence to show that the regime "actually works" (Sharman, 2008, p. 636; see also Chong and López-de-Silanes, 2007, p. 4). Fundamental aspects such as identification of the competent authority or of fair procedures have not emerged from the legal studies research database. This could mean that the FATF had little to build on. On the other hand, it did not show much interest in its own legal foundation in 1989, nor since that date. It is interesting to reflect on the fact that the FATF drafted the first set of Recommendations in 1990 within an extremely tight period of six months with no academic input or consultation (Pieth, 1999). Scholars agree that the FATF was only ever intended for a temporary existence with its initial power base provided by the USA, UK, Australia and France (Levi and Gilmore, 2002; Levi and Reuter, 2006, Pieth, 2002). It quickly succeeded in convincing a sufficient number of other countries of the drug-based threat as a justification for the adoption of a global framework. As Lewisch (2008) points

[14] The 2001 resolution in response to terrorism Resolution 1373, requires that states take a number of actions regarding terrorist finance: prevent and suppress the financing of terrorist acts; and criminalize acts associated with the financial aspect of terrorism. Available at: http://www.un.org/en/sc/ctc/specialmeetings/2012/docs/United%20Nations%20Security%20Council%20Resolution%201373%20(2001).pdf. Accessed 27 November 2014.

out, the heavy political clout that these countries had as 'beneficiary nations' meant that the others had little alternative but to fall into line. Success breeds success and the FATF carried on.

As far as money laundering sentencing statistics are concerned, our literature search yielded no targeted comprehensive studies, though this may be due to the fact that sentencing statistics are in many countries maintained in a step-motherly way. It is also the case that the prosecution of laundering is often only one facet of the whole prosecution which in the final indictment will be listed as the third or lower count, as a kind of safety net if sentencing of the predicate fails (in those countries where a standalone prosecution for laundering is possible). Dependent on the data collection of the national statistical offices, these lower charges are simply not separately recorded. Despite this knowledge gap, the sentencing of money laundering has not gone unnoticed by the FATF: in fact, it has commented frequently on the sentencing practices of the member states, making critical comments when it thinks too lenient sentences have been handed out by the courts. It is noteworthy that legal scholars have paid little attention to an unofficial organisation putting pressure on countries to increase sentence severity to be imposed by an *independent judiciary*. See for example the most recent Mutual Evaluations of Spain and Norway. The relation between the arrogation of semi-imperial powers and the sovereignty of nations needs clearly to be addressed. We will return to this issue in Chapter 10.

6.6 Recovery of assets and restorative justice

Historically, attention has always been devoted to the many facets of CAM, bundled together under the legal construct of money laundering. But how important is the knowledge of CAM if we do not recover the illegal profits? We can make this point even stronger by stating that for any laundering policy there are only two important success measurement points in the whole path from predicate crime to the eventual criminal possession of proceeds: *prevention* and *recovery*. All the AML-steps and Recommendations can be considered as serving prevention and asset recovery: if nothing is prevented and no assets are taken from criminals one might just as well have done nothing. However, there is a knowledge problem with prevention: we can only measure it if we have a baseline against which deviations can be attributed to prevention activities. Unfortunately, we do not have such a baseline in the field of laundering which makes discussions about prevention useless, unless in some anecdotal, qualitative sense – of which the meaning remains indeterminate. This means that by default we will only survey how legal science has dealt with this 'final piece' of the laundering phenomenon: asset recovery.

What is to be theorised about asset recovery? There is little theoretical research about taking back what a perpetrator has acquired by crime. 'Crime doesn't pay' remains an old but valid adage, which is rather a pious wish: crime shouldn't pay, but frequently it does. But there may also be additional objectives to removing the wealth from criminals: part of it may be used to finance further crime and confiscation may disrupt the criminal economy. And otherwise, preventing criminals from showing off their illegal wealth may reduce its recruiting effect on the surrounding neighbourhood. So yes, taking away ill-gotten wealth may also have a preventive value despite measurement defects.

Another aspect of asset recovery is its 'neutralising' effect on laundering. What does this mean? It implies that a recovery sentencing policy makes all laundering irrelevant in view of the obligation to pay back the illegal gains. In whatever way the proceeds have been laundered and become 'white as snow', the recovery order must be fulfilled from all present and future assets, income or loans, laundered or not (Ulph, 2010; Van Duyne *et al.*, 2014). This redemption is an element in the *restoration of justice* and not a punishment, though criminals may feel differently. Given these points, what emerges from the legal science?

Legal researchers have looked at another facet of asset recovery. The origins of confiscation law within the UK are well covered by Alldridge, 2003 (pp. 71 – 88) and Rider (1999) whilst a review of the approach across commonwealth countries is set out in McClean (1989). In search of an underpinning logic, we find that the roots of forfeiture were established under medieval English law, through the concept of the *deodand* (an object forfeited or gifted to God) whereby an inanimate object that caused accidental death was the guilty party (Gordon, 1995; Blum *et al.*, 1999). The second type arose from treason or felony and related to the forfeiture of an estate. However, McClean (1989) points out that the original rules of forfeiture did not easily transfer into this situation in which assets other than property play a role and the largest claimant has become the state. In consequence, the types of activity that could be subject to forfeiture expanded to embrace "virtually any type of property that might be used in the conduct of a criminal enterprise." (Gordon, 1995, p. 747).

Taking the proceeds from criminals was not only seen as 'doing justice', but also as law enforcement revenue. Nadelmann (1986, p. 34) acknowledged that "confiscating the proceeds of criminal activities is a good way to make law enforcement pay for itself". In the UK, the Proceeds of Crime Act (POCA, 2002), added significant new powers, but academics quickly moved to question the motives for its introduction. Levi (2002, p. 189, citing Blumenson and Nilsen, 1998) noted euphemistically "some evidence of goal displacement as enforcement agencies target forfeitable assets rather than serious offenders".

In the USA, which pioneered asset recovery, complaints soon arose that the new policy degenerated into 'legal street robberies', as one sheriff regretfully admitted (Blumenson and Nilsen, 1998, footnote 176). This outcome is not surprising given the attitude which filtered top-down: already in 1990, the Attorney General warned the local attorneys against a "failure to achieve the $ 470 million projection [as this would] expose [us] to criticism and undermine confidence in our budget projections" (Van Duyne and Levi, 2005, p. 16; Blumenson and Nilsen, 1998, note 102; Rasmussen and Benson, 1994). Is this criminal justice or criminal taxation?

One early justification for the application of forfeiture was its usefulness in connection with the enforcement of drug laws. In 1978, the scope was broadened to include property used to facilitate the drug trade, thereby encompassing anything indirectly associated with drug activity: for example, means of transport, safe houses and of course money. This is called the 'facilitation theory'. This description opened an interpretational mine field, as all the mentioned acts of money management, such as hiding or disguising, are activities that can only be attributed to a person and not a financial asset. Bank accounts are bank accounts and should not be personalised.

Fear of 'co-mingling' is evident on the part of policy makers as Young (2013, p. 200) citing Rider (1992) argued: when criminal funds are co-mingled with legitimate ones within the financial system they "have adopted a cloak of legitimacy" such that they become 're-usable' (Buchanan, 2004, p. 117). And regarding this outcome, Rider was of the opinion that "it is almost impossible for evidence to be obtained which would allows a court to establish the derivation of the money" (Rider, 1992, no page for quote). This theory finds no counterpart in the world of financial criminal investigation. In investigative practice the cloak of legitimacy is not formed by simple co-mingling but by constructions, which are formed by a network of legal persons, strew men, forged documents of legal and invoices and disrupted paper-trails.

It is also no longer required by UK law that asset recovery is handled within a criminal law setting, as the UK POCA 2002 can also be applied within civil courts, where the standards of proof are less exacting upon prosecutors, with the burden of proof shifted to the property owner to demonstrate their innocence. This is also observed by King (2013, pp. 267–291). It is one more step, theoretical as well as practical, to arrive in the field of 'unaccountable wealth' and non-conviction based confiscation, a concept which is applied in Eastern Europe to determine the integrity of public office holders (Nicolae, 2013, pp. 293–323). These civil actions can also be an element in restorative justice. However, while there is extensive literature on restorative justice, our search of the literature on criminal profits did not identify substantial research on this aspect.

An area that has not been well explored within the literature is the area of Unexplained Wealth Orders. Already in operation in both Ireland and Australia, they have recently been introduced in the UK through the 2017 Criminal Finances Act. These orders allow the authorities to seize suspected criminal property without the need of a prosecution, transferring the burden of proof concerning the pretended licit source of wealth onto the shoulders of the defendant – the 'reverse burden of proof' (Keen, 2017,vii). They apply specifically to PEPs and to those associated with serious crime. The approach appears to be successful in Ireland (see also King, 2013), though it has only been moderately successful in Australia (Reurts, 2017).

6.7 Conclusion

We introduced this chapter by setting out the legal principles that we might have expected to form the basis of discussions within legal academic literature on the subject of AML. We took stock of a reasonable variety and intensity. Not every subject is as intensively debated, and sometimes the academic literature appears to be scarce.

Interest and harm to the financial system was posed and dealt with in the literature from the beginning of the ALM regime. Most mainstream authors confirm the statement of harm that money laundering causes to the financial system. In contrast to this mainstream confirmation there are a few authors who tried to find corresponding historical evidence. They reported negative outcomes: threat statements were not confirmed. Nevertheless, this had no effect. We observed reproduction of arguments, disregarding these negative findings, and a drift of 'harm' from threat to 'legitimate capital' or to (transnational) organised crime.

The principles of *proportionality* and *subsidiarity* are broadly accepted as legal principles. These principles were addressed but were not comprehensively and systematically covered. To the extent that the AML-regime contains information or intelligence gathering tools, concerns are expressed regarding the protection of the citizens against an intrusive government. The questions about the proportionality of the present system as such or about clearly relevant issues such as the proportionality of punishments, were scarcely raised and struck hardly any chords with other authors.

The principle of legal certainty or *lex certis*, received moderate attention. It was noted that in the initial stages the drug and organised crime scare was used as a 'crowbar' for obtaining international consent to establish the AML-regime. It was also noted that differences in the criminalisation of predicate offences between countries leads to uncertainty: how is cross-border management of monies between two countries where certain acts are criminalised in one, but not in the other?

Another uncertainty discussed concerns the issue of self-laundering, which has which can cover the mere possession to the attempt to commit a crime for profit. A new uncertainty emerging is the management of the profits from tax crime from legal sources of income.

Sanctioning non-compliance is another subject that is connected to maintenance of regulations. Connected to sanctioning is also the principle of proportionality, which the legal literature appears to neglect. Apart from this overlap, a few articles from the legal literature highlighted the sanctioning of non-compliant or non-cooperative countries. A point of concern is the legitimacy of sanctioning by the FATF, which is not resolved. The sanctioning of individual perpetrators received less attention, which is remarkable: after all, the AML-regime should either prevent or punish wrongdoers. However, proper statistics of this aspect prove to be scarce.

Finally, if there is evidence of ill-gotten profits, justice must be restored by recovery of the obtained assets. The principle of *restoration of justice* did not emerge in any meaningful way in combination with criminal asset recovery. This is noteworthy because it is the conceptual connection to the principle of harm, against which the legal system lends protection. More attention was paid to the question of making justice "pay for itself". Some authors point at the corruptive potential of police greed if forfeited assets are used to complement the (local) police budget. Others point at the broad extension of these powers if any object that could be used in the commission of crime were to be forfeitable. Via civil forfeiture the chapter ends with the concept of unaccountable wealth: "wealth you cannot justify must be criminal". This discussion must still unfold.

7

Economists' consensus: models and estimates

7.1 Introduction: the concerns of economists

The interest of economists in crime is not a coincidence or a diversion from the attention of their strict discipline. Apart from personal harm, most crimes concern financial loss and damage or criminal revenue: all of these are economic variables. This interest is traced back by various academics to Becker's seminal 1968 work "Crime and punishment: an economic approach" (see for example, Brennan and Eusepi, 2008; McCarthey *et al.,* 2015; and Arnone and Borlini, 2010). However, the relationship between crime and money and, more generally, the positioning of criminal activity as a natural facet of capitalist society, goes back further in the literature which was mainly focussed on white collar and corporate crime (see for example Bequai, 1979; Braithwaite, 1988). For example, Naylor (2003, p. 82) describes "the inherent economic logic of profit driven offences". Naylor further drew attention to the lack of precision of the definition of 'economic crime'. He noted that the terms economic, profit driven, white collar or financial crime, were freely interchanged though their meanings are different. They cover some different and some overlapping fields of criminal conduct.

As the western economy is underpinned by the profit motive, entrepreneurs devoting themselves to productive or innovative undertakings make a contribution to economic growth, even if it concerns the underground economy. This comes to the surface when facets of the criminal economy become decriminalised: for example, cannabis use (Uruguay) or adult pornography. Apart from this, there are also ". . . largely unproductive activities such as rent

P.C. van Duyne, J.H. Harvey and L.Y. Gelemerova, *The Critical Handbook of Money Laundering*, https://doi.org/10.1057/978-1-137-52398-3_7

seeking[1] or organized crime" (Baumol, 1990, p. 893). Others more clearly positioned crime as a negative facet of the "entrepreneurial spirit" (McCarthy *et al.,* 2015, p. 2; Gnutzmann *et al.*, 2010, p. 245). Within these interpretations, a criminal enterprise is largely seen as taking from, rather than contributing to, economic activity. This dimension is explored further in some of the early literature on the subject of money laundering, which attempted to set out the justification for legislative intervention (see for example Quirk, 1996).

The lack of precision of the concept of economic crime is something that we also found within the field of money laundering. As we discussed in the previous chapter, the legal concept of money laundering (as a criminalised conduct) emerged during the 1980s (Walter, 1989). Other authors (see for example, Bosworth-Davies, 2008; and Buchanan, 2004) position the international anti-laundering as having emerged in the early 1970s with the introduction of the US Bank Secrecy Act of 1970. As we elaborated in Chapter 3, after the adoption of the Money Laundering Control Act of 1986, the broadening of the discussion of money laundering and its launch into public consciousness followed the 'estimate' of the global volume of laundered funds from the IMF and the establishment of FATF in 1989 (Van Duyne *et al.,* 2016, p. 164). It would be reasonable to expect that authors of economic studies publishing within the field would concern themselves with testing the accuracy of these figures to better inform public policy. However, this is not the case (with a few exceptions, for example, Van Duyne, 1994 and Reuter and Greenfield, 2001). Instead, authors within this area of literature constructed theoretical models that fitted the assumption of international policy making (see Keh, 1996). Rather than deducting hypotheses and testing them against facts as an external criterion or inductively constructing alternative explanations as new hypotheses, they based their work on official sources of questionable reliability and validity. As we will show, a great deal of the literature we uncovered was merely explanatory or confirmatory of the AML policy.

Economists have applied both macro and micro approaches to money laundering and in this chapter we discuss those studies intended to measure the size and scale of laundering, as well as papers that model the overall level of laundering activity. The economists' models, can provide a powerful means to prove or disprove the scale of a threat. Schneider (2010) reviewed the literature that, amongst others, included the work of Reuter. The latter argued that it was impossible to produce estimates with any degree of credibility. Walker (1995) thought differently and stated that his input-output model avoided double counting and thus would be superior. Unger *et al.*, (2006)

[1] Those who hold power are able to transform their culturally held system of values, beliefs and norms into a prescriptive system of law which, by definition will also protect their interests (referred to as 'rent seeking' within economic theory a term attributed to Krueger, 1974).

provided something they thought of as the theoretical underpinning for the Walker model. In addition, Schneider discussed the critical work from non-economists such as Van Duyne. Importantly, Schneider (2010, p. 476) observed that ". . . if the phenomenon is ambiguously defined, one cannot determine the volume or extent of its financial threat" whilst also noting that despite such a major shortcoming, the threatening nature of money laundering remains very much part of perceptions within the political landscape. Reuter and Greenfield (2001) set about showing precisely why the figures were not accurate, arriving at far more conservative figures for drug related laundering before concluding that the attempt to hone these data with any degree of accuracy is simply not possible. Others (see for example, Barone and Masciandaro, 2011; Blickman, 2009) are similarly sceptical with regards not only to the IMF data but also to those of Walker. They share the views of Schneider and Windischbauer (2008, p. 117) that "these kinds of results are scientifically doubtful, since they are not reproducible, and unproven". They were joined by Unger *et al.* (2006, p. 102) starkly observing "Most literature on money laundering effects is pure speculation." But despite these critical remarks, their impact on policy making, as cast in the 'IMF-consensus', is negligible: no notable debate evolved.

Therefore, we wonder to what extent economists or authors of economic studies shed light on the shadowy subject of money laundering by providing data with such a validity that they would withstand academic scrutiny. By this we mean that the authors disclose any underlying assumptions in their models and formula so that their findings could be tested and reproduced. In contrast, we found papers repeating the 'truisms' that laundering is 'harmful' to the economy (see for example, Arnone and Borlini, 2010; McCarthy *et al.*, 2015 and Unger, 2007). Other authors recycle 'facts' from other writers or policy papers without verification, or meekly recite the content from official publications. As noted by Soudijn (2014, p. 233), "Because the FATF is an authoritative intergovernmental institution . . . the terminology and examples from the[ir] . . . reports have been adopted by many government bodies and researchers".

Those authors more interested in micro–economic matters tended to focus on regulations considering costs and benefits to the regulated sectors with a particular focus on compliance. These economists contributed to the knowledge of what countermeasures 'should' work theoretically. There is an immediate problem here, however, as while pleasingly plausible on paper, these theories have not yet been tested in the real world.

Walker and Unger (2009, p. 823) are concerned with the measurement of one particular dimension of money laundering, namely "The economics of money laundering . . . aims to explore the scale and impact of illicit funds". We will discuss the sincerity of this statement shortly. But we also discovered a richer landscape of economic literature that included conceptual contributions to economic theory; empirical papers in relation to the volume of crime money; and finally studies that focus on the impact of crime-money on the licit economy.

From the outputs that we reviewed during our research for this book, the largest amount of literature falling within the field of money laundering has been contributed from the discipline of economics. On occasion it is difficult to draw strict lines of demarcation around what falls within the scope of economics and what falls into the more general social sciences, particularly when we cross over into the area of regulation and compliance. We already covered much of the early policy development regarding money laundering in Chapter 3. Now we will present what economists conveyed about money laundering and to evaluate it against the yardsticks of reliability and validity. This entails exploring the rationale for AML policy and the various explanations for the presumed harm caused by the flow of dirty money.

In the opening line of his book on the subject of money laundering law, Alldridge (2003, p. 1)[2] notes the underlying rationale for the AML framework as being based on the premise that "Clean money is worth more than dirty money". Inherent within this statement is the assumption that money identified as the proceeds of crime has less utility to the holder of those funds than the equivalent amount of clean money. As dirty money is laundered so that it may be useable, it follows that the purpose of AML is to prevent this cleaning from taking place. In other words, this framework inhibits the transfer between these two states of dirty and clean. The assumption made by the policy is that the transfer is facilitated by the payments mechanism, a facility made available to the real economy by banks.

Following the search mechanism and lines of enquiry set out in Chapter 2, we located and read a wide number of papers that fall within the field of money laundering from an economic perspective. A large proportion of the literature within this discipline deals with methods of measuring and modelling money-laundering, including ways of measuring AML effectiveness. This work is supported by papers that justify the approach followed by the policy makers. The attentive reader will notice that we revisit issues here that we have already discussed. Consistent with our own methodology, we aim to objectively analyse these important issues.[3]

---

[2] Alldridge also used the same opening line in his paper on the moral limits of money laundering (2002, p. 279).

[3] As noted in Chapter 2, the literature search was concluded in the summer of 2015. This does not mean that we have stopped reading. We have also included here more recent papers that contribute to the chapter. In addition, there are some earlier reports and books that we have found subsequently that although not part of our search were considered important to include.

7.2 Contribution from the conceptual studies

One of the questions most frequently asked by students is "what is the theory of money laundering?" It appears students are not alone in this regard as Unger (2007, p. 32) notes, "a comprehensive economic theory regarding money laundering is still missing", arguing for the inclusion of behavioural interpretations. There was little evidence from others of the existence of a theory. Much of the deductive literature that we located used different 'theories', all of which were borrowed from elsewhere, in order to explain money laundering activity. We think the most apposite answer to this question would be the one-liner already quoted above from Alldridge: "Clean money is worth more than dirty money".

In the absence of a theory directed at the conduct of laundering one has to satisfy oneself with an empirical description of behavioural categories. For example, the interaction with the perfectly legal financial or commercial instruments: launderers may 'invest' in stocks and shares, open savings accounts or purchase valuable art objects. While the launderer may be a criminal none of these activities are of themselves criminal acts, only becoming so by connection to another crime. That implies that they too become risky in the context of predicate offence and money laundering.

The first requirement for successful offending is a rational reduction of risk inherent in undertaking a crime. This provides an area of commonality between legal scholars and economists: the assumption of rationality (see for example, McCarthey *et al.*, 2015; Arnone and Borlini, 2010). The assumed rationality by the criminal is important because under deterrence theory, punishments such as a prison sentence can be set at the level that would deter crime. A further dimension of rationality is that criminals make decisions consistent with the traditional utility theory.[4] This theory assumes that individuals are motivated by self-interest and rationally seek to maximise their personal utility, or what they perceive as such. From this perspective, as crime is driven by the individual motive of personal profit, an effective deterrent to such conduct must impact on this motivation. Therefore, the focus on counter measures should be constructed around manipulating the formula for criminal profit (Gnutzmann *et al.*, 2010, p. 245). This formula operates along two dimensions: the probability of being caught; and the severity of the sanctions imposed if apprehended. In our field of profit-motivated crime this includes taking away the criminal assets: "Crime should not pay" which is strictly not a punishment but a restoration of justice (see Chapter 10). This

[4] Utility underpins classical economic theory, within this framework, *ceteris paribus*, costs are only incurred where they result in an absolute increase in utility which holds under two conditions: marginal utility> marginal cost; resources are distributed in such a way that no additional benefit can be derived by their redistribution. Production is thus regulated through the price mechanism (Dobb M. (1924) 'The Entrepreneur Myth' Economica, No. 10, pp. 66–81).

balancing of the risk of being caught and the threat of sanction severity has a long history in criminological prevention theory. Students of criminology will be familiar with rational choice theory (Clarke and Cornish, 1985; Cornish and Clarke, 1987). Although rational choice was developed to provide a theoretical framework for thinking about situational crime prevention, its objective was to look at the offender's perceptions of risks, effort and accrued rewards.

There is little risk theory concerning money laundering, except Reuter and Truman's (2004) observation that the chances of getting caught are low. This has later been confirmed by UNODC (2011). Moreover, the required skills for managing the crime-money may be quite modest: crime money can be mixed with the expenses of daily life, hoarded or recycled in an informal cash-based market (Van Duyne, 2003; Harvey, 2004): the perpetrator slips almost imperceptibly, or without being aware, into criminal money management. In contrast to the image of a professionally driven criminal money service market, this more earthly state of affairs does not seem to stimulate much risk-based theorising. In the absence of 'theory' there are various schools of thought that attempt to explain money laundering suggesting circumstances in which it would thrive or be impaired. It is this area to which our attention turns, once we have considered how the topic of defining money laundering is dealt with within the economics literature.

7.2.1 Definition

In Chapter 4 we elaborated the requirements of a definition, scientific or otherwise. Here we do not deviate from this stand: economic studies or research projects on money laundering should not start from a different origin than any other scientific endeavour. Hence, the requirement for an unambiguous definition from the literature. Accepting that as basic, we again observe differences which suggest that this principle is little heeded. Unger *et al.* (2006) and Busuioc (2007), do not only observe differences in definitions between, but also within disciplines. As noted in both Chapters 4 and 6, most studies take their starting point from the legal definitions of either the USA 1986 Money Laundering Control Act or of the UN conventions, in particular the 1988 Vienna Convention. Of the 18 definitions Unger *et al.* (2006 ch. 1 Appendix III p. 36), included within their semantic analysis, the majority were taken from 'official' supranational bodies and organisations. They do recognise that six of the definitions reviewed were supplied by academics – they use the term 'scientists' – but note that only two of these appeared in independent academic papers. Of these one was by Van Duyne (2003, p. 69): "Money laundering is falsely claiming a legitimate source for an illegally acquired advantage"; and, the other by Cuéllar (2003, p. 324). Unger *et al.*

(2006) (Appendix 1, p. 36) compressed his definition which we present in full: "The laundering metaphor refers not to any financial transaction to crime, but specifically to the process through which money received from crime is rendered more useful by two means: converting it into a desirable medium (i.e. a bank balance or equity in a company) and erasing its more obvious links to crimes." In the sense of delineation, Cuéllar's definition is more a description than a formal definition. One can argue that the terms 'specific', 'more useful', 'desirable' and 'more obvious' render the whole formulation ambiguous. Moreover, definitions are not 'metaphors'. Accepting such 'definitions' opens the gate to ambiguous theorising. Additionally, laundering does not necessarily entail a conversion into something else. For instance, cash can stay cash as long as it is accompanied with a false invoice or a bogus contract.

Unger *et al.* (2006, p. 22, *et. seq*.) highlight the confusion surrounding the legal interpretation within differing jurisdictions and the disparities that exist in terms of measurement. This confusion can be traced back to the boundaries of what is considered laundering. This can variously include the terms 'money', 'proceeds' and 'property'. Similarly, it interchangeably refers to both the stock (accumulated assets) and the flow of money. There is a further clouding ambiguity in relation to the difficult issue of tax evasion, regarded by Unger as illegal but not criminal. Schneider and Windischbauer (2008, p. 389) distinguish between money laundering and tax evasion and capital flight drawing a line between the informal or grey economy and that which is black or criminal. Helpfully Unger *et al.* (2006, p. 24) go on to note that the most difficult part of a 'legal' definition relates to the scope of assumed predicate offences. Hiding, disposing or disguising the source of funds is clearly money laundering in the eyes of the law if those funds were criminally obtained. This indicates that money laundering is not so much a fact but a criminal law construction. This is the more so where one can be convicted of money laundering in the *absence* of a proven predicate offence, if there is unaccountable wealth and the living conditions of the defendant point at a criminal lifestyle. This looks like a criminal law construction based on an assumption.

As discussed in Chapter 4, the offence of money laundering established by the 1988 Vienna Convention only covers assets derived from drug-related crimes. These include any type of assets deemed to be proceeds of that predicate offence. This list has widened considerably over the intervening years. As we saw in Chapter 4 there are three broad definitions of predicate offences (Arnone and Borloni, 2010; Ping, 2004 cited in Unger *et al.*, 2006). Firstly 'all crimes' as in the Netherlands and the UK; or all crimes tried in a higher court, for example, Australia, Finland and Italy; secondly a 'list approach' – predetermined offences such as in Canada (45 crimes), Greece (20 crimes), USA ('130 plus' crimes); thirdly, a 'threshold approach' with crimes punished with a certain minimum penalty, as in Austria (greater than one year), New Zealand (greater than five years), Switzerland (greater than one year). When rules developed in one jurisdiction are applied on a global basis, De Kocker (2009) points out that care is needed when setting such criteria as *de minimis* limits, as $100 may, for example, not be insignificant within the economies of all countries.

An interesting alternative is proposed by Pellegrina and Masciandaro (2008, p. 14) who, in recognising that it is down to national authorities to determine the relative harm of different crimes, "wonder if it is better to have a stricter list of predicate crimes depending on their relative social costs". A number of academics have noted this problem pointing to the optimal solution of all jurisdictions operating an 'all crimes' approach to avoid its 'Spanish bullfighter' Achilles heel (Busuioc, 2007; Unger *et al.*, 2006). However, we have argued that the 'all crimes' approach does not solve the problem of differences between predicate offences: 'all crimes' concerns the national criminal code, which differs per country. Naylor (2003) draws a distinction between the different types of crime and the outcome of the proceeds of that crime. However, irrespective of the type of crime, the criminal needs to hide and then launder the proceeds so that he can benefit from them.

The diversity of predicate offences is perhaps one of the most obvious areas of conflict between those writing from the perspectives of economics and law. It appears almost obvious to the economists that the 'one size fits all' approach is rational and a way of ensuring the delivery of a global solution. Lawyers have a very different interpretation of the limits of the reach of the criminal justice system within their respective national jurisdiction. For example, writing on the policing of international financial markets, Rider (1990, pp. 179–180) commented "The English criminal law . . . confines itself within the straightjacket of the territorial principle . . . running to the edge of our territorial waters and no further". Although the unexplained wealth orders regime introduced in the UK in January 2018, however, is expected to draw attention to foreign wealth suspected to be illegal. There is very little written on this subject.

If money laundering was criminalised in order to ensure financial intelligence, then, would the 'all-crimes approach' really be helpful from this practical perspective? For instance, should all the revenues of banks from sanctions breaches, cartel arrangements and/or rate rigging, be universally tainted as proceeds and identified as financial intelligence, if the 'all crime' rule differs per country?[5] Are such banks to be treated as high risk clients by financial institutions in countries with another 'all crime' regime. There is barely any

[5] Note the regulatory sanctions for rigging LIBOR and foreign exchange settlement rates. In 2015, Barclays, Royal Bank of Scotland, JPMorgan, UBS, Citigroup and Bank of America had to pay in total approximately $10 billion in fine and settlements to US and UK authorities for FX rate-rigging. Barclays, RBS, JPMorgan and Citigroup pleaded guilty to criminal charges (Titcomb reporting for The Telegraph, 2015). In 2012, the Japanese subsidiary of UBS pleaded guilty to a

guidance on this matter; so regulated entities decide at their own discretion while hoping regulators will concur.

It is perhaps surprising that, having pointed out all of the definitional problems, Unger (2007, p. 26) elected to adopt, without analysis, Walker's 1995 definition: "Money laundering is the process by which illicit source moneys are introduced into an economy and used for legitimate purposes". It is a strange definition, because it equates all criminal *spending* with laundering except if such spending is for illegal purposes (Van Duyne *et al.*, 2016). Secondly, much of the illicit money is already within the economy (for example, proceeds from fraud or illegal tax savings). Using this definition, rather than on grounds of theoretical accuracy, Walker and Unger arrived at a somewhat politically convenient estimate of the volume of laundered funds, predictably a few notches higher than most other estimate studies (see later in this chapter). It is important to underline this point. Any alteration to the definition can result in a sizeable change in the estimated volume of laundered funds. Inevitably, the definitions that produce larger estimates are more likely to be adopted by policy makers and can influence resource allocation, as stated by Van Duyne and Van Koningsveld (2017, p. 150): "words or definitions do matter".

Of course, the scope of offences will determine the scale and amount of laundering within a jurisdiction. This is further impacted by the method of accounting and other conceptual questions. For example, is £1 moved through ten accounts still £1 or £10? Or at what point does £1 laundered last year cease to be considered 'laundered' in the following year (Van Duyne, 1994; *et al.*, 2005; Alldridge, 2003; Tanzi, 1996)? It does appear that the accounting outcomes that produce the largest amount of laundered money (or money identified as 'available' for laundering) tend to be the one preferred by policy makers. This is because a lower estimate would lead those who must implement the rules (the financial industry) to question the non-correlated high costs (Van Duyne *et al.*, 2005, citing Reuter, 2000; Chaikin, 2009).

Though we have reviewed these definitions in the sections above, we need to stress that these are little more than – mostly – juridical constructions which determine an empirical scope *a priori* and often not even unambiguously. As we mentioned before (Chapter 4.2), we do not just observe money laundering, but construct it in a political domain by making political choices. For this reason, it is an unsuitable *empirical* term. What we observe in real life are management actions making use of the mechanisms of the financial payment system with money presumably derived from crime. That CAM is subsequently converted into an indictable 'laundering' according to the Criminal

---

US criminal count of fraud relating to LIBOR manipulation. Several other banks were fined (Bart *et al.*, reporting for Reuters, 2012).

Code.[6] No surprise that with so much careless use of definitions, there are no valid volume estimates and what is presented is more belief than fact, underlining Schneider's observation in the opening section of this chapter.

7.3 Presumed rationality, regulation and the cost-benefit debate

Rationality is a cornerstone of economics underpinning individual decision making. *Homo economicus* is assumed to have perfect knowledge not only of present but also of future risks and rewards and thus is able to make perfect decisions. Writing in the 1970s, Simon introduced the concept of bounded rationality responding to the fact that such perfect foresight did not exist and that decisions frequently were made using less than perfect information.[7] This was later confirmed by Tversky and Kahneman in their classical research on decision making.[8] As mentioned in section 7.2, it is assumed that the hypothetical launderer is not immune to costs variations, being considered a "rational cost-benefit calculator" (Masiandaro, 1998; Harvey, 2004; Blickman, 2009, p. 10). We remind the reader that this is of relevance to only a small portion of the total set of profit making criminals. It is this portion, comprising leading crime-entrepreneurs and financial offenders, to whom Barone and Masciandaro (2011, p. 137) direct their theoretical modelling. These authors express clearly that "we posited a causal link, that more effective regulation produces increasing costs for criminal organizations" (see also Chong and Lopez-de-Silanes, 2007). Remarkably the authors are themselves not sure whether their rational approach will work. They end with the remark: "Let us remember that this assumption is still controversial: see for example the public choice theory of regulation – Coase (1960)[9] and Stigler (1964) – which claims that regulation efforts can be either irrelevant or counterproductive." This is a recognition that increasing the amount of regulation has a limitation, that, if not recognised, can become a non-rational cost driver for all parts of society subject to those regulations.

This rationality concept has long historical roots. In the 1930s, it was already recognised as an important concept with which to understand market pricing. Coase (1937) identified the importance of transaction costs within

---

6 This stepwise conversion from conduct to qualification is routine in criminal investigations, in which first the behavioural components are summed up, followed by a conclusion indicating the charge.

7 H. Simon (1972) *Theories of bounded rationality* chapter 8, pp. 161–176. In C. McGuire and R. Radner R. (eds.) Decision and Organization, North Holland Publishing Co.

8 A. Tversky and D. Kahneman (1974) Judgment under Uncertainty: Heuristics and Biases. *Science* Vol. 185, Issue 4157, pp. 1124–1131.

9 Their citation is in fact incorrect: the correct date of publication is 1937.

the operations of a firm, specifically that access to the 'pricing mechanism' underpinning both consumption and production decisions, has a cost. This cost is that of obtaining pricing information for, as he succinctly states "the operation of a market costs something" (Coase, 1937 p. 398), particularly if information is not a freely accessible commodity. In the same way, intervention in the markets through regulations adds to the costs of operating both legitimate and illicit enterprises in those markets. For example, entrepreneurs in the prohibited substances markets operate at higher costs because prices and products cannot be advertised, staff are not freely recruited while management tools are criminal 'evidence carriers' (Van Duyne *et al.*, 2005, p. 60).

7.4 The vexed topics of efficiency, effectiveness and micro-economics

The desire to demonstrate effectiveness is well illustrated in the UK political arena. Public sector evaluation was introduced by the Blair Labour government and subsequently reinforced by the Conservatives under the post-financial crisis conditions of austerity. In such constrained times, emphasis is placed upon measuring and justifying expenditure from the public purse. Prevalence of such 'evaluation' studies within global criminal justice literature in general and in the UK in particular is commented upon by Alvesalo and Tombs (2005) as being a response to the political desire for 'evidence-led policy'.[10] This inevitably means that greater weight is accorded to evidence that can be quantified – what can be counted and costed as "numbers carry an enormous amount of rhetorical force" (Alvesalo and Tombs, 2005, p. 10). It is also tempting if those numbers can be framed in a way that conveys the desired impression.

Consistent with welfare economics, effectiveness of regulation can be measured using cost benefit analysis (Hantke-Domas, 2003). Harvey (2004, 2008) analysed the main regulatory impact assessments (that purport to have employed cost-benefit analysis) undertaken by the UK government in relation to the introduction of the Money Laundering Regulations (1993, 2001, 2003 and 2007). She noted that costs reported in these assessments were only those directly identifiable by private institutions (thus largely under-reported). These were then set in the context of *un*quantified (but assumed to be 'significant') gains to society that are described as socially desirable outcomes.[11] In

[10] Evidence-led policy making is largely responsible for driving systematic literature review within the social sciences.

[11] There is a statutory requirement in the UK for changes to legislation to be accompanied by cost benefit analysis but while there is a requirement for quantification of costs, it is acceptable to assess benefits in qualitative terms – see for example I. Alfon and P. Andrews (1999) *Cost Benefit Analysis in Financial Regulations: How to do it and how it adds value* FSA Occasional Paper Series 3,

this way it becomes easy to justify any costs when benefits for the relevant commercial sectors cannot be objectively identified, but the unchecked *belief* of 'significant gains' remains upheld which may equally be a kind of self-delusion. With hindsight the costs were undervalued (especially due to the small number of respondents to the survey) which makes any benefit appear bigger. An example of how the estimates come about demonstrates that: the impact assessment accompanying the introduction of the Money Laundering Regulations, 1993, arrived at a cost figure derived from a response rate of 60 out of 1,000 questionnaires (6%) of whom fewer than ten commented on costs and only one attempted their quantification. Against this were balanced benefits derived by the financial institutions from reducing their (unquantifiable) *vulnerability* to laundering (Harvey, 2004, p. 339). How the concept of vulnerability is to be operationalised is left open.

This unjustifiable assessment has been repeated in the most recent Impact Assessment for the 4th Money Laundering Directive which similarly refers to the flow of large sums of illicit funds through the UK, with any reduction leading to unspecified 'significant societal benefits' (p. 2).[12] Van Duyne *et al.* (2018a, pp. 345–374) refer to these impact assessments as a 'politically *soft* cost-benefit assessment'. This rather suggests that rigour was set aside for pre-determined outcomes in accordance with a belief of useful but unproven facts.

Much is said in the literature about whether regulatory intervention within the field of money laundering is efficient; it is almost always followed by the codicil that attempts at efficiency-measurement are well-nigh impossible. Even if it were possible to accurately weigh up the benefits on the one side and the costs on the other, they do not sit on the same account. The benefit derived (to the extent that such exists) from anti-money laundering is a public good, much of the cost of regulation is a private cost that has to be internalised by the regulated institutions and passed through to their customers (see Reuter and Truman, 2004, p. 192).[13] This cost is expected to add to the cost covered by customers.

We find that the terms 'efficiency' and 'effectiveness' are often used interchangeably although accurately, efficiency is a construct based on cost while effectiveness is a construct that can be measured in terms of countable benefits derived or targets hit (or negative events avoided) as a result of implementa-

Available at: http://www.fsa.gov.uk/pubs/occpapers/OP03.pdf and Cabinet Office (2003) Better Policy Making: A Guide to Regulatory Impact Assessment. Available at: http://webarchive.nationalarchives.gov.uk/20040116235945/http://www.cabinet-office.gov.uk/regulation/scrutiny/ria-guidance.pdf. Accessed 7 January 2015.

[12] HM Treasury (2016) "Transposition of the Directive on the prevention of the use of the financial system for money laundering or terrorist financing".

[13] In making this point we are aware of the work of Porter and Van der Linde (1995) who argue that properly designed regulations may induce cost saving innovations that compensates for these internalised costs of compliance. However, for their argument to hold, there is a requirement that regulations are flexible and the firms must be willing to respond.

tion (assuming a proper 'zero-measurement' has been carried out). This difference returns in the various discussions presented below.

Araujo (2010, p. 71) cites Masciandaro (1999) as noting "the lack of efficiency in anti-money laundering regulations" and applies game theory to find optimal conditions for banks' compliance with money laundering regulation.[14] As an external cost, it is not in the interests of banks to comply with these regulations. It is thus assumed that unless forced to comply, they would otherwise seek to ignore or circumvent these rules. Araujo (2010, p. 77) comments that "the crucial variables . . . are related to compliance costs, the probability of being caught and the fine to be paid in case of being caught in the illegal operation". In simple terms, regulated entities will look at the balance between the cost of compliance and the fine they will incur for non-compliance. In consequence, the profit maximising firm will invest in AML systems only up until the costs of their implementation just offsets the costs arising from not undertaking such activity (sanctions for non-compliance). Interestingly although Araujo continues by observing that effort (on the part of the institutions) in AML "is an endogenous variable affected by the ability of the competent authorities to design a proper regulatory system" (Araujo, 2010, p. 77), he does not expand upon what such a system would comprise. To the extent that it is endogenous to the institutions, the cost is externalised by the government. This cost of compliance is not inconsiderable (McCarthy *et al.*, 2015) and evidently, is considerably in excess of the cost estimates included in the impact studies discussed above.

In an attempt to provide an explanation for what constitutes 'effective money laundering policy', Macsiandaro and Filotto (2001, p. 135) also applied the principles of competitive advantage set out in game theory. They explored the circumstances in which independent financial institutions would be prepared to accept this cost burden and determine that it would be beneficial to collaborate with the regulators in enforcement of AML procedures.

Under this scenario the 'effectiveness' of AML is correlated with the ability of the regulators to influence those charged with the execution of the rules within the individual banks in a way that is consistent with the wishes and objectives of the regulator. Of course, this is based on assumptions: first that regulation inhibits the act of money laundering from taking place and secondly that any decline in 'regulatory effectiveness' will directly increase the risk of money laundering. In other words, that there is presumed *ex ante* to be a relationship, not only between regulation and the *risk* of laundering, but between regulation and *actual* laundering.

The nature of this relationship is important because a straightforward causal connection should not be assumed: laundering criminals may be well aware of

[14] Game theory concerns decision making in changing and competitive situations where the outcome of a participant's choice of action depends critically on the actions of other participants.

the regulations and consequently avoid some of the institutions that follow them. Or, they may be aware of the criminal justice penalties imposed. If caught, the launderer will most likely face a prison sentence, and can see the proceeds of his crime removed. The regulatory side enhances the chances of being caught because even if the criminal manages to slip passed the police, his bank manager will have to report the suspicious transactions that appeared in his bank account. Does this have a direct effect on laundering activities? Although assumptions can be made in answer to this question, there are no comprehensive and methodologically strong (statistics-based) studies to prove that it does (see examples below of discussions on this subject, for instance, Chong and López-de-Silanes, 2007). Moreover, there are no comprehensive studies that demonstrate the effectiveness of the whole chain of decision making: from the regulated entities, to the FIU, then right up to the prosecutors and judges.

Of course, one can argue that effectiveness is not only measured by the number of convictions. Firstly, even where there is no criminal conviction for laundering, financial intelligence may be used to identify predicate offences and place criminals on law enforcement's radar. Secondly, in cases where there is no SAR/STR, but merely a de-risking policy, criminals will potentially be affected as regulated entities will decline certain categories of customers perceived to be risky.[15] However, there are no comprehensive studies confirming an effective deterrence in either scenario. Besides, in the de-risking scenario, law-abiding customers may be affected as well as criminals, something that has to be considered in any measurement of effectiveness.

To this scenario comes the laundering criminal with their own perceptions of risks to be avoided. Only a few of them may be accurate but nevertheless attempts at their circumvention increases their costs of laundering. This multifacet relationship refutes the idea of simply attributing outcomes to changes in regulation: if there are effects, they have many causes.

Thus, the direct causal relationship discussed above remains largely unconfirmed at this stage. Further studies are needed to identify the effects of the regulations, also the side-effects, to better understand the full consequences of the AML-regime.

There is, however, another relationship to consider which is often overlooked: and, as in the re-risking example above, that is the decision making by the regulated entity, the financial institution, as an agent of the regulator. To the extent that the interests of the regulator (the principal) can align with those of the regulated entity (the agent), compliance will be achieved more easily. This alignment was explored by both Masciandaro (2005) and Pellegrina

[15] De-risking is understood to be the process of regulated entities declining relationships with customers they consider too risky, for instance, charities, money transmitting businesses, Politically Exposed Persons.

and Masciandaro (2008). In particular, they focussed on the informational advantage retained by the financial institution in relation to the amount of effort they are prepared to expend on AML. Both authors described the asymmetric knowledge of the operational aspects of the regulations that exist between those tasked with executing them (the financial institutions) and those there to police them (the regulatory authority). As regulated entities have to be persuaded to take on these costs, for which they receive no corresponding benefit, micro-economists have considered whether 'carrots or sticks' or a combination of both should be employed.

The case of carrots is considered both by Araujo (2008) and Pellegrina and Masciandaro (2008). These authors questioned why, in the absence of incentives, banks (for example) should share details of the proprietary information they hold on their clients. These authors argue that for AML regulation to work, the difference between the social benefits to society and the private burden on the financial institution must be minimised. Herein lies a problem for academic work that aims to quantify that difference. Harvey (2008) and Sproat (2007) ran up against the unwillingness of institutions to disclose their costs and inability of the authorities to quantify the benefits. Further, Masciandaro and Filotto (2001) suggested that costs and benefits may well differ by jurisdiction.

While it remains difficult to find measurable quantities for the balance of burden and benefit, McCarthy *et al.* (2015) argued that a more equitable solution might be to divert resources to policing adding investment in the form of AML specialists into the FIUs (also see Gordon, 2011). This would have the effect of moving the 'costs' away from the regulated sector and of reducing their burden (this same conclusion was reached by both Ping, 2005 and Takáts, 2011).

Having observed that fines do little to improve compliance with AML, the solution from Pellegrina and Masciandaro (2008) is to emphasise the rewards that might instead be offered to banks in recognition of their compliance efforts. But is this just a wishful fantasy? One imagines that those 'very compliant' banks would both gain benefit because of their reputations and find that other counterparties would be more eager to transact with them.

Masciandaro and Portolano (2003), extending Masciandaro (1998), consider the best design for international regulations. They explore the relationships between what they describe as the "club of virtuous countries" (Masciandaro and Portolano, 2003, p. 322), those preventing laundering and the individual offshore countries deemed likely to flout the rules. They argue that tax havens (in this instance synonymous with offshore centres) exhibit structural characteristics that make them more likely to offer money laundering services.[16] Principally such countries have less to gain from legitimate

[16] Offshore finance centres are revisited in the next chapter.

engagement with the international community. Further, in gaining income from facilitating criminal actions outside their territory, they do not bear the costs of the foreign crime scene. They also concluded that the 'name and shame' approach might prod compliance from slow adopters, however, this would be at the cost of including within the list of those to be shamed, jurisdictions with no deficiencies who would find themselves "*victims of friendly fire*" (p. 326).[17]

Van Duyne *et al.* (2018a) spent some time looking at the rationale underpinning the introduction of the risk-based approach to AML. This approach allows for the regulated entity to align its effort to those areas likely to provide the greatest risk of laundering. This presupposes that regulated entities are able to align their perception of risk with that of their regulator. Failure to do so will result in fines for non-compliance through system weakness, something Van Duyne *et al.* referred to as "interpretation risk". Compliance professionals constantly seek greater certainty: clearer guidance on what is meant by '*risk*' in the eyes of the regulator (Gelemerova, 2009). A number of academics have discussed issues arising from such uncertainty on the part of the compliance professionals (see for example, Araujo, 2008; Favarel-Garrigues *et al.*, 2011; Ross & Hannan, 2007; Tákats, 2011) all of whom argue that where there is uncertainty, there is evidence of over-reporting, 'just to be sure'. Where a rise in STRs (SARs) has been observed without any commensurate impact on crime, this has been described by Pellegrina and Masciandaro (2008, p. 3), as a production of "an overflow of useless AML information".

As sanctions apply in the event of false negatives (failure to report transactions that later prove to be money laundering), a problem lies with false positives (reporting as suspicious, transactions that later prove to be legal). As mentioned above, this has resulted in the unintended incentivisation of reporting all and sundry to avoid the opprobrium of the regulators. Demetis and Angell (2007) highlight the effect of this self-defensive action as passing the risk to the regulator. In various annual reports the FATF condemns this as 'defensive reporting'. A solid intuitive contribution from Takáts (2011, p. 35) is that if banks report everything as suspicious they in effect, report nothing. His solution is for banks to be charged a fee to make reports, although such a suggestion is unlikely to be embraced by the banks. This overlooks more rational solutions such as adopted by the Swiss. They request the reporting institutions to carry out deeper investigations before reporting. For such an approach to work well, however, the authorities need to provide better guidance on what they expect to see and what they do not want to see. We also note that as regulated entities seek to minimise compliance cost, they may simply opt

[17] The Non Cooperative Countries or Territories list was first published by the FATF in June, 2000 'Review of Non Cooperative Countries or Territories: Increasing the Worldwide Effectiveness of Anti-Money Laundering Measures'.

for declining certain categories of clients – de-risking – thereby potentially decreasing the overall volume of valuable financial intelligence.

So far our discussion has focused on the relationship between the regulator and the reporting entity, which is too narrow if the most important actor is left out: the laundering criminal. But the scope can be broadened as done by McCarthy *et al.* (2015) who apply some of the same theoretical principles, using 'bargaining theory' (attributed to Rubinstein, 1982) to this field, whereby agreements can be reached in non-cooperative situations. They use this framework to discuss the fact that the literature generally treats the criminal and launderer as a single entity (the prevailing assumption is of self-laundering). However, their paper considers the launderer as a third person, a separate actor. Within their analysis they argue that one of the key decisions for the launderer is that the chance of getting caught is known to be low (Reuter and Truman, 2004; McCarthy *et al.*, 2015, p. 7): "According to the UN as little as 0.1% to 0.3% of money laundering is detected UNODC (2011)." To the extent that this remains the case, it may be inferred that there is further effectiveness to be gained in increasing the awareness of the authorities of the low risks to the laundering criminal.

7.5 The macro-economic models employed

The original desire to quantify the overall volume of laundered funds came from the IMF, swiftly followed by both the World Bank and the UN[18]. The last attempt by the FATF was in 2001, despite its noting in 1997 that the majority of its member states simply did not have the data required to produce a credible estimate (Harvey, 2011).[19] One of the most recent is "2.7% of global GDP or $1.6 trillion in 2009" (UNODC, 2011). Van Duyne *et al.* (2016, 2018a) provide evidence of the 'fact recycling' by the international bodies that repeat the figures as if they were unassailable truths.

As discussed in Chapter 4.2, in the absence of an operational definition of money laundering it is not possible to 'measure' flows of crime money no matter how sophisticated the constructed model. The complications caused by the lack of clarity over exactly what is being measured leads to a lack of comparable international data. There is also an inherent measurement problem: laundering as a criminal act is counted in addition to the predicate offences. This entails that the dependent variable of 'laundering' is also counted in the

[18] This section includes work produced by the IMF and Inter-American Development Bank that was known to the authors of the book but not recovered as a result of the systematic review of literature. Note that the description of the models included in this section is simplified for the purposes of brevity and readability and for a full exposition, the original works should be consulted.

[19] Financial Action Task Force 1996/97 Report on Money Laundering Typologies, p. 3. Available at www.fatf-gafi.org.

independent variable of 'prevalence of crime', making nonsense of the whole measurement exercise (Reuter and Greenfield, 2001; Ferwerda, 2013). In consequence, researchers have resorted to 'proxy' variables (Harvey, 2011) with a lot of unproven assumptions that only allow hypothetical statements.

The general position is that as an unknown activity, money laundering can distort economic data and thus distort the analysis and policy making reliant on that data (Quirk, 1996). Authors discuss the ability of launderers to co-mingle the illegal and legal funds of a front company, thus undercutting legitimate enterprises, affecting market competition and leading to loss of control on the economic policy making due to adverse impact on macroeconomic estimations (Arnone and Borlini, 2010; Quirk, 1996; Tanzi, 1996). Nevertheless, while some studies focussed on this area (Quirk, 1997 and Masciandaro *et al.*, 2007) found negative effects, others pointed at positive effects on economic growth (studies citied in Arnone and Borlini, 2010). Some researchers (Van Duyne *et al.*, 2005) questioned all of the propositions simply because of the absence of empirical evidence available for substantiation. Unger *et al.* (2006) isolated 25 different effects that they grouped into various categories. Each of these effects was 'negative' (save two). They found that the effect on the growth rate can be either negative or positive as there can be an increase in credit availability or higher demand associated with the inflow of funds into an economy.

The list compiled by Unger *et al.*, (2006, pp. 83–95)[20] is provided below:

- Losses to the victim and gains to the perpetrator
- Distortion of consumption
- Distortion of investment and savings
- Artificial increase in prices
- Unfair competition
- Changes in imports and exports
- Negative (or positive) effect on growth rates
- Effect on output, income and employment
- Lower revenues for the public sector
- Threatens privatisation
- Changes in the demand for money, exchange rates and interest rates
- Increase in the volatility of interest rates and exchange rates
- Greater availability of credit
- Higher capital in- and outflows
- Changes in foreign direct investment
- Risk for the financial sector, solvability, liquidity

[20] Unger (2007) uses two lists of effects: 13 short-term effects and 12 long-term effects (pp. 110–113). The boundary between short- and long-term seems to be thin and sometimes not discernible at all.

- Profits for the financial sector
- Reputation of the financial sector
- Illegal business contaminates legal business
- Distortion economic statistics
- Corruption and bribery
- Increases crime
- Undermines political institutions
- Undermines foreign policy goals
- Increase in terrorism

The legal scholar Alldridge (2002, p. 316) had already done a fairly complete job of dismantling the arguments pointing out that many could be dealt with through existing legislation. Despite this refutation, this list of effects of laundering continued to have a life of its own. In this regard we mention Ferwerda's (2013) test of these claims: one by one he found that there was no underlying empirical evidence, or a different causal relationship to that originally stated. One may wonder whether this outcome will have impact on the status of this list, so favoured by policy makers. Thus far no meaningful debate has been initiated.

From the previous discussions it appears that there is no easy method of measuring the pre- and post-intervention effects. The idea of a proxy variable must be considered as a way out, if proper measurement standards of reliability and validity are met. For example, Sharman (2008, p. 641) notes that the FATF endorsed the use of criminal convictions and amounts confiscated as indicators of effectiveness. With respect to the latter Harvey and Lau (2009) drew attention to the fact that assets recovered had come to be viewed as a performance indicator, but which applies only to a part of the system, further undermining its objectiveness as an encompassing measure.[21] Targets were set for law enforcement over the amounts of assets to be recovered, using confiscation as a yardstick for police performance in general. However, encompassing all crimes, it cannot be used methodologically as a criterion of anti-money laundering policy. In fact, asset recovery does not need to have an operational connection to any anti-laundering measure: it is a consequence of an identified criminal gain (Van Duyne *et al.*, 2014). Developing these ideas, Harvey (2014) observed that the emphasis on what aspect is counted and reported was highly interchangeable, which was in line with the FIU's attempts to demonstrate that it delivers value for money. This produced something like a 'measurement bouquet', which variously encompassed: seizures, restraints,

[21] Rasmusson and Benson (1994) might have been one of the first to observe the goal displacement of enforcement agencies as they targeted forfeitable assets rather than serious offenders. This same observation was also made by Levi (2002) citing Blumenson and Nilsen (1998).

confiscations and something euphemistically referred to as 'interruptions' which could be anything.

It is important to set out in this section the different approaches that have been employed to measure money laundering. We leave the reader to make up their own minds as to whether what follows is an attempt to measure a '*fata morgana*' (Van Duyne, 2006) or "a heroic attempt to measure the immeasurable"' (Gnutzmann *et al.*, 2010, citing Unger, 2007).

The most common areas of focus for building estimates are those that are seen to attract criminal activity: the drugs market, the underground or shadow economy, and tax evasion/capital flight. As direct measurement proves difficult, many of the approaches involve the estimation and measurement of proxy variables. These are variables that are assumed to correlate with the targeted variable. The validity of this assumption is questionable as the level of correlation cannot be determined. Furthermore, the proxy variables may be polluted due to flaws in their definitions and application. As we are focused here on the economic literature there is an inevitable bias toward that which can be quantified, although some econometric models have taken more qualitative aspects into account through employing dummy variables.[22]

The following section discusses examples of some of the main types of models found in the literature and briefly describes the methods that are employed.

a. The early methods of estimation

Estimating a phenomenon that is badly delineated and concerning which there exists a chronic data scarcity, is surrounded with much uncertainty. Despite that circumstance, researchers, policy makers and consultants are not holding back in making attempts to estimate volume. Some represent a genuine effort, others may be serving their own commercial interests. Therefore, we think it proper to give an impression of the enormous spread of the outcomes of these estimation efforts. Table 7.1 does not claim to be complete but rather serves as an illustration.

Basically, two broad methods have been employed: one that is 'top down' employing observed macro-economic data and the other that is 'bottom up' using detailed direct information about expenditures and prices collected by the relevant law enforcement and tax authorities. Both methods have been criticised for specification inaccuracies and over simplification (see the next section) such that they lack statistical robustness (Boorman and Ingves, 2001).

---

[22] Dummy variables are employed in regressions as a way of including non-numerical variables (those signifying certain attributes) assigning 1 for the presence of such information and 0 for its absence. So they are of a nominal level.

Table 7.1 Global Scale – The 'Estimated Guesswork'

Institution/ individual	Estimate (global US$ unless stated otherwise)	Year	Source
OECD	$1.1 trillion (Drugs)	1995	Harvey (2005)
IBRD (World Bank)	$300 - $500 billion	1995	Harvey (2005)
IMF (attributed to Managing Director Michael Camdessus)	2% - 5% GDP ($0.62 – $1.55 trillion)	1998	Arnone and Borlini (2010) (citing Gold and Levi, 1994). Barone and Masciandaro (2011) Buchanan (2004) Harvey (2005) Reuter and Truman (2004)
IMF and Interpol	$500 billion (Organised Crime)	1996	Schneider and Windischbauer (2008) Tanzi (1996)
UN	Up to $1.5 trillion	1999	Harvey (2005)
UN	$700 billion (Organised Crime) $1 trillion	1994 1998	Schneider and Windischbauer (2008)
National Criminal Intelligence Service (USA)	$1.3 trillion (Organised Crime) $1.9 trillion (Organised Crime) $2.1 trillion (Organised Crime)	1998 2001 2003	Schneider and Windischbauer (2008)
FATF	2% global GDP (up to $1.5 trillion)	2001	Harvey (2005)
FATF	US$85 billion (Drugs in USA and Europe)	1990	Arnone and Borlini (2010)
Unsourced	$2.85 trillion and $200-500 billion	No year	Arnone and Borlini (2010)
Costa	$300 billion (Drugs)	2009	Barone and Masciandaro 2011
Walker	$2.85 trillion (4% of world GNP) $2.85 trillion (Drugs)	1999 1999	Barone and Masciandaro (2011) Unger 2013 Schneider and Windischbauer (2008)
FBI	$600 billion - $1.5 trillion	No year	Takáts 2011 (citing Schroeder 2001).
Lal Reuter and Truman	$30 - $225 billion (including self-laundering)	2003 2004	Takáts 2011
UNODC	$1,600 billion	2011	McCarthy ***et al*** (2015)
Reuter and Greenfield	$45 -$280 billion	2001	Unger 2013 Van Duyne ***et al*** (2005)

(continued)

Table 7.1 (continued)

Institution/ individual	Estimate (global US$ unless stated otherwise)	Year	Source
Schneider	$800 billion (Organised Crime)	2001	Schneider and Windischbauer (2008)
	$600-$700 billion (Drugs)		
	$960 billion (Organised Crime)	2002	
	$750 billion (Drugs)		
	$1.2 trillion (Organised Crime)	2003	
	$810 billion (Drugs)		
	$1.4 trillion (Organised Crime)	2004	
	$850 billion (Drugs)		
	$1.5 trillion (Organised Crime)	2005	
	$870 billion (|Drugs)		
	$1.7 trillion (Organised Crime)	2006	
	$910 billion (Drugs)		
The Economist	$400 billion (Drugs)	1997	Schneider and Windischbauer (2008)

Source: the authors

The micro-economic approach relies on crimes reported as a counting unit, which is seen as comprising a subset of all crimes taking place. As discussed by Harvey (2004), this approach was used by the FATF. In its first attempt to produce a global estimate of money laundering in 1989, it took over figures from the UNODC, which were themselves a crude estimation (Van Duyne, *et al.*, 2005; Van Duyne, 1994). This was also criticised as being too country specific (Boorman and Ingves, 2001), or actually requiring huge amounts of data; and also massive effort to collect it (Quirk, 1995).

The macro-economic approaches have traditionally focused on the size of the underground or 'shadow economy'. This point should not be lightly passed over by the reader as convincingly argued by Thomas (1999, p. 387): following this course had led up into a 'blind alley'. Thomas was clearly not a fan of economists concentrating their minds on estimates of what he termed the 'black economy'. He was particularly critical of the lack of theories from which the use of the various parameters of the black economy should be deducted. Reaching a number for an estimated size became an objective in itself.

With the emergence of money laundering as a mainstream theme the economists' occupation was redirected. And with that redirection they took with them their historical academic luggage: the underground economy, relabelled and adapted to the theme of money laundering. They set out to provide a measure of economic activities not captured within official GDP statistics. Within this undertaking it is immediately apparent that the shadow economy not only comprises criminal but also 'informal' economic activity (Schneider and Enste, 2000), although Nardo (2008) interprets this overlap as facilitatory, wherein the grey economy provides hiding places for fiscally unreported monies. This is not as innocent or neutral as it seems: with the inclusion of tax crimes as predicate offences, the circle of criminal earnings (or laundering) has expanded enormously. Apart from that, this method is supposed to additionally pick up errors in specification, statistical sampling and recording (Quirk, 1996; Boorman and Ingves, 2001). The econometric models have employed various methods,[23] with most early studies employing the currency demand[24] and electricity consumption[25] methods to estimate the size of the underground economy. Despite these valiant efforts, neither approach is deemed satisfactory and as expressed by Boorman and Ingves (2001, p. 10 footnote 22): "Representative work in this area is far from convincing or conclusive". Their criticism has good reasons: concept definitions remain imprecise, there is inconsistency in application and proxy variables are applied without independent reliability testing.

---

[23] See Boorman & Ingves, 2001, Annex V for a full discussion.

[24] The first attempts to do this appear to have been Cagan (1958); Guttman (1976) and Feige (1979) and Bhattacharyya (1990) all cited by Quirk (1996) but preceding the money laundering era. The first two citations were made by Chong and López-de-Silanes (2007) to which they acknowledge the further econometric developments by Tanzi (1983). The currency demand approach is one of the most commonly used approaches for measuring the shadow economy and is based on the assumption that shadow or hidden transactions are carried out in cash, thus an increase in the size of the shadow economy will result in an increase in the demand for currency when all conventional explanatory variables are controlled, for such as development of income, payments habits, interest rates and so forth. Variables such as the indirect and direct tax burden, government regulation and complexity of the tax system, assumed to be major factors contributing to people seeking to work in the shadow economy are included in the estimating equation. (See, for example, Schneider and Enste, 2000, p. 31 for an explanation of the model together with a critique of its use).

Tanzi (1983, pp. 289–290, 293), for example, employs a logarithmic model specification (explaining logic for positive signs) that enables him to predict a 'normal' demand for money equation that assumes shadow activity is a direct result of higher taxes and that the main function of currency is store of wealth and transactional:

$$\ln C / M_2 = a_0 + a_1 \ln T + a_2 \ln WS / NIa_3 \ln Ra_4 \ln Y + \in$$

where: C/Y is the ratio of currency holdings to money supply (M2); Y is real per capita income; R is rate of interest on time deposits; WS/NI is the ratio of wages and salaries in national income and T is the rate of income tax. The informal economy is derived in a two-stage process. The predicted C/M_2 can be calculated for each year; rearranging that equation for actual M_2 provides a predicted level of currency holdings $\dot{C}$. Setting T=0 and no change to the other coefficients, the equation can be solved to produce $\ddot{C}$. Tanzi argues that $\dot{C} - C$ provides an indication of goodness of fit and $\ddot{C} - \dot{C}$ shows currency holdings designed to avoid tax and is thus 'illegal' money which multiplied by the velocity of money yields an estimate for the dollar size of the informal economy.

[25] Chong and López-de-Silanes (2007) attribute this approach to Kaufmann and Kaliberda (1996). The physical input (electricity consumption) method measures overall (official and unofficial) economic activity with empirical evidence of observed correlation between the two and an electricity/GDP elasticity of near unity. The difference between the rate of official GDP and the rate of electricity consumption provides an indicator of the growth of the shadow economy. (See, for example, Schneider and Enste, 2000, p. 34 for an explanation of the model together with a critique of its use.)

b. Structural Equation Models (SEM)

More recently, Schneider modified his approach (Schneider *et al.*, 2010; see also Schneider, 2006) to rework his estimates of the size of shadow economies across 162 countries specifically to arrive at an estimate of laundering activity, which looks like a rewrapping of the same material.[26] Recognising the problems inherent in the previous approaches to estimation, he employed structural equation modelling (SEM) through his MIMIC (multiple indicator, multiple causes) method of estimation.[27] This approach provides a method of estimating the value of an abstract or non-tangible endogenous/dependent variable (formally referred to as the latent construct) by taking into account its multiple determinants (causes) and multiple effects (indicators). These multiple measures or explanatory observable variables are combined in multiple regression models where the explanatory variable in one equation can be used as an endogenous variable in another. This approach enables the construction of a picture of the causal relationships amongst all variables used (captured in covariance matrices).

From this it is possible to build, first, a structural model showing all potential causal dependencies between endogenous and exogenous variables, and then the measurement model that describes the relationship between the latent variable and its indicators. Applying principles of parsimony, and employing statistical techniques, the aim is to arrive at the smallest set of observable variables that can be used to best measure the unobserved variable (money laundering).

This MIMIC model identifies (for the 20 highly developed OECD countries using five annual data periods from 1994/95 to 2004/2005), eight causal (of which five are statistically significant) and three indicator variables (two significant) that are used to estimate the turnover of *organised crime* activity, which thus hinges on the preciseness of its definition. The paper does not give details of how each has been measured: thus, the quantum of the turnover of organised crime remains unknown. The causal variables have each a measurement uncertainty of their own.[28]

---

[26] Earlier versions appear as working papers Schneider, F. (2010) "Money Laundering and Financial Means of Organized Crime: Some Preliminary Empirical Findings". Economics of Security Working Paper 26, Berlin: Economics of Security and Schneider, F. (2008) "Money laundering and financial means of organized crime: some preliminary empirical findings". Paolo Baffi Centre Research Paper No. 2008-17.

[27] SEM (also referred to as simultaneous equation models) are multivariate or multi-equation regression models.

[28] Significant *Causal variables*: sales of illegal drugs (+**); sales of illegal weapons (+**); illegal trade in human beings (+*); functioning of the legal system (-**) counterfeit products (+*). *Indicator variables*: Confiscated money per capita (+**); prosecutions (+*). He combined these into the predictive equation to arrive at the turnover figure for organised crime but in order to do so was

Defining organised crime is equally an undertaking with a debatable outcome (Van Duyne, 2006; Von Lampe *et al.*, 2006). However, in a working paper by Schneider and Buehn (2013) the authors substantially self-critiqued this approach. The paper provides a comprehensive review of both theoretical and empirical literature on measuring the shadow economy, detailing the various models used and the precise steps followed in their MIMIC model. Importantly, this work also sets out the criticisms in the literature of SEM as an approach and suggests what further work should be undertaken to improve the overall understanding of the shadow economy and to improve the accuracy of its measurement. We infer that the same shortcomings apply to the measurement of money laundering being a subset of the underground economy: if the wider field has flaws in the definition the subset logically inherits these.

Chong and López-de-Silanes (2007) used data from in excess of 80 countries across two dimensions (estimates of prevalence of money laundering and extent of regulation) which they then fed into a range of models. They calculated proxies for money laundering in the shadow economy using the currency demand approach, the electricity consumption approach and the Dynamic Multiple Indicators Multiple Causes (DYMINIC) approach.[29] Noting the criticisms associated with the macroeconomic approaches they additionally collated data they term "direct, yet subjective" (p. 12), that allowed for the incorporation of *opinion data* from international surveys that looked at the prevalence of money laundering collected on a seven-point Likert scale where 1 was 'pervasive' to 7 'extremely rare'. Interestingly, to this they also added a measure of regulation (more usually the preserve of the micro-economists) that was derived from: financial institutions' disclosure of information; extent of criminal legislation and asset confiscation; and, international cooperation. Inevitably although they are transparent in disclosing their decision making and 'scoring' in order to produce quantitative data sets, there is a degree of subjectivity in arriving at the scores. This does not only apply to the results of the Likert scales, but also to asset confiscation of which the execution may stretch over many years (Van Duyne *et al.*, 2014). To this one should add written-off uncollectable assets, either because all criminal earnings have been dissipated (very often) or sophisticatedly laundered (which occurs in a small number of cases).

They go on to produce a comprehensive set of regressions controlling for various external factors and checking for robustness arguing that the consis-

reliant on the same dataset constructed by Walker for his models reusing the same data without reliability check.

[29] This technique considers a range of possible explanatory cause and effect variables for the size of the shadow economy using factor analysis to determine the most statistically significant. See Schneider, F. (2006) *Shadow economies and corruption all over the world: what do we really know?* (Working Paper No. 0617). Department of Economics Johannes Kepler University of Linz.

tency of results across the different data sources improves confidence in their conclusion that stronger money laundering regulation (especially asset recovery, though, one can argue, this should not be included) impacts on reducing money laundering arising from the main 'feeder activities'. These activities comprise "broad criminal activities, the underground economy and tax evasion" (Chong and López-de-Silanes, 2007, p. 9). The authors do not take account of overlaps between these three categories part of which are not universally criminalised, and so are not a source for laundering in all countries. This casts doubt on the validity of their regression calculations. Indeed, Pickhardt and Pons (2011) drew attention to the wide-ranging criticisms of these models (employing the currency demand approach) on both conceptual as well as econometric specification grounds arguing that the errors in the estimates (to overestimate) have provided misleading information for policy makers. Their own contribution attempted to deal with the mis-specification issues to provide more accurate estimation of the size of the shadow economy for Germany through use of an alternative modified-cash-deposit-ratio (MCDR) approach. Their approach still requires a range of modifying assumptions to hold.

c. Multiple Regression Models

One of the first attempts to model money laundering was undertaken by Quirk (1996). He employed cross-section data for a group comprising 19 industrial countries for two separate time periods: 1983 and 1990. Quirk was not looking to measure the quantity of money laundering but rather looked for evidence of its influence and potential impact on monetary behaviour. Quirk (1996, p. 9) specified the following model to determine the flow of laundered funds into an economy:[30]

$$Mi = Mi\left(y, p^e, i_d, L_j\right) \tag{7.1}$$

Where: Mi = demand for money; y = income (+); p^e = expected inflation (-); i_d = deposit interest rate variable (+/-); L_j = a broad set of variables used as proxies for the influence of money laundering on the demand for money (L_1 crime; L_2 tax evasion, and L_3 unemployment and labour participation rates).[31]

The conclusion of this paper is that where money laundering is on a sufficiently large scale it will impact on economic activity through price distortion and that, if not taken into account, this will result in incorrect policy making.

---

[30] Which he noted was largely based on that of Bhattacharyya (1990).

[31] He used Crime data from Interpol, noting problems of comparability, as a proxy variable for the 'types of money laundering' (p. 10).

This approach has serious flaws in the way reality is disregarded. In the first place price distortion will not go unnoticed and will lead to suspicions and reporting to the authorities of unfair competition or price rigging where that is criminalised. This implies that a rational crime-entrepreneur will avoid the risk of price distortion. In the second place, the reliance on Interpol data for the construction of the proxy variables is debatable given the traditional lack of reliability of police data.

A slightly different approach was followed by Vaithilingam and Nair (2009) who employed factor analysis to identify the 'common features' exhibited by countries identified as having a low incidence of money laundering. Countries so identified were established as a 'benchmark' group that provides for the authors a measure against which progress made by other countries can be assessed. Whilst they identify a number of criteria (factors) that, they suggest, correlate with money laundering, there is no direct evidence available. Instead we are presented with five variables:

- scope of IT coverage;
- irregularity of tax collection;
- bank soundness;
- human capital ('brain drain');
- and, efficiency of the legal system.

While the definition of each variable remained absent, each factor was assessed on an ordinal scale from 1= lowest development to 7= highest development. Whilst the paper provides clarity over how the 'factors' were identified and measured, the authors are less transparent about how they determined 'incidence of money laundering'. This puts the whole undertaking on sandy ground. It is perhaps not surprising that they conclude with

> "the incidence of money laundering will be high when there is a high development in technology but a lack of a comprehensive and enabling environment such as an effective legal framework, tax system and sound financial institutions" (p. 26).

This observation applicable to countries X, Y, Z, does not appear to be generalisable. We are certainly not the first to question some of these approaches that attempt to observe an unobservable phenomenon. In trying to find a more accurate determination of the minimum amount of laundering activity within an economy, Ardizzi *et al.* (2014) focus only on the placement stage of laundering. This is rationalised by the argument that criminals usually deal in cash and that, by default, these tainted funds have to be cleaned through placement into the financial system. They argue that cash is observable and, indeed, can be measured directly as it circulates through the economy. However, this approach virtually excludes financial and economic crime in which cash plays a subordinate role. Their interest is in trying to establish the proportion of cash deposited into banks that could be accounted for by criminals to "provide a lower bound estimate of the amount of money laundered at its very early stage" (p. 1558). The use of *observed* data to construct their model suggests improvement to others, who have merely used theoretical models built from *a priori* assumptions to generate data.

As part of their justification (p. 1558) they highlight important limitations of some of the approaches covered within this literature and critiqued earlier in our book. These are a reliance of 'tacit knowledge and feelings' as a basis for estimation which cannot be independently verified; restriction of models to drugs related data as the 'only' predicate offence; and finally, conflation of the related but different constructs of the illegal and shadow economy.

For their study of Italy, unfortunately they remain bounded by the same constraints of other economists as they apply the currency-demand approach (discussed above) to identify the 'directly observable' variable: cash entering the financial system, with an assumed proportion that might be of (estimated) criminal origin. Through a series of econometric models, they identify different explanatory origins for three different components of cash (p. 1583): money laundering; the legal component; and, the shadow economy component. Their estimates indicate that the laundering component is sizeable for the country. Their conclusion suggests that an appropriate solution for regulation is to limit cash transactions and to move to electronic payments as the best way of controlling laundering by wire tracing.

d. Equilibrium models

Argentiero *et al.* (2008) used a dynamic general equilibrium model under which the choices of economic agents (households and firms) interact with two sectors of the economy: legitimate and criminal.[32] Firms can produce goods in both markets and households can also supply services and consume goods produced in both sectors. It is the criminal market that provides both criminal activity and the money to be subsequently laundered. Naturally, the laundering is also required to obscure the criminal origin of the revenues earned within the legitimate part of the economy (for example, economic and white-collar crime). Both sectors have transaction costs, consistent with the reasoning adopted by Masciandaro (1999): those involved in the criminal sector face a cost determined by the disutility arising from criminal sanctions and

[32] General equilibrium macroeconomic models generally focus on interactions between a small number of markets as a simplification of the economy.

the probability of being caught.[33] Their approach differs in the empirical estimation of the model from that of Masciandaro (1999). Argentiero *et al.* (2008) go on to infer the behaviour of money laundering as an unobservable variable through estimation of observable proxy-variables extracted from the equilibrium model.[34]

The results of their endeavour are to produce a generated series of money laundering as a proportion of GDP that they plot against aggregate GDP (also produced by the model) over the same time period. They suggest that their results point to evidence of a negative correlation between GDP and money laundering, arguing that in times of economic growth, there is greater incentive and opportunity to belong to the legal economy and so criminal activity will decline. Conversely, criminal activity will rise during an economic downturn when the criminal economy acts as 'a buffer' (p. 352). This applies only to the informal economy, which is not necessarily criminal. Traders in prohibited substances are by their nature excluded from the legal economy, unless they succeed in fully laundering the proceeds to the level of integration.

Following from this logic, countries should tighten AML controls in times of recession, although they remain silent on whether the opposite would also be suitable as an option. They suggest that their findings are consistent with Quirk (1996).[35] However, they appear to overlook the fact that the inferred causality they purport is from GDP to laundering whereas Quirk focused on causality from laundering to GDP. Nevertheless, the contribution of this paper is interesting as it suggests that laundering may increase and decrease in contrast to the 'official' literature where the volume of money laundered is presented as increasing year on year.

Gnutzmann *et al.* (2010) took a different approach and explored why some countries were willing to comply with international regulations and others are seemingly prepared to 'tolerate' money laundering. Their study focused on the determinants of the extent to which countries were likely or not to comply with international regulation. They argued that the adopted

---

[33] The classic 'criminal profit formula'.

[34] They (pp. 349–350) include the consumer price index (p1,t) (nominal prices in the legal economy); national consumption time series (C1t) (consumption of legal goods); employment rates (Nt) (labour share in the legal economy); Gross fixed investments (Kt) (investment rate in the legal economy assuming no depreciation); and total factor productivity (Λt) (for both legal and illegal parts of the economy). Finally, transaction costs (Zt) for legal goods (C1t) in the legal economy are set to 0.2 (the rate of VAT). They are still left with the common problem of valuing activity in the criminal sector. Their solution is to resort to an estimate of the value added by the criminal economy across the entire data set as a way of deriving measurement of criminal wages (W2,t). To complete the model, they have to provide values for a number of elasticity/volatility relationships. Although they explain the reasoning behind the values selected they are nevertheless only inferred. Consistent with other approaches to modelling, they attempt to build confidence into their predictions by the incorporation of a sensitivity analysis with a 5% +/- variation in the values ascribed.

[35] Subsequently shown to be highly questionable by Ferwerda (2013) (see later).

position by a country would be determined by whether the economy is closed (social costs and benefits of crime are fully internalised), or open and globally trading. In the latter circumstance, the investment benefits, accruing from 'tolerating' money laundering, move abroad, while the costs of predicate crime remain within the country. These economies are satisfied to see the negative impact of crime externalised because the criminal offences were committed elsewhere. The reason why we do not see a "regulatory race to the bottom" (p. 245) is that those countries with a large legitimate sector will avoid the money laundering market and "smaller, developing countries will be more likely to 'dance with the devil'" (Gnutzmann *et al.*, 2010 p. 245). They attempt to explain the purported relative prevalence of money laundering amongst smaller nations by arguing that larger countries would have more to lose in other areas of financial activity if they were to adopt lower standards of governance. However, the authors do not explain the reasoning used to arrive at these suppositions nor whether they are talking in relative or absolute terms. For example, are they implying that a large legitimate sector in some way crowds out a relatively smaller illegal one or whether a large legal sector can coexist with a large criminal sector? Given the conjunction of the argument with the small developing countries (no mention of large ones), the implication appears that their internal criminal market is equally small. Another weakness is the lack of delineation of exactly what is meant by 'criminal market'. Does this also encompass the informal economy? As a counter hypothesis one may say that in a large economy it may be easier to find a protective niche for money laundering which in a small economy would attract attention.

Similar to Argentiero *et al.* (2008), Gnutzmann, *et al.* (2010) utilise a partial equilibrium model in which economies are both open and closed and consumers are indifferent to whether the goods they consume are legal or illegal, but the latter are produced or provided by criminals. It is interesting to note that Argentiero *et al.* (2008) use a dynamic model and specifically discuss the fact that the size of the illegal sector can change according to the phase of the economic cycle.

By implication here, a simplifying assumption for the purposes of the model is that criminal earnings can only fully be consumed (have value) once laundered. Using uncleaned funds is not without costs or risks: it required the costs of a specific laundering operation and more generally, the costs of avoiding being caught and sanctioned. This is considered equivalent to the cost of laundering (see section 8.2). Consistent with the approaches of Masciandaro (1999) and, to an extent, Argentiero *et al.* (2008) they recognise that there is an exchange rate between clean and dirty money with the latter requiring use of money laundering services. The cost of supply of this service is determined by the transaction cost as set out in other papers. Gnutzmann *et al.* (2010; p. 246) suggest these costs are directly within government control. They argue that it is within the power of governments to completely eradicate laundering services. Obviously, this line of reasoning makes no allowance for the indirect costs placed on the rest of the society through intensified controls, tighter regulation and more repressive criminal law enforcement.

Sadly, much of the theoretical reasoning underpinning these models requires such simplification and abstraction that they are removed from reality, by definition models are simply models. Many academics appear to fall into the trap of finding an explanation for one set of observations and are then lured by the temptation of generalisability, where none exists. Not only geography and national customs make this impossible, also history stands in the way of such attempted general explanations. It is interesting to consider the long-term impact of the early stance of the British authorities who advised their erstwhile colonies to establish offshore centres as a means of economic diversification. This was not without self-interest: it would reduce their continued reliance on the Crown. Some of those territories quickly learned the craft of 'financial secrecy management' (Walter, 1989). It is not without irony that we now observe the UK authorities' recent move to require Britain's remaining overseas territories to adopt a public register of company beneficial ownership by 2020.[36]

e. Gravity Models

One of the best known proponents of the global modelling of money laundering is John Walker. In his first papers on the subject (Walker, 1995, 1998, 1999) he proposed a calculation utilising an input-output matrix to model money laundering flows. Walker's model was uncritically adopted and reinforced by what became the authorities' 'large figure circus' of money laundering. He should be recognised for his bold attempts to 'map' global money laundering. Even though his approach and methods were not always clear they have been accepted by a wide range of policy making bodies. Elaborating on the original 1995 study, Walker (1999) discussed the original method employed that established, bottom-up, an estimate for the proceeds of crime in Australia that started from 'previous work [unattributed] on the costs of crime in Australia in 1991.[37] Data appeared to have been

[36] After having created a register and made it accessible to the UK authorities for several years, with the introduction of the Sanctions and Anti-Money Laundering Act 2018, Britain's overseas territories were now required to make the register public. As UK parliament cannot impose its will on the crown dependencies, the expectation is that they will be persuaded by the UK government to embrace the same standards. See reports in the *Financial Times*, by Mance, 2018, and *The Guardian*, by Sabbagh, 2018. https://www.ft.com/content/5a924560-4d45-11e8-8a8e-22951a2d8493 and https://www.theguardian.com/politics/2018/may/01/uk-to-introduce-public-ownership-registers-for-overseas-territories

[37] A copy of this document was shared with us by the Author, John Walker: Walker J (1999) The Extent of Money Laundering in and through Australia in 2004 AUSTRAC John Walker Crime Trends Analysis RMIT University.

taken from crime victim surveys which identified property lost, triangulated against police and insurance data (p. 33). This was augmented by questionnaires designed to capture the views of law enforcement and criminologists in Australia. We mentioned already in Chapter 4 that in order to get some of the data for inclusion in the model he had relied on testimony from 'experts' with uncertain qualifications. Though fundamentally nothing is inaccurate with such approach by way of reconnaissance, it has not always been immediately apparent that the number of 'expert' respondents was very small; only nine of them provided data and of questionable reliability. The 2004 Report did note the limited nature of the original approach and suggested that the updated version consulted a wider range of respondents. The presentation of the results makes detailed analysis difficult. Within the section 'Survey results' (p. 51) we extract the following:

- Law enforcement and related agencies (12 responses out of 30)
- Australian researchers (one response out of 20)
- Overseas researchers (three responses out of 20)
- FIU and related agencies (21 responses out of 100)

The total response rate was 37 from 170 (22%). Of course, not all respondents answered all questions but the very first table thereafter sums to 15 (Australian) and 24 (overseas), a total of 39; that is two more than indicated by the response rate, though not explained. Further through the report, Walker attempts to update estimates of money laundering using the updated property loss from the crime data, but he applied the criminal income proportions (a percentage income to the offender) derived from his 1995 method.

It transpires that the raw data underlying his estimation model from his 1995 work is seriously deficient. Of the 20 respondents who returned his questionnaire only nine provided an estimate of "Total laundered value (proceeds)": three from Australia; one from Ukraine; one from Belgium; one from Canada; one from Malaysia; one from Thailand; and one from the Dominican Republic. For Australia he gave an average of AUD 28,658,333 and for the other responding countries 10,333, currency not indicated. Only four countries mentioned the "Total laundered value" in cases of recorded conviction. Nothing is mentioned about the competence of these respondents to provide any valid data. His estimation model was based on this weak methodology. Our criticism is not to deride Walker for his efforts, but to point out that the estimates lacked foundations from the very beginning making it all the more worrying that they drove subsequent 'official' estimates while functioning as the foundation of the gravity model used for the Dutch Ministry of Finance.

The models are pleasingly simple to follow, yet the Walker (1995) definition of money laundering as set out in his later papers (see section 7.2.1.) is anything but operational for model testing. Rather, they include an underpinning assumption that crime occurs to varying degrees within different 'types' of countries. Further, that different types of crime generate different average amounts of proceeds to be laundered and that laundering occurs within and across jurisdictions. Thus, Walker focuses on two dimensions.

1. Firstly, on estimating the quantity generated *in* each country (being in broad terms a function of: amount of crime; estimate of amount of laundering per crime reported; and the overall economic environment).
2. Secondly, on the quantity attracted *to* each country (being in broad terms a function of level of banking secrecy; government attitudes to laundering; levels of corruption and regional conflict; relationship between countries either geographic, trade based or cultural/language).

Attractiveness to launderers is set out (1998, p. 6; 1999, p. 30) as

$$= \left[US\$GNP_{per\ capita} \right] x \\ \left[3x_{bank\ secrecy + gov\ attitude + swift\ member} - 3x_{conflict - corruption} + 15 \right] \quad (7.2)$$

Where: *bank secrecy* is an ordinal scale where 0 = no secrecy law and 5 secrecy laws enforced; *gov attitud*e is an ordinal scale where 0 = government is anti-laundering and 4 is tolerant; *swift member* 1 for members and 0 for non-members; *conflict* is on a scale from 0 for no conflict to 4 conflict exists; *corruption* is modified from the TI index from 1 = low to 5 = high. The constant 15 is included to make all results positive.

Movements between countries are calculated (1998, p. 7; 1999, p. 32) as:

$$Proportion\ of\ outgoing\ ML\ from\ country\ X\ to\ country\ Y = \\ \left(attractiveness\ score\ for\ Y\right) / \left(Distance\ between\ X\ and\ Y\right)^2 \quad (7.3)$$

He sets out the assumptions used to construct the spreadsheet and the resulting estimates that are calculated at individual country level. The obvious attraction of this approach is its computational simplicity whilst the disadvantage is that it is time-consuming in its construction. As he constructs variables from the cost of crime, not the estimated profit, he moves to a percentage of these costs assumed to be laundered. He proposes a percentage to be laundered with an interval of 1, 10 and 80%. An expert survey would refine these crude intervals in a survey based on a questionnaire, but there is no evidence of how this is achieved, while we note that the response was extremely low and of uncertain reliability. The author expressed his awareness of the limitations but continued with his methodology nevertheless.

Walker and Unger (2009, p. 830) revisited and attempted to extend Walker's original model on the basis of his old data, providing 'theoretical' underpinning to the gravity model. Others criticise these models as lacking any such grounding (see Ferwerda *et al.*, 2011). They, therefore, modified the presentation:

$$F_{ij} / M_i = Attractiveness_j / Distance_{ij} 2 \qquad (7.4)$$

Where:

$$F_{ij} / M_i = \left[\left(\frac{GNP}{capita} \right)_j x \left(3BS_j + GA_j + SWIFT_j - 3CF_j - CR_j + 15 \right) \right] / Dist_{ij}.^2$$

As specified, F_{ij}/M_i is the proportion of proceeds of crime that country *i* sends to country *j* and all other variables are as specified in the original Walker papers.

This revised version of the model, which achieved little to reinforce its shaky foundation, is also employed by Unger *et al.* in their 2006 calculations for the Netherlands.[38] Here they express relative attractiveness scores (Table 2.14; p. 54), which is rather hypothetical than fact based. It should be noted that unfortunately, these scores do not correspond with reality. Neglecting principles of parsimony, they expanded the number of explanatory variables to include both Egmont Group membership intended to signify 'strict AML policy'; and financial deposits, theorising that countries with large financial centres will prove more attractive to launderers because of having the expertise to 'handle large amounts of money discretely'. They also amended the distance 'deterrence' index by including, as had been suggested by Walker, variables to pick up cultural ties by including language and colonial background (p. 841):[39]

$$P(X, y_i) = \frac{1}{\sum_{i=1}^{n} \frac{attractiveness(y_i)}{dist(X, y_i)}} x \frac{attractiveness(y_i)}{dist(X, y_i)} \qquad (7.5)$$

[38] Unger B, J. r, W. de Kruijf, G. Rawlings, M. Siegel, and K. Wokke (2006) "*The Amounts and the Effects of Money Laundering,*" report for Dutch Ministry of Finance.

[39] For Country X, countries *yi i=1….n*, where **Attractiveness** = *f* {GDP per capita, Bank Secrecy, Anti-Money Laundering Policy, SWIFT Membership, Financial Deposits, Conflict, Corruption, Egmont Group} and **Distance deterrence** = *f* {Language, Colonial Background, Physical Distance}.

Unger *et al.* point at evidence that their results are consistent with others (obtained from different approaches) as an indicator of their method's 'robustness'. They do recognise the need for what they term 'an "economics of crime micro foundation" to further strengthen the model by consultation with criminologists to incorporate behavioural dimensions intending to improve its accuracy and broader acceptance (Walker and Unger, 2009, p. 850). However, this corrective approach remains largely based on the never corrected, flawed initial survey with unsupported assumptions and deducted estimates.

Their model and findings were re-used in the UNODC 2011 report on criminal finances prepared by Thomas Pietschmann (Research Officer, STAS) and John Walker (Consultant). Subsequently this approach was used in the ECOLEF report drafted by the Utrecht School of Economics (2013).[40] While this report makes contributions in terms of setting out the various models of European supervisory architecture (Van Duyne *et al.*, 2016), its methodology can equally be challenged. It largely adopted the earlier approach of Walker, wherein its values from crime types were put together using 'estimates' produced by others. We do not see evidence, however, that before using these data any attempt was made to check their reliability. This approach was further compounded by employing the percentages of proceeds taken from the original Walker (1995; also referring to Walker 1999 and Unger *et al.*, 2006). They then proceeded to employ the same gravity model as set out above and outlined in Walker and Unger (2009). In failing to verify data and assumptions taken from these prior sources, they have inadvertently used what appeared to be deficient data to arrive at new deficient data and conclusions. All this was happily embraced within the mainstream and by authorities such as the Dutch Ministry of Finance and the European Commission.

f. Trade-based models

Others used public source statistical trade data to look for evidence of laundering. De Boyrie *et al.* (2005) modelled abnormal pricing in trade flows between Switzerland and the USA to look for evidence that the imposition of money laundering legislation in Switzerland had increased false invoicing activity through abnormal pricing. Using two different portfolio models, they found an increase in capital outflows, that was explainable by the enactment of the legislation. But they also found that this could not be explained through trade flow pricing. They suggested that this was because the laws only covered the financial sector. In the light of this they suggested that trade provided a relatively easy and tidy way to move capital for a multitude of purposes.

---

40 ECOLEF is a project funded by the European Commission, DG Home Affairs.

Zdanowicz (2009) did not so much offer a model, but a way of analysing trade data looking for abnormalities in pricing using statistical profiling techniques based on an analysis of US imports and exports. He theorised that a mismatch in either could provide the means to move funds into or out of a country in a way that *might be* linked to laundering (moving funds obtained from other illegal activity). However, such a mismatch could equally arise due to capital flight, capital controls or evasion of duties. The method is quite simple: it compares the country average price of an exported product with the world average price for the same (as far as possible) product using the standardised commodity codes employed by all countries. The author suggests that this approach could be used to derive risk based indicators around countries and products. This approach would help financial institutions meet their AML obligations when they have to identify trade finance transactions that require greater scrutiny. While recognising the existence of trade based money laundering, Soudijn (2014, pp. 247–264) questions the capability of this approach to identify cases, relying on impure national and international databases.

Ferwerda *et al.* (2011) tested the model specified by Walker and Unger using data on trade-based laundering (using the data set constructed by Zdanowicz, 2009). The reason for the selection of this particular area was that this type of laundering was observable, being "a special form of trade abuse" (p. 1). However, they rejected the Walker-Unger gravity model in favour of the more traditional version which in the context of international trade is specified as shown below.[41] However, the 'traditional' model was expanded to include the attractiveness indicators in Chapter 7.4 above, as they concluded that this structural model empirically provides the best fit.[42]

$$X_{i,j} = \beta_0 Y_i^{\beta 1} N_i^{\beta 2}\, Y_j^{\beta 3}\, N_j^{\beta 4}\, D_{i,j}^{\beta 5}\, P_{i,j}^{\beta 6} \qquad (7.6)$$

From their results they conclude (as they recognise somewhat counter-intuitively) that countries with strong AML measures in place (proxy variable membership of the Egmont Group) experience more laundering activity through trade. They speculate whether this is a result of criminals avoiding the more tightly regulated financial institutions, although we note that laundering through trade also needs balancing (bank) accounts as a consequence of the under- and over-invoicing through the banks.

Johnson and Lim (2002) were interested in modelling the impact of the introduction of the FATF 40 Recommendations on money laundering.

---

41 Most usually associated with J. Tinbergen (1962) *Shaping the world economy: suggestions for an international economic policy* Twentieth Century Fund, New York.

42 Where *Xij* is the value of trade between countries *i* and *j*; *Yk* is GDP and *Nk* population of country *k*; and *Dij* and *Pij* denote distance between countries *i* and *j* and *Pij* the possible special relationship between them (p. 4).

Although following a macroeconomic approach, they based their study on the attitudes of governments to laundering. In addition, they included the theoretical relationship between banks and the two-sector model of the economy: illegal (crime rate)/legal (standardised GDP) as set out by Masciandaro (1998), discussed below.[43] For the purposes of their analysis they looked at two groups of countries determined by whether or not they were members of the FATF and split their time series data on either side of the establishment of the FATF in 1989. Their analysis pointed to those countries with FATF membership seeing a "weaker bank/money laundering relationship" (p. 18), concluding that the FATF positively impacted on these countries by reducing opportunities for money laundering in them. It should be noted that they recognised the negative impact of data limitations on their work.

7.6 Concluding reflection

What can be concluded from this overview of some of the different approaches employed? The estimates of the scale of money laundering ranged from $30 billion (this lowest figure 'pleased no-one' – Van Duyne *et al.*, 2005, p. 121) to $2.1 trillion, both of which were produced in the same year, 2003. This implies a lot of uncertainty due to imprecise definitions as well as flaws in the databases, which appears to be traditional. Gold and Levi (1994) analysed financial data, including data on 'suspicious transactions', to observe that estimates of money laundering contained errors 'both ways': "suspicious transactions that are actually legitimate" and "legitimate transactions that are actually criminal" (also see Walker and Unger, 2009, p. 827). Certainly, there is evidence of a great deal of effort that should not simply be set aside. Many of the authors were aware of and pointed to the limitations of the approaches they employed, recognising that each simplifying assumption adds further distance from reality. A wise insight that remained subsequently unheeded.

From our review, we note that there is the suggestion that laundering occurs, but that due to definitional ambiguity it is not possible to 'measure' either its size or scale. Perhaps more attention should be paid to the argument of Reuter and Truman (2004) that the success of the system should not be judged by the impact on money laundering but rather on prevalence of *predicate offences* which would mean that the arguments over scale and measurement become pretty meaningless. The beam of light cast into these dark corners still cannot illuminate the looming 'threat'. Either the threats were too small or the beam of light was not strong enough (or both).

[43] GDP expressed per 100,000 population.

Recognising that rationality so beloved by economists cannot properly deal with laundering, Walker and Unger (2009) mentioned the need to incorporate the views of criminologists to shed light on the behavioural dimensions of launderers. We would go much further and note that the behavioural sciences should also be used to explain the actions of those making use of the data without caring for their quality. We have already mentioned the mental 'anchoring' to the large figures from researchers such as Walker, that largely reinforced the IMF consensus and the guesswork of the international bodies.

7.7 The microeconomic models

As discussed earlier in this book, the approach to AML is based on two pillars: the criminal legal framework on the one hand, and the civil regulatory framework on the other. The papers contributed by microeconomists examine criminal decision making and laundering where the 'penalty' imposed is the full weight of the law that can be brought to bear if convicted.[44] Those papers looking at the decision making of regulated entities (the 'agents') consider the 'penalty' as the fine levied for non compliance. Either way, the authors used the theoretical utility model and the rational choice responses of cost and consequence should either the criminal or the institution fail to follow suit. Examples from some of the work in this field are presented in the next sections.

a. Decision making by criminals

The papers looking at the decision-making by criminals largely focus their efforts on "*manipulation of the criminal profit formula*" (Gnutzmann *et al.*, 2010 p. 245). For example, Hinterseer (1997) develops a theoretical model that makes use of underlying microeconomic assumptions drawn from utility theory and incorporates the principles of rational choice. His theoretical model is constructed on a series of underpinning 'principles': The first two effectively incorporate limiting parameters of rationality and risk aversion on the response of the individual. Setting aside considerations of morality, Hinterseer argues (p. 156) that when penalties are known and quantifiable, the instruments through which laundering occurs have an intrinsic tradable

[44] Note that laundering within these models is typically considered as an external service supplied to the criminal, there being no room to look at 'self-laundering'. However, given the all-encompassing legal approach to include self-laundering, this condition implies a serious limitation to the models.

value. In line with normal supply and demand theory, demand for money laundering services is negatively correlated with price (or cost). Applying the principle of rationality which states that individuals faced with two choices with equal return will chose those with the least risk; launderers will choose laundering opportunities or instruments that present a lower risk. To the extent that regulators are able to influence the cost of these laundering services by raising their price, it is assumed demand will fall. However, there are no indications that this is the case: criminal earnings continue unabated leading to a reservoir of unlaundered money. The theory does not account for this consequence. These principles find their way into the underpinning assumptions of other authors: a mutual borrowing of 'shaky ground'.

Masciandaro (1998 and 1999) worked from a definition of laundering that picks up two dimensions: firstly, its *illegality* (that is only associated with criminal or illegal activity); and secondly, that the objective of laundering is the *concealment* of the illegal origin of the funds. The purpose of laundering is to turn *potential* into *actual* or 'effective' (Verhage and Ponsaers, 2009) purchasing power, to enable consumption or investment activity to take place within the upperworld. This logic is applied to the income of the criminal, although not all criminal money has to be cleaned; if it can be intertwined with daily living expenses, it has full earning capacity. Masciandaro argues that by remaining 'un-cleaned' the crime-money has a lower earning capacity. This is because it can only be used in lower profit activities or in endeavours that involve a higher degree of risk of getting caught. Much as set out by Hinterseer (1997), working from the principles of utility, he sets out a series of theoretical propositions that detail the choices faced by the criminal in determining the optimal level of earnings that should be laundered. In particular, he highlights the negative relationship between the utility to the criminal and the probability of detection and strictness of sanctions. As we are dealing with theoretical propositions, an assumed truism is that utility increases as the expected return from investment of laundered funds increases. As discussed already, the function of 'laundering' is not a free one and this is incorporated into the model as a transaction cost. Gnutzmann *et al.* (2010, p. 245) and Argentiero *et al.* (2008) refer to this as effectively a 'tax' on criminal income noting that the rate is equal to the state's enthusiasm for crime prevention. Similarly, Masciandaro theorises about the relationship between the cost of what he terms 'money laundering services' and the amount of money that requires 'cleaning'. As the return to the criminal of his clean money increases, the demand for laundering services will correspondingly increase. Similarly, an increase in the severity of sanctions or probability of detection will produce a downward shift in the demand curve. Employing the familiar two-sector model (one legal and one illegal), discussed above in the section on equilibrium models, he attempts to explain the various influences on money laundering activity. However, as this is a static model, it cannot account for changing behaviour by the criminals in response to changes in the costs they face.

Without reproducing an algebraic proof, if regulation were costless to the criminal, the solution (as arrived at by others) would be to maximise the costs of laundering activities. As this is not the case "the optimal policy will be the one that will succeed in minimising the social costs of regulation while keeping crime at a tolerable level." (Argentiero *et al.*, 2008, p. 231). This implies keeping a sharp eye on unintended costs to keep regulations proportionate to the seriousness of the crime: don't shoot at a mosquito with a cannon (Van Duyne *et al.*, 2016).

Yaniv (1999) was particularly interested in the link between laundering and tax evasion. Following a similar approach to both Masciandaro and Hinterseer, Yaniv employs the algebra of utility theory to illustrate the conditions under which tax evasion/laundering decisions are reached in the light of the prevailing tax and penalty rates in existence.

Ferwerda (2009) also started from the expected utility function derived from committing an offence (using logic established by Becker, 1968). Assuming marginal utility of income to remain positive, he argues that utility derived will be lower the more severe the punishment and the higher the probability of conviction (Ferwerda, 2009, p. 905, citing Becker, 1968, p. 177). The author also examines the utility function expanded in Masciandaro (1999) that extended the utility function into consideration of the costs of money laundering. Ferwerda (2009, p. 910) in mapping out the relationship (indirect) between AML policy and underlying crime, theorises on the existence of a positive relationship between AML policy and the four identified deterrent variables. These are: the likelihood of being caught for money laundering (q); the likelihood of being caught for the predicate offence (z); the average sentence for money laundering (*f*ml); and the transaction cost (tc) (of laundering). As a tightening of money laundering policy will simultaneously increase the deterrent variables, they will also contribute to decreasing crime. That is an interesting hypothesis which must be researched against the counter hypothesis that the present decline in crime rates is due to the ageing of the industrialised world population: fewer youngsters in the crime-prone age of 16-24.

Ferwerda suggests that, at the country level, the degree of compliance with the FATF Recommendations could be used as a proxy for a policy variable. Using an expansion of the compliance scoring applied by Arnone and Borlini (2010), Ferwerda created a database for 17 countries in Europe and North America to quantify a country's compliance with the FATF's first 40 Recommendations. He analysed the recommendations within four different AML policy areas: legal (AML legal framework), private sector (SAR/STR requirements placed on regulated entities), public sector (FIU and regulations) and international cooperation (ratification of conventions and mutual legal assistance) (p. 915).[45] He concluded his work by arguing that international cooperation is particularly important in reducing crime.

b. Modelling regulation and regulatory compliance – utility and game theory

Papers that consider the relationship between the regulators and those subject to the regulations employ the 'principal-agent' relationship as a method of explanation. Araujo (2008, 2010) employed game theory decision trees to explore the range of possible outcomes arising from compliance decision making by banks. Araujo (2008) developed the theoretical structure around a principal-agent model to explain the relationship between the principal – regulator (in this case the FIU) – and the agent – in this case the banks who monitor their customers' activity on behalf of the regulator. Starting with an expression of both cost and demand functions for the supply of AML bank services to the regulator, the paper presents a series of propositions and corollaries (similar in approach to those followed by Masciandaro) under conditions of *imperfect information*. The asymmetry of information is in favour of the agent banks as only they know the circumstances in which they will or will not chose to cooperate. The paper establishes the conditions under which, theoretically, a bank would find it more profitable not to comply with the reporting regime. Araujo (2010) follows a similar approach but this time uses game theory to explore decision making by compliance employees of financial institutions. Illustrating arguments through the algebra of the utility function, he suggests that decisions to comply with regulations are driven by the expected loss arising from non-compliance. A too-obvious conclusion.

---

[45] To this he added four "control variables . . .to prevent the possibility of an omitted variable bias" (p. 916) these included Log GDP per capita; a dummy variable for common law countries; a variable for enforcement and for the extent of corruption. These are specified in the following equation (p. 919)

$$Crime_{ct} = \beta_0 + \beta_1\ Legal_c + \beta_2\ Public_c + \beta_3\ Private_c + \beta_4\ International_c + \beta_5\ Corruption_c + \beta_6\ Common\ law_c + \beta_7\ Enforcement_c + \beta_8 \log(GDPpercap)_{ct} + \beta_9 \log(GDPp/c)_c + U_{ct} +$$

Where: $crime_{ct}$ = total crime rate for country c at time t; $legal_c$ = is the legal AML framework; $public_c$ = institutional AML framework; $Private_c$ = responsibilities of private sector; $international_c$ = international cooperation to fight AML; $corruption_c$ = degree of control of corruption; common law_c = dummy variable for common law country; $enforcement_c$ = public enforcement index; log $(GDP/percap)_{ct}$ = log of GDP per capita at time t and log $(GDP/percap)_c$ = average per capita GDP and U_{ct} is the error term for panel data.

Takáts (2011) takes the same approach as Araujo (2008) and also uses game theory to explore the agency problem between the regulator/ and the banks.[46] He notes that the bank has the objective of maximising private profit (with compliance as a cost, they have to be forced to comply by fines for non-compliance).[47] The government wishes to maximise social welfare (where money laundering is seen to reduce welfare but prosecution is seen to increase social welfare). As we are in a hypothetical world, there is no mention of the 'costs' of enforcement and policing but the paper suggests that the more harmful the impact of laundering, the greater will be the gains from (assumed successful) prosecution.[48] None of which really moves us any further forward in terms of understanding.

Before moving on, it is appropriate to reflect on what these reviewed papers tell us. As already noted, definition, or lack thereof, is a major stumbling block for those writing within the field. A lack of methodological precision concerning what is counted and what is excluded means that there is no single point of departure and an undetermined borderline. This is rather like a mother and a mother-in-law each providing their fail-safe recipe for a Yorkshire pudding to the daughter (in law) that not only contain different amounts of the key ingredients but that is also not consistency in its proportions within the recipes.

The macroeconomic models have employed various approaches but all rely on implied methods of estimation for a variable (laundering) that is unobservable and determined by unclear rules of delineation. The elaboration of the model is achieved by estimating the various dimensions of criminal activity (most usually drugs, the wider underground economy and tax evasion) which are presented by means of proxy variables of which the reliability and validity is highly debatable. Hence, pretended outcomes based on serious methodological transgressions are allowed to pass on, neglecting publicised criticisms.

The microeconomists work within a another hypothetical vacuum in which the ingredients for the pudding recipe are clearly set out and proportions do not alter, but the recipe for the mixing is unclear. However, as all decision making is underpinned by utility, it does not matter for their theory whether they explore decisions by criminals to commission laundering services or those of compliance officers and their employing institutions to adhere to

[46] Note this paper was first published under the same title as an IMF working paper in April 2007 (WP/07/81); and on-line in the journal in 2009; so sometimes appears with this date.

[47] This is consistent with the findings from Sittlington (2015) that banks would certainly neither comply nor report nearly so much if it were not for the regulation (Sittlington, 2015, *"What are the Factors that Influence the Effectiveness of Anti-Money Laundering Policy Implementation in the UK: Exploring Money Laundering Crime and Policy?"* PhD thesis, University of Northumbria at Newcastle).

[48] This is described as a function of utility derived from asset seizure, deterrence of current and of future laundering and predicate crime.

regulations. The outcome for both comes down to the simple risk cost-benefit decision "will I get caught and, if caught, what will be the punishment".

7.8 Critics of the regime

A salutary observation is contributed by Alldridge (2003, p. 5) who, citing Van Duyne (1998), observed that had the amounts of laundered funds been near the sums estimated by economists, the impact would have been noticeable. It appears far from clear that evidence of the 'threat' is concrete enough to justify the exceedingly heavy countermeasures that have been required (Van Duyne and de Miranda, 1999; Van Duyne, 2007; Van Duyne *et al.*, 2018a). Indeed, we are not alone in questioning (see also Levi and Reuter, 2006) if the burden placed on legitimate commerce is justified by the prevention of 'mass criminal action' facilitated by allegedly global money laundering. Others unpick the foundations of the threat imposed by laundering on the integrity foundations of the financial system arguing that integrity is underpinned by trust and that it is this rather than criminal infiltration that is of paramount importance (Van Duyne *et al.*, 2005; Harvey and Lau, 2009). Van Duyne *et al.* also points to the absurdity found in statements by the FATF whereby absence of evidence is used in various ways to validate the existence of a threat: "I believe because I cannot see it" (Van Duyne *et al.*, 2005 p. 129). Rather than underpinned by phenomenological analysis, the threat presentation is determined by nebulae – shifting and reforming as required.

There will remain tension in the relationship between the regulator and the regulated sectors. To alleviate this tension both Masciandaro (1999) and Araujo (2010) argue that unless the objectives of the banks and other regulated sectors align with those of the regulator, the system will never work effectively (see also Bello and Harvey, 2017 and Bello, 2014).

7.9 Conclusion

The chapter has covered the main concerns of the economic literature, looking at both the models to measure laundering and those concerned with effectiveness of countermeasures. Certainly, the move toward greater globalisation over the past 30 years has opened opportunities within the legitimate economy.

We started this chapter by identifying the problems concerning what is and what is not to be counted and the pressure from the economists' corner for a unified definition of predicate offence (see for example Busuioc, 2007).

Within the criminal codes the requirement to criminalise an activity is generally based upon the principle of 'harm'. From that perspective the alleged 'distortion of economic statistics' by itself does not really amount to such criminal law justification (Alldridge, 2002). Both Alldridge (2002) and Van Duyne *et al.* (2016, 2018a) argue strongly in favour of the principle of proportionality in this field. If we think back to the content of Chapter 3.4, the reader will recall that a large part of the justifications for the global approach to AML were drawn from concerns regarding the security of the global financial system. But these were justifications underneath which there were also strong national financial motives fed by concerns of cross-border tax evasion. So, it was almost a foregone conclusion that the rules (originally devised in the USA) would be rolled out on a global basis and enforced with a mixture of coercion and control seemingly without consideration as to appropriateness or indeed necessity. We turn to this in the next chapter.

Overlooking the academic economic output of studies and research on money laundering we find that a number of shortcomings appear to emerge in most publications, though not all of them occur at the same time in a single document or to the same degree. These are the known pitfalls one finds in every discipline and we are certainly not exempt ourselves from falling into such researcher's traps.

- In nearly all publications we find loose definitions of the key concepts, the most basic being that of money laundering. This makes many statements and conclusions undeterminable;
- There is a regular lack of proper methodology: for example data collection is not properly accounted for; test procedures are not transparent or are absent;
- The basic questions of reliability and validity in shared/re-used databases are not raised;
- There is often a gross generalisation over different subpopulations (one fits all), while such heterogeneity requires single analysis first and comparison for general conclusions later;
- There is lack of external criterion testing of models: outcomes of the application of theoretical models must be compared with other data in the field of application to determine the degree of concurrence.

We realise that there may be pressure to meet expectations from principals and the mainstream discourse which can lead to a confirmation bias and retrospective rationalisation. Altogether, the AML is not only a technical system, it is also a political and social system with which researchers have to interact. And while a researcher's models may be high in the air, the AML institutions are right down on the earth with impact on research and fact finding in which they have an interest: their representatives allocate the grants and subsidies and may determine a researcher's next project. Though that is an earthly reality and concern, as a researcher, one cannot walk away from methodology and proper concept analysis.

8

Behaviour and impact 'on the ground'

8.1 Introduction

A book on the subject of money laundering would not be complete without consideration of the impact of the AML framework on those that are subject to its rules. Indeed, any critical inter-disciplinary study within the social sciences would remain incomplete without such discussion. The purpose of this review of literature, identified through the search strategy described in Chapter 2, aims to address that broader impact by examining publications from the fields of regulation, criminology and sociology.

The consequences of a regime of such global importance and scope will have touched upon a very wide range of states, their societies, institutions and indeed individuals. These consequences will inevitably vary in their magnitude depending on how many touch points there have been. By this, we mean the affected parties: the countries, the policy makers, the regulators and law enforcement agencies, the judiciary, the regulated sector, the compliance industry, criminals and indeed tax payers. The earlier chapters in this book identified and explored some of these dimensions. We have considered the justification for the establishment of the regime from its roots in the USA during the 1980s, through to its adoption by the (then) G7 and the creation of the FATF. We have considered the evidence for the global approach (scale of organised crime, drugs, tax evasion) and looked at the sources of the data deployed by way of justification. We have also looked at what has been discussed in the literature about the impact of the adoption of the Recommendations both on national legislative autonomy and on the regulated sector.

P.C. van Duyne, J.H. Harvey and L.Y. Gelemerova, *The Critical Handbook of Money Laundering*, https://doi.org/10.1057/978-1-137-52398-3_8

This book has drawn attention to what is known of the costs of this regime. This is not only from the point of view of the new organisations that have come into existence as a consequence but also from the cost of running the process of mutual evaluation by all members of all members, whether enforced through the FATF itself, or through one of the regional FATF-style regional bodies, the FSRBs. Of course, the costs of running the regime also imply costs for those subject to its inspection: the countries and their own regulators and legislative regimes. Costs fall on the state through firstly, the state mechanisms of law enforcement: the police, the judiciary and the prison systems. Secondly, through the supervision and reporting of this part of the regime through the FIU and respective regulators. The final burden arrives at the door of the regulated sectors and ultimately to a country's citizens, whether law abiding or criminal. As the regulated institutions are mostly private sector, they naturally seek to achieve the objective of minimising the costs to themselves while at the same time pursing profitable business opportunities. An obvious dimension of cost avoidance is by avoiding fines for non-compliance. However, additionally, they will most likely pass on these costs to their customers. Another possible dimension is avoiding cost by avoiding certain categories of risky clients, or 'de-risking'.

Discussion within this chapter is, therefore, organised around the impact of the regime on the states, the regulated sector, its employees and customers and finally on the criminals themselves. As an impact implies a consequence, it is also appropriate to consider the subsequent behaviour of those who have been affected by the AML regime. Of course this 'impact' will vary according to the size of the state and its economy or indeed the number and range of its regulated entities. There may well be instances of 'collateral' impact, or unintended effects. For small countries and those less developed, the burden will be disproportionately heavy, and may require the diversion of financial and other resources from other, much needed, areas. On the other hand, such countries may consider that the accruing benefits of a reduction in crime (including capital flight, if criminalised) or fewer opportunities for corrupt officials to misappropriate funds from the state, would more than compensate for this burden.

8.2 The actions of the states and the persuasiveness of the 'club'

Action at this level can be explored at the level of the individual states through their adoption of the Recommendations in national legislation. It can further be considered across a number of states, *e.g.* those member countries of the FATF who collectively have influenced other countries to join 'the club'. If we go back to examine the 1990 'Financial Action Task Force on Money

Laundering Report' it is clear that the approach was always going to be reliant upon collective action. Their conclusion (p. 28) drew attention to the importance of political support; that their recommendations should be rolled out globally; and, that the process would be expedited through regular assessment of progress. The wider the range of countries applying their recommendations "... the greater their efficiency would be". Nothing was mentioned, however, about how countries would be encouraged to adopt the rules other than by '*political impetus*'. What transpired was recruitment through moral righteousness on the part of those that were early adopters. These countries employed a great deal of persuasion to initially encourage other countries to make the political commitment required to gain their entry into the 'club'. Once the club was formed, further countries did not become members of the FATF for that privilege was restricted to the 35-member jurisdictions and two regional organisations. They could join one of the nine FATF-style regional bodies (FSRBs) who have observer status with the FATF.

However, as things progressed, there was very little to suggest that states had any real choice over whether or not to adopt the Recommendations. As a matter of fact they were persuaded of the need for adherence to the rules through somewhat unsubtle coercion (a 'stiff letter', a 'high level visit' and the early NCCT regime, latterly the 'public list' of deficient countries). Not all academics agreed with this 'pressured' approach. For example, Pieth (1999, p. 530) writing about countries hosting offshore centres, questions "'the legitimacy of collective pressure' brought to bear against countries". It seems that public opinion was brought onto the side of the new regime by the righteousness of the implied actions being taken against organised criminals and its assumed destabilising effects of the international trade in drugs. It is worth reiterating here that the first FATF Report mentioned above was *only* concerned with money laundering arising from the production and trade in drugs and that the 40 Recommendations set out in the appendix to this report were, therefore, drafted from this perspective. We commented in Chapters 4 and 6.1 that the roots of the FATF tree had been planted in the USA in the 1970s and 1980s and it was from here that the threat from drugs and organised crime was linked with the alleged "explosion in the laundering of 'hot money' into the international banking system" (Taylor, 1992, p. 183). This explosion was, as presented by the authorities, entirely attributed to the growth in drug trafficking that occurred in the 1980s. Taylor (1992) suggests that this was the basis of an entirely misleading formulation in the approach to money laundering. This is because it was linked to the activity of drug barons, earning millions in dirty or 'hot' money that, reflecting the dominant discourse at the time, was transferred through the offshore banking sector to be recycled into legitimate business. Having gained legitimacy for the 'war on drugs', US law enforcement were able to extend their reach into the business sector, in particular banking, which was seen as a facilitator of such activity. That the USA was able to conduct this war and indeed extend it to all organised crime was evidence that it had been elevated to a matter of *national security* (Rider, 1999). This is not surprising: from the beginning (1986), an international dimension had been included (see Chapter 3). This made it easier for the Clinton administration to exert influence on a wide range of countries (Harvey, 2005). Naylor (1999) suggested that the US banks, having found themselves subject to a range of reporting restrictions, were supportive to those same restrictions being adopted by other countries (or imposed). For the US banks this was a way of levelling up the regulatory field and restoring their competitive advantage.

It has been suggested (Wechsler, 2001) that this task was made easier through the occurrence of the 1997 South-East Asian financial crisis.[1] This crisis and its rapid contagion, provided support to the arguments of the FATF that financial abuse could undermine the efficiency of the international financial system. The FATF found natural allies in two further organisations. Firstly, the G7's Financial Stability Forum that focused on promoting stability and the reduction of systemic risk in the global financial system. Secondly, the OECD which had a particular focus on tax evasion and offshore finance centres (OFCs) (Wechsler, 2001). The OFCs were regarded as the main culprit, undermining the tax regimes of other countries through differential treatment of domestic and non-domestic residents (Harvey, 2005). However, as mentioned in the chapter 7, what is conveniently overlooked is that such centres were set up in a number of former British colonies to provide sustainable sources of income as they became independent.

The international community has long been interested in OFCs because of concerns over their lack of transparency. Firstly because they enable legitimate tax avoidance schemes and, from there, diversify into the arena of illegitimate tax evasion. Secondly, their perceived attractiveness to money launderers. However, the difference between on- and offshore is not just a question of geography; offshore centres operate across the globe in developed financial centres (for example, Singapore and Hong Kong) as well as in micro economies such as Niue. Neither is it possible to locate a clear definitional dividing line between on- and offshore with offshore activity legitimately taking place within global financial markets such as New York and London and within specific parts of a country (Delaware in the USA, Macau in China). Lately a debate emerged whether the Netherlands, otherwise an 'unsuspected coun-

[1] The Asian financial crisis saw a series of currency devaluations that started with the de-pegging of the Thai Bhat from the US dollar that spread through the Asian markets during the summer of 1997. The large currency declines in turn caused stock market falls and reduced import revenues and required IMF and World Bank intervention to stem the contagion.

try', should be considered an off-shore centre because of its generous tax rulings for multi-nationals.[2]

It is, therefore, important that this approach should be subject to critical examination. The AML framework has girdled the earth and found its way into the national legislation of some 190 countries. Given this spread it might be hoped that this has been achieved in a way that is totally transparent and safeguards the basic means of democratic control and the rule of law. Absence of transparency and vagueness are serious matters that should not be waved away as pedantic pettiness, as it facilitates the usurpation of power and influence. As we discussed in Chapter 3, there has been a dual approach to tackling money laundering: the road of legality through treaties and (UN) conventions and the road of informality as chosen by the G-7 in 1989 by installing the FATF as an informal policy advisory club (Goldbarsht and Michaelsen, 2017). This informal advisory group had the advantage of circumventing the formalities of traditional international approaches requiring democratic votes and formal adoption procedures. For the USA, the initiator and leading force in this field and in light of the discussion above, the democratic route was not an attractive option (Wechsler, 2001). Not only because of the built-in uncertainty of outcome, but also because a formal treaty course only would bind the signatory countries, potentially, restricting its adoption to a far smaller group of member countries and jurisdictions. Goldbarsht and Michaelsen (2017) further point out that the FATF has arrogated an enforcement authority that is at odds with the principles of the rule of law operating in the civilised world. As we discussed in Chapters 3 and 5, the FATF itself (the Plenary as the collective voice of its members), investigates whether a country is compliant. On this basis it determines the seriousness of non-compliance, gives a judgment and determines what sanctions to impose. While authors have raised concerns at the ability of the FATF to override the role of national legislature (Stessens, 2001; Pieth, 1999) there has been no apparent public, meaningful debate of this fundamental matter. Are the national parliaments not the final responsible organs of state? In theory yes, but Goldbarsht and Michaelsen (2017, p. 215) observe critically with respect to the response of Australia to the third round of its MER "this process of norm-development reduces domestic parliaments to rubber stamping institutions".

Noting that the USA supported the informal influencing approach, it suited the Reagan Administration to make use of informal mechanisms to reinforce the need for action to tackle the problems of drugs and organised

[2] Van Koningsveld (2015) took stock of the many definitions of 'off-shore' to conclude that there is little discipline in providing a precise delineation to this concept.

crime by having the media sound the alarm. Indeed, the support of the media no doubt assisted in the creation of a new category of crime and a criminal 'problem' from something (money laundering) that was not criminal at the time (Nichols, 1997, p. 324, see also van Duyne *et al.*, 2005, Hulsse, 2007 and Alldridge, 2008). Hulsse (2007, p. 156) examines the extent to which the phenomenon of money laundering was a politically created problem, an occurrence that he terms "problematisation." Elsewhere in the literature, this is referred to as 'claims-making' in relation to conditions that ought not to exist and about which apparently something needs to be done (Nichols, 1997; Harvey and Ashton, 2015).

Under this scenario, once other countries were persuaded that the 'problem' of money laundering existed, the methods and procedures proposed for problem-solving quickly become seen as both justified and necessary. In this way, an abstract problem-creation became underpinned and reinforced by untrue or fake 'facts'. In the case of money laundering these facts were the volume of laundered funds in existence. The FATF quickly became elevated as *the* authority on the issue such that its statements were attributed a great deal of objective value. Statements on the alleged scale of the problem, on its apparent undermining of the financial system and of adversely impacting on economic activity, were swallowed as absolute truths. However, as we have already pointed out in chapter 7, these facts were not always as certain as they were presented. For as vividly stated by Naylor (1999, p. 6) "it is not necessary to take the square root of a negative sum to arrive at a purely imaginary number". In less colourful but similar fashion, Steinko (2012) is astonished that the international AML regime has managed to penetrate so many legal systems in so many countries without any actual evidence of threat. That omission was skilfully circumvented by what van Duyne and Nelemans (2011) called "the indicative bias": the sliding of the subjunctive formulation (may, might, could) towards the indicative '*is*'. After two or more quotations or cross-references in other official documents the subjunctive has slid to "is" and become a generally accepted *fact*. Further, where laundering does occur (see section 8.4) it is far more mundane than the way presented in the official discourse. There appears to be no evidence that it occurs on such a scale that it can threaten the stability of the financial system. We do not claim money laundering is harmless but a broad and all-sweeping 'one size fits all' approach at this stage appears disproportionate and, therefore, less effective.

Despite a lack of evidence and as already discussed in Chapter 3, as more countries were persuaded of the value of the cause, those opposing found themselves not simply in opposition to the FATF, but against the collective stand of all other (rich and powerful) countries. It is small wonder that the majority of them readily fell into line. States that were members of the FATF were able to use persuasion and coercion, although they preferred to couch their action in the language of cooperation and encouragement. Thus they came to embrace the more recalcitrant countries and those who nominally had little to gain through adherence to the AML-rules (Hulsse, 2007; Levi and Gilmore, 2002). For these latter countries, persuasion took on a more forceful character (see for example, Sharman, 2008). We have already discussed the emergence of the formal public blacklisting through the pillory of the NCCT (see Chapter 5). The source of these blacklists was examined by Stessens (2001). He argued that in 1990, the FATF explicitly rejected the idea of a 'black list' of 'non-cooperative jurisdictions'. He noted that this same position was adopted by the European Parliament at the same time. This was in its debate on the then draft Money Laundering Directive in 1991 when it rejected an amendment to "prohibit financial transactions with third countries that did not apply comparative standards against money laundering to those established by the Community" (Stessens, 2001, footnote 22, p. 206). Nevertheless, it did appear in a "watered-down form" in the preamble. Hulsse (2008) extended the idea of the 'club' model of regulation, arguing that the FATF suspended the use of the 'successful' coercive method of blacklisting because it only ensured formal compliance (*i.e.* box ticking and ducks in a row) rather than actual compliance. He helpfully highlights the authors that have drawn attention to such superficial compliance as set out in Table 8.1:

Actual compliance implies that those subject to the rules are willing to conform because they accept the legitimacy of such rules, or feel compelled to do so. Hulsse (2007) suggested that the third round Mutual Evaluation process was evidence of the FATF shifting towards a more accommodating or persuasive, 'softer' approach to compliance with its Recommendations. Although, at the same time, Hulsse (2007) acknowledged that the blacklist

Table 8.1 Authors drawing attention to superficial compliance

Types of compliance	Authors
'paper compliance'	Biersteker, *et al.* 2008, p. 241
'compliance in the books'	Unger & Ferwerda, 2008, p. 4
'form is elevated over substance'	Simmons 2000; Williams and Baudin-O'Hayon 2002; Harvey 2005; Gardner 2007; Roberge, 2007; Tsingou, 2007; Biersteker, *et al.* 2008
'mimicry'	Sharman 2008, p. 646
'engaging in cosmetic forms of conformity but doing little to implement their obligations'	Williams and Baudin-O'Hayon, 2002, p. 140
"simply results in a 'window-dressing' exercise by 'non-cooperative' jurisdictions so that their names can be removed from the list"	Leong, 2007, p. 152; see also Daepp, 2006
'It has increased formal compliance with the FATF rules, but it has – according to most observers – done little to reduce, leave alone rule out money laundering'	Sica, 2000; Doyle, 2002; Kremer, 2004; Sharman 2008; Reuter and Truman, 2004; see also Levi 2008; Naylor, 2002

Source: Hulsse (2008, p. 467), adapted and expanded by the authors.

approach had achieved its objective (also see for example, Gallant, 2010). Hulsse also noted that this may have been partly influenced by both the IMF and the World Bank, institutions that were against the idea of blacklisting (Hulsse, 2007, p. 167). The IMF Report (2011, p. 13 note 21) clearly states "In 2002, the Executive Board conditioned the Fund's involvement in AML/CFT assessments and cooperation with the FATF on the suspension of the NCCT initiative".[3] The note goes on to state that "in 2004, in the context of the decision to make AML/CFT assessments a regular part of the ROSC program, Directors agreed on the importance of continuing collaboration with the FATF and welcomed the fact that the FATF had no plans to conduct a further round of the NCCT exercise".[4]

Stessens (2001) went so far as to suggest that the FATF was more stringent with its standards and requirements where states were not OECD members, although he did not provide specific examples. Nevertheless he concluded that its credibility would have been enhanced had it been "more critical of its own members" (p. 208). Differential application in standards is perhaps most obvious in the case of the USA which operates within its own 'onshore state' a number of offshore centres in: Delaware, Wyoming, Utah, and Nevada (Levi and Gilmore, 2002). This difference in standards according to geographic location was also observed by Rosdol (2007) who noted in her review of crown dependencies and British overseas territories of Bermuda and the Cayman Islands that they had in place more stringent AML measures than the equivalent on-shore financial centres of the UK, Australia and the USA. While earlier, Hampton and Levi (1999), suggested that the chances of a country being targeted by the FATF was far higher if they were recipients of international aid, had small defence forces, and were considered strategically unimportant (Hampton and Levi, 1999). However, this argument was subsequently partially refuted by the fact that both Russia and Israel found themselves added to the black list in 2000-2001, though they do not fulfil these characteristics.

Chapters 1 and 3 of this book have discussed the early origins of money laundering policy in the legislation of the USA, commencing in 1970 with The Bank Secrecy Act. It is apparent that laundering received a boost in the public attention because of the Bank of Boston affair. For its apparent contravention of the currency reporting required under the 1970 Bank Secrecy Act, the Bank of Boston agreed to pay a criminal fine of $0.5 million (Abramovsky, 1986; Nichols, 1997). Although this bank was singled out, it was not alone in

[3] International Monetary Fund (2011) Anti-Money Laundering and Combating the Financing of Terrorism (AML/CFT) – Report on the Review of the Effectiveness of the Program Prepared by the Legal Department (in consultation with other departments). Approved by Sean Hagan, 11 May 2011.

[4] Reports on the Observance of Standards and Codes.

its failure to report (Hinterseer, 2001, cited in van Duyne *et al.*, 2005). A number of banks at the time were in violation of the currency reporting requirements that required them to record transactions over $10,000 together with a description of the customer. However, "The transition to major scandal was effected through a crucial rhetorical move that transformed 'non-reporting' into 'money laundering'" (Nichols, 1997, p. 327). We discussed in Chapter 3, that non-reporting of suspicious transactions, among other reasons, paved the way for the passage of the Money Laundering Control Act, 1986. Academics critical of this legislation argued that the currency reporting requirements were "an example of over-trumpeted intelligence gathering methodology" (Levi, 1991 cited in van Duyne *et al.,* 2005, p. 120). Uppermost in the minds of critics was concern that this legislation gave police access to confidential tax and financial records (Naylor, 1999 and Rider, 1999). They suggested that while ostensibly introduced under the banner of the fight against drug trafficking (see Gelemerova, 2011), it also enabled a focus on tax evasion.

Nevertheless, the extent to which a small group of countries was able to influence the actions of just about every other country within the global financial system, is an important observation. As indicated above, whether such state of affairs is justified, would largely depend on the effectiveness of the regime (Hulsse, 2007). Indeed, measuring effectiveness is essential if we are to justify the resources diverted into compliance activity by both the regulated entities and those tasked with their policing. However, Goldby (2013, pp. 368–369) argues that "there is no consensus on the exact meaning of 'effectiveness' and the correct method of measuring it". Both Goldby (2013) and Harvey (2009) noted the difficulty of the approach. Theoretically, effectiveness of AML would correspond to a reduction in laundering and, by implication, profit directed (organised) crime. In a scientific setting, a 'control' experiment would be employed to determine the positive impact of the regime as it would be possible to look at changes of crime rate before (a baseline) and after the introduction of the AML legislation. That is not an easy approach, because there are many other intervening variables that may influence crime rates, such as population composition ('greying') or criminal market changes. Hence, the focus on indirect measures. The FATF had set out in Recommendation 33, Interpretive Note, that effectiveness can be assessed through:

> "statistics on the [suspicious transaction reports (STRs)] received and disseminated; on money laundering and terrorist financing investigations, prosecutions and convictions; on property frozen, seized and confiscated; and on mutual legal assistance or other international requests for co-operation."

To call these 'indirect measures' of effectiveness is methodologically wrong. With the exception of convictions and confiscations these are rather *internal system* measurements, measuring various outputs within the system. These can measure internal effectiveness, but for measuring the main AML aims, integrity of the financial system and crime reduction, they are unsuitable. For example, the number of STRs/SARs received reflects the interaction between the obliged entities and the FIU plus background 'noise', such as the cleaning up of backlogs. It was noted that the focus on STRs was quietly dropped (with attention being shifted to what constitutes suspicious activity and, later, with a focus on a risk-based approach) when it became apparent that the number of reports began to rise exponentially and that the data capture systems of the FIUs became clogged with meaningless information. Reporting all and sundry was a method to avoid a reproach for having missed a suspicious case, which was difficult to recognise: so, if in doubt you rather report. This led to what the FATF called 'defensive reporting', while filing STRs should be *risk based*. In Chapter 7 we commented on the limited quantitative information contained within MERs on ML, prosecutions and convictions. Harvey (2009) suggested that a more valuable measure of effectiveness here might be the conversion rate of prosecutions to convictions. However, that is also an internal criterion. Could asset recovery be considered an external effect measure? "*Hitting criminals where it hurts them most*", is an often-quoted phrase. Though this phrase sounds more revengeful than aiming for effectiveness, it must be rejected on two grounds: (a) it remains within the criminal law system as it does not indicate a change in crime rate and (b) it is not an AML component but has been absorbed into the AML discourse. Further, asset recovery is a consequence of another principle: restorative justice. We return to this question in Chapter 9.

Apart from these considerations hard data on AML effects are rarely found within the MERs. The presentation in the MERs of quantitative data is anything but professional and is frequently at odds with the FATF Recommendation on AML statistics (R. 33). This point is a frequent criticism by the assessors to the evaluated member states. But despite the, nothing happens. It is the FATF, which by neglecting database building from the beginning, remained in a state of *camera obscura* (van Duyne *et al.*, 2005; pp. 69–95). At present, reliable and valid data on criminal law processing of cases up to assets recovery is not widely reported within the MERs. Further, data reported by the FIUs is often modified year on year making analysis of trends difficult (Harvey, 2014). There has been criticism of the 'cost effectiveness' of AML measures as discussed in Section 7.4 where we looked at the regulatory impact assessments. This criticism concerns particularly the asset recovery regime where authors (see for example, Harvey, 2008; Chaikin, 2009; Sproat, 2007, 2009a and 2009b) have analysed the cost of recovering for each criminal pound or dollar.

As it has, therefore, proved difficult to demonstrate any reduction in actual money laundering, emphasis has, as a result, shifted instead towards demonstrating effectiveness with compliance (but that is internal to the system). This is something to which we turn our attention in the next sections.

8.2.1 Joining the club and adhering to the rules; enforcement and mutual evaluation

Persuading others of the moral value of the objectives of the FATF club is only one dimension of the collective behaviour of the states. Once a country has been persuaded of the benefit of membership (either voluntarily or because it is considerably colder to be left outside), their continued membership has to be regulated and evaluated against the club rules, in this case the 40 Recommendations and guidance notes. These are the cornerstone to the approach of the FATF and, as discussed in Chapter 3, they are expensive to operate.

The evaluations are conducted by a small group of 'peers' and assesses compliance for each of the FATF Recommendations. This involves visits across the whole of a country and meetings with representatives of all involved, from the civil servants, through to the regulators, judiciary, law enforcement and FIU. In addition, there are meetings with representatives from a range of regulated bodies and organisations. All this must be achieved by a group of seven to eleven assessors in about two weeks. Prior to the visit, there is a desk-based review of submitted documentation. Following the visit, the report has to be drafted and then circulated to the reviewed country for the correction of factual inaccuracy prior to it being discussed and adopted at one of the plenary meetings.

In the present (fourth) evaluation round the recommendations of the evaluation team are reviewed by a different team of three reviewers in an attempt to provide consistency with other evaluations in interpretation and recommendation. Depending on the outcome, there may be follow-up and further reviews and reporting. A summary of the approaches followed during both the third round and the current fourth round are presented in the Tables 8.2 and 8.4 below. It is worth reminding ourselves of the extensive nature of the evaluation process. There were a total of 151 countries inspected over the period 2006 to 2014 during the third round.[5] Looking forward to the fourth Round, the FATF identifies 132 states that have been scheduled for evaluation

[5] Data taken from FATF website page 'Assessments Calendar' available at: http://www.fatf-gafi.org/calendar/assessmentcalendar/?hf=10&b=10&s=asc(document_lastmodifieddate)&table=1. Accessed 22 September 2017.

visits over the period from 2016 to 2024. In addition, there are a further 42 states identified as requiring inclusion in the programme, bringing the total to 174.

It might seem reasonable to infer, given the cost and scale of this exercise, not to mention its impact on each of the reviewed countries, that this would be an area that would evoke the interest of scholars. Such interest has been apparent, although the numbers that have undertaken any detailed enquiry in the area are relatively small (see, for example, Sharman, 2008; Ferwerda, 2009; Arnone and Padoan, 2008; Johnson, 2008; Chaikin, 2009; and Gordon, 2011).

Arnone and Padoan (2008) looked specifically at the degree of compliance by Recommendation for 20 countries for whom information was available on the FATF website, by attributing a numerical score to the ratings whereby Not Applicable = 0; Partially Compliant = 1; Largely Compliant = 2; and Compliant = 3.[6] This enabled them to identify for their sample, a range of overall average compliance levels and specific weaknesses against each of the areas covered by the Recommendations. They concluded their paper by considering the problems of the approach specifically noting (p. 382) "too many assessors, uneven quality of reports" alongside inconsistency in the layout of the reports.

Similarly, Ferwerda (2009) found that the MERs differed substantially in terms of underlying quality as well as in the size of the reports themselves. However, he was also of the opinion that the assessment of degree of compliance was influenced by the resources available to the country being assessed (with more expected of more developed countries). In consequence, he argues that the scores for different countries should not be compared in the manner of Arnone and Padoan (2008). Instead, he proposed an alternative scoring system that he applied to a sample of 17 countries.[7] This scale went from 0 for no action performed through to 5 which is comprehensive implementation. He cross tabulated against the work of Arnone and Padoan (2008) for those countries that appeared in both samples in an attempt to provide evidence of consistency. Johnson (2008) also applied a numeric scale to convert the assessment but chose instead Not Compliant (0), Partially Compliant (0.33), Largely Compliant (0.67) and Compliant (1.0) before undertaking a similar assessment of compliance for 16 countries.[8] Her contribution is to consider average levels of compliance before and after 2003 (from the self-assessment

6 Australia, Belgium, Czech Republic, France, Guatemala, Honduras, Iceland, Ireland, Italy, Jamaica, Luxembourg, Norway, Portugal Samoa, Sri Lanka, Spain, Sweden, Switzerland, the USA and Venezuela.

7 Australia, Austria, Belgium, Denmark, France, Germany, Greece, Ireland, Italy, Luxembourg, the Netherlands, Norway, Portugal, Spain, Sweden, the UK and the USA.

8 Australia, Belgium, China, Denmark, Greece, Iceland, Ireland, Italy, Norway, Portugal, Spain, Sweden, Switzerland, Turkey, the UK and the USA.

method to the third round mutual evaluation) concluding that there had been a reduction in levels of compliance, a finding which does not accord with the FATF mention of "significant progress" being made.

Chaikin (2009, pp. 242–244) provides a good overview of the approach followed under the third round and its limitations – in particular that 'effectiveness' is subjective. He is focussed on outputs (in particular STRs /SARs) but ignores the costs associated with any system. Sharman (2008, p. 641) noted that the appropriate measure of 'effectiveness' for the FATF in both 2004 and 2007 was both "number of convictions and asset confiscation". However, as we earlier discussed, many of the MERs show little quantitative data around either of these two measures. And when they are included the numbers are low, which can be interpreted in two opposite ways: there is a serious underscoring or there is a serious overestimation of the prevalence of laundering. Unsurprisingly the FATF thinks the answer is the underscoring.

Those that have discussed the effectiveness of the evaluation process have included considerations of the impact or reality of what it actually means to adhere to a regime imposing a set of Recommendations designed to meet the needs of large OECD countries with highly developed financial systems (Sharman, 2008; Rider, 1999). Sharman (2008, pp. 642–643) looked in detail at Barbados, Vanuatu and Mauritius as part of his consideration of evidence of regime effectiveness.[9] He observes what he termed the absurdity of Vanuatu drafting its AML legislation as "a word for word copy of the UN model" while there was nothing intrinsically wrong with such an enthusiastic approach, he does point to the inclusion of "provisions for complex financial derivatives that do not exist in the country" (p. 642). Despite this considerable compliance effort by Vanuatu, as discussed by van Duyne *et al.* (2018a) this did not mean that it had an easy time, finding itself placed on the serious warning list.

As mentioned above, the MER process itself has been criticised for only being able to determine the effectiveness of the compliance systems (input measures) rather than the reduction of money laundering or terrorist financing (output measures) (Gordon, 2011). van Duyne *et al.* (2016) also drew attention to the variability in quality of the reports and to the fact that some countries might have warranted more care and attention. For example, Uganda with a Transparency International (TI) rating of 2.7 in 2005 and an average compliance rating of 1.2; a modal rating of 1 (non-compliant) had a visit by a team of only four persons who produced a report of 82 pages. Contrast this with France, visited in 2011. France has a TI rating of 7.4 and an average compliance score of 2.9, modal rating of 3 (largely compliant), but was visited by a team of seven people who produced a report that ran to 664 pages.

---

9 Sharman also usefully includes estimates of the cost of compliance for these countries ranging from $10 m p.a. for Barbados and Mauritius to $1.5 m p.a. for Vanuatu for the period 2002-05.

Table 8.2 Summary of approach under the third round MER

Area	Observation
Purpose of MER	Assessment of formal compliance with Recommendations and assessment of effectiveness of implementation. Rating for each recommendation as Compliant (C); Largely Compliance (LC); Partially Compliant (PC); and Non-Compliant (NC); Not Applicable (NA).
Assessment team	Appointed by FATF Secretariat from FATF members, associate members, FATF-style regional bodies or international organisations with observer status.
Skills	The team will include experts in law, law enforcement and financial regulation with expertise in AML/CFT and includes a member of FATF secretariat. They will not necessarily have country specific knowledge
Scope of review	Institutional framework; AML/CFT laws, regulations and guidance including both law and regulatory enforcement; assessment of effectiveness of the system to deter ML and CFT
Documentation	FATF Methodology for Assessing Compliance with the FATF 40+9 and a Handbook for Countries and Assessors.
Approach	Pre-visit completion of a questionnaire, team visit for a period of 2 weeks comprising meetings with government officials and with private sector; post visit drafting of the report in consultation with officials within the country. The report is tabled and further discussed at one of the Plenary meetings when the ratings can be amended and once consensus is reached the report is published. Within 2 years the inspected country has to report back to the plenary on progress made in addressing identified deficiencies.

Source: van Duyne *et al.* (2016) and original adapted from Chaikin, 2009, pp. 242–244, but see also Levi and Gilmore (2002, p. 346), Halliday, Levi and Reuter (2014, p. 27).

As commented upon by van Duyne *et al.* (2016) the third round was hamstrung by its subjectivity. As teams were effectively assessing compliance with recommendations, each team appeared to have its own interpretation and hence a unique 'measuring rod'. This came clearly to the fore in the application of the score 'partially compliant' which provided such a range of interpretations that it almost required its own mini calibration to distinguish between almost compliant at the one end and just better than non-compliant at the other!

The tabular representation in Table 8.2 above of the third round MER implies a closed process that is complete at least within two years of the report being accepted. This is in fact far from the end of the matter. To give an idea how this worked under the third round, we will present a few examples from this procedure of monitoring and follow-up homework, highlighting how they have little relation to the size of country, the complexity of its financial sector, or its apparent vulnerability to criminal infiltration. This observation is illustrated by Table 8.3 which contains information on the follow-up procedure (or its absence) for a selection of countries. From this table it can be observed that the CFATF is the most assiduous group in the post evaluation follow-up requirements that are placed upon individual countries. Despite this it also took a decision at its El Salvador Plenary that all Members who had

Table 8.3 Examples of follow-up to a Mutual Evaluation

Country	Date of MER	Regional body	Average compliance score	Modal compliance rating	TPI 2006	Follow up reports
Colombia	Dec. 2008	GAFILAT	3.2	3	3.9	One follow-up report for 2009 nothing further in public domain
Uruguay	Dec. 2009	GAFILAT	2.9	3	6.4	Four follow-up reports from earlier MER 2006 nothing further in public domain after 2009
Paraguay	Dec. 2008	GAFILAT	1.5	1	2.6	Also evaluated in 2005; two follow up reports both in 2009
Dominican Republic	Oct. 2006	CFATF	1.9	2	2.8	13 follow-up reports latest May 2015 Looking to the future mutual evaluation it is suggested that Dominican Republic report to the November Plenary 2015 with a view to fully rectify outstanding deficiencies for the third round.
Barbados	June 2008	CFATF	2.5	2	6.7	13 follow-up reports latest May 2015 As a result of the late submission of the matrix by Barbados, the Secretariat was not able to prepare the relevant follow-up report for the consideration of the Plenary. As such, it is recommended to Plenary that the Secretariat should complete the present report by July 15, 2015 and submit it for approval of delegates via round robin process.
Anguilla	July 2010	CFATF	2.7	2	1.3 (2010)	Seven follow-up reports latest May 2015 The El Salvador Plenary decided that Anguilla would remain in regular expedited follow-up and report back to Plenary in May 2015, at which time a determination would be made as to whether Anguilla would remain in regular expedited follow-up or be assigned to another category of follow-up reporting.
Norway	June 2005	FATF	2.7	3	8.8	Four follow-up and 1 biennial, the last follow up report (fourth) February 2009 recommended that the Plenary exercise its flexibility and remove Norway from the regular follow up process, with a view to having it present its first biennial update in June 2011. That report makes no comment on when the next report be submitted and no others are on the FATF site

(*continued*)

Table 8.3 (continued)

Country	Date of MER	Regional body	Average compliance score	Modal compliance rating	TPI 2006	Follow up reports
Belgium	June 2005	FATF	3.2	4	7.3	Three biennial reports none of the reports are published, 3rd update was in June 2011, in 2015 Belgium was reviewed under the 4th round
USA	June 2006	FATF and APG	3.1	3	7.3	No documents other than the MER in the public domain
Sri Lanka	July 2006	APG	1.8	2	3.1	No documents other than the MER in the public domain
Australia	Oct. 2005	APG	2.6	3	8.7	No follow up evaluated April 2015 under the fourth round
Vietnam	July 2009	APG	1.7	2	2.6	No documents other than the MER in the public domain
Bahrain	Nov. 2006	MENAFATF	2.5	2	5.7	Four follow-up reports, 4th report in 2012 recommended removal of Bahrain from follow up process to biennial updating
Tunisia	April 2007	MENAFATF/ World Bank	2.4	2	4.6	Six follow-up reports, latest June 2014 recommended removal from regular follow up to biennial updates
Sudan	Nov. 2012	MENAFATF	1.7	1	1.3 (2014)	No documents other than the MER in the public domain
Sierra Leonne	June 2007	GIABA/World Bank	1.3	1	2.2	12 follow-up reports, latest May 2015
Ghana	Nov. 2009	GIABA	1.7	2	3.3	Four follow-up reports, most recent, November 2012
Lithuania	Nov. 2006	MONEYVAL	2.8	2	4.8	Two biennial reports latest follow-up March 2010; 4th full visit 5th Dec 2012 updated the compliance scoring but was not a new MER, this 283-page report revisited some but not all of recommendations
Georgia	July 2007	MONEYVAL	2.1	2	2.8	2 follow-up progress report in July 2008 and March 2010 with a fourth assessment visit under the 3rd round July 2012 and a 466-page report that included reassessment of compliance against recommendations
Botswana	Aug. 2007	ESAAMLG/ World Bank	1.7	1	5.6	No documents other than the MER in the public domain
China	June 2007	FATF/EAG	2.5	2	3.3	Eight follow-up reports with recommendation in 8th Report February 2012 to move to Biennial reporting with next report in 2014. This is not in the public domain

(continued)

Table 8.3 (continued)

Notes:
Country Compliance score translated from: 0 - N/A to Country; 1 - Non-compliant; 2 - Partially compliant; 3 - Largely compliant; and 4 - Compliant
TPI 2006 country assessment rating where scale is 0-10 (corrupt to clean)
TPI country assessment for Sudan refers to 2014
GAFILAT: The Financial Action Task Force of Latin America (secretariat based in Argentina)
CFATF: Caribbean Financial Action Task Force (secretariat based in Trinidad and Tobago)
FATF: Financial Action Task Force (secretariat based in France)
APG: Asia Pacific Group (secretariat based in Australia)
MENAFATF: Middle East & North Africa Financial Action Task Force (secretariat based in Bahrain)
GIABA: Inter-Governmental Action Group against Money Laundering in West Africa (secretariat based in Senegal)
MONEYVAL: Council of Europe - Committee of Experts on the Evaluation of Anti-Money Laundering Measures and the Financing of Terrorism
ESAAMLG: Eastern and Southern Africa 'Anti-Money' Laundering Group (secretariat based in Tanzania)
EAG: Eurasian Group on combating money laundering and financing of terrorism (secretariat based in the Russian Federation)
Source: The authors, based on annual reports of the FATF and FATF-style Regional Bodies.

Table 8.4 Summary of approach under the fourth round MER

Area	Observation
Purpose of MER	The assessment is conducted on the basis of 11 immediate outcomes, which represent key goals that an effective AML/CFT system should achieve. Assessed on a four-point scale from high level of effectiveness (HE); substantial (SE); Moderate (ME) and low (LE). Technical compliance with the Recommendations is on a 4-point scale with N/A only in rare circumstances. Expressed from no shortcomings (C) to minor (LC); moderate (PC) and major (NC).
Assessment team	The composition of teams appears to be unchanged. The reviewers are drawn from a pool of volunteer experts but all from the FATF and FSRBs – from countries other than those of the assessors. A list of reviewers is to be maintained and monitored by ECG
Skills	Although not explicitly stated it may be assumed that collectively the team requires (a) a fair knowledge of statistics and methodology, (b) a study on the reliability of the national crime statistics and the FIU database; (c) knowledge of the economy and sociology of the assessed country; (d) knowledge of the criminal law, fiscal law, administrative law and commercial law.
Scope of review	Separation of technical compliance from effectiveness assessment with increasing emphasis on risk with the view of the evaluators having precedence over those of countries.
Documentation	(a) the 40 Recommendations; (b) the methodology; (c) the guide on data and statistics and (d) the procedure and the Interpretative Notes.
Approach	The review for technical compliance (with the 40 Recommendations) will be desk based and start at least six months prior to visit with a draft reading three months before visit. The on-site visit will focus on the eleven immediate outcomes (effectiveness). There is an expectation that the visit will last for ten days. The time line appears to provide for a greater number of iterations of the draft (including a revisit to the country). The first draft is sent back to the country for comments and input, a second draft and executive summary then goes to a new stage – a team that provide a 'quality and consistency review'. This panel is drawn from the pool of qualified volunteer expects from FATF, FSRB delegates, FSRB secretariat and IFIs (suggesting a team of three to review each second draft MER to feed into a third draft). At this stage it is possible to revisit the country to agree the report prior to tabling the fourth draft at the Plenary.

Source: The authors using information from FATF (2013) 'Procedures for the FATF Fourth Round of AML/CTF Mutual Evaluations' October and updated June 2014.

not exited the third round follow-up process should do so by November 2015. Did they just 'empty the shelves'? We could find no explanation for this remarkable outcome, whether from the CFATF or the Plenary of the FATF itself.

For other countries reviewed under the auspices of APG nothing further appears to be warranted or if it was, is not then publicly disclosed. MONEYVAL appear to execute the most thorough of procedures including re-visits and reassessments.

The FATF has now moved onto the fourth round of mutual evaluation[10] in response to the revised set of Recommendations and its proposed methodology for compliance assessment.[11] It is interesting to note that the latter comprises a detailed 164-page document that sets out the approach to be adopted under the new system without showing how the proposed changes address any of the shortcomings identified in the third round. To some extent, this task is ably performed by Halliday, Levi and Reuter (2014). Their report sets about unpicking the new methodology and setting this in the context of both the previously identified problems together with their recommendations of further adjustments that would still be needed. Despite the fact that the independent study was undertaken in cooperation with both the IMF and the FATF, it is not clear whether the fourth round has been adjusted in any way in order to respond to the observations covered by Halliday *et al.* (2014).

It is interesting to consider the changes in the approach between the two rounds. The list of reviewers (past and proposed) is to be maintained and monitored by the Evaluations and Compliance Group (ECG) (para 50 p. 14, FATF 2013b). The FATF members should provide qualified experts as reviewers of the concept MERs. Point 17 on page 6 (FATF 4th round procedures) states that "countries with greater capacity should provide more assessors". The reviewers comprise a pool of volunteer experts (all from the FATF and FSRBs) but from countries other than those of the assessors (point 42 on page 12). This distinction being thought necessary to ensure that the new stage of 'quality and consistency review' is conducted by a separate group from those conducting the assessment.

There is a separation of *technical compliance* from *effectiveness assessment*: the adequacy of implementation, compliance and maintenance of the regime. Effectiveness is defined as the extent to which the defined outcomes are achieved. That is the "extent to which financial systems and economies mitigate the risk and threats of ML and financing of terrorism" (para. 38 p. 14). In fact, "Effectiveness is assessed in a fundamentally different way to technical compliance." And "Therefore, assessors need to be flexible and to use their judgement and experience when reaching conclusions." (Point 60 p. 19). The problem over determining effectiveness through application of flexible judgment remains a problem of the revised approach. Perhaps the new concept of "flexible effectiveness" will be added to our vocabulary as another linguistic veil of lack of precision and proper methodology.

---

[10] FATF (2013b) 'Procedures for the FATF Fourth Round of AML/CTF Mutual Evaluations' October and updated June 2014.

[11] FATF (2013c) 'Methodology for assessing technical compliance with the FATF recommendations and the effectiveness of the AML/CFT systems', as updated by FATF (2017), 'Consolidated Processes and Procedures for Mutual Evaluations and Follow-Up "Universal Procedures"', February 2017.

Following the discussion and adoption of a MER, the country could be placed in either regular or an enhanced follow-up. The FATF states that the default mechanism for monitoring is that of regular follow-up, which requires a report three years after the MER is adopted and a follow-up assessment completed after five years from the date of the MER.

Countries considered to exhibit significant deficiencies (for technical compliance or effectiveness) will be placed in the enhanced follow-up procedure requiring up to three reports prior to the follow-up assessment at year five. The report in year five is intended to be "a targeted but more comprehensive report on the countries' progress, with the main focus being on areas in which there have been changes, high risk areas identified in the MER or subsequently, on the priority areas for action."[12] To date 35 countries have been evaluated under the fourth round and thus far no follow-up procedures have been disclosed on the FATF website.

We have looked at a sample of fourth round evaluations (see section 9.2.3.) and it is evident that assessment teams are just as enthusiastic as those that carried out the third round. The reports range in length from 105 pages for Ethiopia to 230 for Italy. Size of teams was between seven and ten people (largest teams for Australia, Norway and Spain) and took between ten days (Ethiopia) and 17 days (Belgium, Australia and Sri Lanka) to complete. Norway and Ethiopia received a low ranking: Norway because it does not consider the whole issue very important (perhaps reasonably with such a low crime rate) and Ethiopia because all matters appear to go slowly there in any case. Spain displays a highly valued risk-based approach. But, looking closer, one might suspect that they collated a range of information that was then rather smartly lined up in support of their policies. There is also evidence that when a phenomenon is rated as 'high risk' it is accepted blindly, but a 'low risk' qualification seems to evoke some dispute and warrant further investigation by the evaluation team. At the time of writing, there has been no academic engagement with the fourth round.

Our discussion so far has focused on the impact of the AML framework at the level of the nation state. In particular, this has been with an eye on why and how countries are subject to the rules of the FATF. Part of that adherence requires that each nation establishes the internal mechanisms for policing those sectors within their economies that are subject to the FATF's rules and regulations. A key element of the AML regime is the *regulated sector*, *i.e.* all those entities and professional groups required to report suspicious financial transactions. Harvey *et al.* (2014) pointed out that the implied complexity of money laundering makes prevention via regulation 'manifestly difficult' but

[12] Procedures for the FATF Fourth Round Of AML/CFT Mutual Evaluations, updated June 2017 p. 20. Available at: http://www.fatf-gafi.org/media/fatf/documents/methodology/FATF-4th-Round-Procedures.pdf. Accessed 22 September 2017.

that this has not deterred an enthusiastic implementation by the authorities. Just as in Chapter 6, where we considered some of the problems of imposing a single solution on countries with very different criminal legal frameworks, it is similarly difficult to impose one set of rules on countries that traditionally have very different models of regulation.

8.3 The regulated sector and reasons for compliance

In principle, governments have a public duty to ensure their regulations are fair and proportional to the problem; targeted to avoid unintended consequences; and consistent to avoid uncertainty in their interpretation and application (Baldwin and Cave, 1999, p. 77; Kirkpatrick 2006, p. 236). Naturally, for any system to be transparent, the regulators themselves should also be open to external scrutiny about their own objectives and associated actions. This public accountability includes three components:

1. being able to provide reasons for decisions;
2. making such decisions available for scrutiny; and
3. submitting themselves (if required) to independent review.

It is not entirely clear how these general principles of 'good regulation' can apply to AML. In particular, the question of proportionality proves particularly thorny (for an extensive discussion of proportionality of the AML regime, refer to van Duyne *et al.*, 2016 and van Duyne *et al.*, 2018a). Further, the historical development of regulations within financial sectors has differed between countries. Therefore, while a more prescriptive and rules-based approach to regulation is consistent with the American system of enforcement, it is largely at odds with the approach within financial markets in the UK. In this country, institutions were used to self-policing and regulatory compliance was more a matter of persuasion (Mascini, 2013). Reuter and Truman (2004) contrasted the American enforcement approach to money laundering to that of Switzerland. The former had generated tonnes of useless reports by banks whipped into line by the threat of swingeing penalties. By contrast, Switzerland operated on a collaborative and trust based model under which banks undertook more extensive pre-investigation prior to lodging a report with the FIU. As a result, there were a smaller number of reports lodged, each of which were apparently more effectively acted upon. Of course, this smaller number of reports created different problems when the number of reports was being considered an important (if irrelevant) measure of performance. But research is lacking to show where – in the US or Switzerland – financial intelligence captures all that is needed for a detailed comparison.

Van den Broek (2015) compared the supervisory regimes in existence in Spain, the Netherlands, the UK and Sweden. These four jurisdictions were selected as exemplifiers of the main types of supervisory model: (a) FIU Model (the FIU is the supervisor); (b) the external model (supervision is through public administration or government); (c) the internal model (professional body associations); and, finally (d) the hybrid model. Not surprisingly, she found (p. 410) that "effective supervision requires that (substantive) legislation is clear, precise, foreseeable, predictable and enforceable". Equally important is that supervisors be able to carry out their roles free from political influence and that, for purpose of legitimacy, decision-making should be transparent, making use of persuasion that is enforced where needed and legitimised by sanctions.

Four and a half decades after the introduction of the first money laundering legislation, the AML landscape is so much more complex, not only because of the changing requirements arising from the regime but also because banking itself has become much more complex. The regulated sector has to watch out for suspicious signs or 'red-flags' that could relate not only to drug trafficking but to a vast range of issues from white-collar crime and corruption to terrorist financing and economic sanctions. Banks, among the regulated entities, seem to be the ones most often under fire from law enforcement and regulatory agencies and the ones spending most on AML measures.

Whether or not the approach is proportional, the need for compliance creates an internal cost and a decision-making process on the part of the banks. They must determine just how much resource should be devoted to the required activities. This dimension opens up an area of literature that has focused on the reasons behind bank compliance and the mechanism by which they are persuaded to assume what is, essentially, an external cost (Levi and Reuter, 2006; Favarel-Garrigues *et al.*, 2011). Many of these authors have also considered whether the benefits of the regime in the way it has developed so far justify (let alone outweigh) the costs. Professional groups (lawyers, accountants and notaries as well as representatives of the regulated businesses) have also voiced concerns over the costs. Details of the composition of these costs are discussed in the next section.

8.3.1 Costs of compliance

Although not specific to money laundering, Alfon and Andrews (1999, p. 16) provide a definition of compliance costs as comprising "the costs to firms and individuals of those activities required by regulators that would not have been undertaken in the absence of regulation". Unfortunately, just as it is difficult to arrive at an estimate of benefits (see Chapters 3, 7 and 9), total costs data is fragmented across the various parts of the regulated sector and across jurisdictions. As discussed in previous chapters, there have been attempts, particularly among the larger audit and risk management firms, to collect costs data for the regulated sectors. Such firms have also undertaken surveys to identify trends and to establish changes in estimated percentage costs (see van Duyne *et al.*, 2018a and Chapter 3). However, such surveys only capture costs directly arising from the implementation of AML measures. Another difficulty is that many reporting entities, particularly banks, undertake their anti-fraud and AML activities within the same department, making it difficult to disentangle those specific to AML. Otherwise, banks are not necessarily able and/or willing to provide specific details or a breakdown of AML-related costs.

The costs of compliance are generally thought of as comprising those tangible operational costs required to carry out the compliance function (Masciandaro and Filotto, 2001, p. 136). *Ceteris paribus*, these are likely to be higher the more extensive the regulation (Harvey, 2008, p. 191). In detail these costs might reasonably include the following:

1. *administrative costs* at any stage of compliance, including any related administrative paperwork, administrative correspondence with clients (for example, in relation to obtaining KYC documents); these can be general as well as case-/client-specific
2. *legal costs*, such as legal fees for the preparation of contract clauses relating to AML, sanctions, anti-corruption assurances; legal fees for the interpretation of regulation and legal consultancy; the legal costs can also be general as well as case-/client-specific
3. *operational costs*: these can include (i) KYC (for example, costs for retrieving KYC documents such as corporation documents from UK Companies House; (ii) (enhanced) due diligence costs (such as database charges for media research and sanctions screening and fees to external consultants; these can be incurred at the early stage of a potential relationship or post on-boarding); (iii) monitoring, for instance, where high-risk clients are subject to on-going sanctions and media screening for adverse news, as well as transactions monitoring; (iv) compliance audit and remediation reviews; operational costs can entail fees and charges for external services paid for client-/case-specific matters separately or flat fees that are paid over a certain period of time rather than for separate matters
4. *investment in technical products* and software to assist compliance
5. *investment in staff*, this includes salaries and training (training could also include subscription fees for membership of compliance associations and conferences)
6. *fines and settlements*, which are arguably paid for (alleged) non-compliance to demonstrate compliance is re-instated.

Even the above costs will have elements that are difficult to fully capture. For instance, while compliance specialist personnel's remuneration is a clear-cut figure, the time devoted to compliance matters by other, non-specialist, personnel and senior management is difficult to record and measure. Apart from these direct costs, there are other indirect opportunity costs, for example, lost business through delays in on-boarding of new clients or through damage to reputation through non-compliance (which comes with an additional direct cost of a penalty for failure to comply). It is not possible to fully capture financial data on decisions such as de-risking (as already discussed). Even if banks kept track of decisions on de-risking, they would be unlikely to disclose such data to the public. It could even be argued that through the de-risking process, banks actually minimise future AML compliance costs as they limit their exposure to risk. However, the de-risking process is associated both with administrative costs (related paperwork, legal costs *etc.*) and, often, irrecoverable enhanced due diligence costs. Due diligence is a mandatory AML requirement. For a bank to determine whether a client falls within its acceptable risk parameters, often the first-hand data about the client, such as nationality and occupation, is not enough. Banks may have to undertake deeper checks if there is a high-risk factor such as political exposure or wealth that has come from a jurisdiction of perceived heightened risk. At the end of the due diligence process a bank may decide not to on-board a prospective client because there is not enough in terms of information on his or her source of wealth or because of alleged misconduct, or simply because the prospective client turns out be a highly prominent political figure, which translates into a bigger risk. A bank's due diligence costs can run into six-digit figures or even exceed a million dollars a year, particularly if they do not result in any business. Furthermore, there is the possibility of opportunity costs if the de-risked wealthy client proves to be no ML risk.

A more difficult area of cost concerns the risks arising from non-compliance, or failure to fully comply, which would generally impact on the reputation of the institution that might find itself subject to investigation and fines. In weighing up the arguments as to why banks would or alternatively, would not, be prepared to absorb the costs, Chong and López-de-Silanes (2007) considered whether the reputational concerns of financial institutions would be sufficient to ensure they do not contaminate themselves with criminals or their money without the need for additional AML controls. Within this frame, the imposition of regulations simply increases operational costs while reducing the speed of operations.[13] Harvey and Lau (2008) argue that reputation is peculiar within this context as it is not a public notion, but specific to the

[13] However as detailed in section 8.4 they ultimately conclude that there is no support for this hypothesis.

opinion of the regulator. From the public perspective, account holders would be concerned about the security of their own bank accounts and funds and less concerned about who else maintains accounts with their bank. One only has to look at the queues that formed outside of Northern Rock in the UK during the financial crisis. The account holders thought there was a chance that their monies would no longer be safe and thus sought to withdraw their capital. The situation was only halted by the UK Government stepping in to support the bank's viability. No such queues have formed in front of the doors of banks fined for failures in money laundering compliance such as HSBC or Deutsche Bank. This is despite the fact that the total overall penalty costs that are imposed on banks can be severe. As set out in Chapter 3.8. as part of the fine handed out, banks are required to undertake remedial measures and pay for the services of a firm to inspect, monitor and improve their internal controls. As discussed, such a cost is not inconsiderable because this 'consulting' can be imposed for periods of a year or more.

Academics have looked at the mechanism by which compliance is enforced. Mostly this has been through the use of penalties for the breach of regulations. Levi and Maguire (2004, p. 417) indicate that it was widely assumed that bankers, amongst others, could be made 'capable guardians' of the AML system simply by penalising them when they failed in this duty. Harvey (2008) provided a list of banks that were fined for breaches of AML compliance but concluded that these types of sanctions appeared to have little impact on the reputation of the bank involved. The most recent example of such fines concerns Deutsche Bank which, in February 2017, was fined by the UK's financial regulator, the Financial Conduct Authority (FCA). The penalty of £163 million was imposed for a failure to maintain an adequate anti-money laundering (AML) control framework during the period between 1 January 2012 and 31 December 2015, *not* because the FCA found evidence that Deutsche Bank had facilitated any laundering scheme or that laundering had been established (see Gelemerova *et al.*, 2018).

Seeking to understand the reasons for compliance (and the costs involved), a number of qualitative studies have been carried out. For example, Favarel-Garrigues, *et al.* (2008) studied compliance in France, Magnusson (2009) examined compliance in Sweden, Verhage (2009) considered Belgium, Sathye (2008) looked at Australia and Harvey and Lau (2008), the UK. Sandulescu (2014, 2016) evaluated how the Swiss banking system has adapted to an AML compliant culture. Some have speculated that the evident lack of enthusiasm by banks for providing details on costs means that they have adopted the cheapest acceptable 'tick box' approach they are able to get away with (Gelemerova, 2010; Harvey and Lau, 2009). Although some banks have learned through bitter experience that their definition of compliance might not wholly accord with what the regulator sees as 'acceptable' their argument in case of reproach is often "lost in obfuscation", especially under the risk-based approach (Gelemerova, 2010, p. 34).

Magnusson (2009, p. 105) used interviews with representatives of the regulated sector in Sweden to arrive at estimates of the costs of compliance for the commercial and savings banks. The data were reported without comment of the precise system under which the estimates were derived. As part of an attempt to provide an estimate of the costs of compliance in Australia Sathye (2008), drew together a range of problems highlighted in earlier studies by Reuter and Truman (2004); Dolar and Shughart (2007); Harvey (2004); and Ryder (2008):

- Due to scale economies, costs fall disproportionately on smaller firms and institutions;
- As costs are passed through to customers, compliance costs raise the overall cost of credit;
- Due to the sensitivity of data, there is a general reluctance for firms to disclose their compliance costs;
- And, that it is actually difficult to estimate the total costs involved if, in addition to direct costs, indirect and opportunity costs are to be considered.

For his own contribution, Sathye (2008), took data from similar compliance cost exercises, although not the ones concerning money laundering. For example, one of the estimates entails unpicking the costs reported by a single bank (as the main data available) concerning its compliance with a different piece of regulation (Uniform Consumer Credit Code). He then assumes that AML compliance will entail the same degree of effort. Although it is not entirely clear why this should be the case as one of the main drivers for 'effort' is, one imagines, the penalty enforced for non–compliance. He then employs 'management accounting' techniques to break down these costs against various accounting expenditure items to arrive at a percentage cost that is then scaled up to current prices and extended across the sector. Following this effort, he arrives at AUS$1.02 billion (2007 prices) as an estimate of compliance costs for Australia.

In light of the costs of establishing and maintaining an entire middle office devoted to compliance, institutions do consider outsourcing or buying in bespoke solutions and packages, including those with respect to suspicious transaction monitoring (see Chapter 3.9). A simple 'google' search returns many such service suppliers. Recognising the industry that has been built up around AML-compliance, Verhage (2009) looked at the suppliers of compliance services and the ways in which they are able to sell 'solutions' to the banks' for their money laundering 'risk'. Verhage demonstrates the tendency for the solution providers to create increasingly comprehensive packages that enable the banks to scan their accounts or to monitor PEPs. Importantly, she points out that once a critical number of banks employ these techniques others have no choice but to follow. This is particularly the case, where the regulator considers such problem-solving packages as 'best practice' and in so doing, unintentionally (one assumes) promotes them to more institutions for purchase. If one was inclined to cynicism it might appear that we have inadvertently created an elaborate 'hustle'. Indeed, as long ago as 1998, van Duyne (also see, Verhage and Ponsaers, 2009) drew attention to what he termed the Threat Assessment Industry (van Duyne, 2004).

Normal cost benefit analysis would enable the policy makers and other beneficiaries of the regime to set on a single account, the costs incurred against the benefits gained. As has been discussed in this book, it is impossible to see the assessment of the benefits of the AML regime as an exact science. It can be argued that if financial intelligence provides valuable leads, for instance, in a kidnapping investigation and helps save a life, then all the compliance efforts of the regulated sector is worth it. In that sense, financial intelligence is priceless. This can be considered a valid argument. Red-flag indicators in the financial world, for instance, have helped solve human trafficking cases (as, for instance, the FATF's human trafficking typologies report of 2011 indicates). However, those who use this argument to dismiss the need for evidence-based regulation and a cost-benefit analysis are missing the point. While the concept of collecting financial intelligence has, undoubtedly, its merits, it is the extent and effect of *uncertainty* of regulations and their enforcement that need to be re-considered. Is the AML regime going to become more effective, with less uncertainty, but further increases in regulations, and as a result, increases of AML spending? Ultimately, much of the more obvious costs are passed on to ordinary customers of the regulated sector without, as it appears, directly translating into any evidence of decrease in crime. This will be further discussed in Chapter 9.

If one thinks of where it all started and where we are now, expectations of what is required of the regulated sector are so far beyond what was originally laid down. This means that cost is so much higher now (2018) than it was three and a half decades earlier. Currently, in addition to red-flags relating to the 'usual suspect' crimes such as drug trafficking, financial institutions have to watch out for clean money financing terrorism and also transactions that may be undertaken in breach of trade sanctions. The latter is particularly challenging as it can involve perfectly legitimate businesses unrelated to money laundering. The case of Red Bull agreeing to pay $89,775 (a relatively small amount compared to the fines paid by others for sanctions breaches in the past ten years) for unauthorised travel to Cuba to film a documentary in 2009 shows how unpredictable and subjective the sanction system can be.

Without dismissing the potential value of financial intelligence, there must be some understanding of the cost incurred by the regulated sector that would enable us to understand better how the system works and what the scope for improvement is. Costs of bank regulation become a particularly topical issue at a time of financial crisis – banks' expenditures and efficiency attract more scrutiny. As Elliehausen (1998, p. 2) observed in his study of the cost of bank regulation in the USA in 1998, "The cost of government regulation of business has become a political issue." After all, as noted previously, this cost is passed onto ordinary customers. In a transparent financial world reputable organisations should strive to make sure resources are not misplaced and the interests of *bona-fide* customers are protected.

As costs of AML compliance within the industry are substantial and show little sign of decreasing (see Chapter 3.9), it is appropriate to look at the institutions' decision making to see how that is being influenced.

8.3.2 'Persuading' compliance by other means

Obviously, involving the banks in the development of the regulatory framework is a good way to ensure their compliance (Araujo, 2008; Ping, 2005; and Masciandaro, 1999). Indeed, this consultative approach was incorporated into the fourth Directive and the most recent iteration of the rules. One of the central problems of AML is that the costs accrue (mostly) to the regulated sector while the benefits accrue to the government that is able to demonstrate compliance with the international community, and in theory, to broader society which is supposed to see less (organised) criminal activity.

In pondering this difficulty, some authors (Araujo, 2008; Masciandaro, 1999, 2005; Masciandaro & Filotto, 2001; Pellegrina & Masciandaro, 2009; Takáts, 2011) have borrowed agency theory from management studies to look at the ways in which the AML compliance system can be improved. Within the theoretical paradigm, there is recognition that the 'agent' (in this case the regulated bank) acts in a way that promotes the objectives of the principal (in this case the regulator) over and above their own objectives. Of particular interest to their studies is how banks can be incentivised to capture information that they would not ordinarily require and to share it with the regulatory authorities. However, this sharing of client sensitive information is not a natural position for the banking sector. A peculiarity of money laundering regulation is its reliance on the execution of enforcement activity by non-police actors. Certainly, the banks were at first reluctant to take on this role (Marshall, 2004; Favarel-Garrigues *et al.*, 2008; Canhoto, 2008), although it has been suggested they were more willing following the events of 9-11 (Bergström *et al.*, 2011). As a side note, it should be mentioned that in the UK, for example, there is no general duty on citizens to report criminal activity to the police as this was abolished in 1967 (Alldridge, 2003). Indeed, it is strange that money laundering legislation relies on such compelled disclosure (van Duyne *et al.*, 2005; Alldridge, 2003).

One way in which compliance can be promoted is through aligning the objective of the financial institutions with those of the regulators (Bello and Harvey, 2017). This can be achieved by framing both as ensuring the safety and soundness of the banks and the banking system as outlined by the BIS and the Basle Accords. Strengthening financial sector integrity is more explicitly addressed in the FATF's 2013 methodology as one of the three high level objectives (see Chapter 9). There appears still to be hope that this emphasis on outcome effectiveness, may be more successful in linking AML/CFT measures to safety and soundness of the banking system (Halliday *et al.*, 2014). As discussed, however, there is no solid evidence to show laundering is taking place at such a scale that it is affecting the soundness of the financial system. In that case there is very little to measure.

8.3.3 The apparent benefits of the risk based approach

Discussion in the literature on the risk based approach was covered in Chapter 7 but is also relevant here. Ryder (2008) noted the industry wide support for the introduction of the risk-based approach, seeing the rules based approach as overly burdensome and "too severe for the risk involved" (Ryder, 2008, p. 647). Ostensibly, the rationale for the move to a risk-based approach to compliance was to reduce the costs of compliance (Sathye, 2008, also see FSA DP 22.[14] The advantage over the prior rule-based approach was the perceived flexibility it offered to banks such that ". . . resources should be directed in accordance with priorities so that the greatest risks receive the highest attention" (FATF, 2007 p. 2). It was also introduced with the hope of addressing the problem of excessive reporting: the generation of large amounts of mostly useless information that had been associated with the rules based approach (Ross and Hannan, 2007; Pellegrina and Masciandaro, 2009). As discussed, the risk-based approach was introduced in 2003 by the FATF following its revision of the 40 Recommendations (de Koker, 2009), and was accompanied by the development of the Guidance on the Risk-Based Approach to combating money laundering and terrorist financing (FATF, 2007). The Guidance was developed in the aftermath of the introduction of the third Money Laundering (which launched the risk-based approach) and following a meeting in 2005 between the FATF and representatives of the banking and securi-

[14] In its consultation paper, DP22 "Reducing money laundering risk: know your customer and AML monitoring", 2003, the FSA discussed the practical application of the then proposed risk based approach to AML, noting that without its adoption "firms' costs will be disproportionate" (section 2.6 p. 7).

ties sectors. At that meeting, a group was formed to look at developing the risk-based approach (FATF, 2007). The main purpose of the Guidance was to foster a common understanding and interpretation of what was implied by the approach. The resulting explanation was that a risk-based approach "... encompasses recognising the existence of the risk(s), undertaking an assessment of the risk(s) and developing strategies to manage and mitigate the identified risks" (FATF, 2007 p. 2).

There is a distinct difference between 'risk-taking' (according to risk appetite), on the one hand and 'being at risk', on the other. The latter was the approach promoted by the regulators (FATF, 2007; BIS, 2004; Financial Conduct Authority, 2013). This difference has also been articulated by Demetis and Angell (2007, p. 4) where taking a risk is "where an action is taken in search of opportunities, but with the possibility of facing hazards" as distinct from being at risk "where outside forces threaten". Financial institutions are used to measuring and hedging risk for regulatory purposes and the majority of large banks use VaR[15] models. For purposes of measurement they draw a distinction between risk (probability of an event occurring is known but the outcome is unknown) and uncertainty (both probability and outcome remain unknown and thus cannot be ascribed a value). This distinction is ascribed to Frank Knight, whose name is synonymous with 'Knightian Uncertainty'.[16] As rational individuals, we are uncomfortable with uncertainty and prefer the quantification of risk (Demetis and Angell, 2007; Bello and Harvey, 2017). One may assume that banks are able to quantify risk and thus would embrace the idea of the risk-based approach (Anna, 2011; Demetis and Angell, 2007). Especially as one of the reasons given for the move was the anticipated reduction in costs it was anticipated to provide.

However, the reality has been different, primarily because as we have discussed in this Chapter, the shift has increased uncertainty. This was a very specific type of uncertainty: it was 'interpretation risk' (van Duyne *et al.*, 2018a) that refers to the gap between the institution's judgment of money laundering risks and that of the regulator. In consequence, the risk-based assessment is in two stages:

1. the bank assesses the risk of the client, business partner, counterparty, transaction, country and so on;
2. in addition it has to consider whether it's judgment will meet the approval of the regulator.

[15] Value at Risk (VaR) is a measure of market risk that estimates, for a given probability, the largest loss likely to be suffered on a position over a given period.

[16] Frank Knight (1921) formalised a distinction between risk and uncertainty in his book: *Risk, Uncertainty, and Profit.* Hart, Schaffner, and Marx Prize Essays, no. 31. Boston and New York: Houghton Mifflin.

This is not something that is always as easy to judge. This is because the FATF failed to provide a conceptual definition of 'risk' within a risk based approach. Moreover, the FATF and national regulators have not provided sufficient guidance on what mitigates risk. Although there are copious guidance notes on how the RBA should be implemented it remained, for instance, unclear whether the amount of laundering and the nature and extent of its harm mattered. In fact, the approach continued to be all-encompassing. If an account was being funded by small amounts of money, mostly legitimate funds and, only occasionally, proceeds such as from marijuana sales, the red-flags might not be raised. Although the approach varies across jurisdictions, in the UK, for instance, a bank would be expected to invest the same amount of effort in investigating trivial sums as they would with larger sums of money, because there is no SAR reporting threshold. Such a broad scope and vagueness of definition severely hampers institutions from arriving at indicators of low, medium or high risk (De Koker, 2009, p. 334 and p. 340; also see Gelemerova, 2009, 2011; Ross and Hannan, 2007; Killick and Parody, 2007; Sathye and Islam, 2011). It is ironic that while the FATF did not define risk, it nevertheless provides "key elements of an effective risk-based approach" (FATF, 2007 p. 1). In addition, the FATF (through its assessors in the mutual evaluations) effectively argued that ML should be prioritised in National Risk Assessment relative to predicate offences and reprimanded countries and law enforcement agencies for not doing so. But can the authorities prioritise unspecified risks over very specific predicate offences of which the public requires a reduction? The FATF is unhelpful on this point while remaining quick to reproach.

Sathye and Islam (2011) examined one of the empirically underpinned AML risk assessment models. This model categorises the risk of money laundering into business and regulatory risk and further subdivides business risk into inherent and residual risk. However, there is a problem with this categorisation because some of the inherent risks are determined, as illustrated by Ross and Hannan (2007), according to what regulators *think* are risks rather than following the industry recognised risk assessment framework. For example, there is an expectation that a regulator would want to see a customer rated a high risk if he is a politically exposed person (PEP), by virtue of being a top government official or a relation or close associate of such a person (unless there are compelling mitigating factors). This applies to both domestic, foreign and international PEPs (FATF, 2013a) irrespective of whether they show any criminal intent. Gelemerova *et al.* (2018) provide a detailed analysis of the problems faced by banks in AML risk assessment with respect to corruption. The authors point out that the regulatory focus on country risks rather than case-specific ones means banks' primary driver in the risk-categorising of partners and clients is their country of origin or nationality rather than their conduct, lending an unhelpful bias against a class of potential clients. Consequently, banks might decide it is easier to follow a blanket approach of de-risking by deeming clients in specific countries too risky and thus declining potentially profitable and legitimate business opportunities. A similar observation was made by the *Economist* (2017, p. 8) that reported on banks de-risking "money transfer firms handling remittances to poor countries, and charities that work in conflict zones" and closing down correspondent banking relationships for banks in countries in, for example, Africa and Latin America, affecting their ability to clear hard currency transactions.[17]

The classification of countries may also be arbitrary (Sharman, 2008). What are the criteria for designating a country as being at a high risk from money laundering? Should it be based on evidence of a lack of political will by those in government or due to a weak regulatory framework for dealing with money laundering? Or should it be based on the amount and frequency of money laundering activity of which there are usually no statistics? The USA, for example, has, arguably, the highest level of money laundering in the world (Dolar and Shughart II, 2011) but is commonly considered a low risk country. In contrast, countries with fewer incidents of money laundering, in both value and frequency, are considered high risk because of alleged lax control and lack of 'political will' towards compliance. In consequence, a transaction from California may not be considered a high risk even when it may be riskier than an equivalent transaction emanating from Kenya. Van Duyne *et al.* (2018a) went further in pointing out that although using the same term 'risk', the meaning within AML is different from its use within general banking activity. Within the latter, risk is quantified as the outcome of probability and impact and an outcome that results from the bank's own actions such as lending to a certain counterparty, or trading a currency which is miscalculated, which will result in a direct loss on the bank's books. Within AML, however, risk is a far more elusive and subjective concept. It becomes a judgement about risk, namely that a counterparty or transaction might be associated with criminal funds. On-boarding the risky client does not of itself necessarily result in any loss to the bank: the techniques of financial transactions remain the same irrespective of the origin of the funds (see also Mitsilegas, 2003).

8.4 Impact on the criminals – evidence of changing behaviour?

If it is often difficult to distinguish between legitimate and illegitimate banking transactions. Does the AML framework impact on the behaviour of criminals? We think of organised (economic) criminals, the drug smuggling cartels

[17] The Economist (2017) 'Financial de-risking "Forget Whiter than White" Leader pp. 8–9 and 'Financial derisking: The great unbanking', pp. 53–54, Print edition 8 July. Within the industrialised countries there is the "postcode exclusion": mortgage applicants from 'risky' neighbourhoods are deemed too big a mortgage risk.

and those intent upon avoiding tax or capital controls. Not just in abstract terms, but also thinking of the kind of stimuli to which criminals are supposed to respond. Just as was seen in the late 1990s in the UK, a criminal re-orientation away from armed robbery to the drug market.. According to Ruggiero and South (1995) this was in response to the risk of receiving lengthy sentences or of being shot on the job (see also Harvey and Hornsby, 2016). So yes, criminals are not unresponsive to negative, discouraging stimuli, but that is only in very general terms.

There is no easy way to connect 'cause and effect' in such cases because criminals respond to many stimuli beyond the actions of the state. It is evident that the crime rate is declining in the industrialised world and in tandem there has been a reduction in crime for profit, as will be set out in the next chapter. For example, while recently, we observe a fall in traditional acquisitive crimes such as burglary, there seems to be a switch towards the less 'risky' web based fraud. But such a 'switch' does not need to be a personal decision in the criminal's career: criminals may just as well quit their career as 'too old, and too risky' while potential successors move to a relatively safer and less demanding criminal field. Further, as set out in the next chapter, there is evidence of a rise in criminal activities in response to the recent economic recession.

So, is it possible to infer any causal relationship between the impact of anti-money laundering and the activity of criminals? There is no solid data when it comes to serious organised crime. There appears to be a 'shortcoming' of the literature, possibly induced by lack of proper operational definitions (van Duyne and Vander Beken, 2009). Harvey (2009) observed that it is well-nigh impossible to show in any measurable way how criminals have adjusted their volume of laundering in response to the introduction of the AML-framework. For argument's sake we abstract from the earlier discussed attempts to approximate the volume of laundering (Walker, 1995; Unger, 2007) or to re-visit the 'availability riddle' again.

The impact of AML operates along two dimensions: firstly, the *regulatory* side discussed in Section 8.3; and, secondly through the *criminal legal structure* that enables prosecution and sanctioning in the event of conviction. Looking at the former, the paper from Chong and López-de-Silanes (2007) published by the Inter-American Development Bank, argued by way of their '*law matters*' hypothesis for the imposition of a regulatory framework as a way of providing an important contribution to controlling illegal activity. This is because immediate short-term gains provide criminals too great a temptation to break the rules and alternative criminal litigation can be too expensive or cumbersome to serve as an adequate deterrent. They accept that the enforcement of AML comes at a cost, however, launderers providing services are rational and, therefore, the additional legal framework can enhance deterrence (refer to Chapter 7.2.). According to the authors, this is particularly the case when there is a greater likelihood of catching launderers through the SAR/

STRs. Secondly, they argue that there is a powerful negative impact of confiscation on decision making by launderers. Indeed, from their empirical work they conclude that the hypothesis that the law is irrelevant is not supported.

Asset recovery has lately received much attention, though we must emphasise that it is largely independent from the AML-regime, even if it is often discussed within this framework. This is further elaborated in Chapter10. It must be acknowledged, however, that if the STR/SAR regime had been better operationalised, it would have rendered more valuable support to asset tracing and recovery. Sittlington and Harvey (2018) assess the effectiveness of asset recovery legislation through its impact on the decision-making by the individual criminal. They conclude that the choice by individuals to commit money laundering offences is not bound by the deterrent effect of going to prison; this is simply part of the job. However, criminals do fear losing their assets from the asset recovery that follows (Vruggink, 2001). The focus of Sittlington and Harvey is on criminal decision-making rather than the more usual consideration of the volume of assets recovered. Studies looking at this dimension criticised the AML-regime, indicating that those caught showed a lack of sophistication and did not appear to be the type of criminals that had been the original target of the legislation (see for example, van Duyne and Levi, 2005; van Duyne, 2013; van Duyne and Soudijn, 2010; Levi, 2015; and, Harvey and Lau, 2009). Going through the asset recovery procedure can be a raw deal: the criminal is not only being stripped of present wealth, but, if that is insufficient, also faces the prospect of remaining indebted to the state or victims for years (van Duyne *et al.*, 2014).

In contrast to the views of Sittlington and Harvey, Levi and Reuter (2006), noted that despite the plausibility of the arguments, the impact of asset recovery had not been verified "on a large sample of offenders" (Levi and Reuter, 2006, p. 349). Further doubt had already been cast by Pieth (2002), who stated that asset recovery was rarely effective. Pieth considered the balance between the huge effort and cost of AML and the 'catch' that has resulted in a small number of criminal cases from which the profits were forfeited. These were but a drop in the ocean compared to the estimates of the size of the drug market (reinforcing the findings of Sproat, 2009b and comments by Ryder, 2008).

To obtain more empirical evidence about the potential of multi-billion Euro asset recovery van Duyne *et al.* (2014) analysed 10,012 Dutch asset recovery cases. They re-affirmed what was already known for 15 years: the criminal wealth distribution is extremely skewed with most 'criminal income' below €10,000 and only a tiny minority of criminals in the category of "one million plus". Recovery was partly successful, but not without the coercive measure of custody when unwillingness was suspected. On average, recovery was not an 'easy and speedy' process: its execution could take between 2.3 to 3.5 years, an outcome confirmed by Kruisbergen *et al.* (2016).

If there is limited or contradictory evidence of the deterrence effect on criminals, it is interesting to consider how the AML regime has impacted in other ways. Levi (2015) addressed this problem by considering the structures of financing of 'organised crimes' and their similarities and differences to methods of financing businesses within the licit economy. He points to the importance of the social capital of offenders as entry into a criminal enterprise (as with licit organisation) requires access to credit or start-up capital. In addition to market entry, capital may also be required to meet ongoing operational expenses (purchases and payments); one-off costs such as legal expenses; assets confiscations; and, to finance business expansion beyond what is fundable via reinvestment. Given the lack of independent credit ratings or assessment of risk, the lender/investor emphasises their knowledge of the enterprise and of the criminal. This knowledge is reinforced by personal connections and their power to recover advanced funds. Levi's study makes an important contribution to our chapter by setting out the mechanisms by which AML works (similar to those identified by Chong and López-de-Silanes, 2007). In summary (pp. 291–292), he identifies a range of individual and collective controls: individual prevention (due diligence and SARs reporting); individual incapacitation (asset recovery); individual deterrence (fear of apprehension and the sentencing consequences); group deterrence (prevention of organised groups exploiting differences between jurisdictions); and community support for the rule of law and government (criminals not being able to benefit from crime). In acknowledging some of the studies referenced above, Levi notes that little is known about the laundering choices and risk assessment thinking of criminals. However, he concludes that ease of access to illicit finance may somewhat ironically be easier if controls make it harder to launder money. This is because if it is difficult to execute real 'laundering' of illegal funds, it is inevitable that criminal funds will simply stay within the criminal economy and continue as a supply fund for investment. This reference to 'real' laundering highlights the paradox that financing future crimes from past illegality still counts as laundering as does self-laundering or spending by criminals beyond daily consumption. Thus, "no-one could rationally think that AML controls in general or financial investigation in particular will 'solve' organised crime completely or eliminate high-level offending" (Levi, 2015, p. 294) as illegal activity can continue simply by continued re-cycling of criminal funds.

Others also looked at the spending and investment choices of criminals. Kruisbergen *et al.* (2015b) uses a dataset of 150 criminal cases extracted from the Dutch Organized Crime Monitor from 1996-2011, to look at the decisions made by organised crime offenders when they invest their money in the legal economy. They identifies in which 1,196 individual possessions: firms and properties. In particular they were interested in the types of assets purchased and where these assets are located. Their results indicate that offenders predominantly invest in their country of origin or in their country of residence and that, their investments consist of tangible, familiar assets such as real estate and (small) companies from sectors well-known to them such as pubs. This confirms earlier research findings by Suendorf (2001) and van Duyne (1995; 1996; 2003). The latter identified the criminal asset management as "own yard investment", where 'yard' stands for the social and economic area around the criminal which he thinks he knows and can manage (van Duyne, 1996; p. 365). There was limited investment in financial products such as shares or bonds: as a matter of fact, they were very conservative investments. Steinko (2012) found very similar results for Spain with purchase of 'conspicuous' consumer goods concluding that there is little evidence in Spain of the existence of professional launderers. This lack of sophistication in investment choices and investment in familiar areas such as property was also observed by van Duyne and Levi (2005); van Duyne (2013); van Duyne and Soudijn (2010); Levi (2015); and Harvey and Lau (2009).

One of the main arguments for the requirement for the adoption of the AML standards on a global basis was the feared potential for criminals to exploit differences between legal systems. However, there is little evidence to show that most average criminals would venture further than their own social and economic circle: their own 'yard'. In Chapter 7.2 we discussed the difference in approach between economists who consider it rational to apply the same rules on a global basis to avoid such game playing and the lawyers who have a very different interpretation of the limits of the reach of criminal justice system within their respective national jurisdictions. We have discussed some of the absurdities of this 'one-size' approach in Section 8.2.1, however, there is little written on this criminal circumvention of rules apart from tax havens and offshore banking.

Writing at the same time, Blum *et al.* (1999) and Naylor (1999) expressed similar views on the role of the offshore banking sector in facilitating laundering. However, this theme can still be found in more recent literature. Both Young (2013), and Otusanya *et al.* (2011) considered the attraction of money laundering by offshore finance centres (OFCs). They suggest that such places were in some way less honest than onshore banks as they are home to funds from drugs, organised crime and those evading tax. There appears, however, to be little solid research to corroborate the idea that all international financial centres operate in that way. Johannesen and Zucman (2014), highlighted the G20 crackdown on tax havens initiated at the G20 summit in April 2009. This initiative required tax havens to enter into information exchange treaties (under threat of economic sanctions) to improve tax enforcement. For the countries with such treaties in place, the authors carried out an empirical study that made use of BIS locational banking statistics. This latter source provided them with bilateral deposit data. They argued that their evidence challenged the view that the tightening of laws had indeed been successful because there was little evidence of a reduction in the total amount of funds held offshore. Rather there had simply been a reallocation in favour of less compliant jurisdictions. They did suggest that further work was needed to understand why tax havens might abandon the benefits of bank secrecy, wondering if an improvement in reputation would attract other financial activities. To some extent this work has already been carried out as set out in the last chapter (see for example Gutzman *et al.* 2010). The leak of the Panama papers in 2016 indicates that the attraction of OFCs is still evident.

Somewhat unusually, Panama had the privilege of receiving two mutual evaluations under the third round, both of which were undertaken by the IMF. The first visit took place in 2005 as part of the Financial Sector Assessment Programme (FSAP), and overall it received a reasonably clean bill of health (both the arithmetic and modal average compliance scores were 3.[18] This included R20 (preventive measures – Designated Non-Financial Business and Professions) being assessed as largely compliant – despite concern about the Colon Free Zone whereby the independent agency charged with overseeing compliance lacked the "minimum human and technological resources needed to perform [. . .] inspections and audits". It is also curious why Panama should have requested that the IMF conduct the assessment rather than GAFILAT when the IMF state that "FSAPs are required to be associated with an AML-CFT assessment conducted either by the IMF's Legal Department or by FATF or a FATF-style regional body". Further and at odds with the procedure followed for other MERs this report did not appear to have been discussed and accepted at any plenary and indeed does not appear on either the FATF or GAFILAT websites, being marked as 'confidential- restricted use only'. There is no evidence that the country then went into the subsequent monitoring rounds. To set this in context, both the British Virgin Islands (average 3.0 and modal 4) and the Cayman Islands (average 3.0 and modal 3) were reviewed in 2007 by CFATF and went into a series of follow up annual and then biennial reporting.

The second visit by the IMF took place in October 2012 and was carried out by a different team and resulted in a far longer report (348 pages against 99) and a marked deterioration in compliance assessment (average 1.7 and modal 2) although it is not immediately clear what had happened to warrant either a second visit or the apparent deterioration in standards. This report was published in February 2014 (presumably having allowed the Panamanian authorities time to digest and respond) and although still not appearing on the FATF or GAFILAT websites, the country, in June 2014, found itself featured on the list of 'monitored jurisdictions'. It should be noted that Panama made the required high-level political commitment to work with the FATF and GAFILAT to address its apparent strategic AML/CFT deficiencies. Panama was removed from the list on February 19th 2016 apparently having established the required legal and regulatory frameworks. It is not without irony that the OECD had publicly adopted a '***we told you so***' stance drawing attention to their warnings of Panamanian back-tracking on tax transparency.

Source: the authors

[18] Creating the scale of 0=not applicable; 1=not compliant; 2=partially compliant; 3= largely compliant; and 4=compliant.

The relative anonymity allowed by Panama's offshore regulations makes its corporate services not only attractive to criminals, but also to politically exposed persons (PEP) for legal tax planning and/or tax evasion. A well known example is the Prime Minister of Iceland, who had to resign; the President of Ukraine, also mentioned, did not resign. Baker (1999) in an early exposition on the main drivers for laundering looked at the role of capital flight (usually moving funds out of developing economies into developed ones) arising from tax evasion and the proceeds of corruption. He provided various examples of the trade based mechanisms by which such movement was being facilitated through under- or over-pricing of goods. Trade-based methods of laundering were discussed in Chapter 7. Of interest here is that these types of laundering are actually difficult to detect and have probably grown in sophistication in line with opportunities presented from financial markets (the Deutche Bank mirror trades bear evidence to this). This rather suggests that the AML regime has had no great impact on criminals, they have merely adapted their methods and it is business as usual.

8.5 Conclusion

This final section on the literature has examined the impact of the AML-rules. The AML-regime has expanded well beyond its original rationale and focus on drugs to encompass a range of internationally determined 'threats'. This mission creep has had a range of impacts that could not have been foreseen in 1990. For this reason, we have considered what is known about the impact of the regime on the states, the regulated sector and its employees and finally on the criminals themselves. As an impact implies consequences, it is also appropriate to consider the subsequent behaviour of those that have been affected by the AML regime. Behaviour and response is of course a difficult area in particular because of the uncertain causality between the (AML) stimulus and response as both are inaccurately delineated. This applies not so much to criminal conduct, where little change is observed, but to the costs incurred by the financial 'gate keepers'.

The rules and regimes have all been constructed from a pre-determined expectation of how the addressed persons or institutions might respond. Deterrence theory suggests that imposition of penalties can be set at a level that will ensure that potential offenders will choose to stay on the right side of the law. The introduction of asset recovery is one such example. It is 'rational' that criminals will desist from crime when faced with seeing their 'hard earned' money and valuables forfeited. In the same way it is assumed that banks can apply a risk based approach to AML and allocate their resources accordingly. However, this is not a straightforward undertaking. One of the classic weaknesses of the 'risk-matrix' approach is the occurrence of low frequency but high impact events.[19] Hence, the savvy will focus their attention on that potential vulnerability. Can it be argued that the hypothetical 'Mr Big' would fall into this category? Most likely, as long as we realise that this is a label for a very heterogeneous class of high-earners who are few and far between: the set contains top drug dealers and mega-fraudsters like Madoff. Also, we are not completely awash with their illegal funds: the real large flows of money could be observed during the credit crisis. And there is little evidence for the assumed high level of sophistication?

What is troubling about the general representation of 'big money' is the evidence supplied from the output data. The data on assets recovered discussed above points to low economic sophistication and low criminal income. If there is impact, it is mainly at a low criminal level. We have pointed out in Chapter 6 that it is debatable whether asset recovery is an inherent aspect of AML, being part of restorative justice.

The vulnerability of any risk-based model is its human interface. Those making decisions – the individuals within FIUs, within regulators and within financial institutions. They are supposed to act rationally and sincerely believe they actually do. However, humans very often act far from rational in decision-making. The pioneering work of Kahneman and Tversky (1984) (briefly mentioned in Chapter 7.3) is relevant again here as they also showed how individuals can be influenced according to how information is 'framed' by a scheme of interpretation.[20] In the narrative of the FATF 'money laundering' is such a scheme, to which we opposed the scheme of 'criminal money management'. They lead to different interpretations and connected decision making. Both Hulsse (2007) and Nichols (1997) drew attention to how easily problems can be created about which action quickly becomes imperative. But to what extent is this interpretation of urgency determined by psychological or political frames or schemata? This book has unpicked the official discourse in the policy documents partly derived from such schemes and tried to find corresponding evidence to support the concluded 'threat'. Not much evidence was dug up while the few bits and pieces of facts were neatly arranged with economic models (or schemes) containing built-in conclusions.

This points to a very real area of vulnerability: the fallacy of self-exception. The whole approach to AML has incorporated the human biases and social consensus about the precise nature, form and extent of the problem and has

---

[19] In simple terms imagine a box comprised on four quadrants with likelihood on one access and impact on the other. Rationally a bank will focus AML resources on the quadrant where there is maximum likelihood of a risk being realised and that when such realisation occurs, it will have the most negative impact on the organisation.

[20] A. Kahneman and D. Tversky (1984) 'Choices, values and frames' *American Psychologist,* 39 (3): 341–350.

designed a response specific to the assumed nature and level of that 'threat', that suited the political decision makers beforehand. Once in motion it was supported by the many profit seeking hangers-on: the AML-service industry. This course of events looks like a collective fyke net in which one can only move forward. This is not unique, as well as it is also not unique to deny that: "We don't fall into that trap". But this is a self-excepting tendency that has haunted many other organisation: giant multinational companies come to mind. They hung on, believing in an outdated business schemes, and while ignoring contrary information until they were ultimately outmanoeuvred by new market entrants.

9

"What is all this good for?" A layman's question

9.1 Introduction: questions from a *tabula rasa*

It can often be elucidatory to explain to a layman what one is doing and for what reasons. The '*tabula rasa*' of the layman forces one to explain what has been taken for granted in the development of the mainstream discourse and routines. So, let us allow that hypothetical layman, as a kind of modern *Candide*[1], already briefly presented in the introduction, to wander through the AML territory. We will try to answer the questions bubbling up from his pure, 'child-like' ignorance.

In the AML field there is, indeed, a lot of activity to be observed that may raise the curiosity of our 'ignorant' visitor, who may ask: "Why do so many FATF and related staff travel to and fro and meet so often; what comes out of all these activities; is there an ultimate objective to be achieved and what effects do all these activities have on that superordinate aim?" After the first questions and answers the visitor, now less naïve, will return with new questions: "What is the impact of the AML regime compared to the pre-AML state of affairs: the 'dark pre-historic ages' of unfettered laundering". And, from the present transparency perspective a further important question: "Who is in charge that can be held accountable in case something goes wrong? Whom to address if the system fails to function as intended or is even harmful, or if a sovereign state

[1] To paraphrase the novel *Candide ou l'optimisme*, by the 18th Century philosopher Voltaire, who describes how a naïve person walked on this earth full of war, cruelty and misery. It was a satire of his colleague, philosopher Leibniz who claimed we live in the best of all possible worlds.

P.C. van Duyne, J.H. Harvey and L.Y. Gelemerova, *The Critical Handbook of Money Laundering*, https://doi.org/10.1057/978-1-137-52398-3_9

simply does not want all these AML regulations because it has not chosen them?" Or the layman visitor may summarise these detailed questions with a simple "*What is all this good for?*"

Naturally, as our ignorant visitor has not read through the huge volume of papers issued by the anti-laundering community, some of his questions have already been discussed in another setting in previous chapters of this book. Nevertheless, we will re-order or rephrase them here to accommodate our hypothetical questioner.

9.2 "What is all this good for?" Duality of aims and knowledge sources

The answer to the naïve question "What is all this good for?", was originally focussed on the problem of drug money laundering (FATF 1990). As set out in the introduction to the FATF document (1990, p. 3) the mandate of the group was to assess the extent of existing cooperation to "prevent the utilisation of the banking system and financial institutions for the purposes of money laundering . . ." This has subsequently evolved into: "to further and preserve the integrity of the financial system".[2] Despite the rationale for this general doctrine having been repeated very many times, our questioner may remain unsatisfied. Does this doctrine denote an observable aim? No, it is a formula that requires the specification of the term 'integrity'. To that end we consult the online Oxford Dictionary which provides the following definition: "The quality of being honest and having strong moral principles." This leads to further definitions of the constituting elements: honesty and moral principles indicating truthfulness and high standards of behaviour. We believe that it should be straightforward to define 'honesty' and 'moral principles' to which one remains loyal. In our context they imply the ethics of the institutions and of its staff surrounding the kind of financial transactions that any honest person would seek to avoid, namely handling (potentially) criminal funds. This is a person and behaviour bound interpretation: integrity is a personal and psychological attribute. Integrity may spread through an institution which, as a kind of derivative, may be considered a 'person' in many legal systems.

To someone like our unknowing visitor this still sounds like an abstract formula with limited tangible relevance to her/his primary question "What is all this good for?" This requires more than explanatory semantics but also something tangible or observable as outcomes. This requires a specification of

[2] Directive 2005/60/EC 26 October 2005 (p. 1) on 'the prevention of the use of the financial system for the purpose of money laundering and terrorist financing', available from: http://eur-lex.europa.eu/legal-content/EN/TXT/?uri=celex:32005L0060. Accessed 19 October 2015.

the effects of AML on the financial system (and designated non-financial sectors) and *beyond*. We have to look at the field of criminality, the proceeds of which allegedly threaten our financial system's integrity. Positive developments may answer this question, of course, for example evidence of the assumed causal connection between criminal phenomena and the AML-regime. However, the idea of causality related to some specified external crime measurement seems not to have been elaborated theoretically or investigated empirically, which should be a part of a proper evaluation. This has never taken place, despite mention of such by the G-7 in the 2004 FATF annual report. Apparently nobody was eager to see this executed: a fateful sign for transparency.

Following this, there is a clear duality in the AML aims. While integrity is a primary aim, there must also be tangible positive effects in terms of *crime reduction*: less profit oriented crime and consequently a lowered laundering-threat posed to the integrity of 'gate keepers': the 'designated financial sectors and professions'. These two aims must remain connected. If we separate them we may get a divided outcome. For example, the pursued integrity and the AML-regime becomes an internal ordering of its own: a rule compliance world. Meanwhile in the 'outside world', the aim of crime-reduction may be reached by other simpler, less demanding approaches, such as a stringent asset recovery regime or other criminal law measures. If we cannot identify mutually connected outside effects, inside and outside the financial industry, we must assume that the criminal world running is its own autonomous course. That implies a relinquishing of a causal connection between the AML regime and its targeted crime for profit, which implies we cannot answer the question: "What is all this good for?".

Before we continue with setting out this question, we have to carry out a '*tour d'horizon*' of our knowledge sources, anticipating the question of our naïve visitor: "where is the evidence for the alleged effects?" The visitor will rightly assume that, given the importance of this global regime, there is an established statistical database. This requirement was, indeed, recognised shortly after the FATF had been established. There was no specific requirement within the original 1990 FATF report for evidence or data gathering, although the 1990-91 annual report referred to the need for operational data sharing by Interpol and the Customs Cooperation Council.[3] But this concerns operational data specifically about the proceeds of criminal activities (p. 12). The need for quantitative data finally found its expression in an Interpol resolution in 1997. In its meeting in New Delhi the ICPO-Interpol

[3] Financial Action Task Force on Money Laundering Report 1990-1991 available from: http://www.fatf-gafi.org/. Accessed 29 September 2017. http://www.fatf-gafi.org/media/fatf/documents/reports/1990%201991%20ENG.pdf. Accessed 29 September 2017.

General Assembly recommended that "member countries collect and circulate such data, particularly through Interpol channels" and also that such data "include at least

- the number of reports on suspicious transactions received from financial institutions and the number of such reports referred for further investigation (giving the outcome of the case where known),
- the number of convictions for money laundering and related charges,
- the number of cases where assets were seized and/or confiscated and the value of the assets forfeited."[4]

Nothing has since been heard of this lofty resolution unless it has silently found its way into the Recommendations of 2003. We have already referred to the intention of the G-7 to evaluate the AML-regime through the FATF in 2004, which met the same fate. Nevertheless, the FATF stressed in its Recommendation 32 (later renumbered 33) that "Countries should ensure that their competent authorities can review the effectiveness of their systems [. . .] by maintaining comprehensive statistics on matters relevant to the effectiveness and efficiency of such systems", after which it mentions the same kind of data as in the Interpol resolution. With a few exceptions, the compliance with this Recommendation has been defective. Most quantitative presentations in the MERs display little more than crude and deficient statistics with limited analysis. For example, there are no interconnections between the phases of case processing: filing a SAR/STR, criminal investigation, prosecution and conviction. There are unconnected information/data columns which are used by the assessors in the MERs for assessing a country's compliance to the Recommendations. Such assessment is bound to remain superficial because with these separate data columns that do not feed into each other, it is not possible to link the number of convictions as a result of prosecutions or the number of prosecutions as a result of investigations, and so on. The reason is simple: there is no *unique reference number* on a case-by-case basis that can be used to make connections between these various columns and across different years. For example, developing the discussion of this point in the previous chapter: to determine effectiveness one must know the ratio of STRs/SARs or investigations related to prosecutions and convictions, which requires an integrated database across all phases. Lacking such information, the 'system' remains opaque and non-transparent which undermines the aim of integrity. How can the AML-regime contribute to the integrity aim if there is no feedback of results? This issue is particularly pressing against the background of the risk-based AML policy: there is no proper risk assessment with-

[4] Resolution No AGN/66/RES/18.

out feedback from criterion variables. Another consequence is the possible 'interpretation gap' (as we earlier identified in Chapter 3) in risk assessment between the regulated sector and its regulators; and indeed, between assessors and the evaluated countries.

We are not alone in drawing attention to the lack of consistency which also affects statistics. Levi *et al.* (2018) point to the tendency of evaluators to report the statistics used within a country because of, firstly a lack of time and secondly, citing Eurostat as an example, the apparent inability of international bodies to be able to pull together a standard set of criminal justice statistics. It should be possible that all countries asked would be able to design a standard database with comparable counting units. Once that is in place, comparative standard statistics can be deducted. Countries are, for example, used to recasting national accounting and banking data into a standardised template in preparation for the IMF Article IV consultations. Why are they not invited to do the same in the field of AML?

Despite these obvious flaws, as long as the evaluated country can present sufficient crude statistics, the FATF considers it as compliant to the relevant Recommendation. We should note that the FATF Data and Statistics report, 2015 E33 'maintenance of statistics' drew attention to the significant problems with the statistics collected within the third round. Indeed, they are incomplete and lack reliability and where available, do not consistently measure the same things. Surprisingly, however, rather than address this lack of consistency, the report seems almost to argue instead for a move away from data. The 2015 document sets out a non-binding guidance on collection and analysis of country data (p. 8) instead of imposing strict methodological rules.

This part of the empirical horizon concerns what happens within the system of the AML-regime. Another part concerns the outside world: changes in the field of profitable crime, whether in the illegal drug market, human trafficking, or any variety of economic or financial crime, including tax evasion. Regretfully, the MERs do not contain statistical information on such *outside* effects: FATF data on effectiveness concern the 'inside' of the AML-regime. Fortunately, as far as *illegal drugs* and related criminality are concerned we are partly served by the UNODC. Nevertheless, these data on drug trafficking, seizures and consumption have not been collected to answer more detailed questions relevant from our AML perspective. The same applies to the UNODC survey of a select number of *property crimes*, which have the advantage of covering a period from 2003-2015, though that does not apply to all responding countries: some started a few years later or did not return the questionnaire in the last or previous years. Economic crime data are more meagrely served. Most overviews are provided by the audit firm PWC in its *Global Economic Crime Survey* (2016). This glossy report presents its questionnaire-based findings in pictures rather than concrete databases.

It should be remarked that all these data have been collected outside the subject of money laundering: the word 'laundering' does not occur in the statistical surveys on drug trafficking, property crime or human trafficking, though it was (without connected data) mentioned in passing three times in the UNODC World Drug Report 2012. The exception is the UNODC (2011) report on assessing illegal money flows. It looks as if the data collections of the FATF and those of the other assessing institutions of criminality in general do not communicate with each other. In consequence databases cannot be connected through similarly defined concepts: a negative finding we cannot explain to our naïve visitor because it is so basic. There is, however, a flipside to this: the data we find are at least not biased by FATF interests. We return to the statistics in section 9.2.2. For now it is sufficient to have shown our visitor the kind of data we have, or do not have.

9.2.1 Integrity and uncertainty

We quoted earlier the online Cambridge dictionary interpretation of integrity (the quality of being honest and having strong moral principles that you refuse to change). This leads to further definitions of the constituting elements: 'honesty' and 'moral principles' indicating truthfulness and standards of behaviour to which one should adhere. It should not be too difficult to give content to 'honesty' and 'moral principles' to which one remains loyal. In the first section of this chapter we provided content to these concepts in our context: avoid involvement with 'fishy' funds, personally and institutionally. Furthermore, the legal person must be sound and honest too.

Our hypothetical naïve visitor may feel amazed and ask the question "Is that all?", suspecting that this simplicity is just the prelude to something more complex. Unfortunately, he is right as there is a subjective 'knowledge' element underlying the attitude to integrity. One must 'know that', a concept that finds its expression in the well-known 'Know Your Customer' principle. Indeed, integrity assumes knowing and within the execution of money laundering it is not a static quality but an on-going process of learning and updating.

In theory, this sounds elegant: a dynamic knowledge supported process as a psychological foundation of integrity. However, in practice it is not that simple because of cognitive uncertainties: how well do you really know your customer? And, if you have strong doubts and file an STR/SAR do you get feedback to confirm or refute your suspicion about your reported customer? As previously remarked, the growth of knowledge is fed by proper feedback: from the FIU to the obliged entities, from the police to the FIU and from the prosecution and courts to the police. As a police officer remarked it should not be that: "I learn the trial outcomes from the newspapers".

Defects in feedback create uncertainty and a feeling of risk. Does this affect the integrity of decision-making? Not necessarily, but it adds another psychological dimension: *risk avoidance* (or de-risking). Even where a bank is sure there are no crime proceeds, the amount of work arising from the legal and regulatory obligations associated with 'high-risk' client relationships, can be disheartening. The lack of clarity with regards to how to mitigate risk and, more importantly, how to satisfy a regulator that risk is being mitigated, means a regulator can interpret the law in many ways and, consequently, can always build a case for a fine (see Gelemerova *et al.* 2018). In the end, reporting institutions may be managing the risk of being fined as opposed to the risk arising from AML/TF. The impression that the revised risk-based approach seems to be advocating greater flexibility in interpretation can result in arbitrary conclusions. For instance, "To what extent has the country sought legal assistance for international co-operation in an appropriate and timely manner to pursue domestic ML, associated predicate offences and TF cases which have transnational elements?"[5] What is a 'timely manner'? Unless there are uniform channels for cooperation and exchange of information where every country has to adhere to the same timeframe, it is difficult to say what 'timely' is. This means that in the case of uncertainty, a risk-avoidance routine may be preferred: either (i) don't run risks and avoid taking on 'high-risk' clients, or (ii) hold off with the transaction and report it to the FIU if you do not have the capacity to fully investigate a red-flag. If such a routine becomes prevalent it may lead to what the FATF calls 'defensive reporting': obliged institutions report anything associated with what a regulator can broadly deem as a laundering risk just to make sure they will not be reproached. Does this affect the aim of integrity? Again, not necessarily, but it may be undermined by such a risk avoidance. It can result, as discussed in Chapter 8, in widespread de-risking and an associated removal of access to the financial system for perfectly legitimate aid agencies or money transfer companies or migrant workers who send their savings home, to what happens to be a 'risky country'.

As was discussed in Chapters 3 and 8, to counter this risk avoidance, in what came to look like an "over-zealous effort to counter the risks", the FATF together with the Electronic Advisory Group introduced guidance on the *risk approach* in 2007, which became the official policy with the new methodology in 2012/13.[6] The financial industry also lobbied for a less prescriptive approach allowing it to devote fewer resources to low-risk cases. The essence of the new approach is a simple and common policy in any insurance, or other financial

---

[5] The FATF consolidated standard on information sharing. Updated November 2017. http://www.fatf-gafi.org/media/fatf/documents/recommendations/pdfs/Consolidated-FATF-Standards-information-sharing.pdf. Accessed 24 January 2018.

[6] FATF (2007) *Guidance on the risk based approach to combat money laundering and terrorist financing. High-level principles and procedures*; p. 16. See also: FATF (2013) *National money laundering and terrorist financing risk assessment.*

institution: efforts aimed at damage control or reduction must be commensurate to their impact and prevalence. Earlier we used the metaphor: "don't kill a mosquito with a cannon" (Van Duyne *et al.*, 2016). Nevertheless, while this is a sound principle, it does not reduce uncertainty surrounding decision making in the regulated sectors. What are the criteria for 'less risk' and, therefore, the associated lower levels of customer due diligence? These cannot be spelled out globally and will have to be specified on a country or even sector level. Albeit from the perspective of corruption, Gelemerova *et al.* (2018) drew attention to the difficulty faced by banks arising from the regulators' focus on country risk, as opposed to case-specific risk. The reality of this means that partners and clients get the risk qualification of their country rather than one based on their conduct. Something that they see as creating an unhelpful bias. Meanwhile the commensurate risk approach does imply an acceptance of letting many small fishes slip through the net. It is plausible to assume that most of these small fishes are 'self-launderers', a category that the FATF has always insisted should be criminalised. In the past twenty years every country that has resisted criminalisation of self-laundering, such as Austria, has been reproached by the FATF; now they are (under conditions) presented by the FATF as below the risk threshold.

Does this affect the integrity? At any rate it affects the concept as a binary requirement. While still heeding to the demand of integrity, we have to accept a scaling in its practical implementation. That was the intention of the 2007 FATF Guidance report (p. 16), warning that an 'over-zealous' focus on tasks may do more harm than good.[7] While this is a good management principle, it increases uncertainties and, thereby, the risks to financial institutions. These risks are manifold, but two are omnipresent: (1) the risk of letting actual laundering slip through and (2) the risk of not having installed or used the required prevention measures. Gelemerova *et al.* (2018) present an interesting example of an activity risking a fine without proof of actual laundering: overlooking the reputation of a customer's country.

> In 2017, the UK's Financial Conduct Authority (FCA) fined Deutsche Bank (DB) £163 million for failing to maintain adequate AML controls from 2012 to 2015. According to the FCA (2017), Deutsche Bank was unable to assess and manage its money laundering risk and engaged in suspicious transactions enabling customers to transfer $10 billion from Russia to overseas, via Deutsche Bank in the UK, 'without detection'. The Financial Conduct Authority's reproach was that Deutsche Bank failed to categorise Russian customers as 'high-risk'."

[7] *Guidance on the risk based approach to combatting money laundering and terrorist financing. High-level principles and procedures*. 2007, FATF/OECD.

This consideration implies weighing a customer's personal integrity risk against his country's corruption reputation. The next important question concerns the political status of the customer: is he or she politically connected or exposed? If this is the case, the customer is a Politically Exposed Person (PEP), requiring a higher level of due diligence. One can imagine that the combination of these two variables produces a category of customers –'politically exposed', plus 'from a high-level corrupt country', which banks seek to avoid. To reduce uncertainty, the circle of 'politically exposed' may be drawn broadly: from sons and daughters to a whole clan. Therefore, the FATF warns that,

> "Refusing a business relationship with a person simply on the basis of the determination that he or she is a [PEP] is contrary to the letter and spirit of this Directive and of the revised FATF Recommendations" [. . .] All to no avail: "by focusing on geography and prominence, and without providing adequate guidance on mitigation and how to factor in product risk, the authorities in the US and the UK have made it difficult for banks to service PEPs." (Gelemerova *et al.*, 2018)

This suggests that PEPs from countries with a negative Corruption Perception Index are unlikely to be on-boarded or such existing clients are likely to be off-loaded (institutions will de-risk). This may be reinforced by the requirement to have a closer look at family relationships and associates. In cases where a customer has risky political connections and is from a country with an 'extended family' tradition (and the country itself has a high-risk score), this would be a rational procedure. However, how deep should regulated entities, from large banks to designated businesses and professions, dig to show it heeds the aim of integrity?

> Sometimes by hindsight, there are reasons to dig deeper than was thought of before. This was the case with 'Putin's cellist' and lifelong friend Roldugin. Seemingly a man of modest means, he remained under the radar when in 2014, the USA imposed sanctions against Russians connected to the Kremlin. Later, in 2016, the Panama Papers brought a serious miser to light: 'Putin's cellist' was a very important but possibly passive link in a global transaction carrousel to handle unaccounted monies from and to Russia. US law enforcement agents investigate whether this money flow is connected to the alleged Magnitsky scheme of $230 million, siphoned off from the Russian tax administration.
>
> Source: The Panama Papers, The International Consortium of Investigative Journalists, available at https://panamapapers.icij.org/

In this case the Panama Papers brought to light that reporting institutions should have been aware of sensitive political connections, requiring a deeper look into this individuals' sources of wealth. But regulators' expectations of how the various PEPs needed to be treated, are not completely clear either: there are no objective yardsticks. This can lead to heightened requirements such as those imposed by the US and the UK regulators. These make their own more stringent demands, forcing regulators in other countries to also accept their requirements. International economic sanctions are a good example. Ignoring economic sanctions against a country appears to be treated in a similar way to money laundering.

Indeed, where adequate guidance and yardsticks are missing, there is a risk of subjectivity or even arbitrariness in deciding on whether and how to embark on an extensive PEP-due diligence. Does this observation also apply to wider circles of the AML policy implementation? For example, policies concerning remittances by migrant workers or informal value transfers ('underground banking'): what do we know of their cross-border implementation? Are the reporting standards for SARs/STRs the same for the sending as for the receiving countries? In that case the figures of the FIUs in the sending and receiving countries should be roughly the same. In an older study Van Duyne (2007; pp. 78 and 86) found that this was not the case: for example, what was reported as wired from country A to country B was not found as incoming money in country B, and the other way round (a similar finding was reported by Johannesen and Zucman, 2014). Such inconsistences in national financial flows were traditionally attributed to 'errors and omissions' in the national accounts. These are usually small in nature and likely to occur as positive or negative. However, newspaper reports have found consistent flows to and within the UK that appear linked to the escalation of London house prices. Also here we find no connections between organisations aiding the flows of information. Is this due to differences in data gathering, policy implementation or just the usual organisational opaqueness and lack of interest in data transparency? Nobody knows.

Meanwhile, with so many questions unanswered and so many ambiguous explanations, the prime aim of integrity, while still fully valid, has become less clear. Our hypothetical naïve visitor has good reasons to wonder why it is so difficult to get an answer to his basic question: "What is all this good for?"

9.2.2 Crime reduction: the external criterion

As we remarked in the introduction to this chapter: integrity is fine, but it must contribute towards something other than integrity itself. Otherwise it becomes a kind of inward directed, pious but introverted praying. Given the basic nature of profit-oriented crime, reducing it by fighting 'criminal financing' is an obvious, but not an exclusive or even the best option. However, it has an important motivational foundation: making it difficult for criminals to use financial institutions to enjoy the fruits of their crimes, has a demotivating and, thereby, a crime reducing effect (as is assumed). At first sight this looks plausible, but it neglects the finding that most proceeds are at the low end of the criminal income scale and are usually spent without entering the financial institutions. As mentioned in Chapter 2, analysis of Dutch confiscation databases shows that the median of bank accounts and hoarded cash (also qualified as laundering) is around €5,000 (Van Duyne and Soudijn, 2010). This is confirmed by the Dutch assets recovery data from 1995-2011 which showed an even lower median value: €3,300. Only 2% of those convicted were served a recovery order for more than €100,000 (Van Duyne *et al.*, 2014; pp. 245–247).[8] We can conclude that most of the profit directed crime is at the low end of the criminal income range and that only a small rich minority may face laundering problems: they get stuck with unlaundered cash. If this cash constitutes the frequently mentioned threat of 'money available-for-laundering', the discouragement policy must work on this sub-population of richer criminals. Discouraging this smaller rich criminal sub-population also means taking into account their financial management behaviour and style. An all-encompassing approach appears to be of little efficiency and effectiveness.

Addressing the higher earning criminals may have an effect on criminal markets as it is likely that these individuals have more leverage in the flow of contraband. Whether this also applies to common property crime is uncertain. Plain thieves and burglars are more likely to need a trusted fence than a trusted bank for laundering. The present legal construct of money laundering does not distinguish between the two types of criminals. This makes studying the phenomenon, and addressing it, more difficult.

Moreover, the 'rational' discouragement or deterrence hypothesis may underestimate the impulsiveness of much property crime: a quick 'grabber' is probably not discouraged by AML measures assuming that he knows of them in the first place.

Though there are theoretical doubts about the effectiveness of the deterrence hypothesis, it has been mentioned so often in working papers of the FATF, IMF and World Bank, that a proper inspection of the available data is required. As we discussed previously and will see further below, there are indications that undermine the plausibility of this hypothesis. The very fact that these organisations claim that laundering still occurs on such a massive scale suggests the AML regime is not as effective as expected. This is not a hypothesis testing as is usual in behavioural science: the concepts are not operationalised and the available data have many *caveats* (under-reporting of crime

---

[8] See also Van Duyne and Levi (2005), Van Duyne (2013), Levi (2015); and Harvey and Lau (2009).

('dark numbers') police inaccuracy and so on). The best one can do is to make rough trend comparisons at the ordinal level and then look for the most plausible fit of the theory to the data.

A few critical methodological annotations must be made more explicitly, because we use the UNODC data, as this allows for better cross-country comparisons.[9] In the first place, the data are collected according to crime categories, with the main subdivisions of drug crimes, property crimes and violent crimes. The important lucrative category of financial and economic crime/fraud is not mentioned on the UNODC website database: a serious omission of this category of offenders to whom the 'rational' discouragement approach could be relevant. We found no explanation for this omission.

Thus, we have:

a. the UNODC World Drug Reports providing trends on the four main markets: opiates, cocaine, cannabis and synthetic drugs;
b. property crimes: kidnapping (for money), robbery, theft and burglary (dwellings).

For each of these categories we look at the main global trends and will only occasionally single out separate countries or events. Our two main questions are (1) do the documents make any reference to the AML-regime as a mitigating factor in the drugs market or the commitment of property crimes? (2) even if there is no mention, can we discern in the trends some connection to AML developments, such as the risk-based approach?

Before turning to this task, we should note that we are not the first to ask searching questions about the relationship between AML and drug crime prevalence. For example, the IMF Review of Effectiveness, 2011 (footnote 12) states "The analysis of global compliance with the AML/CFT standard reveals an absence of correlation, however, between a given country's compliance with the standard and its contribution to global drug production, consumption, and trafficking, a crime known to generate significant proceeds that need laundering". This observation is drawn from Verdugo Yepes (2011, p. 20) who states "there are countries with high levels of AML/CFT compliance and low levels of involvement in the drug trade and countries with high AML/CFT compliance and that contribute a great deal to the global drug problem".[10] This absence of correlation implies at least that modesty is required in claiming effects from the AML-regime.

---

[9] UNODC Publication Reports 2017.

[10] Concha Verdugo Yepes, IMF Working Paper WP/11/177 Compliance with the AML/CFT International Standard: lessons from a Cross-Country Analysis, 1 July 2011.

a. The drug market

To find references and trends in the four drug markets we inspected the UNODC World Drug Reports 2012-2017; the UNODC Illegal Financial Flows 2011; UNODC Overview of Drug Demand and Health; and the European Drug Report 2015 of the EMCDDA.

First we inspected the documents for the occurrence of 'laundering/launder' and 'FATF'. With the exception of the UNODC Illegal Financial Flow 2011, which exclusively elaborated the laundering issue, and three short mentions in the World Drug Report 2016 in a section on deforestation resulting from drug production (pp. 89–90) we found no reference to money laundering or the FATF. For a global threat and the worldwide standard bearer this does not look impressive. Given the extensive reporting on illegal financial flows of the UNODC 2011 report, this absence cannot be explained as 'bureaucratically forgotten'. Or does it reflect the less than modest influence of the AML-regime and the FATF on crime control? We have little meaningful data to answer this question. The authors of the UNODC 2011 report expressed their despair for their estimate:

> "Data collected by the US State Department suggest that some $3.1 billion were seized in connection with money-laundering activities in 38 countries [. . .] This would be equivalent to some 0.2% of the best estimate of the extent of money-laundering at the global level. In comparison, more than 20% of the globally produced illicit opiates are being seized and more than 40% of the cocaine."

This observation leads to the question whether money-launderers really are so much smarter than drug traffickers, or is there something wrong with the existing AML-control system? The authors of the report think "more likely, shortcomings in the implementation of existing instruments" (UNODC, 2011; p. 41). So, by implication: Has the new instrument, the RBA, made any difference?

In the absence of references to the FATF and laundering we have to design AML-impact criteria ourselves. The FATF documents are of little help in this regard. As pointed out in the literature sections of this book, there is no AML-theory from which to deduct hypotheses spelling out 'if . . . then . . .' statements: for example a correlation between levels of dissuasive AML measures and drug crime reduction, in terms of something like interception rates, prices or consumption prevalence. So, what is likely to happen if well-earning drug criminals are discouraged because they cannot launder their proceeds due to the effective due diligence thresholds? They have cash but cannot spend it in the regulated sectors: from banks to real estate, car dealers or jewellers, there are alert gate watchers everywhere. If the AML-policy is effective, crime-entrepreneurs do not have many options:

- they leave the market;
- they scale down their business;
- or, as mentioned in the last chapter, they continue their criminal re-investments and recycling outside of the formal economy to avoid paper trails.

Big earners will be spending some of their income on day-to-day ordinary life activities (such as food, consumer and household products, transport). However, spending more than they legitimately earn (for instance, on a luxury lifestyle) will likely attract attention. Given the supposedly effective AML-policy, we also assume that the 'supply holes' created by the exiting drug entrepreneurs are not immediately filled by rising opportunist traders, as this would contradict the assumption of an AML success. If all this holds and given an unchanged demand, we would expect a supply reduction, rising prices or lower purity.

However, the hypothesis of discouragement and drug market changes could not be confirmed from the UNODC graphs and tables. In the first place, because these representations of global developments lack the necessary granularity to deduce detailed correlations between a non-operationalised independent variable (AML-discouragement policy) and the dependent (supply reduction) variable. The available UNODC comments on the variations from year to year and country to country make clear that in this field, for every illegal commodity we always have to account for (a) multi-variable determined causality and (b) missing or polluted data. Against this background the global drug markets look rather stable and certainly not very receptive to subtle psychological influences such as AML-discouragement. The data as well as comments also make clear that wholesale entrepreneurs are active in smoothing shortages due to interceptions: for example with opiates "The build-up or depletion of previous years' opium inventories may be used to offset annual changes in production and maintain the supply of heroin." (UNODC, 2016). Indeed, despite some temporal and regional seizure peaks, the timelines of consumption prevalence 1998-2015 look smooth. Clearly, if anti-money laundering measures had any effect on these crime markets, the UNODC statistical presentations need a further detailed analysis beyond the data presented in the diagrams. As the UNODC also uses raw data from the European Monitoring Centre of Drugs and Drugs Addiction (EMCDDA) and its archive allows the download of excel files, we explored this material looking for traces of AML-effects

The EMCDDA archive is very extensive: from prevalence of drug use to problematic use in prisons and health and social responses. However, there is

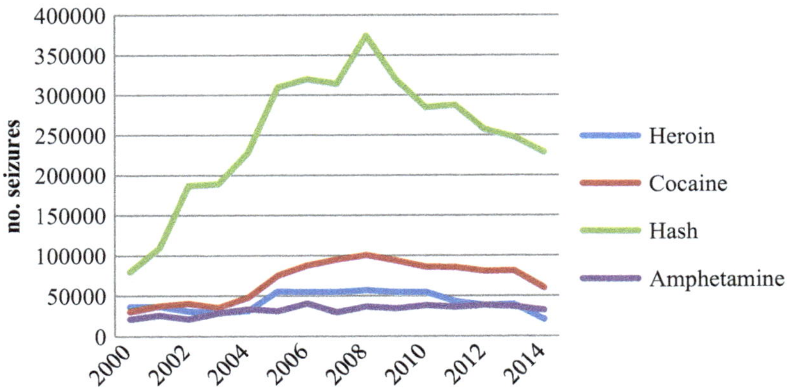

Fig. 9.1 Number of seizures in the EU: 2000-2014. Source: The authors based on data available from EMCDDA website, http://emcdda.europa.eu/data/stats2017_enc

no mention of the FATF and AML. Nevertheless, we thought it best to look for the statistics about interceptions as presented in Figure 9.1. We assume that these figures would, to a large extent, reflect law enforcement priorities, efforts, budget *and* the bad luck of smugglers who lose their contraband. This is something financial and perhaps relevant to AML: under normal market conditions, it is plausible that there is an inverse relationship between seizures and proceeds. Thus, if the seizure rate goes up, the money laundering threat declines. Moreover, if the seizure rate remains 'flat' we can assume a more or less stable market and a corresponding regular flow of proceeds with related money laundering transactions.

It sounds like an easy and elegant hypothesis, but the quality of the data is insufficient to test it. In the first place, the compiled excel files show many gaps, due to countries not submitting their data every year. Whether this was caused by national organisational impediments or for reasons of methodological principles, at this stage, can only be answered in the case of the Netherlands. It stopped submitting the yearly compiled drug figures in 2001 as it thought these methodologically misleading. France, otherwise a country with many interceptions, showed numerous data gaps from 2009 onwards, as did Poland for seven to eight years, depending on the nature of the commodity. Concerning the steep rise in seizures from 2003/4 onwards we must warn of a participation effect: Italy and England and Wales started their participation in 2004, Romania in 2005. Apart from that, from 2003 onwards Spain appears to have intensified its seizure policy contributing to a large proportion of the total seizures.

To obtain a better picture, the data have to be detailed with figures about the volume or prices of the seizures, in order to differentiate according to value: if the focus is on impacting serious crime the 'big money' should have priority. This requires a differentiation based on raw data in order to determine significant changes. In the absence of access to raw data we must be guided by aggregate data as presented in Figure 9.1. Searching for signs of impact it may be efficient to inspect the cannabis data first: this is the only law enforcement field where we observe more variation. However, any correlation with AML measures is purely speculative. The other crime markets reflect the observations from the UNODC annual drug reports: after some peaking, seizures revert to their long-term average trend, underlining the resilience of drug markets (a point that was also observed more than a decade ago, see Van Duyne and Levi, 2005).

Inspecting the cannabis resin excel table we also looked at the weight in terms of kilos as an indication of commercial value. We also looked at the proportion of the countries in terms of total numbers of seizures and related weight, in order to determine the relative importance of one or more countries within the whole picture.

It appears that in this regard Spain is absolutely dominant: 55% of the reported seizures during the period 2000-2014 came from Spain. Only France also had a percentage in double figures: 14.3% to which should be added that it did not submit any statistics in the last 6 years (a hint to the messy methodology on which policy makers must rely). The UK is the third largest with 8%.

As indicated, weight is important because it represents value. Indeed, with an easy sweep among users, for example at festivals, the authorities can score high numbers but with a low average (consumption) weight. Where do we have the highest weight: relatively and in average kilos? With its share of the total kilos seized Spain was again on top: while it has 55% of all seizures, it accounted for 71% of the total seized volume in kilos. The remainder was scattered over the 29 other countries. But this does not represent a high mean seizure weight: with a mean weight of 2.8 kilo for all countries Spain, with 3.2 kilos, was well above that average, but much lower than Italy (7 kilos but only 4.2% of total seizured weight) and Turkey (4.4 kilos but with only 2.3% of total seizured weight).. The UK, third with 8% of the seizures, had a mean of 0.7 kilos, indicating primarily low weight catches and corresponding low monetary value.

This reconnaissance is as far as we can get with the present data: interesting differences, a kind of mosaic, but only a first step towards addressing the question: what does the dissuasive AML policy do to the drug market? With all the ups and downs of temporary law enforcement success (but not mentioned as attributable to the AML policy) any discouragement does not seem to be perceptible. If law enforcement takes a bite out of the market it is a setback, but it soon returns to 'business as usual'.

b. Property criminality

In addition to the profitable criminality of the illegal drug market there are criminal revenues from common predatory property crimes about which

UNODC issued a report in 2017, covering the time span 2003-2015.[11] From this data set we selected the common profit motivated crime categories: theft, robbery, kidnapping and burglary for trend inspection for the EU member states, the USA, Canada, Australia and New Zealand. The developments in this time span for these categories per 100,000 inhabitants showed in general a significant reduction in crime rate:

Kidnapping:	- 32%
Theft:	- 36%
Robbery:	- 63%
Burglary:	- 37%

Obviously, these data, presented without background, do not give an explanation for this crime rate decrease. The AML regime may have played a role in discouraging criminals, but this remains an implausible speculation: these are crime categories with total profits smaller than profits generated in the drug market. The impact of the generally ageing population in the industrialised countries may be a more plausible hypothesis.[12]

However, this hypothesis does not hold for all countries. Greece showed an increase in all property crimes and France, Luxembourg, Romania and Germany for some of them.

> During and after the financial crises *Greece* showed an increase in all property crimes. Kidnapping increased from 0.22 in 2013 to 1.55 in 2010 per 100,000 inhabitants; theft increased from 510 to 1,158 a year later; robbery went up from 21 to 59 (2011) and burglary from 240 to 781 (2011).
>
> *Luxembourg* saw its property crime rate rising too, though little is known about the effects of the credit crises in this small, wealthy country. Over the whole period theft and burglary increased by respectively 31 incidents and 28%. The violent forms of property crime, kidnapping and robbery, increased by 156 and 64%.
>
> *France* showed an increase in kidnapping of 84% and theft of 38%.
>
> The prevalence of *kidnapping* increased throughout this period in Poland (121%), Italy (109%), Lithuania (56%), Ireland (49%), Belgium (5%) and Romania (2%).

As such these are interesting findings deserving more background knowledge. Unfortunately, we cannot dwell on them further, as we only explored these data

---

[11] UNODC (2017) Theft national level, police records. Financial and economic crime is lacking.

[12] The Dutch Statistics Office. In a press release it was noticed that crime reduction appeared to be due to an aging population with younger people tending to stay at home, clinging to their smart phones and tablets.

in order to address the question of our naïve visitor about the effects of AML policy on profit-directed crime. With the interesting exceptions annotated above, there is a general reduction in the profit generating crime rates. Interestingly, the MERs do not mention this trend, let alone claim this as evidence of AML success. Either it was silently recognised that the general ageing population hypothesis is more plausible or, most likely, the assessors were simply unaware of these statistical trends. The same applied to the FATF as a whole.

9.2.3 Comparison with the Mutual Evaluation Reports fourth round

As there are no clear cross-references between FATF Annual Reports or other AML-documents and empirical documents on profit directed criminality as discussed in the previous section, we decided to inspect the mutual evaluation reports of the fourth round which are drawn up from the perspective of the Risk Based Approach (RBA). Our question is: do the MERs mention the effects of the new RBA on profit making criminality? It is not our intention to evaluate these MERs. Nonetheless, we will look at various connected aspects through the lens of the assessments. One aspect is the FATF's demand: do the authorities understand the RBA? If there is no understanding one cannot expect much of a result. Of course, we also looked at what risks were mentioned, some indications about the size of the organisations facing the challenge and some outcome variables, for which we also looked at the nature of the statistics. From our perspective, claiming effectiveness without statistical underpinning must be considered as a non-valid statement.

At the time of writing only the fourth round MERs of the countries that also featured in our UNODC sample of property crime have been selected: Australia; Austria; Belgium; Canada; Hungary; Italy; Norway; Spain; Sweden; and the USA.

The following abstracts summarise the respective MERs:

Australia

- **Risk understanding**: 'good' but little specific detail; there is a national Organised Crime-strategy, a threat assessment but no AML /CFT strategy or risk-based resource allocation.
- **Risk profile**: country is attractive to foreign syndicates; banking sector vulnerable to complex financial structures; inward and outward money flows; no further specification.
- **Crime-money laundering threats**: illegal drugs, tax and other fraud: mainly 'usual suspects'. No data for proceeds estimation.

- **Organisations**: 13 bodies (from central to federal) for formulating and implementation.
- **Prioritisation**: "disrupt and deter predicate crime", not ML. No results data.
- **Assets recovery**: defective statistics but stable pattern nonetheless.
- **Risk mitigation**: 'some' (unspecified), but not regarding drug predicate offences.
- **Statistics**: crude, no breakdowns by specific variables; absent statistics concerning freezing; differences at federal/state & territory level; no private sector data, no feedback and deficient for evaluation.[13]
- **Predicate crime rate**: no reduction (contradiction with UNODC: data from the same office); no mention of success in making (drug) crime unprofitable;
- **Investigation, prosecution and conviction for ML**: only crude statistics presented; no breakdown by predicate offences;
- **Correspondence with risks**: ". . . the overall results are lower than they could be relative to the nature and scale of the risks".(p. 8; para. 10). But 'scale of risks' is not indicated, nor a baseline as a point of comparison.

From the text of the MER of Australia the risk and outcome of risk-based policy are indeterminable. Actually, this MER does not say very much of the outside world of crime.

Austria

- **Risk understanding**: mixed understanding: "no holistic picture" but list of separate risk factors; no formal risk assessment, rather subjective perceptions; no single national picture of ML risk.
- **Risk profile**: complex ML cases, professional money launderers, and ML related to foreign predicate Italian and East European Organised Crime; no specification.
- **Crime/ML-threats**: mainly 'usual suspects': organised crime, human trafficking, smuggling, drug trafficking, corruption, VAT fraud and other types of fraud, such as phishing, theft and customs/excise tax evasion;
- **Organisation**: 18 ministries and authorities involved; no formalised AML strategy or policy; authorities determine their own priorities.
- **Prioritisation**: "undue focus on predicate offences" and self-ML, not on complex ML as expected of an international financial centre and risk profile.

[13] R 33 'largely compliant' looks very flattering and is not supported by assessors' own annotations throughout the report with 64 instances of 'statistics'.

- **Assets recovery**: not in line with its risk profile; limited results due to court approval and less focus; low level of profit making crime: mean = €12.000. Ambiguous statistics.
- **Risk mitigation**: three references, no description or specification;
- **Statistics**: Not clear to what extent statistics from various authorities/departments are integrated in one database;
- **Predicate crime rate**: not specified;
- **Investigation, prosecution and conviction**: too little and too low sanctions for ML;
- **Correspondence with risks**: "suboptimal effectiveness"

The MER contains no risk or risk profile specification, just the word 'risk' used for comparison and judgments, but lacking content.[14] No reference is made to a relevant predicate crime level. Instead, reference was made to the general international profile as an 'international financial centre', fitting many other countries as well. There is mention of insufficient staff, small courts and small prosecution offices. 'Effectiveness' concerns matters *inside* the AML-regime and is otherwise indeterminable.[15]

Belgium

- **Risk understanding**: actions based on risk but understanding is fragmented and incomplete (although not for all authorities); there is no synthesis, no ranking of risks and no direction to new trends (this requirement is not found in other MERs).
- **Risk profile**: transit country for illegal funds; cash sectors; underground economy.
- **Crime/ML threats**: (tax) fraud, economic crime, organised crime (drugs): 'usual suspects'.
- **Organisation**: AML cooperation and coordination institutionalised.
- **Prioritisation**: there is an overall approach and corresponding resources allocation, but the local focus is primarily on predicate offences and the potential of confiscation.
- **Assets recovery**: no clear statistics; lack of resources; but still also a driver for investigation: hoped-for assets are a criterion for prioritisation in the case of tax fraud and drugs; new recovery law February 2014: too early for effect measurement.

---

[14] Issued September 2016; 206 pages. Assessment team: eight staff; three reviewers 3.

[15] The report observes in para 178 that "Austria has not shown results in line with Austria's ML/FT risk profile as an international financial centre, with funds transiting through Austria where no predicate offence may have taken place."

- **Risk mitigation**: two references relating to the diamond trade and Belgian National Bank
- **Statistics**: partly good, but available statistics not used; not up to date concerning asset recovery.
- **Predicate crime rate**: not presented.
- **Investigation, prosecution and conviction**: Sanction regime satisfactory; third party ML convictions are rare; still no general criminal policy guidance of investigation and prosecution derived from National RBA.
- **Correspondence with risks**: "substantial results in international co-operation, use of financial information", though the 'risk' is only roughly referred to.

The MER contains insufficient specifications to gauge the effectiveness of Belgium's risk approach. Local prosecution, "on the ground" offices, seem to determine their own priorities based on local needs and resources. In contrast, the MER prioritises the ML prosecution above predicate crime mitigation. [16]

Canada

- **Risk understanding**: all authorities have a good understanding. Loophole: legal firms, councils and Quebec notaries do not have to comply with the AML regime due to a 2015 Supreme Court of Canada ruling.
- **Risk profile**: estimate of proceeds of crime generated: 3-5% of GDP. Laundered: between CAD5-15 billion. 650 OC groups; third party laundering; risk of foreign funds. NRAC carries out a gap analysis for 'residual risks' after mitigation.
- **Crime/ML threats**: FINTRAC: drugs related offences; fraud and tax evasion, organised crime, involved in illegal trafficking (drugs, tobacco, humans). NRA: fraud (marketing, mortgage, payment cards, trade); counterfeiting; corruption; foreign funds.
- **Organisation**: established in the Proceeds of Crime Money Laundering and Terrorist Financing Act (PCMLTFA): Finance Canada is lead agency which chairs four main government bodies of AML regime; 14 authorities involved for policy and coordination, prevention and detection, investigation and disruption. Staffing and budget not mentioned.
- **Prioritisation**: LEAs (Royal Canadian Mounted Police) have a prioritisation of their own mainly focused on drugs and fraud; insufficiently focused on ML as a main risk.

---

[16] Issued April 2015: 213 pages. Assessment team: seven staff; three reviewers.

- **Assets recovery**: federally seized amount (CAD44 million) show a downward trend from 2009 onwards. Cross-border cash possessions: 9% was forfeited: also a downward trend
- **Risk mitigation**: powers legally arranged under the PCMLTFA.
- **Statistics**: breakdown by ML, proceeds of crime, drugs, fraud and 'other'.
- **Predicate crime rate**: presented time series of ML-related prosecutions and proceeds of crime cases (prosecution and conviction) show a decreasing trend.
- **Investigation, prosecution and conviction**: ML emerges mainly from predicate crimes investigations; RCMP prioritises with own weights, not matching to identified risks in the NRA. Tension with National Security priorities is not elaborated. What must have priority: National Security or NRA? And in weighing this choice, to whom are policy makers accountable: Parliament and voters or FATF?
- **Correspondence with risks**: law enforcement agencies prioritise predicate offences, drugs and OCGs: numbers of ML convictions too low in view of assumed but unspecified risks.

Is Canada successful in mitigating predicate crime? There is statistically a downward trend, but the MER does not take notice of this, let alone attribute it to the AML-regime but makes a negative comparison with the assumed higher NRA-risk profile: there must be more. The statistics are still too crude for any causal attribution of effectiveness. [17]

Hungary

- **Risk understanding**: rather 'mixed' understanding; no clear picture; Hungarian FIU and LEAs show more understanding of RBA. No critical (financial) analysis: superficial, no breakdown with little attention to organised crime, corruption or professional laundering. Because of lack of statistics, risk-based supervision cannot be determined, except for the HFIU.
- **Risk profile**: cash-based (shadow) economy (unexplained transactions in payment accounts) attractive to OC, increase of payment institutions, casino and card-room operators plus lawyers as company service providers; evasive beneficial ownership and misuse of (foreign) legal persons (straw men).
- **Crime/ML threats**: because of cash-based economy and financial industry, the country is attractive to foreign OC. Fraud (high), corruption (medium)

[17] Issued September 2016; 216 pages. Assessment team: ten staff; five reviewers.

and trafficking drug and humans (low threat rating). Increase of OCGs using cybercrime.

- **Organisation**: AML Subcommittee composed of 6 ministries and other bodies. For AM policy and implementation there are 17 responsible bodies.
- **Prioritisation**: no articulated strategy; no ML priorities deducted from the NRA;
- **Assets recovery**: recovery (also of equivalent value) is mandatory for prosecution. Central role of Asset Recovery Office, though the yield is very modest. Role also for HFIU for suspending transactions and freezing accounts.
- **Risk mitigation**: no coordination of actions for mitigating resource allocation. Otherwise also not much implementation by supervisors or DNFBPs.
- **Statistics**: shortcoming, incoherent throughout the Law Enforcement organisation (except HFIU); serious impediment for assessment.
- **Predicate crime rate**: no specific mentions or crime rate is no issue.[18]
- **Investigation, prosecution and conviction**: no cases based on NRA risk rating: main trigger for investigation is predicate offence instead of ML.
- **Correspondence with risks**: difficult to determine. The risk assessment is not very convincing and any statement about a deviation from some risk profile lacks proper foundation.[19]

To all effects it is impossible to determine any effect of the AML measures relative to a particular crime prevalence, let alone risk profile.[20]

Italy

- **Risk understanding**: the main authorities have a good understanding of risk: the LEAs, financial institutions, but to lesser extent the non-financial sector. Italy has not yet developed a nationally coordinated strategy informed by NRA but is in the process of doing so (p. 7 para.18).
- **Risk profile**: tax evasion is the main source of proceeds (criminal savings). Then comes organised crime and corruption though not enough is known (from the MER) about this issue.
- **Crime/ML threats**: Foreign legal arrangements; tax evasion is the "biggest single" ML threat. New OCGs next to traditional mafia.
- **Organisation**: 17 ministries, authorities and entities with public functions in this domain.

---

18 The MER (p. 21) does, however, refer to the NRA as identifying fraud as high risk.

19 It seems that the assessment team has also used the reports on the situation in Hungary, issued by the US Department of State.

20 Issued September 2016; 223 pages. Assessment team: seven assessors; three reviewers.

- **Prioritisation**: LEAs focus on domestic predicate crime with ML following.
- **Assets recovery**: comprehensive framework. Priority: tax evasion as well as organised crime: conviction and prevention based. Italy is a member of (informal) Camden Asset Recovery Interagency Network. Increase in mafia confiscations: €2 billion in 2014.
- **Risk mitigation**: no exemptions from AML requirements.
- **Statistics:** comprehensive statistics, but no integration of the databases of the different authorities. No detailed breakdowns.
- **Predicate crime rate**: tables unsuitable for crime rate assessment even if most figures show a decreasing trend.
- **Investigation, prosecution and conviction**: prosecution and conviction rate for corruption is difficult to interpret; prosecution is possible in cases where a suspect habitually lives from proceeds: no statistics for this option.
- **Correspondence with risks**: figures in most time series show a downward trend suggesting a lower figure than the projected magnitude (high) of the risk presentation, which, however, is unspecified. Next follows a jumping to conclusions from the unspecified high risk: because 'there must be more'.

Italy has the best laws, regulations and institutions, according to the MER, but it cannot be determined whether it is effective in terms of crime prevention. The AML-regime seems to be effective internally, but outside effects are not mentioned. [21]

Norway

- **Risk understanding**: the authorities have insufficient understanding of ML risks, according to the MER: policies not based on risks; no *overarching* strategy, except an Action Plan against Economic Crime (not translated); not well framed. NRA seriously flawed: procedurally not all stakeholders participating or not all available data involved.
- **Risk profile**: no risk profile apart from a few threat assessments. Cash deposits and withdrawals; handling high-value assets (by professionals); Money Value Transfer System (MVTS); many NOKs smuggled out of the country (€195 million).
- **Crime/ML threats**: Norwegian organised crime gangs (motor cycle), Swedish and Baltic criminals.

[21] Issued February 2016; 230 pages. Assessment team: eight staff; three reviewers.

- **Organisation**: 14 ministries, authorities and entities with public functions in this domain. However, no principal body or coordination mechanism developing national policies.
- **Prioritisation**: focus on predicate offences rather than ML and economic crime. Self-laundering reserved for obvious cases.
- **Assets recovery**: 5-year average: €8.3 million (2009-2013), slightly decreasing.
- **Risk mitigation**: with no proper NRA, mitigation is also indeterminable.
- **Statistics**: shortcomings.
- **Predicate crime rate**: no proper statistics in place: flaws due to wrong classification.
- **Investigation, prosecution and conviction**: from 2010: 18 ML prosecutions and 15 convictions; eight cases began as ML but pursued for predicate crime (Økokrim). Majority of ML offences consist of 'receiving' (fencing). ML added as an extension of the charge (subsidiary).
- **Correspondence with risks**: many ML cases were drug-related or concerned tax evasion. With little reliable data as a substantiation of statements on risk, the ML magnitude remains unspecified, let alone being able to have a role in comparisons and judgments.[22]

Spain

- **Risk understanding**: risk assessments are carried out by most obliged sectors or their supervisors, but there is no RA at a national level. The non-financial sector does not have a risk-based pro-active approach.
- **Risk profile**: the country is a transhipment territory for drugs from Latin America and North Africa (declining slightly).
- **Crime/ML threats**: high intensity criminal organisations: drugs and human trafficking. Foreign criminals residing in Spain, possibly laundering in real estate. Illegal flow of cash (MVTS). Tax crimes.
- **Organisation**: the Commission for the Prevention of Money Laundering and Monetary Offences. There are numerous interagency working groups and mechanisms to facilitate operational coordination.
- **Prioritisation**: high intensity criminal organisations. Parallel financial investigation mentioned as routine.
- **Assets recovery**: an increase in confiscation volume but no exact figures; instead, general global information.
- **Risk mitigation**: disrupting and dismantling criminal organisations in Spain.

---

[22] Issued December 2014; 206 pages. Assessment staff: ten assessors; three reviewers.

- **Statistics: predicate crime rate**: compliant, but no statistics on crime rate. Time series is too short (three years) and no breakdowns of crime-type against other variables.
- **Investigation, prosecution and conviction**: modest number of investigations through FIU dissemination. Prosecution and conviction numbers are also modest, still the rating is "substantial". Sentencing: sanction too lenient.
- **Correspondence with risks**: the assessors are of the opinion that investigation and prosecution are consistent with threats and risks.

Though Spain is praised for its compliance, the numbers are modest and a baseline for comparison is lacking: many compliance statements cannot be underpinned by figures.[23]

Sweden

- **Risk understanding**: generally "sound", but with key agencies more sound than in the NRA 2013-14. The NRA is more detailed in drawing on earlier trend reports. Lack of quantitative data and knowledge. Few pieces of legislation are actually based on risk or are dragged in *post hoc*. Some of the national policies are without a mechanism for updating.
- **Risk profile**: cash money transfers; cash as tools for criminals; tax crime.
- **Crime/ML threats**: financial and tax crimes; misuse of legal persons; cash intensive businesses (MVTS); theft (including of vehicles); black labour market.
- **Organisation**: 16 authorities and self-regulatory bodies. Single authority for ML: Brå. There are five main groups: LEAs, supervisory and directory authorities, self-regulatory bodies and obliged entities. Complex structure for coordination with weak inter-institution feedback.
- **Prioritisation**: "disconnects": (local) agencies have their own agendas and predicate crimes remain a first priority.
- **Assets recovery**: Measure Prohibition on Disposal of Property. Poor statistics; figures of tax reclaims sliding down. Proceeds recovered in line of risks.
- **Risk mitigation**: general formulation, no mention of concrete mitigation.
- **Statistics:** crime statistics is of "uneven quality" whether on sentencing or asset recovery.
- **Predicate crime rate**: no information

[23] Issued December 2014; 206 pages. Assessment team: ten staff; three reviewers.

- **Investigation, prosecution and conviction**: new ML law July 2014 with lower evidence threshold and self-laundering (not many cases recorded). Prosecution rate 53%. The principle of concurrent offences applies: predicate plus ML offence. The possibility of low sentences for ML is 'regretted' by the FATF+.
- **Correspondence with risks**: the report makes a statement that lack of data limits the understanding of the authorities. This applied to all layers of LEAs. Observation of 'aquarium economy' is an illustration of low risk of impact. Also, otherwise the main risk factor, tax crimes, "is not believed to be large compared to other countries".

The scarce availability of quantitative data impedes any assessment of impact on money-making crime. The anecdotal evidence is illustrative, but gives the impression of being scraped together. No mention of crime rate or similar concepts.[24]

The USA

- **Risk understanding**: good understanding at all levels.
- **Risk profile**: frauds of various sorts (health fraud), drugs trafficking, (transnational) organised crime.
- **Crime/ML threats**: big complex cases; significant frauds; drugs.
- **Organisation**: seven ministries and a host of other authorities: 49, ranging from National Security Council to Counter Intelligence and Export Control Section.
- **Prioritisation**: large impact cases in states like California, Florida, New York or Texas. Most states do not prioritise ML but, instead, predicate offences.
- **Assets recovery**: $4,4 billion 2014 by Federal Authorities: mean = $100,054. High value in large complex cases may have shifted the mean upwards. Median not known. No information at state level.
- **Risk mitigation**: three mentions related to banks and Designated Non-Financial Businesses and Professionals (DNFBPs), but no content specification.
- **Statistics:** 1,973,813 SARs received 2014. Conviction figures contaminated by results of plea bargaining or only pursuing the more serious offences.
- **Predicate crime rate**: no figures in report.

[24] Issued April 2017; 216 pages. Assessment team: 7 staff; 3 reviewers.

- **Investigation, prosecution and conviction**: 1,967 ML convictions in 2014; SARs to FinCEN are often used for their intelligence usefulness (for instance, IRS, DEA). Information dissemination also more pro-active to LEAs.
- **Correspondence with risks**: conviction rate does not look like in agreement to the US risk profile. Huge efforts with modest outcomes: 1,732,765 SARS against around 2,000 convictions.

The picture is obscured because real estate agents, trust and company service providers, lawyers and accountants are not under the AML-regime.[25]

This should have changed by 2018.[26]

9.2.4 The AML supremacy

What does this bird's eye view tell us and our naïve visitor about the basic question ("what is all this good for") concerning the positive effects of the RBA leading to less crime for profit? Given our selective approach via the UNODC statistics on property crime and this limited sample of MERs our answer must be preliminary: in the fourth round, a further 20 more MERs have been issued. These have been studied, but not included in this comparison.

Our first observation is that the MERs show little attention to the criminal developments in the 'outside world' where the effects are supposed to take place and which should be the ultimate *external* criterion of effectiveness. If there are references to such external criteria, it is only in passing. The asset recovery results in various countries can serve as a critical example. Collecting valid data on asset recovery would be a first step in learning the effects in the outside world by obtaining financial insight into the ultimate aim of criminal discouragement. This basic requirement appears neglected: proper databases are few and far between (such as real estate and banks: Van Duyne *et al.*, 2009; Van Duyne and Soudijn, 2010), not only in the past but also in these MERs. To determine the ultimate effects of the AML-policy one needs a long-term analysis of what is happening 'on the ground'. It is remarkable that without exception the eight to ten assessors and three reviewers in the analysed MERs have been satisfied with crude asset recovery tables that usually cover a recent three-year period.

---

[25] Issued December 2016; 266 pages. Assessment team: ten staff; three reviewers.

[26] The FATF seems to have shown a great degree of leniency given the gaps it has observed in US' AML framework over the years. As admitted by the FATF: "The BSA AML/CFT regulatory framework has a number of exemptions, gaps and thresholds which do not appear to be justified or in line with the vulnerabilities identified through the risk assessment process." MER USA 2016, para 10. p. 6.

Dealing with a core concept such as 'risk' requires equally critical attention to what is taking place on the ground. This comes to the fore in the way risk is formulated in the FATF policy document *National Money Laundering and Terrorist Financing Threat Assessment* (2013a). In that document, the requirements of which must be followed worldwide, risk is presented as "a function of three factors: threat, vulnerability and consequence" (p. 7). These are the three legs which make a 'risk stool'. However, about the factor 'consequence' the FATF remarks on the next page that "Given the challenges in determining or estimating the consequences of ML and TF it is accepted that incorporating consequence into risk assessments may not involve particularly sophisticated approaches, and that countries may instead opt to focus primarily on achieving a comprehensive understanding of their threats and vulnerabilities." With this concession to leave consequences (*i.e.* what happens on the ground) out of the picture, the risk-based approach is reduced to a wobbly stool with two legs. Not only is this instrument wobbling, we have also an overdose of subjunctives verbs: 'can', 'may', 'potential', all pointing at events that have not yet have happened. With close reading, the sharp mind will recognise that the formulations of the concept of threat and consequence have a puzzling overlap: on the one hand, "*the potential to cause harm*" (threat) and on the other hand, "*impact or harm that ML or TF may cause to*" *etc.* (consequence). Anyhow, one does not need to look too closely, as the category of 'consequences' can be addressed without particularly sophisticated approaches or 'comprehensive understanding' of the two remaining factors. We assume it is some 'holistic' method again.

Given such formulations one cannot blame the Norwegians for their alleged lack of understanding (according to the assessors), while there are serious reasons to suspect the marks of 'good understanding' given to the authorities in highly praised countries such as the USA or Italy.

Another uncertainty in this policy document as well as in the MERs concerns the frequently mentioned focal point: *harm by the predicate offence* versus that caused by *laundering*. With predicate offences one does not usually need to dispute the harm in real life. However, with money laundering as an additional or even exclusive harm, this is much less certain. For example, VAT fraud undeniably inflicts harm on the public fund, but what is the additional harm if the tax authorities wrongly refund one's VAT claim into the bank account? Is the bank victimised in such as case? If that is true, the financial institutions as well as the populations of international financial centres, such as Luxembourg or the British Virgin Islands, can be ranked as the richest global 'victims'. Indeed, if one follows the texts of the FATF documents, one finds no simple answer for our naïve visitor (who should have lost much of his innocence by now). The reason for this is not only conceptual fuzziness, but a fundamental political orientation which is 'recommended' to law enforcement: Laundering First.

Hence, laundering must not be a subsidiary element in the investigation and indictment, but must either come first or be treated singularly. This developed as follows. In the previous chapters we described the gradual arrogation of (unaccountable) power by the FATF. While the AML-policy found its home and justification in the financial system the FATF soon extended its reach to the criminal law domain, where the predicate offences generate the proceeds that to be laundered. This, as well as the superordinate aim of crime reduction, suggests a focus on predicate offences. However, in the evaluations we now observe a shift to the prioritisation of money laundering. With the exception of the MER of Spain we find the explicit criticism, that law enforcement agencies, police and prosecutors, prioritise by looking at the seriousness of predicate offences or other priority points of their local law enforcement agendas instead of putting ML investigations and prosecutions first. In the FATF Guidance 2013a (p. 23) this is one of the defects criticised: "Law enforcement fails to investigate ML due to their focus on predicate crime only." This is a strange statement assuming that the population as well as the Prosecution Office want to have predicate crimes solved and brought to justice in the first place. It is also remarkable in view of the aim of crime mitigation. What counts more: less crime or more money laundering investigations? And what counts most: accountability to the people represented in Parliament or the unaccountable FATF convened in its Plenary?

Nevertheless, given this repeated criticism it becomes less clear what the risk assessment approach strives for: anti-money laundering or mitigating the risks of predicate offences? Statements in the individual MERs point at the first orientation, given also the ways the assessors deplore the usual efficiency considerations in prosecution practice. These imply that prosecutors aim at convictions and if an addition ML charge has no added value for proof or sentencing, it is dropped or included only as a subsidiary charge. This has the consequence that it may disappear from the prosecution/court database. For the FATF this is interpreted as a sign of lower priority and consequently the evaluated country gets a bad mark, making it clear: We, the FATF, go for AML supremacy. Or should that be FATF-supremacy?

9.3 The National Risk Assessment Dome

Following this detour, we must admit that from our study of the documentation (discussed throughout this book as well as within this chapter) we cannot answer our visitor's question "what is all this good for". The keen reader will also note that we have not yet reconsidered the contribution from the academic community to find if they cast any light on this hypothetical question: this consideration is included in the final chapter. External criteria fed from data on the ground are few and far between: in its place is anecdotal evidence of big cases, crude statistics and time series truncated to a few years. If we maintain the two aims of the integrity of the financial system and crime reduction we have not much to offer on either count. Integrity is a lofty moral principle which must be pursued as an ethical value *in se* even if it remains elusive. The aim of crime reduction is rarely mentioned in the FATF documents: appearing three times in the FATF Guidance 2013a (as a synonym of mitigation) it is hardly discussed, let alone analysed, as a superior effect worthy of all the collective efforts.

This does not mean that we are left entirely empty-handed. What the FATF has presented to and then imposed upon the global community with the RBA is a kind of 'dome of risks': after "identifying, assessing and understanding" the ML (and TF) risks, action must be taken. One of those actions is the establishment of an *authority* or a *mechanism to coordinate actions*: an overarching structure. For this reason, we introduce the idea of a 'dome' as an architectural metaphor. From the apex of the dome various tasks must be fulfilled and coordinated, one of them being the allocation of resources. That means: "to make sure that measures to prevent or mitigate ML are commensurate with the risks identified". In simple terms this implies that higher money laundering risks get more financial attention, while lower risks may be dealt with in simpler, less demanding ways. However, there is a difference on which the interpretive note to Recommendation 1 is specific: lower risks must be *proven*. Clearly, risks must not be downgraded light-heartedly. Apparently high risks need no proof: a simple statement is enough.[27]

Such decisions can be fed by bottom-up information, but given the emphasis on *national* risk assessment, the 'dome' is intended to work top down and in a formal way. For example, Norway was reproached by its assessors for operating on an informal basis, without a formal authority or a designated formal committee.[28] While Recommendation 1 and its Interpretive Note are not clear about the implementation of "authority or mechanism", the Guidance is more specific: there must be "a clear commitment from high-level government officials [. . .] to recognise, understand and acknowledge" any ML-risk. Here is a clear imperative warning: let government officials (or competent authorities) "not purposely fail to identify risks in their countries . . ."

---

[27] There is a systematic bias in risk assessment: as the Recommendations use a dichotomy of 'high' and 'low' risks, while contrary to 'high risk' proposing a 'low risk' requires a burden of proof (and "strictly limited circumstances"), it is likely that the consequence will be a bias towards 'high risk'. Sometimes an in-between 'medium' risk is mentioned, though without many consequences attached. The Interpretive Notes to Recommendation 1 mentions only "higher" and "lower" risk (pp 32–33).

[28] The assessors did not raise the question whether such a bureaucratic layer would be commensurate to a low-crime country such as Norway.

for whatever national or commercial reason (p. 12). Also undue lobbying influence must be avoided. Between the lines one reads also a recognition of the political sensitiveness of this task.

Therefore, in the following section on the planning and organisation of the assessment, we find a clear preference towards institutionalisation, though not mandatory but 'ideally': "However, ideally there should be a clear determination and designation of the specific agency, organisation or 'task force' in charge of leading and co-ordinating the process" (p. 13). The FATF Guidance recognises that the composition of a national risk assessment can be a lengthy undertaking, including collecting information and working according to project plans. The requirement of the inclusion of a maximum number of stakeholders certainly adds to the complexity and efforts of the undertaking. This requires many resources in terms of time and staff. What do countries get in return for this, or in the direct question mode of our meanwhile impatient visitor: "what is all this good for?"

The results consist of the dome like structure with some interaction between the apex and the lower galleries where the financial institutions and DNFBPs reside. It is not necessarily a one-way direction, but in the end, everything must be ordered in a hierarchical way, even if that term is not used. But in the end the FATF asserts that all "should be consistent with national requirements and with guidance from competent authorities and Self Regulating Bodies." Though the text of the Recommendations and Interpretive Notes are not more specific, the assessors clearly interpret them such that the national risk assessment is *overarching* and that lower-level risk assessments are 'derived from' or at least 'consistent with' it. This interpretation is underlined with documentation and closely supervised, while this also applies to any undertaking or entity that "*do not fall under the definition of financial institution or DNFBPs*". Even if according to the law entities are outside the perimeter of the FATF, authorities can ignore that if they determine "through their risk assessments that there are types of institutions [etc.] that are at risk of abuse of money laundering . . ." (note 2, Recommendations 2012, updated 2017, p. 29). Bear in mind that it is not required that *actual* laundering is observed. For extending the rule of the AML regime it is sufficiently justified if a country's risk assessment provides a justifying indication. It is almost a blank cheque.

This constitutes an impressive 'imperial' achievement: an extension of the FATF's power to assess and judge, without limitations and with only unproven risks as leverage. Unproven, because as soon as they are proven they stop being 'risks' and become part of the probability formulation $\sum x/N$. But that is not what is intended with 'risk assessment. We must go back to the beginning: Risk = function of *threat, vulnerability* and *consequence*. We remind the reader that we indicated earlier that threat and vulnerability were both very much in the subjunctive mode (can, could, may, might) but shifted to the indicative mode later. We have also seen that the FATF Guidance (p. 8) considers the inclusion of 'consequences' as optional due to their complexity and the uncertainty of sufficient sophistication being available to address this factor. The Guidance made an attempt to facilitate the work on this factor by presenting a list of the consequences of laundering in box 1 (p. 26). Unfortunately, as Ferwerda *et al.* (2011) has made clear, there is not much empirical evidence for this causality outlined in this box. Apparently this finding escaped the attention of the authors of the FATF Guidance (see also Chapter 7.5) as well as of the FATF supporting researchers, who base part of their research on these alleged consequences (Dawe, 2013; Savona and Riccardi, 2017). This is the way to maintain the mainstream. Under the dome of risk they look like frescos which can have some resemblance with reality. How much? That is difficult to say as we know so little of that reality. We recall the sad state of most of the money laundering statistics. Also, throughout its history the FATF has shown little understanding of this crucial foundation of any risk approach. The relevant formulation of Recommendation 33 contains a list of the required separate statistics per subject, but no indication of an *integrated* database for a detailed analysis across subjects.

The FATF Guidance seems to compensate such shortcomings by stating that the aim of analysis is "to gain a *holistic* understanding of each of the risks". However, from a methodological perspective we are afraid that this wholism will produce little more than an undifferentiated global porridge with a few lumps: anecdotal evidence, outdated statistics and a truncated risk scale biased towards many unproven 'high risks' and very few proven 'low risks'.[29]

"Is this all?" asks the no longer naïve visitor. "Where are the real effects on the outside world? You are only checking yourselves and your compliance behaviour under your Dome. But where do I observe discouragement in terms of crime reduction?" These are justified questions and we will sit down with this persistent visitor (and reader) to discuss these in the last chapter.

9.4 Conclusion

In this Chapter we were again accompanied by our hypothetical, naïve layman, who looked around and asked the essential simple question: "*What is all this good for*?" To answer this question we provided the almost self-evident answer: "to further and preserve the integrity of the financial system". However, this is a very abstract aim with a large latitude of interpretation. Also, it says

[29] This is not unlike the phenomenological school of the 1950s and 1960s, with its emphasis on total understanding ('Verstehen') which could mean anything.

nothing of the effects of AML in the *outside* world. That is the place where profit motivated crimes are committed and crime-money is earned that consequently has to be laundered. And it is here that we should demonstrate to our layman Candide what all this is good for: *crime reduction* leading to less laundering.

Subsequently we made a *tour d'horizon* through the FATF and took stock of many AML-knowledge documents. Here we faced a severe deficiency: the continuous neglect of proper basic statistics. As a result we can declare the FATF to be in a state of continuous ignorance. This is despite its Recommendation about statistics and even the production of a special guidance report for this topic. This situation of flawed statistics creates uncertainty about the aims that the FATF desires to reach, in addition to inherent uncertainties about the moral objective of integrity.

As the massive efforts of the Mutual Evaluations do not provide us with proper national data about the AML effectiveness in terms of the decrease of *external* crime prevalence, we looked at other statistics about drug and property crimes from the EMCDDA and UNODC. Naturally with much caution, because these statistics are unrelated to the AML issue. In fact, within these data bases, AML is not even mentioned. The survey of the drug market (mainly interceptions) showed a statistically general resilience that flattens most temporary outliers in the market. This does not appear to bear evidence that the AML-regime has an effect. The statistical trend of property crimes is for most categories downwards, more likely reflecting the ageing of the population than a hypothetical impact by the AML-regime.

Subsequently we looked at a sample of countries to find out whether there is a discernible impact from the understanding of the new Risk Based Approach, whether or not in combination with an overarching National Strategy. Does it matter in terms of effects? Actually, we found that, whether or not there was a good understanding, there were no unambiguously discernible effects in terms of risk mitigation. However, the required understanding of the Risk Based Approach (Recommendation 1) remains an *internal* matter and is not reflected in external criteria. This is underlined by other MERs which pay little attention to potential effects in the 'outside world': again no 'facts and figures' or even a sign of interest. This is reinforced by the FATF itself, which proposes that a risk model is "a function of three factors: threat, vulnerability and consequence" and subsequently declares that determining these consequences may not be 'particularly sophisticated'. In this way, by virtually taking out the consequences as external effects, the FATF does not encourage accuracy in reporting on the money-laundering threat. Given the present lack of sophistication in this field, our naïve visitor has a reason to feel surprised.

What is a recurrent issue is the uncertainty in determining most of the AML-tenets, concepts and aims. This applies not only to the moral aim of financial integrity, but also to many facets of harm, that are indeterminable in many transactions. Despite that, the FATF chooses a clear policy of pressing for '*Laundering First*' as a national priority for investigations and prosecutions. Any country that does not do so gets a bad mark in its mutual evaluation. Actually, the FATF through this tool, seems to interfere in the independence of national judiciaries.

Though the question "what is all this good for" remains unanswered, one cannot deny the FATF displays a considerable zeal for extending its remit, or rather its grip by building an elaborately constructed system. The FATF's drive for the Risk Based Approach and the National Risk Assessment are examples of this striving for a system from the apex downwards. We used the metaphor of a Dome, with naturally the FATF at its apex. It is not really bureaucratic, but it is undeniably hierarchical, with a touch of an imperial tone with its repeated hammering assertion that "*the country should . . . the country should*" in the mutual evaluations and guidelines.

Is such a hierarchy conductive to transparent policy making? A concluding warning here is appropriate: hierarchies and transparency are not necessarily mutual companions. We have repeatedly pointed at conceptual vagueness and lack of 'facts and figures', a deficiency not compensated by its suggested 'holistic understanding'. Such a suggestion is rather something that may feel good under the Dome but is no replacement for knowledge of 'the outside world'.

10

Conclusion: back to the essence and the future

We started this work by looking back to the late 1980s and introduced in the first chapter a hypothetical layman questioning the gravity of the laundering threat that has loomed above our heads for decades without it actually coming down. In the previous chapter we reintroduced this layman with his persistent plain question "What is all this good for?" In relation to the two main aims of combating money laundering: *integrity* and *crime reduction*. Trying to answer this question left us rather speechless. Must we admit that there is not sufficient material for a satisfactory answer? Or shall we prevaricate and say the question is not well phrased? That would be nonsense: the question is perfectly clear and simple. Maybe it is a matter of a disorderly 'conceptual cupboard' which needs a severe tidying-up. While doing so we may find the outlines of a correspondingly simple answer, provided there is adequate material.

In the last chapter we used the metaphor of the 'Dome of Risk' which has to be enlarged to a Laundering Dome. On purpose written in capitals as we imagine an impressive baroque building with galleries and walled-in chapels. This metaphor presents the elaborated present-day global AML-regime with all the regional bodies, working groups, typologies, guidelines and so forth. Opposed to this stands our layman with his plain question we cannot properly answer by using information coming from that Laundering Dome. If that is the case it may be wise to leave that Dome and look outside for elementary principles as building stones from which to construct our answer. Naturally we will also look over our shoulders at the Laundering Dome from which we can borrow anything that may be useful. We look at that structure from a distance and reflect on whether it stands on the correct spot and is built the right way?

P.C. van Duyne, J.H. Harvey and L.Y. Gelemerova, *The Critical Handbook of Money Laundering*, https://doi.org/10.1057/978-1-137-52398-3_10

10.1 A legal axiom and the 'least effort principle'

Our approach looks somewhat Euclidean or Cartesian: first one must find a theorem or axiom, which is elementary and indisputable and then start a deductive process from that proposition. Descartes found his axiom in the following proposition: "I think, therefore, I am" (*cogito ergo sum*). That is doubtless true and a tried and tested method. Concerning our field –profit making crime– we think of the thesis "*crime should not pay*" as the first and most obvious candidate proposition. The reason for this elementary proposition is its direct bearing on laundering: because of this proposition, a sound criminal must carry out follow-up actions to safeguard the obtained criminal revenues and make sure they remain untouchable. Every behaviour to achieve that is a form of criminal asset management as we discussed in Chapter 3. This ranges from the simple act of burying assets in the ground to the most sophisticated off-shore investment or multi-layered loan-back scheme. Obviously, this formulation contravenes the basic axiom, but that is implied and intended: committing a crime for profit makes no sense if the surrounding legal world can be easily informed about the perpetrator or of the whereabouts of the loot. It is a tautological implication of committing crimes for profit. Given this implied status, one could dispute whether laundering should be considered extra blameworthy such that it must be penalised in addition to the predicate offence. Being in the crime business and not laundering is a guarantee for being caught.

As we analysed in Chapter 4, hiding and disguising are at the core of criminal asset management and naturally qualified as laundering. Looking at them more closely, there is more to it, because of two aspects. The first regards the commission of the predicate offence itself. Obviously the perpetrator will attempt to hide or disguise his identity as a criminal actor, for example by wearing a mask. Or, in the case of a skilful fraudster he will attempt, by forging and deception to hide the evidence that any crime has been committed by making it look legal. Shouldn't these acts of hiding and disguising also have been criminalised?

Perhaps, but at the moment there are no penal clauses which say: "he who wears a mask at a robbery is guilty of the offence of . . ." or "he who for the purpose of committing fraud, tampers with his accountancy . . ." The *Modus operandi* of disguised predicate offences are not further penalised unless additional harm is inflicted on persons or goods through some kind of aggravating circumstances. Therefore, one could wonder why that disguising behaviour in the commissioning of the predicate offence is not qualified as a crime, while hiding and/or disguising the proceeds arising *after* the completion of the offence are criminalised. Sometimes there is no technical difference between 'at the time of' and 'after the crime' as mentioned in Chapter 4. For example, with tax fraud, the false tax return serves as part of the *modus operandi* and as the instrument for disguising and concealment (Van Duyne *et al.*, 2005).

Lifting this differentiation has an interesting implication for countries where self-laundering has been criminalised as elaborated in Chapter 4.3.1. In these jurisdictions (tax) fraud and tax evasion can automatically additionally be prosecuted as laundering. In fact, this applies to all economic crime, where the corporate accounting is the 'cover-up tool' for the commission as well as for the profits, whether for illegal waste dumping, logging, or in relation to provenance fraud of fake antiques or illegally excavated artefacts. As frequently mentioned earlier, Van Duyne *et al.* (2005) called this 'canned laundering': with the predicate crime and the concealment contained as it were in the same can. This built-in presence of laundering also applies to the *attempt* to commit a crime for profit. Preparing such a crime also contains preparing for laundering because otherwise the crime makes no sense unless the criminal proceeds are intended for mere possession (as proposed by the European Parliament and Commission) or to be consumed on the spot or shortly thereafter.

In this way the circle of the application of the criminal law is expanded tremendously, simply by criminalising 'canned laundering' and its attempt. However, is this necessary? Why should we have two possibilities for prosecution when one of the offences is inherent to, or contained within, the original one? This goes against the basic principle of *subsidiarity* or the 'rule of the least effort', which states: "don't use a heavier legal tool when a simple one is also available". However, what the reader might observe here is the opposite of subsidiarity: an ongoing pressure to bring a heavier criminal law armoury without first applying the fundamental rule of the 'least effort'. As a matter of fact, the law makers have already created many legal tools with which to address criminal money management. This was not taken into account: instead of rearranging the existing legal architecture, the Laundering Dome was built and expanded piecemeal whenever legal loopholes were identified. What was not done, was investigate whether the basic axiom of 'crime should not pay' and the rule of least effort would be enough for designing a robust and simple criminal law architecture. For example, comparing the situation of countries before and after a change of law, such as self-laundering: what are the observed changes in criminal input and law enforcement output compared to the situation before the new criminalisation: a baseline measurement.

10.2 The circle of reasoning

It should be observed that a failure to criminalise self-laundering does not imply that the perpetrator escapes punishment for any of his own criminal asset management activities. In the follow-up actions from his predicate crime, the self-launderer can commit new offences that are instrumental to hiding and disguising the criminal origin of his proceeds. For example: constructing a fraudulent loan back scheme; forging import or export invoices or a document of provenance for an ancient find from an illegal excavation. It is worthwhile musing on the ironic hoped-for outcome of a 'whitened' criminal income being presented to the tax office: the figures are correct but the origin is nonetheless fraudulent. This is still tax fraud even if the state is not harmed and receives the income tax due on the presented, but laundered income. It is a myth that self-laundering is free of legal consequences. As soon as the self-launderer moves with his crime-money into the regulated economy, he is at risk of money laundering. Spending large amounts on daily household items beyond one's legitimate earnings, may attract attention whether or not self-laundering has been criminalised. If self-laundering is criminalised, any handling of such income would potentially qualify as laundering. For example, if you fail to spend the funds sufficiently quickly, then you are saving or hoarding, which is then also laundering. In terms of the FATF jargon, this saving means that the proceeds remain '*available for laundering*' which is legally constructed as laundering although it should not be confused with real laundering (in the strict sense of the term). And if self-laundering is not criminalised one has the case of unexplained wealth and an intentional violation of income and wealth tax. What does an extra criminalisation add?

Let us also apply this simplifying line of reasoning to laundering by more than one person: the predicate offender is in need of assistance in managing his criminal assets and involves other persons. Applying the 'rule of least effort', do we need the laundering article or can this be covered by the general criminal code clauses on complicity and fencing? If these clauses are a good enough legal tool to cover all crimes, what value has been added by the separate criminalisation of money laundering? If assisting and abetting in the safeguarding of the profits of crime can be considered as complicity, then we have the same desired result. For this complicit involvement, we have the general gradations of intent, criminal negligence or culpability ("should have known that"). This can be deduced from factual circumstances and knowledge of the assisting person.

Engaging another person in the criminal asset management is itself also punishable as incitement to obstruct the course of justice or to commit other crimes such as fraudulent accounting to disguise the profits of crime. To this, of course, can be added the traditional crime of receiving goods from a criminal origin.

With this proposed simplification, we question the added value of many of the anti-money laundering legal tools. If the existing legal arsenal of complicity, incitement, fraud, fencing and receiving is good enough for general purposes, it must be proven that the whole money laundering armoury, as a legal newcomer, has added value. Criminal law is sufficiently complex: why add more complexity?

Such a comparison would require a juxtaposition of the old and new situation and an independent assessment. Regretfully, this has never been adequately tried: as we have seen in Chapter 3, as soon as the USA went global with their anti-money laundering package, their legal model became a political requirement. Once accepted, there was little interest in, or patience with, legal principles such as the rule of least effort, simply as these might stand in the way of the G-7 politics. One can say that the principle of least effort and existing legal tools were ignored. Instead, the banner of Money Laundering was unfurled and was endowed from the beginning with a high symbolic value which had to remain clearly visible – that of threat. Hence, money laundering became a separate offence, a new title in the national Criminal Codes was adopted worldwide, driven by a new organisation tasked with setting and guarding the new standards. Did this add to clarity?

10.3 Conceptual opaqueness

In this mainly political setting in which basic legal principles could be ignored, it is not surprising that the requirement of conceptual precision was not always heeded. We elaborated this issue in Chapter 4. We began with lining up various definitions of the concept of money laundering and noticed that there were many semantic differences between countries.

That is not surprising, given the many national angles from which the phrase draws its content. We have seen that descriptions in criminal law could range from just one lengthy sentence as a formula (the Netherlands) to several pages (the USA and UK), with Belgium not even mentioning the phrase 'money laundering', but complying through its other wording with the FATF's criminalisation requirements. In the end we asked: does it matter? Yes, it does matter, but few care. As long as minimum requirements are fulfilled, we find that the stakeholder institutions (the FATF, IMF/World Bank, the Council of Europe and the UNODC) or law enforcement agencies, declare themselves satisfied (see Chapter 4.3). From that side one must not expect a drive to sharpen the concepts used.

This is a strange finding: an intellectual laxity amidst a climate of serious warnings about the harm caused by money laundering. Notably, despite the definitional vaguenesses, the FATF still imposes severe measures against countries who showed deficiencies in their compliance or who were judged to be non-compliant for other reasons, with the consequence of a public call by the FATF for 'countermeasures'. We have repeatedly pointed at amateurish statistics and, alongside, given examples of how a lack of precision can lead to double counting. For example, as with the example of a bribe given and accepted, both counted as laundered, even though the bribe may come from a licit source transferred to an illicit slush fund. What has been laundered? What are just 'murky' finances and where is the laundering?

For instance, in the case of the recently reported financial transactions involving the Azeri elite in 2017, the goal of the transactions largely varied. Some of the transactions, reportedly, involved purchases of luxury items, private school fees for the elite's children and paying for PR, apparently to benefit Azerbaijan.[1] And although the media indiscriminately labelled the transactions as 'laundering', it is debatable whether laundering in the strict sense of the term was involved. Paying PR specialists to lobby is not in itself illegal and is a common practice in the industrialised world. Naturally, such activities will be surrounded by secrecy. Would the same 'laundering' label have been used if this was a powerful Middle Eastern monarchy?

Similarly, in the case of Deutsche Bank's Russian mirror trades, for which the bank was fined in 2017, it remains questionable whether they entailed crime proceeds. Further, the leaked Panama papers exposed the lack of transparency regarding the affairs of some senior political figures, but in itself did not necessarily always contain evidence of crime proceeds. While we would not necessarily expect the media to be specific, we are also seeing a tendency among regulators to lump disparate things together. This results in uncertainty for the regulated sector where the only certain thing is that transactions involving certain jurisdictions and / or PEPs will have to be investigated more closely.

Against the background of these foggy dealings, sharp conceptualisation in criminal law is not a luxury. In view of the inclusion of tax crimes (related to direct and indirect taxes) into the list of predicate offences ('*designated offences*', Recommendations 2012, pp. 112–113), one would expect more specification and a better delineation of laundering from the predicate offence. This is all the more important as in the course of law enforcement the scope of application of penalty clauses has tended to broaden. At first the combat against money laundering concerned serious international drug trafficking, then all serious crimes, of which the threshold was soon lowered to offences threatened with a maximum penalty of one year, covering practically all profit-motivated crimes. In parallel to this development one can observe that to the initial charge, money laundering has increasingly also been added among others to justify an arrest, house search or other investigative actions. Often it is added as the third or lower point in the charge. It can be used as a prosecutorial safety net in case of acquittal on other points: for example, the predicate crime cannot be proven, but there are still unexplained suspicious transactions or unexplained wealth. Additionally, the laundering count can even be

[1] Organised Crime and Corruption Report Project: The Azerbaijani Laundromat. newsletter@transparency.org. 8 September 2017.

dropped in the final indictment if it had no procedural added value.[2] In short, the use of money laundering can be determined by opportunistic or pragmatic reasons. From the MERs of the fourth round we can deduce that the assessors want a prime place for criminal money laundering charges, while they reproach prosecutors who put the predicate first. However, such reproaches may be premature. Given our argumentation concerning 'canned laundering', it may become opportune to combine a charge of tax crime routinely with a subsidiary charge of money laundering. Not reporting deposited money from legal sources in one's bank account may automatically provide evidence.

Surveying the official AML literature, one may wonder whether there has been any attempt to provide conceptual clarity, despite numerous guidance documents. Perhaps fuzzy concepts are felt to be useful, because they allow a circumvention of the sharp edges of precision. The risk-based approach is an example of this fuzziness as discussed in Chapter 5. We have seen that it is based on three ill-defined concepts: threat, vulnerability and consequences. The latter can either be dropped or be approached in a 'less sophisticated' but still 'comprehensive way' (FATF, 2013a, p. 8). It is not quite certain what this implies, but it may be connected to the analysis phase which should lead to a "*holistic* understanding of each of the risks" (p. 21). As discussed earlier, the meaning of this term remains unexplained, but it may indicate an interconnected whole that is more than the sum of the parts, though that is our interpretation. At any rate this undefined concept is considered important enough to have been adopted by the European Commission and Parliament in the Directive 2015/849. The Directive recommends, without further explanation, that "a holistic, risk-based approach should be used" (para. 22). Whether this had any effect is difficult to determine because, though we do find this concept back again in the research report of the European Commission of 2017, it remains undefined. And, undefined things have undefined effects.

This is a truism, not worth mentioning if it did not also apply to the other essential concepts of the research report "*Assessing the risk of money laundering in Europe; final report of the project IARM*". The project adopted the reasoning and concepts of the FATF (2013a) guidelines to the Risk Based Approach and consequently we find the concepts 'threat', 'vulnerability' and 'consequences' back, but again without any additional operationalisation. Such an adoption without proper content analysis can lead to strange counterfactual statements, which go unnoticed because they fit so conveniently into the 'holistic' approach. In consequence, the 'whole' soon crumbles under closer dissection and proves to be less than the sum of the parts. Take the statement about cash as a vulnerability and tax evasion: "*Cash is a facilitator for committing crimes (first of all tax evasion) and for concealing and laundering the proceeds of crime.*"

[2] The order of the indictment is often: predicate offence + organised crime + money laundering.

This statement combines a platitude with nonsense by presenting the cash as an evil actor instead of the coveted loot. Apart from that, had the authors carried out a proper literature review, their interpretation may have been different. Tax evasion is not in the first place a matter of hiding cash revenues, unless the FATF referred to the various small cash transactions in the shadow economy such as paying a taxi driver or tipping a waiter. When it comes to higher level tax crimes rather than cash, one finds more false invoices (canned laundering) and bank deposits. Moreover, in cases of money being siphoned off, the international wiring of criminal tax savings and returns is more important than the awkward dragging around of cash-filled bags. Finally, cash is fine for hiding by comingling small amounts of black money, but in the end cannot be the instrument of real laundering: *white* washing. Instead of unquestioningly following the FATF holistic framework of semi-defined concepts, the researchers should rather have looked into their own (scarce) data (and relevant research) on cash payments. For example, while Italy is marked as one of the EU countries with the highest levels of cash use, and hence, according to the assumptions about cash, the most vulnerable to laundering, the data on cash payments shed doubt on this conclusion. In table 11, p. 55 of the *IARM* report (Savona and Riccardi, 2017), one can read that though Italy has the most small-cash transactions of less than 20 Euros, namely 91%, only 4% of the transactions were cash-based, in the highest transaction category of more than 10,000 Euros, whereas Austria has the highest percentage of large cash transactions, namely 10% (IARM, 2017; p. 55). But neither Italy nor Austria are commonly seen as high-risk jurisdictions in the banking industry.[3] The Dun and Bradstreet country risk ratings from 2017 rate Italy 'DB4a' and Austria 'DB2c'.[4]

It should be observed that "Given the difficulties of measurement, consequences are not considered in the analysis and they are not covered by the final indicator. This choice is in line with previous NRAs and with the EU SNRA." (IARM, p. 29). This appears to imply that the project has not tested validity of findings against external criteria. Because of this shortcoming, the IARM-project is little different from other assessment undertakings: a risk picture exhibition about what happens within the Laundering Dome, but unfortunately, falsely presented as a picture of the outside threats.

[3] No mention is made to Germany where according to *Die Welt* Germans hoard a lot of savings cash at home (€ 200 billion) and show the highest preference to pay cash for shopping. How 'vulnerable' is Germany and how much is 'available for laundering' is there in this country? https://www.welt.de/finanzen/verbraucher/article180413460/Waehrungen-Die-manische-Liebe-der-Deutschen-zum-Bargeld.html.

[4] Dun and Bradstreet's Country Risk Indicator is a commercial database that provides a comparative, cross-border assessment of the risk of doing business in a country. The risk indicator is divided into seven bands, ranging from DB1 to DB7 sub-divided into quartiles (from 1a to 6d) where 1 is the lowest risk and 7 the greatest. Those countries classified as 5 and above are high risk with advice that companies limit their exposure.

Our observation reflects the poor knowledge position of the FATF, the FSRBs, law enforcement agencies and the regulated sectors. One does not need to be a genius to recognise a problem with efficiency determination. If the effects in terms of consequences remain immeasurable, we know nothing about aims reached, whether they are in relation to prevention, integrity or short-term repression. We are missing the numerator and denominator from the effort and effect fraction both of which should be supplied by the outside reality. However, the knowledge situation is such that from the outside only glimpses penetrate through the stained glass windows of the Launder Dome, depicting the horrors of the risks of threats that have not happened and their non-described consequences. Perhaps this is what is meant by the word 'holistic'.

10.4 The FATF repressive drone and the independent judiciary

A difficult issue in this field concerns the exercise of power to enforce compliance. At present we are used to an FATF that praises and reproaches, warns and offers assistance in a manner that a country can not refuse. It conveys one opinion, that of the Plenary whose messages seem to have an imperial or commanding tone.

It was clear that when the G-7 launched the combat against money laundering in 1989, it meant serious business: it was a matter of grave concern which should be treated severely. Or, that is the kind of combat language that one would expect given the somewhat harsh and imperial FATF tone in its later years. However, that was not the tone initially adopted. As mentioned in the last chapter, the first report with the 40 recommendations was more intended as a text to stimulate discussion (the commanding, uppercase 'R' did not appear until the second edition). It stressed "the need for rapid and tough action" and the "need for practical measures", but it did not have the commanding tone of later years. Sometimes it mentioned discussions about differences of opinion in the group. There was no mention of severe sanctions against non-compliance. Rather, as seen in the subsequent first Annual Report, the text referred to the need to encourage and to use a "White List" instead of a "Black List" approach (FATF AR, 1991-91; p. 16). The recommendations were still real recommendations, not veiled commands written with a capital letter. However, whether or not this was only a velvet appearance, Recommendation 21 already meant serious business, as we discussed in Chapters 3 and 5. It recommends that financial institutions in compliant countries should pay special attention to transactions from non-compliant countries. That means that all bank transactions would be 'held up against the light' and through such close examination, cause delays in handling and loss of customers.

This velvet appearance did not last long. We have already seen that there were soon compliance problems with Turkey and Austria and the Plenary pondered aloud how to deal with this non-compliance situation short of suspending membership after a stiff letter and 'high-level visit' (FATF AR, 1995-96; p. 15. See also Chapter 3). Turkey and Austria were put under pressure for not having passed the required legislation. The FATF threatened to apply Recommendation 21 (FATF AR, 1996-97; p. 11). Soon Turkey backed down and complied. For internal political reasons Austria was more persistent but in the end capitulated.

One can say that the FATF gradually recognised the power derived from a more sanction-driven compliance policy. For example, in discussion of the evaluation of Luxembourg it was observed that the legal framework broadly conformed to the FATF Recommendations. However, the small number of suspicious transaction reports were disappointing to the FATF. The FATF made a number of suggestions to improve the performance, but if that did not help, Luxembourg was recommended (=must) to be the subject of sanctions: "the exemplary value of formal procedures of sanctions should be duly acknowledged, whether they are penal or administrative." (FATF AR, 1998-99; p. 12).

Luxembourg was just one example of a broader challenge to the aims of the FATF: the countries that offer services to circumvent AML-measures or deviate from the basic suspicious transaction reporting rule. It would be damaging to the regime "if there is a lack of criminal or administrative sanctions for financial institutions in respect to the obligation to report suspicious or unusual transactions." (FATF AR, 1999-2000; p. 49). Naturally, this should not be allowed. As such circumventing services were assumed to be offered by non-cooperative countries and territories (NCCTs), since the end of 1998, the FATF had embarked on bringing these in line with its policy.

This endeavour involved broad preparation requiring the weight of the OECD, special *Ad Hoc* groups and meetings outside the regular Plenary meeting (FATF AR, 1999-2000; p. 6). Counter-measures were announced. In the following years the pressure on (or the hunt of) non-cooperative countries was intensified with sometimes eyebrow-raising consequences, such as pressure on the tiny Faroe Islands because of defects in its terrorist financing rules.

To make countries compliant it has been realised that one essential element in the demanded compliance to FATF standards would be the presence of a *sanction system*. Obviously, the FATF itself cannot impose sanctions: it can only call on others to take 'countermeasures' against hardened 'non-compliant' states such as North Korea and Iran. We think such a call differs only in words from international sanctions. But by way of indirect rule the FATF can recommend that countries adopt a sanction system for enforcing the implementation of and compliance with the 40 Recommendations. The imposition (or

Recommendation) of a sanction system was effected in the FATF Recommendations, October, 2003 in Recommendation 2 and 17. For Recommendation 2 that concerned legal persons and for Recommendation 17 "natural or legal persons covered by these Recommendations that fail to comply with anti-money laundering or terrorist financing requirements." Does this also apply to ordinary citizens who do not comply with the requirements, for example if being occasionally involved in a large cash transaction? We do not think so, albeit many MERs based on the 2012 Recommendations did not make this subtle difference.

What is more important, the FATF 2012 Recommendations, updated in 2017, makes this difference obsolete: from 2012, the Recommendation on sanctions concerns *all* persons, natural or legal, who had anything to do with the financial system, whether in a serving or customer function. Was this necessary? As a matter of fact, Recommendation 3 already requires that "Countries should criminalise money laundering on the basis of the Vienna Convention and the Palermo Convention." Further, what system of law will criminalise specific conduct without connecting sanctions? Though this is already over-obvious, the FATF thought it necessary to emphasise in the Interpretive Note to this Recommendation concerning legal and natural persons convicted of money laundering that "all sanctions should be effective, proportionate and dissuasive" (p. 33)

This formulation is repeated 19 times in this FATF Recommendation document and further, within virtually all MERs from 2004 onwards. It is a strange as well as an ominous formulation. It is strange because the term 'effective' is redundant as it is tied to the aim of being dissuasive: if the sanction is not dissuasive neither is it effective, and the other way around. Proportionate is redundant as well: it is a built-in characteristic of sanction systems without which sanctioning would turn into boundless revenge. So we have only the criminal law platitude of dissuading punishments, repeated as if it is of the highest importance. Should this not also be deleted as redundant?

No, all this is not redundant. In fact it contains a very specific but implicit message: that is *that* the FATF has not only the right to demand from every country that it criminalises a particular behaviour. It arrogates also the right to impose implicit levels of punishment: effective, proportionate and dissuading. The FATF should first have raised the question of whether this is the domain of the independent judiciary as it should be in a democratic rule of law. There is no written evidence of such a discussion and if there has been one, how the discussion led to this outcome.

One can argue that these specifications, *effective, proportionate and dissuasive*, are just empty words concatenated into a sonorously sounding mumble which one can ignore. We think this would be a gross misjudgment. Accepting this formula is tantamount to accepting that an informal extra-democratic body (no-one has ever called the FATF democratic) has the right to impose sentencing characteristics on sovereign states. In the whole context of the FATF this comes down to demanding more severity in money laundering policy. In Chapter 6, we compared the ruling of the FATF with the indirect rule of the English and French colonial empires which we rephrase as 'ruling the financial natives through the local chiefs', in this case that would be the judges. One could label this a 'benign' rule. But as soon as it is opportune, such indirect rule can easily turn into a more direct one. For example, the FATF thinks it has the right to look (through the MERs) over the shoulder of criminal law policy makers and pressure them for a more repressive approach to money laundering. We think this was already the case when the FATF reproached countries for lenient sentences (Spain, Norway, among others) and demanded more severe treatment by the courts.

To get an impression of how this works, go through the MERs and look at every occurrence of the phrase "*effective, proportionate and dissuasive*". Though we think this rather a "follow-up research project", we have nevertheless gone through 22 MERs of the third as well as the fourth round and made a bouquet of the most salient findings. The general repressive attitude is best expressed in the MER of the Netherlands (MER, 2011; para. 238): "it is clear that the sanctions regime has been effective to a certain degree in that it has resulted in significant number of prison sentences." Handing out prison sentences is presented as a triumph of repression, but not of a successful prevention policy. How have countries been valued against this repressive background?

First, the positive findings. In the MER of the USA there was no reproachful mention of "*not* effective, proportionate and dissuasive" despite the FATF recognising the gaps in the US AML regime. For the UK there were only a few remarks about the sanctioning of infringements of EU regulations. It is not mentioned whether this is due to a generally high 'punitive climate' in both countries or to a tradition of high compliance. Another, more or less positive judgement is about the punishing of money laundering in Malaysia (MER fourth round): sentences "appear to be proportionate to the seriousness of the ML conduct . . ." (MER 2015, para. 381) which certainly does not refer to leniency. Unfortunately, the information on predicate offences was incomplete. Therefore, it was not entirely clear what defines 'proportionate' and 'seriousness'.

In the MERs of the other countries the general judgment was summarised as: the sanctioning is *not* effective, proportionate and dissuasive. The FATF does not show much understanding of sentencing policy or tradition in many jurisdictions. For example, in Germany and Austria a first prison sentence is usually on probation unless there are counter-indications. However, the FATF observed peevishly: "Sanctions applied by the courts for ML are not dissuasive, as penalties actually applied are very low (normally probation for a first time offense)". (MER Austria, 2017; para. 20). The same applies to the Scandinavian countries which have a lenient sentencing tradition for which the FATF shows equally little appreciation.

The following underlines that there is every appearance that the FATF thinks it appropriate to take its place in the chair of the judge, prosecutor or even the legislator. In the 2017 MER (para. 194) of Sweden the FATF is of the opinion that "the maximum sentence applied may not be fully dissuasive and effective, particularly where money laundering is the sole offence or the most serious offence. Prosecutors should identify the appropriate serious ML cases for the Supreme Court to establish court practice for the level of sanctions." We note that the FATF recommends that Swedish prosecutors go beyond the legally arranged maximum sentence or that it enters into debate with the Supreme Court about its sentencing guidelines. We think this is constitutionally a matter of Sweden and not of the FATF.

In the case of Spain, the FATF seems to go one step further. For both the third as well as for the fourth mutual evaluation rounds, the FATF expresses its dissatisfaction with the low sentencing by the Spanish Courts. The courts sentence the majority of money laundering defendants to a prison term in the lower range of six months to two years. Penalties of six or more years imprisonment are rarely imposed (MER Spain 2014, p. 43). A tougher policy is not even enough for the FATF: "Since the 2010 reform of the Penal Code, tougher sentences have been imposed in practice, but remain very low." (para. 3.44). The FATF then gives a lesson of what the judges must do: "When imposing sentences, judges must take into account mitigating and aggravating circumstances, and the general and special rules for the application of penalties: Penal Code art.21, 22, 61-79. The maximum six year penalty could be elevated up to nine years if it is a continuing offence (art.302 Penal Code)." Spain might have been given a lower rating because of the lenient level of its sanctions if it had not demonstrated that it disrupted and dismantled organised crime groups.

The phrase *effective, proportionate and dissuasive* is a mantra with an ominous message. From below its semantic redundancy emerges an evident claim of the right to press for more repressive national policies, which must not be taken lightly. About prevention there is no word.

10.5 Dissuasion and restorative justice

The last section may suggest that we distance ourselves from an 'effective, proportionate and dissuasive' policy. This is not correct: but the emptiness of this phrase allows the MER assessors to apply it *ad hoc*, at risk of arbitrariness of judgment with the noted repressive bias. In our opinion it must be attached to general criminal law principles. We suggest, therefore, it should be connected to our simple point of departure: 'crime should not pay'. Indeed, this principle must be maintained effectively, in proportion to the seriousness of the law breaking, such that it has a dissuasive effect on the commission of the predicate crimes as well as the support lent to the management of the ill-gotten gains; that is third person laundering. To heed the principle of subsidiarity we must then address the question: "How much do we need for a minimally satisfactory effect?" And every bit more effort must be justified by evidence, preferably found outside the Laundering Dome to counter-balance the bias of self-confirmation.

Proposing the minimum measures to reduce crime for profit remains difficult given that subsidiarity contains no built-in yardsticks for making choices. Naturally, making a yardstick concrete requires heeding the national and economic contexts. What is a serious issue in one country may only be a matter of nuisance in another. Why should the Swedish law enforcement authority chase the underground cash based "aquarium economy" when the country had a very high level of non-cash transactions? Should Sweden devote extra effort simply to avoid a bad rating by the FATF? That in itself would be rational and effective, but from the perspective of the Laundering Dome only for compliance with the Recommendation in the MER: "Currently, Sweden does not sufficiently investigate ML which occurs in the 'aquarium economy' and does not interface with the legal economy".[5] What would be a rational yardstick for devoting resources to this "aquarium economy"? This depends on its valuation which may range from a "big risk" to be rooted out, to a nuisance to be contained within manageable proportions.

As the commission of profit-driven crime also has strong emotional drivers, such as plain greed and need, keeping up appearances or challenging 'the system', it remains an illusion that the FATF approach will do better in the next 25 years than it has in the past quarter Century. One could argue that the only country where money laundering has been eradicated is North-Korea, the principal country on the FATF's blacklist. The method of that 'success' is simple: total compliance requires total control; and total control is only achieved by a totalitarian state. The argument that this solution is fully disproportional may be challenged by pointing at the big crime-money threat that is still looming over our heads (after more than 25 years of continuous efforts).

[5] With "aquarium economy" the authorities mean that a "great deal of the criminal assets never comes into contact with the legal sector; rather, it is spent in the illegal economy, with purchases occurring in cash or through bank accounts." MER Sweden, April 2017; p. 59. Meanwhile the Swedish law enforcement faces a contradiction: it is not very inclined to go after this "aquarium economy" laundering despite "the fact that the new money laundering offence targets consumption of criminal gains without the intent to laundering". Hence, steal the cake but don't eat it, because that would be laundering. But keeping the cake would also be laundering.

Whether one likes the regime or not, North-Korean style financial control is, at least, laundering-proof, and so is that of Cuba, according to its MER. We can imagine that even stiff proponents of tough and ever increasing money laundering controls may be prepared to lower the threat level to avoid having to choose for a North-Korean compliance model. A multi-dimensional weighing of options is never purely rational if one realises such final consequences.

If we do not want to end up with copying the most 'virtuous' country on our planet (North Korea), we have to look at our contradictory crime risk and control options: in principle we want zero crime risk but not 100% control. How can this balance be achieved? We may have to think of the break-even point: "how many fishes do we allow to slip through the net against the expenses of further tightening the meshes?" This is the usual risk control question in business, that can also be applied to crimes for profit while nibbling at the 'crime does not pay' axiom. The norm is absolute, but a quota of violations can be accepted. As is the case with most issues of criminal policy making, policy makers and law enforcement know this and are forced to think of a slip-through and/or an alternative treatment quota. For example, the police cannot deal with all apprehended shoplifters or other small time offenders and have to balance their input against the seriousness of the law that has been transgressed and which must be restored. So some are let off with a sharp word of warning to save police time filing the required paperwork.

This balancing of interests must in principle be the same for all kinds of criminality. There are no valid reasons why there should be an exception for anti-money laundering polity. Nevertheless, the FATF documents suggest differently. At least the mutual evaluation reports clearly claim an exceptional position by stressing the '*ML-first*' principle and reproaching countries for not complying with this demand. To this we add: without much debate or justification. It is just stated with much aplomb, after which it remains silent. With no discussion evolving. As time passes by, the claim has become a 'truth'. Unfortunately, it is only an 'alternative truth'. In reality the FATF serves only a limited interest: the integrity of the global financial system, which is part of a legal whole and not a high-level exception. This claim contrasts with the fact that it is neither possible to measure the size of the global system nor its integrity.

As is clear throughout this work, we acknowledge this task and discussed it in Chapters 3-5 and 8. We also stress that this task should not be fulfilled under the Laundering Dome, but within a transparent system of law, which is, amongst others, instrumental to the restoration of justice. This principle transcends any claim of the FATF. In our field, the restoration of justice can be broad and is not always easily measurable, but one aim is clearly unambiguous and literally 'countable': the restoration of the axiomatic rule 'crime should not pay'. Hence, to restore the injustice of illegally obtained advantages, these must be returned or be otherwise annulled. This redirects our focus to *asset recovery*.

Contrary to what is regularly maintained, this is not a punishment, but a civil action, even if it is mostly executed at a criminal trial. Of course, criminals feel differently, which seems to have some entertaining value, given the encouraging statement: "Hit them where it hurts them most –in their wallet". However, restoring is not about revenge but redress. This redress is *laundering-neutral*: it does not matter whether all the acquired assets have been squandered, lost or in fact fully 'whitened'. The rule is: "Thou shall pay back what does not belong to thee", which is the direct consequence of the violation of the basic axiom that crime should not pay. And this rule must be pursued relentlessly. Except for some awareness raising, it does not need the Laundering Dome of the FATF.

So, while it is lofty to have the asset recovery obligation included in the list of FATF Recommendations, it transcends the domain of the FATF, which seems to have absorbed it. This is historically, and as a matter of legal principle, incorrect. In the Netherlands the focus was already redirected on "plucking criminals" ("Pluk-ze") in 1987. To that end it the Dutch Task Group investigating this subject only needed one axiom as expressed in the first page: "Crime should not pay".[6] This policy initiative came before the onset of the FATF or the invasion of US law enforcement missionaries.

As far as the integrity of the financial system is concerned, restoring justice does not necessarily impact on financial institutions, unless they have become victims themselves. But launderers do no usually victimise banks. Again, this raises the question whether we need the armoury of the FATF to pursue this restorative task. It should be part and parcel of law enforcement independent of money laundering. This does not imply that the penalty clause for laundering or managing someone's criminal assets has no function. The investigation and prosecution of 'criminal asset management services' offered to predicate offenders may for investigation be strategically important and otherwise equally of value to restoring justice.

Looking from this perspective at the outgrowth of the AML-regime we think there is a need to simplify its abundance. But even then we must ask the question: does this overgrown garden justify the present global anti-money laundering apparatus and the FATF as a kind of Superintendent Gardener? Do we need the heavy consultative structure, a debatable risk assessment methodology and a costly mutual evaluation procedure? This is not a rhetorical question. In Chapter 9 we have tried to answer our hypothetical visitor's simple question: "What is all this good for" and we remained speechless for want of a proper answer. We looked for properly specified external criteria,

---

6 Financiële Facetten van Ernstige Vormen van Criminaliteit. Editor P.C. van Duyne; Ministry of Justice, 1987.

but did not find these in the FATF documentation. We found a multitude of effectivity indicators, but these were all internal, under the Laundering Dome, rather than from outside. The FATF presents an impressive organisational chart of working groups, but their effects do not radiate through the glass stained window.

Having returned to the general level of maintaining the rule of law, we have space for a discussion of criminal law policy issues regarding criminal asset management without giving it an exceptional position. For example, what additional injustice must be redressed in cases of self-laundering given it is a built-in act? Or, must the seriousness of the criminal money management not be related to the seriousness of the predicate offence? If the basic requirement of restoration has been fulfilled, are there still reasons for a criminal law action or are there alternatives that are proportional and subsidiary or less harmful? Naturally there are also other aims, such as the reduction of profit directed crimes.

These and similar criminal law reflections are few and far between in the money laundering literature and absent in the FATF documentation. This is not a reproach, having the metaphor of the Superintendent Gardener in mind: we admit that he had to supervise a big garden, but we think he let it overgrow. Now that it has been raked up, the question should be raised: do we need the FATF? And if 'yes', do we need it in its full capacity and in its current form? While recognising the valuable contribution of the FATF to the awareness raising of criminal asset management and stressing the importance of the integrity of the financial system (however undefined that is), there are no reasons why the structure and functioning of the FATF should not be held against the light of the basic principles of law as elaborated in this and previous chapters.

10.6 Outside of the Laundering Dome

Our visitor poses the question again: "what is it all this for?" Has the academic literature in the field provided clarity and a sense of purpose for the AML regime? We reviewed a large body of existing academic work with the purpose of understanding the issues that have been explored and to determine what had been found out as a result. This was to share what is already known, but also to point to those areas to which further research could fruitfully contribute. Looking back at the contents of Chapters 6 to 8, there are areas of commonality in the different disciplines of our enquiry. Many authors have worked within the Laundering Dome, accepting the prevailing basic premises and principles set out in the official discourse. Some, however, strayed outside or were never let in and cast a critical eye over the entire edifice, probing the solidity of the foundations and the strength of the walls.

What can we draw from this critical discourse that will provide an answer as to the purpose of the AML-regime? Given the emphasis that has been placed on the integrity of the financial system, a number of academics have considered the harm caused by money laundering and the notion of morality. Within the legal literature, this is approached by looking at the use of the legal framework to redress harm from money laundering. However, as has been set out in this chapter, one has to question the degree of harm caused by money laundering over and beyond the predicate offence. We have already questioned whether laundering can be viewed as being harmful in its own capacity (other than in the moral sense) because it thwarts the axiom of 'crime should not pay'. How does this compare with 'moral harm' to the financial system being caused by criminally tainted funds being mixed with all other funds already in bank accounts? Moreover, whilst some of the earliest papers attempted to line up the evidence of financial and economic harm (see for example, Quirk, 1996), others (Ferwerda, 2013) could find no such justification. Similarly, Reuter (2013) from a review of the literature, has not located endangered sectors of the financial system. These refutations were never reacted upon: did they really penetrate into the Laundering Dome?

Nevertheless, within the official discourse, the idea of harm arising from money laundering has been framed in the context a major global threat requiring and justifying action by countries around the world. Many mainstream authors seem to accept this as a statement of fact. Such uncritical acceptance seems to be at odds with the role and function of the academic. There are notable exceptions: see, for example, Alldridge (2003); Naylor (1999); Van Duyne and De Miranda (1999); Sharman (2008); Pieth (1999); Harvey (2005); Levi and Reuter (2006) and Hulsse (2008). Some authors explored the mandate and authority of the FATF (Gallant, 2010) and its ability to sanction those countries that are strategically deficient in implementing the Recommendations (see Comstock, 1994). There have been no empirical studies of whether such punishments have been proportional, although a number of authors looked at the scope of predicate offences as the list has gradually crept beyond drug trafficking (see for example Unger *et al.*, 2006; Gelemerova, 2011). Given the interest in the moral imperative 'crime must not pay', some authors looked at the principle of restorative justice and the recovery of criminal assets to the state (Alldridge, 2003; Rider, 1999; McClean, 1989; Gordon, 1995). Other authors considered whether the nature and scale of the recovered assets would provide evidence to support the threatening nature of these monies to the financial system.

Economists tend to adopt positivism as a research philosophy, searching for facts, data and the testing of theory through its reproducibility. The literature covered both the models that have aimed to measure the volume of laundering activity and those concerned with the effectiveness of countermeasures reducing opportunities for it to take place. Certainly, the move toward greater globalisation over the past thirty years has opened opportunities within the legitimate economy. It is a doctrine that it has also facilitated global organised crime. It goes without saying, that if one is intent upon measuring the quantum of something, that it is necessary to be very clear about what is to be included within the measure. Furthermore, in considering effectiveness, as already outlined in the chapter here, in a scientific approach it should be possible to measure the amount before the intervention and the commensurate change arising from the intervention evidenced by the different amount at the end. So as discussed, do we line up all or only some predicate offences; do we count all or only some types of laundering and how do we account for the inevitable double counting? Economists tend to support the all-crimes approach (see for example Busuioc, 2007). Within the criminal code, the requirement to criminalise an activity is generally based upon the extent of 'harm' caused to society. From that perspective the alleged 'distortion of economic statistics' by itself does not really amount to such criminal law justification (Alldridge, 2002). Both Alldridge (2002) and Van Duyne *et al.* (2016, 2018a) argue strongly in favour of the principle of proportionality in this field. Despite the apparently simple outlines above about approaches to scientific measurement, studies have failed to arrive at reliable estimates of the sums involved. Often using gross generalisation over different subpopulations of criminality there is an in-built bias towards large numbers (although other academics have consistently questioned these assumptions, see, for example, Reuter (2013)).

The cross-disciplinary literature was presented from the point of view of the impact that the regime has had upon those subject to it. This, therefore, considered the behavioural responses of the countries, the regulated sectors and, finally, the criminal fraternity. Behaviour and response is, of course, a difficult area in particular because of the uncertain causality between (AML) stimulus and response in view of the fact that both are inaccurately delineated. This applies not so much to criminal conduct, where little change has apparently been observed, but more to the costs incurred by the financial 'gate keepers'.

One important aspect of this literature base has brought forward is the role and contribution of asset recovery and the deterring impact it may have upon criminals. Despite its importance, there does not appear to have been any serious enquiry to determine whether criminals have modified or (preferably) reduced their criminality. They may have modified their *modus operandi*, though the FATF reports on methods and trends has little criminal laundering innovation to present: usually variations on old *modus operandi* like trade-based laundering and loan-back constructions.

What is troubling about this ambiguous representation is the evidence supplied from the output data. The data on assets recovered discussed above rather points to low economic sophistication and relatively low criminal income among the majority of criminals, which does not require laundering in the strict sense of the term. If there is impact, it is mainly at a low criminal level.

A principal contribution from this final section of literature was to draw attention to how individuals are far removed from the rational *homo economicus* beloved of economists. Distancing from the assumption of rationality does not only relate to criminals. Policy makers are equally vulnerable to the way information is framed in an unrational threat image and thus subject to the consequent risk of an upward spiral of more laws, regulations and repression (see for example, Hulsse, 2007; Nichols, 1997; Van Duyne, 1998, 2004). It seems unlikely that there will be any lessening in requirements. Given the existence of the global legal and regulatory framework that is AML, it will be very tempting to the international community to use it for the solutions of the next generation of issues and problems. Witness how taxation and corruption have been incorporated within its scope.

10.7 To launder or not to launder: that is the question

Looking back at our extensive reconnaissance, accompanied by our naïve questioning companion, we covered a broad field and hit on many unanswered questions. We have also not been complete in the sense that we have not touched the wide field of economic and financial crime, in view of its huge revenues no doubt highly relevant for money laundering policy. We will see whether that assumption holds true.

It does not require deeper wisdom to recognise that profit generating crimes are part and parcel of the economy, and therefore ML-relevant. The FATF also recognises this intermittently: see its typologies on trade based laundering, the gold sector and its more recent attention to tax crimes (direct and indirect taxes). The list of categories of predicate economic crimes contained in the General Glossary of the FATF Recommendations 2012 range from fraud to environmental crimes to tax crimes, insider trading and market manipulation. Managing the proceeds from such crimes is of course laundering. Or not?

That is not certain, given the added annotation to the categories of predicate crimes which we discussed in Chapter 6.2.: "each country may decide [. . .] how it will define those [predicate] offences and the nature of any particular elements of those offences that make them serious offences" (Recommendations 2012; updated June 2017; p. 113). This can lead to remarkable outcomes. We point at the historical fact that in 2003, Prime Minister Berlusconi *avoided the consequences of his acts* by introducing a bill which downgraded his reported offence to a lower (civil law) qualification.

Further, the Italian Parliament '*abetted*' this disguise of its PM's alleged crimes in broad daylight by passing the law. Is that not laundering? It could rather be qualified as 'Grand Laundering' in conjunction with 'Grand Corruption', which the FATF let pass without any critical comment.

In the field of economic crime, such downgrading can involve most profitable offences moved out of the money laundering range. For example, illegal logging and trading the resulting product may be still punishable, but it may no longer be defined as a predicate offence for laundering. Hence, managing the proceeds would not be qualified as an offence. In this field in which probably most of the illegal profits are made this allows a substantial eroding of the AML-regime. For example, if Indonesia or the USA have an interest in respectively illegal logging or oil pollution, they can avoid laundering charges by downgrading the applicable offences (assuming the prosecution wants to initiate an investigation in the first place).

Is it possible to neutralise this defect? A simple approach to counter such erosion would be to make the *all-crime* regime general. Actually, there is no reason to make the application of the ML-regime dependent of national political preferences for predicate offences. However, though the all-crime approach looks simple and elegant, it does not solve the diversity of national criminal law: there will always remain differences in national criminalisation.

We think that pursuing this discussion diverts from the fact that there is more in life than laundering. In the first place, there is no reason to attribute laundering cases a kind of 'primacy' as we have seen in various MERs: there should be no 'laundering first'. Ultimately, AML-policy does not serve itself but the application of the axiom that crime should not pay. If the AML has a meaning, it is within a criminal law architecture that strives for the restoration of justice. This implies undoing all illegal advantages.

In the second place, in economic and financial crime there is a problem with the recognisability of laundering, connected to the phenomenon of 'canned laundering: as soon as the false paperwork is completed the money is 'clean in the can'. To be clear, this means it is already fully in the legal economy and not just vaguely 'available for laundering'. Some forms of economic crime require even less in terms of laundering effort: the profits can consist of illegal savings. For example, dumping chemical waste instead of undertaking expensive processing. The disguise consists of making goods disappear, but where is the laundering? Labour fraud is another example: making products more cheaply by keeping the taxes and social security contributions, aggravated by cost saving exploitation and neglect of safety conditions. The principal takes knowing advantage of these forms of criminal cost reduction. So, here too are proceeds, but where is the laundering? And who is criminally liable: the principal or those further along the supply chain? Another example is food fraud: making profit by adulteration of the product and deceiving by means of a false label description does not lead to a clear criminal money trace. Neither does the production of counterfeit goods that might find a ready market amongst consumers but undermine the copyright holder. This takes on a more sinister form when those substandard products might endanger life such as medicines, or vehicle and machine parts. The emission fraud by the car industry may justifiably be approached from a laundering angle as well.

This discussion should be intensified and broadened, because there are reasons to believe that mainstream discourse remains biased to the 'usual suspect' thinking. Above that there is the overarching subject of restoring justice which the FATF papers leave fully untouched.

The independent, rather overarching position of restorative justice comes to the fore in the policy of asset recovery. Under the title of Confiscation it has its correct place in Recommendations 4, 30, 36 and 38. Though these mentions are technically correct, they do not emerge from any proper reflection on doing justice. As a matter of fact, asset recovery is indifferent to any laundering device and has a long history pre-dating the FATF. In the Netherlands, the first initiatives were unfolded in 1987 while in the UK forfeiture were established under medieval English law. The basic approach is simple. If a Court determines in its sentence that a defendant had obtained a certain illegal financial gain (or its equivalent), he or she has to pay that sum to the state or victimised persons. It does not matter whether it is the original money, or has been co-mingled, whitewashed or squandered on a grandiose lifestyle: that amount must be paid, even if it comes from the 'white' inheritance of the old grandmother. In formal terms: such a recovery is not a punishment but a *measure*, although convicted persons may feel it differently (Vruggink, 2001). Nevertheless, there is a transition zone between asset recovery and punishment, for example, when such a recovery is realised by means of a fine, estimated as equal to the illegal gains (Borgers, 2001). Nevertheless, irrespective of this legal transition zone, we consider asset recovery as a *restorative measure* in addition to the punishment for the predicate offence.

While restoring justice is a superordinate principle, it has some uncertain fringes. One of them concerns 'the unexplained wealth', a phrase which speaks for itself. This looks almost like the opposite of laundering: there are assets or life-style expenditures, but the owner of these possessions cannot explain where he bought them or how he could afford them. Unexplained also means that a criminal explanation is lacking. One can also call this '*un*laundered wealth' because of the absence of a justifying, 'white' origin.

This is a difficult field beset with many pitfalls when there is no evidence of criminal origins of the wealth. Based on circumstantial evidence the wealth can be seized and forfeited in a civil procedure (King, 2013). The approach is also used against (unproven) corruption of office holders in Romania, though at this stage, with little success (Nicolae, 2013). Naturally, 'unexplained wealth' could be seen to at least imply a tax offence if no other predicate offence is found: withholding information about income and possessions. However, does the unexplained wealth imply a full *criminal* income that can be forfeited forthwith and in full? What i*njustice* must be redressed if there is no other law breaking?

This is a recent development about which we should sound a note of caution. The unexplained wealth orders (as for example introduced recently in the UK through the Criminal Finances Act, 2017) remains a legal problem. Does this mean an opening of the door to 'open fishing expeditions' and harassment of 'usual suspects'?

In the Netherlands, Rotterdam and Amsterdam, there are 'take away' experiments, implying that the police check suspects who are known to have no licit income (called 'air biters'), but who, nevertheless, display much visible wealth in terms of cars, watches and expensive branded clothes. The police question them in the street, requiring that they produce evidence of the legal origin of their status symbols: receipts, invoices or other evidence to explain their lawful acquisition. If not, the objects are taken to the police station and the suspect may be prosecuted for laundering: the judge invites the suspect to give an explanation and lacking that, decides whether there is sufficient circumstantial evidence of predicate offences (no proof required) to convict the defendant for laundering and declare the seized objects forfeited.

While this represents a visibly targeted action, popular with the police, there is criticism that it focuses on petty criminals, profiling young, often ethnic minority 'usual suspects'.

In such cases of unexplained wealth there is a non-evidenced suspicion of one or more predicate offences and evidence of (self) laundering, consisting of mere possession of valuables for which a punishment is applied. What about cases with a proven predicate offence and self-laundering? Should self-laundering be considered as an *aggravating* circumstance? What is the added value in terms of the restoration of justice?

We discussed this earlier in section 10.1 and cast doubt on the usefulness of applying the anti-money laundering tools everywhere and on all occasions. If our doubts are correct, we should raise the question: given the present enormous ramification of the ALM-regime, are all its components in their proper place?

10.8 Putting things in proper places

Having come at the end of our journey it is appropriate to look back at the AML-regime as it unfolded. The FATF started as an informal advisory organ concerning the laundering of drug money and ended as a mighty global (but still informal) organisation with sanctioning powers but without any corporate accountability. Meanwhile its tasks have been extended: it not only has to guard the integrity of the worldwide financial system, it also assumed a role in preventing and repressing (for profit) crime. We have set out how willingly and eagerly it adopted these roles with its latest manifestation focused upon corruption. It arrogated the right to criticise the work of independent law enforcement agencies, such as prosecutors and the courts, for prioritising predicate offences above laundering and for passing down sentences that it (in the guise of its assessors) considered too lenient. It has also formulated policies outside the range of money laundering, such as those concerning asset recovery. For all these diverse fields it drew up Recommendations. Given this outgrowth, one may wonder whether this is something of an overgrowth.

To this end it is appropriate to decompose the FATF website statement about its mission "*Who we are*": "The objectives of the FATF are to set standards and promote effective implementation of legal, regulatory and operational measures for combating money laundering, terrorist financing and other related threats to the integrity of the international financial system."[7] This is an elaborate sentence of which the last part constitutes the final justification: *the threats to the integrity of the international financial system*. The question is whether the outgrowth mentioned above is indeed supported by this broad justification.

We have discussed the integrity issue and noted in Chapter 9.2.1. that the aim of integrity is very much shrouded in uncertainty. Can this aim really function as the foundation of all the aspects of the AML-regime? We have pointed out that the uncertainty of the concept of integrity does not allow for proper feedback of what measure does or does not contribute to global financial integrity. This implies that there is little to be built upon: as stated by Alldridge fifteen years ago it is a moral call for a financial crusade. There is nothing wrong with this moral position (as long as these financial crusaders behave better than their medieval ancestors), but this is not an evidence base for the conclusions reached by the FATF. Take the following sentence: "The FATF is *therefore* a policy making body". This is odd: there is nothing to which "therefore" refers or which allows for such a deduction. There is no foundation for this essential statement. So, despite all international acceptance, we will have to create some order ourselves, while staying as close as possible to the FATF's wording.

Firstly, we examine the place of the FATF itself: a policy making body. What does that mean? Giving policy advice or establishing a set of binding rules? Given that the FATF is still an informal body, it lacks any kind of sovereign authority to impose rules of national conduct. The FATF is and remains an inter-ministerial creature and the G-20 ministers have made it clear: they are the principals. Therefore, under the current circumstances, the FATF can

[7] Available from: http://www.fatf-gafi.org/about/whoweare/. Accessed 2 January 2018.

only be a policy *advisory* body. We arrived at this conclusion earlier (Chapter 5.5), but here we connect it to the Recommendations, the recognised international standards. We have seen that these Recommendations were intended as commands with the word "should" to be read as "must", while their compliance is monitored by the same FATF that issued these commands. In this role it does not behave as an advisory body at all: we have noted a distinctly imperial appearance and tone. We are of the opinion, therefore, that this approach should be reconsidered: drafting recommendations (with lower case r); monitoring their compliance and sanctioning non-performers are distinct tasks that should not be held in one hand. A policy making body should not at the same time be a policy controlling body and it certainly should not arrogate the power to sanction AML-sinners. We suggest, therefore, that the policy making side of the FATF should be separated from and monitored by a different operational compliance or implementation group. This body should have clear legally identified structures of governance.

With regard to the recommendations (by us in lower case) it makes sense to reconsider their position in terms of their content on the one hand, and national sovereignty on the other hand. In the first place, concerning content, we have the recommendations that are more directly connected to the aims of financial integrity. These mainly concern section D of the FATF 2012: recommendations 9-23, directed at the gatekeepers of the financial institutions and the designated non-financial businesses and professions. Summarised: know your customer well and if he is a PEP, know him better. We think it appropriate that the FATF admonishes the private sector to heed these principles.

Section E addresses the governments, telling them to see to it that there should be no possibility of civil or commercial law enabling beneficial owners to hide behind screens of anonymity. No corporate veil should exist, as indicated by the OECD in 2001.[8] Aside from whether or not states should be 'admonished', what the recommendations require is actually a proper anti-fraud provision within the Criminal Code. This is already in place in most jurisdictions. What applies to fraud or financial or other crime for profit applies *ipso facto* also to money laundering. If this is not the case, one should look for defects in the general criminal law provisions and not only for money laundering.

The section F of the Recommendations looks like a mixed reservoir: it deals with regulation and supervision as well as the powers and responsibilities of the authorities and other institutional matters. One can argue that the *regulation* and *supervision* of financial institutions and designated non-financial businesses and professions, is within the circle of financial integrity (recom-

---

[8] *Behind the corporate veil: Using corporate entities for illicit purposes*. OECD, 2001.

mendation 26-28). Is that also the case with the subsequent recommendations in this section?

In the subsection *Operational and Law enforcement* the FATF makes demands about the structure and functioning of the organs of state. It begins with the demand that a Financial Intelligence Unit (FIU) will be established as a hinge or transition point between the regulated private sector and law enforcement. Having an FIU is even a condition for being a member of the FATF. We do not know of a comparable example of a demand by an informal organisation to all countries worldwide to create an institution. This makes it difficult to determine its appropriateness or legitimacy. We can only think of a hypothetical case such as a (badly needed) "Climate Action Task Force on money laundering", which would demand the establishment of a Climate Intelligence Unit to monitor and process shady financial 'agro-deals'. In fact, every good cause can have an Intelligence Unit, but should that be a demand? And how would the international community respond to this? Of course, it is no transgression for the FATF to suggest such a thing: the sovereign states have to consider whether or not they are willing to accept this with or without the threat of the big 'sanctions' stick the FATF wields.

From recommendation 30 onwards, the direct connection to the justifying integrity aim becomes looser. The attention is rather directed to the national law enforcement authorities: investigation (basic level), cross-border cash flow intervention, general requirements (among them statistics (*sic*!) in r. 33), sanctions and international cooperation.

Looking back at these demands, we observe again that they are most basic and already mostly implemented as a matter of routine by any state that takes the investigation and prosecution of serious profit motivated crime seriously. Therefore, for most states these recommendations are superfluous. So, one may wonder whether we need the FATF to be reminded of the importance of these routines. Casting them in a new recommendation document looks like 'old wine in new sacks'. More importantly, do we need the FATF to express its view on the autonomous prosecution office and the sentencing of the independent Courts? What the FATF conveys is a clear punitive view, exhorting member states to ever more severe punishment and criticising evident leniency. What has this to do with the aim of integrity of the financial system? Does a punitive regime contribute to more integrity? If not, these recommendation might just as well be deleted because they can be considered as contradicting the independence of the judiciary.

Finally, what we have saved to the end as 'last but not least', the first two – strategic – demands: the risk based approach and the national coordination thereof. We have already seen that this is quite demanding: "Countries should identify, assess, and understand . . . and take action . . . and designate an authority . . . and have a national policy", and so on. Should the FATF be the appropriate body to impose such a complicated demand in which the connection with the integrity of the financial system looks indirect? We do not disqualify this as a bad idea, though the usual lack of statistical material and imprecise concepts (see Chapter 9.3) make it very uncertain and difficult to evaluate. Only the evaluation teams seem to have the mental capacity to assess whether all these risk requirements are fulfilled, including the 'understanding'. However, on what methodological basis do these assessor teams work? Resorting to a qualitative, 'holistic' approach does not add much sharpness and will not save their approach from an eventual vagueness. What is needed is a stern methodological hand, thus far not provided by the FATF. Therefore, while it is laudable that the FATF encourages this line of thinking, it is also not the appropriate body to impose it as a demand: let the member states sort that out.

Putting things in proper places looks indeed like tidying up: when we look at which of the recommendations are already routine for police and prosecution, or at least enshrined in the various Criminal and Procedural Codes, one can simplify the 40 recommendations. Consequently, one can also simplify and economise on the Mutual Evaluations, which according to Halliday *et al.* (2014) cost the staggering sum of $300,000 each; they belong to the innerworks of the Laundering Dome. Time and energy can then be saved for other threats: our Climate Action Task Force is not a pun, and the huge proceeds from corrupt environmental businesses is concern for us all (Levi, 2018). It would be proper to open the windows of the Laundering Dome and look outside at what more has to be done.

Chapter 2 Appendix 1

Details of the sample of 69 countries selected for the purposes of this study shown in chronological order of review third round

Report Date	Country	FATF or FSBR leading the Review	No. pages	No. evaluators
10 June 2005	Norway	FATF	160	6
10 June 2005	Belgium	FATF	187	6
14 October 2005	Australia	FATF	180	7
14 October 2005	Switzerland	FATF	252	6
15 October 2005	Jamaica	CFATF	136	4
17 February 2006	Sweden	FATF	211	6
28 February 2006	Italy	IMF/FATF	128	5
16 June 2006	Ireland	IMF/FATF	197	6
23 June 2006	The United States	FATF	311	9
23 June 2006	Spain	FATF	177	6
5 July 2006	Sri Lanka	APG	142	5
22 Sept. 2006	Denmark	IMF	248	5
13 October 2006	Iceland	FATF	179	5
19 October 2006	Portugal	FATF	165	6
25 October 2006	Dominican Republic	CFATF	212	4
14 November 2006	Mauretania	MENAFATF	109	4
14 November 2006	Bahrain	MENAFATF	93	4
15 November 2006	Syria	MENAFATF	157	5
16 November 2006	Vanuatu	APG	164	4
30 November 2006	Lithuania	MONEYVAL	185	5
23 February 2007	Turkey	FATF	231	7
03 April 2007	Tunisia	MENAFATF	114	5
15 May 2007	Trinidad and Tobago	CFATF	179	4
6 June 2007	Latvia	MONEYVAL	187	5
12 June 2007	Sierra Leone	GIABA	97	3

P.C. van Duyne, J.H. Harvey and L.Y. Gelemerova, *The Critical Handbook of Money Laundering*, https://doi.org/10.1057/978-1-137-52398-3

Report Date	Country	FATF or FSBR leading the Review	No. pages	No. evaluators
13 June 2007	UK & Northern Ireland	FATF	328	7
14 June 2007	Kyrgyzstan	EAG	135	7
29 June 2007	Greece	FATF	233	7
1 July 2007	Fiji	APG/WORLD BANK	144	3
4 July 2007	Samoa	APG	146	6
12 July 2007	Georgia	MONEYVAL	212	7
24 July 2007	Macao-China	APG	236	5
24 July 2007	Mongolia	APG	147	5
24 July 2007	Chinese Taipei	APG	226	5
24 July 2007	Thailand	APG/IMF	308	5
15 August 2007	Uganda	ESAAMLG	82	4
15 August 2007	Zimbabwe	ESAAMLG	240	7
20 August 2007	China	FATF/EAG	165	9
24 August 2007	Botswana	ESAAMLG	165	3
24 August 2007	Namibia	ESAAMLG	102	4
14 September 2007	Malta	MONEYVAL	177	4
2 October 2007	Moldova	MONEYVAL	299	7
12 October 2007	Finland	FATF	248	6
06 November 2007	Morocco	MENAFATF	123	5
22 November 2007	Poland	MONEYVAL	165	5
23 November 2007	Bahamas	CFATF	285	6
23 November 2007	Cayman Islands	CFATF	163	5
29 February 2008	Singapore	CFATF/IMF	237	8
29 February 2008	Canada	FATF	311	9
01 April 2008	Bulgaria	MONEYVAL	200	6
09 April 2008	United Arab Emirates	MENAFATF	222	4
09 April 2008	Qatar	IMF	217	5
10 April 2008	Croatia	MONEYVAL	234	4
7 May 2008	Nigeria	GIABA	210	7
7 May 2008	Senegal	GIABA	211	8
20 June 2008	Russia	FATF, EAG AND MONEYVAL	199	11
20 June 2008	Hong Kong	FATF	378	7
23 June 2008	Antigua and Barbuda	CFATF	210	7
23 June 2008	Barbados	CFATF	175	5
23 June 2008	Haiti	WORLD BANK/ CFATF	124	3
8 July 2008	Romania	MONEYVAL	218	5
9 July 2008	Indonesia	APG	220	6
10 July 2008	Palau	IMF	268	5
10 July 2008	Myanmar	APG	207	6
16 June 2008	Macedonia	MONEYVAL	238	5
23 July 2008	Andorra	MONEYVAL	176	3
20 August 2008	Zambia	ESAAMLG	234	6
22 August 2008	Seychelles	ESAAMLG	230	7
22 August 2008	Israel	MONEYVAL	226	4

Chapter 2 Appendix 2

Details of the sample of 13 countries selected for the purposes of this study shown in chronological order of review fourth round

Month and year of report	Country	No. pages	No. evaluators
December 2014	Spain	206	10
December 2014	Norway	206	10
April 2015	Belgium	213	7
April 2015	Australia	198	10
May 2015	Ethiopia	105	7
July 2015	Sri Lanka	170	8
September 2015	Samoa	187	8
September 2015	Vanuatu	167	7
September 2015	Malaysia	211	7
December 2015	Armenia	182	7
December 2015	Costa Rica	169	8
December 2015	Cuba	186	9
February 2016	Italy	230	8

P.C. van Duyne, J.H. Harvey and L.Y. Gelemerova, *The Critical Handbook of Money Laundering*, https://doi.org/10.1057/978-1-137-52398-3

Chapter 2 Appendix 3

Scope of study "money laundering" OR "anti-money laundering"
Search undertaken on 26 September 2014

Database	Search terms employed	Number of entries	Years covered by database	Relevant Publications prior to 1st January 1990
Emerald Insight	'money laundering' OR 'anti-money laundering' *abstract, articles and chapters [Note returning just 'money laundering gives same number]*	527	1993-2014	0
Scopus (Elsevier) (Social sciences)	'money laundering' OR 'anti-money laundering' *article title, abstract and key words*	526	1991-2014	0
Science Direct (Elsevier)	'money laundering' OR 'anti-money laundering' (Limited to: social sciences; economics, econometrics and finance; Business management and accounting; and arts and humanities) *article title, abstract and key words*	48	2004-2014	0
British Humanities Index (ProQuest)	'money laundering' OR 'anti-money laundering' *abstract, peer review, English, bibliography, conference reports, journal article and literature review*	11	Not provided	0

P.C. van Duyne, J.H. Harvey and L.Y. Gelemerova, *The Critical Handbook of Money Laundering*, https://doi.org/10.1057/978-1-137-52398-3

Database	Search terms employed	Number of entries	Years covered by database	Relevant Publications prior to 1st January 1990
Web of Science (Thomson Reuter)	'money laundering' OR 'anti-money laundering' *Topic Note returning just 'money laundering gives same number*	455	1950-2014	6
Ebsco host	'money laundering' OR 'anti-money laundering' in Business Source Premier, e-Books International Political Science Abstract, *abstract, peer reviewed journals, English produces different numbers for ml apart from AML*	1037	1988-2014	0
IEEE Xplore	'money laundering' OR 'anti-money laundering' *Metadata only across all sources of conference proceedings, journals and magazines and books and ebooks*	67	1995-2014	0
JISC Journal Archives	'money laundering' OR 'anti-money laundering'	369	1980-2010	4
JSTOR Collections	'money laundering' OR 'anti-money laundering' *content access journal articles and archive books, English: Business, Business and economics, Economics, Finance, General Law, Law, Political Science; Public Policy and administrations, social sciences, sociology*	0	Not provided	0
Oxford Journals archive	'money laundering' *Social sciences*	12	Feb 1827- Jan 2015	0
Westlaw UK	'money laundering' *document title, journals*	1461	Not provided	4
Wiley online	'money laundering' OR 'anti-money laundering' *Abstract, journals and books*	70	1991-2014	0
Zetoc	'money laundering' *general search, title*	1687	Not provided	0
Social Science Research Network (SSRN)*	'money laundering' *title abstract and key words*	331	Not provided	0

Database	Search terms employed	Number of entries	Years covered by database	Relevant Publications prior to 1st January 1990
Northumbria University Library catalogue**	'money laundering' *books, ebook and book chapters* in the library catalogue	155	Not provided	3
Total		**6,756**		

* indicates open access database
** indicates University of Northumbria on line search facility – this search covered the library catalogue separately from the e-journals.
Note: no adjustment has been made to remove duplicates or articles that might not be relevant.

Chapter 2 Appendix 4

Themes that emerged from the 21 papers.

Our allocated Parent theme	Topics supporting theme	Number of papers*	Authors of the 21 papers
Definition	Definition	6	Arnone and Borlini (2010); Gordon (1995); McCarthy *et al.* (2015); Naylor (2003)*; Schneider and Windischbauer (2008); Waris and Latif (2014).
International standards	Assessment of compliance with FATF	1	Arnone and Borlini (2010)
	Typologies and methods	2	Arnone and Borlini (2010); Schneider and Windischbauer (2008)
Impact on economy	Negative effect on economic activity	4	Alldridge (2002); Arnone and Borlini (2010); Aurojo (2010); Otusanya *et al.* (2011)
	Impact on economic variables	5	Alldridge (2002); Arnone and Borlini (2010); Coleman (1992); Mccarthy *et al.* (2015); Schneider and Windischbauer (2008)
	Capital flight	3	Arnone and Borlini (2010); Otusanya *et al.* (2011); Otusanya and Lauwu (2012)
	Impact on growth in developing countries	2	Arnone and Borlini (2010); Araujo (2010)

P.C. van Duyne, J.H. Harvey and L.Y. Gelemerova, *The Critical Handbook of Money Laundering*, https://doi.org/10.1057/978-1-137-52398-3

Our allocated Parent theme	Topics supporting theme	Number of papers*	Authors of the 21 papers
Impact of globalisation	OFCs	4	Arnone and Borlini (2010); Otusanya *et al.* (2011); Otusanya and Lauwu (2012); Young (2013);
	Facilitating AML	3	Alldridge (2002); Gordon (1995); Nardo (2006)
	Global wealth chains	1	Waris and Latif (2014)
Attractiveness of countries to criminals	corruption	2	Otusanya *et al.* (2011); Young (2013)
	Laxity in controls	1	Barone & Massiandaro (2011)
	Bank secrecy	4	Aruajo (2008); Aurojo (2010); Otusanya and Lauwu (2012); Young (2013)
	Potential for criminals to exploit differences between legal systems	2	Alldridge (2002); Arnone and Borlini (2010)
Predicate offences	Drugs	2	Arnone and Borlini (2010); Taylor (1992)
	General including white-collar	5	Alldridge (2002); Arnone and Borlini (2010); Coleman (1992); Naylor (2003); Pellegrina and Masciandaro (2008)
Deterrent effect of increasing costs of money laundering	Risk of detection	3	Arnone and Borlini (2010); Mccarthy *et al.* (2015); Nardo (2006)
	Rational actors	2	Arnone and Borlini (2010); Mccarthy *et al.* (2015)
Microeconomic models	Game theory/bargaining theory/prisoners' dilemma	4	Alldridge (2002); Arnone and Borlini (2010); Araujo (2010); Mccarthy *et al.* (2015)
	Principal agent (compliance)	3	Aurojo (2008); Pellegrina and Masciandaro (2008); Takats (2011)
Macro-economic models	Trade-based gravity model	2	Arnone and Borlini (2010); Walker and Unger (2009)
	Dynamic general equilibrium modelling	2	Argentiero, Bagella, and Busato (2008); Barone and Masciandaro (2011)
	Multiplier effect	2	Arnone and Borlini (2010); Barone and Masciandaro (2011)
	Dynamic macro model of measurement	1	Barone and Masciandaro (2011)
	DYMIMIC estimation, (dynamic multiple-indicators multiple-causes)	1	Schneider and Windischbauer (2008)
	General measurement/size of problem	3	Arnone and Borlini (2010); McCarthey *et al.* (2014); Pellegrina and Masciandaro (2008)

Our allocated Parent theme	Topics supporting theme	Number of papers*	Authors of the 21 papers
Efficiency of regulation and impact on regulated sector	Risk-based approach	2	Arnone and Borlini (2010); Pellegrina and Masciandaro (2008)
	Incentives based approach	3	Aurojo (2008); Pellegrina and Masciandaro (2008); Takats (2011)
	Suspicious activity	4	Arnone and Borlini (2010); Aruajo (2008); Nardo (2006); Takats (2011)
	Costs of non-compliance	2	Aurojo (2010); Pellegrina and Masciandaro (2008)
	Burden on banks	2	McCarthey *et al.* (2014); Takats (2011)
	Reputational risk and undermining of trust	1	Arnone and Borlini (2010)
	Corporate liability failure in controls	2	Arnone and Borlini (2010); McCarthey *et al.* (2014)
Moral perspective	Claims makers	1	Nichols (1997)
	Moral Limits	1	Alldridge (2002)
	Lack of morals	2	Otusanya and Lauwu (2011); Otusanya and Lauwu (2012)
	Hot money	1	Taylor (1992)

* Each of the 21 papers appears at least once and can be categorised multiple times where their content covers more than one topic area

References

Abadinsky, H., (1994), *Organised crime*. Chicago: Nelson-Hall Publishers. 4th ed.

Abadinsky, H., (2003), Organized Crime (7th edn), Wadsworth/Thomson Learning, Belmont, CA.

Abramovsky, A., (1986), Money-laundering and narcotics prosecution, *Fordham Law Review,* 54(4), 471–507.

Akopyan, E. (2010), Money Laundering, *American Criminal Law Review*, 47(2), 821–845.

Alfon, I. and Andrews, P., (1999), *Cost Benefit Analysis in Financial Regulations: How to do it and how it adds value*, FSA Occasional Paper Series 3, September, Available at http://www.fsa.gov.uk/pubs/occpapers/OP03.pdf

Alldridge, P., (2002), Moral Limits of the Crime of Money Laundering, *Buff. Crim. L. Rev,* 5, 279–320.

Alldridge, P., (2003), Money Laundering Law: Forfeiture, confiscation, civil recovery, criminal laundering and taxation of the proceeds of crime, Oxford –Portland Oregon: Hart Publishing.

Alldridge, P., (2008), Money Laundering and Globalization, *Journal of Law and Society,* 35(4), 437–463.

Alvesalo, A. and Tombs, S., (2005), Evaluating Economic Crime Control? *Security Journal,* 18(4), 7–15.

Amann, D.M., (2000), Spotting money launderers: a better way to fight organized crime? *Syracuse Journal of International Law and Commerce, 27*(2), 199–231.

Argentiero, A., Bagella, M., and Busato, F., (2008), Money laundering in a two-sector model: using theory for measurement. *European Journal of Law and Economics*, 26(3), 341–359.

Armitage, A. and Keeble-Allen, D., (2008), "Undertaking a Structured Literature Review or Structuring a Literature Review: Tales from the Field." *The Electronic Journal of Business Research Methods*, 6 (2), 103–114, available online at www.ejbrm.com

P.C. van Duyne, J.H. Harvey and L.Y. Gelemerova, *The Critical Handbook of Money Laundering*, https://doi.org/10.1057/978-1-137-52398-3

Anna, S., (2011), The risk-based approach to anti-money laundering: problems and solutions, *Journal of Money Laundering Control,* 14(4), 346–358.

Araujo, R.A., (2008), Assessing the efficiency of the anti-money laundering regulation: an incentive-based approach, *Journal of Money Laundering Control,* 11(1), 67–75.

Araujo, R.A., (2010), An evolutionary game theory approach to combat money laundering, *Journal of Money Laundering Control,* 13(1), 70–78.

Ardizzi, G., Petraglia, C., Piacenza, M., Schneider, F., and Turati, G. (2014), Money Laundering as a Crime in the Financial Sector: A New Approach to Quantitative Assessment, with an Application to Italy. *Journal of Money, Credit and Banking, 46*(8), 1555–1590.

Argentiero, A., Bagella, M. and Busato, F., (2008). Money laundering in a two-sector model: using theory for measurement. *European Journal of Law and Economics,* 26(3), 341–359.

Arnone, M. and Borlini, L., (2010), International anti-money laundering programs. Empirical assessment and issues in criminal regulation. *Journal of Money Laundering Control,* 13(3), 226–271.

Arnone, M. and Padoan, P.C., (2008), Anti-money laundering by international institutions: a preliminary assessment. *European Journal of Law and Economics,* 26(3), 361–386.

Baker, R.W., (1999), The Biggest Loophole in the Free-Market System. *Washington Quarterly,* 22(4), 29–46.

Balcells, M, (2015), Left Behind? Cultural Destruction, the Role of the International Criminal Tribunal for the Former Yugoslavia in Deterring it and Cultural Heritage Prevention Policies in the Aftermath of the Balkan Wars *Eur J Crim Policy Res* 21(1), 1–13.

Baldwin, R. and Cave, M., (1999), "*Understanding Regulation: theory strategy and practice"* Oxford: Oxford University Press.

Ball, M., (2011), 'Images, language and numbers in company reports: a study of documents that are occasioned by a legal requirements for financial disclosure' *Qualitative Research* 11(2): 115–139.

Bank for International Settlements, (2004) *Sound Management of Risks Related to Money Laundering and Financing of Terrorism.* Basel.

Barlett, B., (2002). "The negative effects of money laundering on economic development", Countering Money Laundering in the Asian and Pacific Region. *For the Asian Development Bank, Regional Technical Assistance Project No. 5967.*

Barone, R., and Masciandaro, D., (2011), Organized crime, money laundering and legal economy: Theory and simulations. *European Journal of Law and Economics, 32*(1), 115–142.

Barro, R.J., (1991), Economic growth in a cross-selection of countries. *Quarterly Journal of Economics,* May.

Bart, K., Miles, T. and Viswanatha, A., (2012), UBS traders charged, bank fined $1.5 billion in Libor scandal, Reuters, 19 December 2012, https://www.reuters.com/article/us-ubs-libor/ubs-traders-charged-bank-fined-1-5-billion-in-libor-scandal-idUSBRE8BI00020121219?feedType=RSS&feedName=wtMostRead&utm_source=twitterfeed&utm_medium=twitter&utm_campaign=Feed%3A+reuters%2FMostRead+%28News+%2F+US+%2F+Most+Read+Articles%29. Accessed 6 January 2018.

Baumol, W., (1990), Entrepreneurship: productive, unproductive and destructive. *J. Pol. Econ.*, 98(5), 893–921.

Gary S. Becker, (1968) "Crime and Punishment: An Economic Approach," *Journal of Political Economy* 76 (2): 169–217.

Bell, R.E., (2003), Abolishing the concept of 'predicate offence'. *Journal of Money Laundering Control,* 6(2), 137–140.

Bello, A.U., (2014), Self-protecting theory a classical grounded theory study of money laundering reporting officers (MLROs), Ph. D. Thesis, University of Northumbria at Newcastle. Faculty of Business and Law, Northumbria University.

Bello, A.U. and Harvey, J.H., (2017), From a risk-based to an uncertainty-based approach to anti-money laundering compliance, *Security Journal,* 30(1), 24–38.

Bennett, T., Holloway, K., and Farrington, D., (2006), Does neighbourhood watch reduce crime? A systematic review and meta-analysis, *Journal of Experimental Criminology* 2(4), 437–458.

Bequai, A., (1979), *White collar crime: a 20th-Century crisis.* Lexington: Heath and Company.

Bergström, M., Helgesson, K.S., Morth, U., Uppsala, U., Humanistisk-samhällsvetenskapliga, V., Juridiska, F., and Juridiska, I., (2011), A New Role for For-Profit Actors?: The Case of Anti-Money Laundering and Risk Management. *Journal of Common Market Studies,* 49(5), 1043–1064.

Bewley-Taylor, D.R., (1999), The United States and international drug control, 1909–1997. London, Pinter.

Biersteker, T.J., Eckert, S.E., Romaniuk, P. (2008), International Initiatives to Combat the Financing of Terrorism. In Biersteker, T.J., Eckert, S.E. (Eds.), *Countering the Financing of Terrorism,* pp. 234–259. London: Routledge.

Blastland, M., and Dilnot, A., (2008) The Tiger that Isn't: seeing through a world of numbers Profile Books Ltd, London.

Blickman, T., (2009), Countering Illicit and Unregulated Money Flows: Money Laundering, Tax Evasion and Financial Regulation. *Crime and Globalisation Debate Papers, TNI Briefing Series.*

Blum, J.A., Levi, M., Naylor, R.T., and Williams, P., (1999), Financial havens, banking secrecy and money laundering: Double Issue 34 and 35 of the Crime Prevention and Criminal Justice Newsletter, Issue 8 of the UNDCP Technical Series, May 1998. *Trends in Organized Crime,* 4(4), 68–71.

Blumenson, E., and Nilsen, E., (1998), Policing for Profit: The Drug War's Hidden Economic Agenda. *University of Chicago Law Review,* 65(1), 35–113.

Boorman, J., and Ingves, S., (2001), Financial system abuse, financial crime and money laundering—background paper. Washington: Monetary and Exchange Affairs and Policy Development and Review Departments, International Monetary Fund.

Boran, C., (2003), Money laundering. *American Criminal Law Review,* 40(2), 847–871.

Borgers, M.J., (2001), *De ontnemingsmaatregel.* Boom Juridische Uitgevers.

Bosworth-Davies, R., (2008), The influence of Christian moral ideology in the development of anti-money laundering compliance in the west and its impact, post 9-11, upon the South Asian Market. *Journal of Money Laundering Control,* 11(2), 179–192.

Boylston, L.D., (1987), Attorneys' fees and the Money Laundering Control Act of 1986: further erosion of criminal defense advocacy. *Georgia Law Review,* 21(4), 929–965.

Braithwaite, J., (1988), White-Collar Crime, Competition, and Capitalism: Comment on Coleman. *American Journal of Sociology,* 94(3), 627–632.

Brennan, G. and Eusepi, G., (2008), Guest Editorial: Introduction. *European Journal of Law and Economics, 26,* 233–235.

Briner, R. and Denyer, D., (2012), Systematic review and evidence synthesis as a practice and scholarship tool. In: Rousseau, D. (ed.) The Oxford Handbook of Evidence-Based Management. Oxford University Press, New York, U. S. A, pp. 112–129. Available at: http://www.cebma.org/wp-content/uploads/Briner-Denyer-Systematic-Review-Evidence-Synthesis.pdf where manuscript pages run from 328–374 (accessed 7/9/14).

Brown, C., (2007), *Economic theories of the entrepreneur: a systematic review of the literature.* MRes thesis, Cranfield University School of Management, available at: http://dspace.lib.cranfield.ac.uk/handle/1826/2152 (accessed 2/9/14).

Bruun, K., Pan, L. Rexed, I. (1975), *The gentleman's club: International control of drugs and alcohol,* University of Chicago Press.

Buchanan, B., (2004), Money laundering - A global obstacle. *Research in International Business and Finance,* 18(1), 115–127.

Busuioc, M., (2007), Defining Money Laundering. Predicate Offences-The Achilles' Heel of Anti-Money Laundering Legislation. In B. Unger (ed.), *The Scale and Impacts of Money Laundering* Cheltenham: Edward Elgar.

Canhoto, A.I., (2008), Barriers to segmentation implementation in money laundering detection. *The marketing review,* 8(2), 163–181.

Chaikin, D., (2009). How effective are suspicious transaction reporting systems? *Journal of Money Laundering Control,* 12(3), 238–253.

Charney, N. (ed.) (2009), *Art and crime. Exploring the dark side of the art world.* Santa Barbara (Ca).

Chong, A. and López-de-Silanes, F., (2007), *Money Laundering and its regulation.* Washington, D.C: Inter-American Development Bank.

Clarke, R.V. and Cornish, D.B., (1985), "'Modelling Offenders' Decisions: A Framework for Research and Policy" In M. Tonry and M. Morris, (eds.) *Crime and Justice: An Annual Review of Research,* Vol 6. Chicago, IL: University of Chicago Press.

Coase, R., (1937), The nature of the firm. *Economica,* 4(16), 386–405.

Coleman, J.W., (1992), Crime and Money: Motivation and Opportunity in a Monetarized Economy. *American Behavioral Scientist,* 35(6), 827–836.

Comstock, M.B., (1994), GATT and GATS: A public morals attack on money laundering. *Northwestern Journal of International Law and Business,* 15(1), 139–177.

Conklin, J.E., (1977), "*Illegal but not criminal*". *Business crime in America.* Englewood Cliffs, New Jersey.

Cook, D., Mulrow, C. and Haynes, R., (1997), Systematic Reviews: Synthesis of Best Evidence for Clinical Decisions. *Annals of Internal Medicine,* 126 (5) March, 376–380, cited in Tranfield, D., Denyer, D. and Palminder, S., (2003) Towards a Methodology for Developing Evidence-Informed Management Knowledge by Means of Systematic Review. *British Journal of Management,* 14, 207–222.

Cornish, D. and Clarke, R., (1987), Understanding crime displacement: An application of rational choice theory. *Criminology*, 25(4): 933–947.

Cuéllar, M-F., (2003), The tenuous relationship between the fight against money laundering and the disruption of criminal finance. *The Journal of Criminal Law and Criminology*, 93(2/3), 311–466.

Cummings, L. and Stepnowsky, P., (2011), My Brother's Keeper: An empirical study of attorney facilitation of money laundering through commercial transactions. *Journal of the Professional Lawyer*, (1), 1–36.

Daepp, K., (2006). Le Re-Re´gulation Se´lective de la Finance Internationale: L'Initiative sur les Pays ou Territoires Non Coope´ratifs du GAFI. Universite´ de Lausanne. Travaux de Science Politique. Political Science Working Paper Series.

Dawe, S., (2013), Conducting national money laundering or financing of terrorism risk assessment. Chapter 9, 110–126. In Unger, B and Van de Linde D (eds.) *Research Handbook on Money Laundering* Edward Elgar, Cheltenham.

de Boyrie, M.E., Pak, S. J., Zdanowicz, J. S., (2005), The impact of Switzerland's money laundering law on capital flows through abnormal pricing in international trade *Applied Financial Economics*, 15(4), 217–230.

de Koker, L., (2009), Identifying and managing low money laundering risk. *Journal of Financial Crime*, 16(4), 334–352.

de Koker, L., (2011), Aligning anti-money laundering, combating of financing of terror and financial inclusion. *Journal of Financial Crime*, 18(4), 361–386.

Demetis, D. S. and Angell, I. O., (2007), The risk-based approach to AML: representation, paradox, and the 3rd directive. *Journal of Money Laundering Control*, 10(4), 412–428.

Denyer, D. and Tranfield, D., (2009) "Producing a systematic review" pp. 671–689, in Buchanan, D. and Brymans, A. (eds.), *The SAGE handbook of organizational research methods*. London: Sage Publications Ltd.

Dolar, B. and Shughart, W.F., (2007), The wealth effects of the USA Patriot Act: evidence from the banking and thrift industries. *Journal of Money Laundering Control*, 10(3), 300–317.

Dolar, B., and Shughart, W.F., (2011), Enforcement of the USA Patriot Act's anti-money laundering provisions: Have regulators followed a risk-based approach? *Global Finance Journal*, *22*(1), 19–31.

Dombrink, J. and Meeker, J.W., (1986), Beyond 'Buy and Bust': non-traditional sanctions in federal drug law enforcement. *Contemporary Drug Problems*, 13(4), 711–740.

Doyle, T., (2002), Cleaning Up Anti-Money Laundering Strategies: Current FATF Tactics Needlessly Violate International Law. *Houston Journal of International Law* 24(2): reprinted in Entrepreneur.com.

Duyne, P. C. van, (1994), Money-laundering: estimates in fog. *The Journal of Asset Protection and Financial Crime*, 19, 103–142.

Duyne, P.C. van, (1995), *Het spook en de dreiging van de georganiseerde misdaad*, SDU, 's-Gravenhage.

Duyne, P.C. van, (1996), The phantom and threat of organized crime. *Crime, Law and Social Change*, 4, 241–377.

Duyne, P.C. van, (1998), Money-laundering, Pavlov's dog and beyond. *The Howard Journal*, 37(4), 395–374.

Duyne, P.C. van., (2003), Money laundering policy. Fears and facts. In van Duyne, P.C., von Lampe, K, Newell, J (eds.), *Criminal Finances and Organised Crime in Europe*. (pp. 67–104). Tilburg, The Netherlands: Wolf Legal.

Duyne, P.C. van, (2004), The creation of a threat image: Media, policy making and organised crime. In: P.C. van Duyne, M. Jager, K. von Lampe and J.L. Newell (eds.), *Threats and phantoms of organised crime, corruption and terrorism*. Nijmegen: Wolf Legal Publishers.

Duyne, P.C. van., (2007), Criminal finances and state of the art. Case for concern? In van Duyne, P. C., A. Maljevic, M. van Dijck, K. von Lampe and J. Harvey (eds.), *Crime business and crime money in Europe. The dirty linen of illicit enterprise*. (pp. 69–98). Nijmegen: Wolf Legal Publishers.

Duyne, P.C. van, (2013), Crime money and financial conduct, Ch 19 pp. 232–250, in Unger, E. and van der Linde, D., (*Eds.*), *Research handbook on money laundering*. Cheltenham: Edward Elgar.

Duyne, P.C. van and S. Donati, (2009), In search of crime-money management in Serbia. In: P.C. van Duyne, J. Harvey, A. Maljevic, K. von Lampe and M. Scheinost (eds.), *European crime-markets at cross-roads. Extended and extending criminal Europe*. Nijmegen, Wolf Legal Publishers.

Duyne, P.C. van and A. Kabki, (2016), Investment and long firm fraud. Local and cross-border. In: P.C. van Duyne *et al.*, *Narratives on organised crime in Europe. Criminals, corrupters and policy*. Oisterwijk: Wolf Legal Publishers.

Duyne, P.C. van and van Koningsveld, T.J. (2017), The offshore world: nebulous finances. In: P.C. van Duyne *et al.* (eds.), *The many faces of crime for profit and ways of tackling it*. Oisterwijk: Wolf Legal Publishers.

Duyne, P.C. van and Levi, M., (2005) *Drugs and money. Managing the drug trade and crime-money in Europe*. London, Routledge.

Duyne, P.C. van and de Miranda, H., (1999), The emperor's cloths of disclosure: Hot money and suspect disclosures. *Crime, Law and Social Change,* 31(3), 245–271.

Duyne, P.C. van and Nelemans, M.D.H., (2011), Transnational organised crime: thinking in and out of Plato's cave. *Handbook of transnational organised crime*, In: F. Allum and S. Gilmour (eds.) London: Routledge.

Duyne, P.C. van and Soudijn, M.R.J., (2010), Crime-money in the financial system: what we fear and what we know. In: M. Herzog-Evans (ed.), *Transnational Criminology Manual, Volume 2,* Nijmegen, Wolf Legal Publishers.

Duyne, P.C. van, Vander Beken, T., (2009), The incantations of the EU organised crime policy making. *Crime Law and Social Change,* 51, 261–281.

Duyne, P.C. van and Vorm, B van der. (2015), From organized crime threat to nuisance control. In P.C. van Duyne *et al., The relativity of wrongdoing: Corruption, organised crime, fraud and money laundering in perspective.* Oisterwijk: Wolf Legal Publishers.

Duyne, P.C. van, Groenhuijsen, M.S. and Schudelaro, A.A.P., (2005), Balancing financial threats and legal interests in money-laundering policy. *Crime, Law and Social Change,* 43(2-3), 117–147.

Duyne, P.C. van, Harvey J., and Gelemerova, L., (2016), 'The Monty Python Flying Circus of Money Laundering and the Question of Proportionality' Chapter 10 in 'Illegal Entrepreneurship, Organized Crime and Social Control: Essays in Honour of Professor Dick Hobbs' (ed) G. Antonopolous, Springer, Studies in Organized Crime 14.

Duyne, P.C. van, Harvey J. and Gelemerova, L., (2018a), A 'Risky' Risk Approach: Proportionality in ML/TF Regulation. Chapter 15 in C. King, C. Walker J. Gurulé. (eds.) *The Palgrave Handbook of Criminal and Terrorist Financing Law*, Palgrave, 978-3-319-64497-4, 420951.

Duyne, P.C. van, Harvey J. and Gelemerova, L., (2018b), The crusade for purity: Corruption and laundering. P.C. van Duyne *et al.* (eds.), *The Janus faces of cross-border crime in Europe*. Den Haag: Boom Uitgevers.

Duyne, P.C. van, M. Soudijn and T. Kint, (2009), Bricks don't talk. Searching for crime money in real estate. In: P.C. van Duyne, S. Donati, J. Harvey, A. Maljevic and K. von Lampe (eds.), *Crime, money and criminal mobility in Europe*. Nijmegen, Wolf Legal Publishers.

Duyne, P.C. van, de Zanger, W., and Kristen, F.H.G. (2014), Greedy of crime-money. The reality and ethics of asset recovery. In P.C. van Duyne *et al.*, *Corruption, greed and crime money. Sleaze and shady economy in Europe and beyond.* Wolf Legal Publishers, Nijmegen.

Easterby-Smith, M., (1997), Disciplines of Organizational Learning: Contributions and Critiques". *Human Relations*, 50 (9), 1085–1113.

ECOLEF Report, (2013), Utrecht School of Economics, project funded by the European Commission, DG Home Affairs.

Elliehausen, G.E., (1998), The cost of banking regulation: a review of the evidence, No 171, Staff Studies, Board of Governors of the Federal Reserve System (U.S.).

Engdahl, O., (2008), "The role of money in economic crime". *British Journal of Criminology*, 48(2), 154–170.

Ensign, R.L. and Colchester, M., (2015) Meet the Private Watchdogs Who Police Financial Institutions, Wall Street Journal, 31 August 2015, https://www.wsj.com/articles/meet-the-private-watchdogs-who-police-financial-institutions-1440983917, (accessed 16 October 2017).

European Monitoring Centre for Drugs and Drug Addition (EMCDDA) (2015) *European Drug Report: Trends and Developments*, Lisbon.

FATF (1990) *The Forty Recommendations of the Financial Action Task Force on Money Laundering.* Paris.

FATF, (2000), *'Review of Non Cooperative Countries or Territories: Increasing the Worldwide Effectiveness of Anti-Money Laundering Measures'*, June, Paris.

FATF, (2007), *Guidance on the risk-based approach to combating money laundering and terrorist financing; High level principles and procedures,* Paris.

FATF, (2008), *Money laundering and Terrorist Financing risk assessment strategies*. Paris.

FATF, (2012), *High-level principles and objectives for FATF and FATF-style regional bodies*. Paris.

FATF, (2013a), *Guidance: National money laundering and terrorist financing risk assessment Strategies*, February Paris.

FATF, (2013b), *'Procedures for the FATF Fourth Round of AML/CTF Mutual Evaluations'* October and updated June 2014, Paris.

FATF, (2013c), *'Methodology for assessing technical compliance with the FATF recommendations and the effectiveness of the AML/CFT systems'* February, Paris.

FATF, (2015), Guidance on AML/CFT Related Data and Statistics. October, Paris.

FATF, (2017), *'Consolidated Processes and Procedures for Mutual Evaluations and Follow-Up "Universal Procedures"'*, February, Paris.

FATF Annual Reports (1990 to date) are all available from www.fatf-gafi.org/publications/

FATF money laundering & terrorist financing typologies 2004–2005, 10 June 2005, available at: http://www.fatf-gafi.org/media/fatf/documents/reports/2004_2005_ML_Typologies_ENG.pdf. Accessed 3 February 2017.

FATF Mutual Evaluations (MER) are all available from http://www.fatf-gafi.org/publications/mutualevaluations/?hf=10&b=0&s=desc(fatf_releasedate)

Favarel-Garrigues, G., Godefroy, T. and Lascoumes, P., (2008), Sentinels in the banking industry: Private actors and the fight against money laundering in France. *British Journal of Criminology,* 48(1), 1–19.

Favarel-Garrigues, G., Godefroy, T., and Lascoumes, P., (2011), Reluctant partners?: Banks in the fight against money laundering and terrorism financing in France. *Security Dialogue,* 42(2), 179–196.

Ferwerda, J., (2009), The economics of crime and money laundering: Does anti-money laundering policy reduce crime? *Review of Law and Economics,* 5(2), 903–929.

Ferwerda, J., (2013), The effects of money laundering, part III, chapter 3 in Unger, B. and van der Linde, D. (2013). *Research Handbook on Money Laundering.* Cheltenham: Edward Elgar Publishing.

Ferwerda, J. and Unger, B., (2013), Detecting money laundering in the real estate sector chapter in Unger, B. and van der Linde, D. (2013). *Research Handbook on Money Laundering.* Cheltenham: Edward Elgar Publishing.

Ferwerda J., Staring, R., De Vries Robbé, E. and van de Bunt J., (2007) J. *Malafide activiteiten in de vastgoed sector.* Amsterdam: BV Uitgeverij SWP.

Ferwerda, J., Kattenberg, M., Chang, H., Unger, B., Groot, L., & Bikker, J., (2013), "Gravity models of trade-based money laundering". *Applied Economics,* 45(22), pp. 3170–3182.

Ferwerda, J., Kattenberg, M.A.C., Chang, H.-H., Unger, B., Groot, L.F.M. and Bikker, J.A., (2011), Gravity Models of Trade-based Money Laundering. In Tjalling C. E., (*Ed.*), Vol. 11 (16). Utrecht.: Koopmans Research Instituten.

Financial Conduct Authority. (2013) Handbook: SYSC. Retrieved http://fshandbook.info/FS/html/FCA/

FinCEN, (n.d.) History of Anti-Money Laundering Laws, https://www.fincen.gov/history-anti-money-laundering-laws (accessed 1 January 2018).

FinCEN (Financial Crimes Enforcement Network) (2004), In The Matter Of Riggs Bank, N.A. Assessment Of Civil Money Penalty, No. 2004-01, 13 May.

Fisse, B. and David, F., (1993), Some Antipodean Skepticisms about Forfeiture, Confiscation of Proceeds of Crime, and Money Laundering Offenses; *Alabama Law Review,* 44, 737–762.

Freiberg A. and Fox, R., (1992), Forfeiture, confiscation and sentencing. In B. Fisse, D. Fraser and G. Coss (eds.), *The money trail. Confiscation of proceeds of crime, money laundering and cash transaction reporting.* Sydney: The Law Book Comp. Ltd.

FSA (2003) consultation paper, DP22 "Reducing money laundering risk: know your customer and AML monitoring".

Gallant, M.M. (2010). Promise and perils: the making of global money laundering, terrorist finance norms. *Journal of Money Laundering Control,* 13(3), 175–183.

Gardin, J-C., (1973), Document analysis and linguistic Theory, *Journal of Documentation*, 29(2), 137–168.

Gardner, K.L. (2007), Fighting Terrorism the FATF Way. *Global Governance* 13, 325–345.

Gelemerova, L., (2009), On the frontline against money-laundering: The regulatory minefield. *Crime, Law and Social Change,* 52(1), 33–55.

Gelemerova, L., (2010), Fighting foreign bribery: the stick or the carrot? In van Duyne, P.C., Harvey, J, Maljevic, A, Vander Beker, T, and von Lampe K. (eds.), *Cross Border Crime Inroads on Integrity in Europe*. Nijmegen: Wolf Legal Publishers.

Gelemerova, L., (2011), *The anti-money laundering system in the context of globalisation a panopticom built on quicksand*, Nijmegen: Wolf Legal Publishers.

Gelemerova, L., Harvey, J., and van Duyne, P.C. (2018) 'Banks assessing corruption risk – a Risky undertaking' in Campbell L and Lord, N Corruption (2018) Chapter 10, pp. 182–198 in Commercial Enterprise: Law, Theory and Practice, Oxford: Routledge.

Gnutzmann, H., McCarthy, K. J., and Unger, B., (2010), Dancing with the devil: Country size and the incentive to tolerate money laundering. *International Review of Law and Economics*, 30(3), 244–252.

Gold, M., and Levi, M., (1994), *Money-Laundering in the UK: an Appraisal of Suspicion-Based Reporting*, London: Police Foundation. http://orca.cf.ac.uk/id/eprint/58055

Goldbarsht, D. and Michaelsen, C., (2017), International legal and quasi-legal approaches to combatting money laundering: an Australian perspective on norm-development. In van Duyne P.C., Harvey J, Antonopoulis, G.A,. and von Lampe K (eds.), *The many faces of crime for profit and ways of tackling it.*, Oisterwijk: Wolf Legal Publishers.

Goldby, M. (2013). Anti-money laundering reporting requirements imposed by English law: measuring effectiveness and gauging the need for reform. *Journal of Business Law,* June (4), 367–397.

Gordon, J.E., (1995), Prosecutors who seize too much and the theories they love: money laundering, facilitation, and forfeiture notes. *Duke Law Journal,* 44(4), 744–776.

Gordon, R.K., (2011), Losing the war against dirty money: rethinking global standards on preventing money laundering and terrorism financing. *Duke Journal of Comparative and International Law,* Spring 21(3), 503–568.

Greenfield, H.I., (1993), *Invisible, outlawed and untaxed: America's underground economy.* Westport: Praeger.

Hakkio, C. and Higgins, B., (1985), Costs and benefits of reducing inflation *Economic Review,* 70(1), 3–15.

Halliday, T., Levi, M. and Reuter P., (2014). *Global Surveillance of Dirty Money: Assessing Assessments of Regimes to Control Money-Laundering and Combat the Financing of Terrorism* (pp. 1–61): Centre on Law and Globalisation.

Hampton, M. P., and Levi, M., (1999), Fast spinning into oblivion?: Recent developments in money-laundering policies and offshore finance centres. *Third World Quarterly*, 20(3), 645–656.

Hantke-Domas, M., (2003), The Public Interest Theory of regulation: non-existence or misinterpretation. *European Journal of Law and Economics*, 15, 165–194.

Harmon, J. D., Jr. (1988). United States money laundering laws: international implications. *New York Law School Journal of International and Comparative Law*, 9(1), 1–45.

Harvey, J., (2004), Compliance and reporting issues arising for financial institutions from money laundering regulations: a preliminary cost benefit study. *Journal of Money Laundering Control*, 7(4), 333–346.

Harvey, J., (2005), "Controlling the Flow of Money-Laundering or Satisfying the Regulators", In van Duyne P.C., von Lampe, K., van Dijck, M. and Newell, J. (*Eds.*), *The Organised Crime Economy: Managing Crime Markets in Europe*, Tilburg, The Netherlands: Wolf Legal.

Harvey, J., (2008), Just How Effective is Money Laundering Legislation? *Security Journal*, 21(3), 189–211.

Harvey, J., (2009), The search for crime money – debunking the myth: facts versus imagery: Guest Editorial. *Journal of Money Laundering Control*, 12(2), 97–100.

Harvey, J., (2011), Money Laundering Phantoms, Imagery and Facts. In G. Antonopoulos, Groenhuijsen, M, Harvey, J., Kooijmans, T., Maljevic, A., and von Lampe, K. (Ed.), *Usual and Unusual Organising Criminals in Europe and Beyond: Profitable crimes, from underworld to upperworld: Liber Amicorum Petrus van Duyne* (pp. 81–104). Antwerp: Maklu.

Harvey, J., (2014), Asset Recovery Substantive or Symbolic In C. King, and Walker, C. (*Eds.*), *Dirty Assets: Emerging Issues in the Regulation of Criminal and Terrorist Assets*: Kent: Ashgate Publishing.

Harvey J., (2015), Engendering confidence in the financial system – challenges and observations, Chapter 18 pp. 219–228 in the *Research Handbook on International Financial Crimes*, Rider, B.A.K (*Ed.),* London: Edward Elgar Publishing Ltd.

Harvey, J. and Ashton, S., (2015), Anti-money laundering policy: A response to the activity of criminals or of agencies? chapter 12, pp. 283–307 in van Duyne, P.C., Maljević, A., Antonopoulos, G., Harvey, J., von Lampe, K (*eds*) (2015) *"The relativity of wrongdoing: Corruption, organised crime, fraud and money laundering in perspective"* Nijmegen: Wolf Legal Publishers.

Harvey, J. and Hornsby, R., (2016), The Criminal Entrepreneur: a case study of an organised criminal family pp. 167–192 in van Duyne, P.C., Scheinost, M., Antonopoulos, G., Harvey, J. and von Lampe, K. (*Eds.*) *Narratives on organised crime in Europe: criminals, corrupters and policy*. Nijmegen: Wolf Legal Publishers.

Harvey, J. and Lau, S.F., (2008), "Crime-money Records, Recovery and their Meaning" pp. 285–307 in van Duyne, P.C., Harvey, J., Maljevic, A., von Lampe, K., Miroslav, S (*Eds*) *"European crime-markets at cross-roads: Extended and extending criminal Europe"* Tilburg, The Netherlands: Wolf Legal.

Harvey, J. and Lau, S.F., (2009), Crime-money, reputation and reporting. *Crime, Law and Social Change*, 52(1), 57–72.

Harvey, J., Hutchinson, M. and Peacock, A., (2014), AML and the political powerweight. In Van Duyne P.C., Antonopolous G, von Lampe K, Maljevic A.,

Markovska., A. (*Eds*), *Corruption, Greed and crime money: Sleaze and shady economy in Europe and beyond*. Nijmegen: Wolf Legal.

Haynes, A., (1997), Securitisation, money laundering and fraud. *Journal of Money Laundering Control*, 1(2), 148–153.

Haynes, A., (2008), Money laundering: from failure to absurdity. *Journal of Money Laundering Control*, 11(4), 303–319.

Hidalgo Landa, A., Szabo, I., Le Brun, L., Owen, I. and Fletcher, G. (2011), "Evidence Based Scoping Reviews", *The Electronic Journal Information Systems Evaluation*, 14(1), pp. 46–52. Available online at www.ejise.com (accessed 9/9/14).

Hindes, T.L., (1977), Morality Enforcement Through the Criminal Law and the Modern Doctrine of Substantive Due Process, 126 *U. PA. L. REV.* 344, 346, December, http://scholarship.law.upenn.edu/cgi/viewcontent.cgi?article=4895&context=penn_law_review. Accessed 1 January 2018.

Hinterseer, K., (1997), An economic analysis of money laundering. *Journal of Money Laundering Control*, 1(2), 154–164.

Hinterseer, K., (2001), The Wolfsberg Anti-Money Laundering Principles. *Journal of Money Laundering Control*, 5(1), 25–41.

HM Treasury (2016) *"Transposition of the Directive on the prevention of the use of the financial system for money laundering or terrorist financing"*, London: HM Stationery Office.

Hoekje, C.L., Gaal, C.K. and Schmid K., (1993), State of New Jersey Commission of Investigation Report of Money Laundering. Two day public hearing on money laundering held on 9 and 14 December.

Hulsse, R., (2007), Creating demand for global governance: the making of a global money-laundering problem. *Global Society*, 21(2), 155–178.

Hulsse, R., (2008), Even clubs can't do without legitimacy: Why the anti-money laundering blacklist was suspended. *Regulation and Governance*, 2(4), 459–479.

International Monetary Fund (IMF), Working Paper WP/11/177 *Compliance with the AML/CFT International Standard: lessons from a Cross-Country Analysis*, Washington: IMF.

International Monetary Fund (IMF), (2016), Germany financial sector assessment program. Anti-money laundering and combating the financing of terrorism—technical note, IMF Country Report No. 16/190, June, https://www.imf.org/external/pubs/ft/scr/2016/cr16190.pdf. Accessed 25 December 2016.

International Monetary Fund (IMF/Hagan) (2011) *Anti-Money Laundering and Combating the Financing of Terrorism (AML/CFT)*—Report on the Review of the Effectiveness of the Program Prepared by the Legal Department (in consultation with other departments) Approved by Sean Hagan, 11 May, Washington: IMF.

Institute of Internal Auditors, Chartered (2013) *Guidance on Effective Internal Audit in the Financial Services Sector*, July.

IRS, Bank Secrecy Act History and Law, https://www.irs.gov/irm/part4/irm_04-026-005#idm139674432055184. Accessed 13 December 2017.

Jacobs, J.B., (2006), *Mobsters, unions, and Feds. The Mafia and the American labor movement*. New York: New York University Press.

Johannesen, N. and Zucman, G., (2014), The end of bank secrecy? An evaluation of the G20 tax haven crackdown. *American Economic Journal: Economic Policy*, 6(1), 65–91.

Johnson, J., (2008), Third round FATF mutual evaluations indicate declining compliance. *Journal of Money Laundering Control,* 11(1), 47–66.
Johnson, J., and Lim, D., (2002), Money laundering: has the Financial Action Task Force made a difference? *Journal of Financial Crime*, 10(1), 7–22.
KPMG, (2014), *Global Anti-Money Laundering Survey*, London.
Keen, F., (2017) *Unexplained Wealth Orders Global Lessons for the UK Ahead of Implementation,* RUSI Occasional Paper, September.
Keh, D.I. (1996). *Drug money in a changing world: economic reform and criminal finance*. Vienna: UNDCP.
Keršmanc C. and Ahtik, M., (2013), Learning the ABCs of deceptive practices in banking, pp. 177–201 in van Duyne, P.C., Harvey, J., Antonopoulos, G.A., von Lampe, K., Maljević, A. and Spencer, J., (Eds.) *Human dimensions in organised crime, money laundering and corruption,* Nijmegen: Wolf Legal Publishers.
Kessler, R. (1996), *The sins of the father*. New York, Warner Books.
Killick, M., and Parody, D., (2007), Implementing AML/CFT measures that address the risks and not tick boxes. *Journal of Financial Regulation and Compliance,* 15(2), 210–216.
King, C., (2013), Following the money trail: Civil forfeiture of criminal assets in Ireland. In P.C. Van Duyne *et al.*, *Human dimensions in organised crime, money laundering and corruption*. Nijmegen, Wolf Legal Publishers.
Kirkpatrick, C., (2006), Regulatory impact assessment Chapter 11, 232–251 in Crew, M. and Parker, D., *"International handbook on economic regulation"* London: Edward Elgar.
Koh, J., (2006), Suppressing Terrorist Financing and Money Laundering, Springer Science & Business Media, 25 July.
Koningsveld, T.J. van. (2015) *De offshore wereld ontmaserd.* Uitgeverij erckebosch, Zeist.
Krueger, A.O., (1974), The Political economy of the rent-seeking society, *The American Economic Review,* June, 64(3), 291–303.
Kruisbergen, E.W.K., Kleemans, E.R., and Kouwenberg, R.F., (2015a), Profitability, power, or proximity? Organized crime offenders investing their money in legal economy. *European Journal of Criminal Policy*, (21), 237–256.
Kruisbergen, E.W.K., Kleemans, E.R. and Kouwenberg, R.F. (2015b), Wat doen daders met hun geld? Uitkomsten van de Monitor Georganiseerde Criminaliteit. Justitiële Verkenningen, 1, 84–102.
Kruisbergen, E.W.K., Kleemans, E.R., and Kouwenberg, R.F., (2016), Explaining attrition. Investigating and confiscating the profits of organised crime. *European Journal of Criminology*, 13(6), 677–695.
Kurdrle, R.T., (2008), Did blacklisting hurt the tax havens? *Journal of Money Laundering Control,* 12(1), 33–49.
Lacey, R., (1991), *Little man; Meyer Lansky and the gangster life*. London Random Century.
Leong, A.V.M., (2007), Chasing Dirty Money: Domestic and International Measures against Money Laundering. *Journal of Money Laundering Control* 10, 140–156.
Levi, M., (1991), Regulating money laundering - The death of Bank Secrecy in the UK. *British Journal of Criminology,* 31(2), 109–125.

Levi, M., (1997), Evaluating the 'New Policing': attacking the money trail of organised crime. *The Australian and New Zealand Journal of Criminology,* 1, 1–25.
Levi, M,. (2002), Money laundering and its regulation. *Annals of the American Academy of Political and Social Science, 582*(July), 181–194.
Levi, M., (2003), Following the Criminal and Terrorist Money Trails. In van Duyne, P.C., von Lampe, K. and Newell, J. (*eds*) Criminal Finances and Organising Crime in Europe. Nijmegen, The Netherlands: Wolf Legal Publishers.
Levi, M., (2007), Pecunia Non Olet? The control of money-laundering revisited. In Bovenkerk, F. and Levi. M., (*Eds.*), *The organised crime community* (pp. 161–182). New York: Springer.
Levi, M., (2008), Lessons for Countering Terrorist Financing from the War on Serious and Organized Crime. In Biersteker, T.J., Eckert, S.E. (Eds.), *Countering the Financing of Terrorism*, pp. 260–288. London: Routledge.
Levi, M., (2010), Combating The financing of terrorism, a history and assessment of the control of 'Threat Finance'. *British Journal of Criminology*, 50, 650–669.
Levi, M. (2012), The Organization of Serious Crimes for Gain. In M. Maguire, R. Morgan, and R. Steiner (Eds.), *The Oxford Handbook of Criminology* (5th ed., pp. 595–622). Oxford: Oxford University Press.
Levi, M., (2015), Money for Crime and Money from Crime: Financing Crime and Laundering Crime Proceeds *Eur J Crim Policy Res* (21), 275–297.
Levi, M., (2018), 'Green with envy: Environmental crimes and black money, chapter 9 in Spapens, T., White, R., van Uhm, D. and Huisman, W. (Eds.), *Green Crimes and Dirty Money*. London: Routledge.
Levi, M., and Burrows, J., (2008). Measuring the Impact of Fraud in the UK: A Conceptual and Empirical Journey. *British Journal of Criminology,* 48(3), 293–318.
Levi, M., and Gilmore, B., (2002), Terrorist finance, money laundering and the rise and rise of mutual evaluation: A new paradigm for crime control? *European Journal of Law Reform,* 4(2), 337–364.
Levi, M., and Maguire, M., (2004), Reducing and preventing organised crime: An evidence-based critique. *Crime, Law and Social Change*, 41(5), 397–469.
Levi, M and Osofsky, L., (1995*), Investigating, seizing and confiscating the proceeds of crime,* Police Research Group, Crime Detection And Prevention Series: Paper No 61, London: Home Office Police Department.
Levi, M., and Reuter, P., (2006), Money Laundering. *Crime and Justice*, 34(1), 289–375.
Levi, M., and Reuter, P. (2009), Money Laundering. In M. Tonry (Ed.), *Handbook on Crime and Public Policy* (pp. 356–380). New York: Oxford University Press.
Levi, M., Reuter, P. and Halliday, T., (2018), Can the AML system be evaluated without better data?' *Crime Law and Social Change*, (69), 307–328.
Lewisch, P., (2008), Money laundering laws as a political instrument: the social cost of arbitrary money laundering enforcement. *European Journal of Law and Economics,* 26(3), 405–417.
Lissack, R. QC, Leslie, N., Morvillo, C.J., McGrath, T. and Ferguson, K., Monitorships, (2017), *Global Investigations Review* Clifford Chance LLP, Fountain Court Chambers, 04 January, http://globalinvestigationsreview.com/insight/the-practitioner%E2%80%99s-guide-to-global-investigations/1079360/monitorships (accessed 18 December 2017).

Magnusson, D., (2009), The costs of implementing the anti-money laundering regulations in Sweden. *Journal of Money Laundering Control,* 12(2), 101–112.

Malm, A., and Bichler, G. (2013), Using friends for money: the positional importance of money-launderers in organized crime. *Trends in Organized Crime*, 16(4), 365–381.

Marshall, P., (2004), Part 7 of the Proceeds of Crime Act 2002: double criminality, legal certainty, proportionality and trouble ahead. *Journal of Financial Crime*, 11(2), 111–126.

Masciandaro, D., (1998), Money laundering regulation: the micro economics. *Journal of Money Laundering Control,* 2(1), 49–58.

Masciandaro, D., (1999), Money laundering: the economics of regulation. *European Journal of Law and Economics,* 7(3), 225–240.

Masciandaro, D., (2005) False and Reluctant Friends? National Money Laundering Regulation, International Compliance and Non-Cooperative Countries, *European Journal of Law and Economics* 20(1), 17–30.

Masciandaro, D. and Filotto, U., (2001), Money laundering regulation and bank compliance costs: what do your customers know? economics and the Italian experience. *Journal of Money Laundering Control,* 5(2), 133–145.

Masciandaro, D. and Portolano, A., (2003), It takes two to tango: international financial regulation and offshore centres, *Journal of Money Laundering Control,* 6(4), 311–330.

Masciandaro, D., Takats, E. and Unger B. (2007), *Black finance: the economics of money laundering*. Cheltenham, UK, Edward Elgar.

Mascini, P., (2013), Why was the enforcement pyramid so influential? And what price was paid? *Regulation and Governance,* 7, 48–60.

McCarthy, K.J., van Santen, P. and Fiedler, I., (2015), Modeling the money launderer: Micro-theoretical arguments on anti-money laundering policy. *International Review of Law and Economics,* (43), 148–155.

McClean, D. (1989). Seizing the Proceeds of Crime: The State of the Art. *International and Comparative Law Quarterly, 38*(2), 334–360.

Ministry of Justice (2008), New Zealand: *Assessment of business compliance costs of the indicative anti-money laundering regulatory requirements,* July.

Mitsilegas, V., (2003), Countering the Chameleon Threat of Dirty Money: 'Hard' and 'Soft' Law in the Emergence of a Global Regime against Money Laundering and Terrorist Finance. Chapter in A. Edwards and P. Gill (eds.), *Transnational Organised Crime: Perspectives on Global Security,* London, Routledge.

Moorman, M., (2005), Cutting off the money. *SAS, Banking,* 26–29.

Nadelmann, E.A., (1986), Unlaundering Dirty Money Abroad: U.S. Foreign Policy and Financial Secrecy Jurisdictions. *The University of Miami Inter-American Law Review,* 18(1), 33–81.

Nardo, M., (2008), Organised crime and networking economy: models, features, dynamics and related approaches. *Journal of Money Laundering Control,* 11(2), 172–178.

Naylor, R.T., (1999), "Wash-Out: A Critique of the Follow-The-Money Methods in Crime Control Policy,". *Crime, Law and Social Change,* 32, 1–57.

Naylor, R.T., (2002), *Wages of Crime: Black Markets, Illegal Finance, and the Underworld Economy*. Ithaca, NY: Cornell University Press.

Naylor, R.T., (2003), Towards a general theory of profit-driven crimes. *British Journal of Criminology,* 43(1), 81–101.

Nelen, H. (2004). Hit them where it hurts most? The proceeds-of-crime ap-proach in the Netherlands. *Crime, Law and Social Change*, 41(5), 517–534.

Newland, L.S., (2008), Money laundering. *American Criminal Law Review,* 45(2), 741–764.

Nichols, L.T., (1997), Social problems as landmark narratives: Bank of Boston, mass media and "money laundering". *Social Problems,* 44, 324–341.

Nicolae, R., (2013), Peculiarities of unjustified wealth confiscation policy in Romania. pp. 293–323, in Van Duyne, P.C., Harvey, J., Antonopoulos, G.A., von Lampe, K., Maljević, A. and Spencer, J., (Eds.), (2013), *Human dimensions in organised crime, money laundering and corruption*. Nijmegen, Wolf Legal Publishers.

Office of the Comptroller of the Currency (OCC) (2006) finCEN, Feasibility of a Cross-Border Electronic Funds Transfer Reporting System under the Bank Secrecy Act, Appendix A, October.

Otusanya, O.J. and Lauwo, S., (2012), The role of offshore financial centres in elite money laundering practices: evidence from Nigeria. *Journal of Money Laundering Control,* 15(3), 336–361.

Otusanya, O.J., Omobola, A.S. and Olajide O.E., (2011). The role of financial intermediaries in elite money laundering practices. *Journal of Money Laundering Control,* 15(1), 58–84.

Pellegrina, L.D. and Masciandaro, D., (2008), The risk based approach in the new European anti-money laundering legislation: A law and economics view. *Paolo Baffi Centre Research Paper No. 2008-22.*

Pellegrina, L. D. and Masciandaro, D., (2009), The risk-based approach in the new European anti-money laundering legislation: A law and economics view. *Review of Law and Economics,* 5(2), 931–952.

Pickhardt, M. and Pons, S.J., (2011), The size of the underground economy in Germany: a correction of the record and new evidence from the modified-cash-deposit-ratio approach. *European Journal of Law and Economics,* 32(1), 143–163.

Pieth, M. (1998). The Prevention of money laundering: a comparative analysis. *European Journal of Crime, Criminal Law and Criminal Justice,* 6(2), 159.

Pieth, M. (1999). The Harmonization of Law against Economic Crime, *European Journal Law Reform*, 527–546.

Pieth, M. (2002). Financing of Terrorism: Following the Money. *European Journal of Law Reform, 4*(2), 365–376.

Ping, H. (2004). *Fight Against Money Laundering. A Comparative Perspective.* Rotterdam: Erasmus University.

Ping, H., (2005) The suspicious transactions reporting system, *Journal of Money Laundering Control*, 8(3), 252–259.

Pittaway, L., Robertson, M., Munir, K., Denyer, D. and Neely, A., (2004) Networking and innovation: a systematic review of the evidence". *International Journal of Management Reviews.* 5/6(3 and 4), 137–168.

Popper, K.R., (1969), *Conjectures and refutations. The growth of scientific knowledge.* London, Routledge and Keegan Paul.

Porter, M.E. and van der Linde C., (1995) Toward a New Conception of the Environment-Competitiveness Relationship. *Journal of Economic Perspectives* Fall, 9(4), 97–118.

Provost, M.A., (2009), Money laundering. *American Criminal Law Review,* 46(2), 837–861.

Quirk, P., (1996), "Macroeconomic implications of money laundering". *IMF Working Paper, WP/96/66, Monetary and Exchange Affairs Department, IMF, Washington, DC.*

Quirk, P., (1997), Money Laundering: Muddying the Macro-economy. *Finance and Development*, 7–9.

Rasmussen, D.W. and Benson, B., (1994), *The economic economy of a drug war. Criminal justice in the commons.* Lanham, Rowman and Littlefield.

Reuter, P., (2013), Are the estimates of the volume of money laundering either feasible or useful? In: Unger, B and van der Linde, D. (*Eds.*), *Research handbook on money laundering*. Cheltenham, Edward Elgar.

Reuter, P. and Greenfield, V., (2001), "Measuring Global Drug Markets. How Good Are the Numbers and Why Should We Care About Them?" *World Economics,* 4, 159–173.

Reuter, P. and Truman, E.M., (2004), *Chasing dirty money: the fight against money laundering*. Washington, DC: Institute for International Economics.

Reuter, P. and Truman, E.M., (2005), Anti-money laundering Overkill? It's time to ask how well the system is working. *The International Economy, Winter*, 56–60.

Reurts, N. (2017), 'Unexplained Wealth Laws: The Overseas Experience', in *Unexplained Wealth Orders: thoughts on scope and effect in the UK,* Briefing Papers, January, The White Collar Crime Centre.

Rhodes, R., QC, and Palastrand, S., (2005), A guide to money laundering legislation. *Journal of Money Laundering Control*, 8(1), 9–18.

Rider, B. (1992), Fei Ch'ien laundries: the pursuit of the flying money (part 1), *Journal of International Planning*, 1(2), 77–89.

Rider, B.A.K., (1990), Policing the International Financial Markets: An English Perspective. *Brooklyn Journal of International Law,* 16, 179–222.

Rider, B.A.K., (1996), The practical and legal aspects of interdicting the flow of dirty money. *Journal of Financial Crime*, 3, 234–254.

Rider, B.A.K., (1999), The Crusade against Money Laundering - Time to Think. *European. Journal Law Reform*, 501–527.

Roberge, I., (2007), Misguided Policies in the War on Terror? The Case for Disentangling Terrorist Financing from Money Laundering. *Politics* 27, 196–203.

Rogers, C. and Spector, M., (2017), Judge Slaps VW With $2.8 Billion Criminal Fine in Emissions Fraud, Wall Street Journal, 21 April, https://www.wsj.com/articles/judge-slaps-vw-with-2-8-billion-criminal-fine-in-emissions-fraud-1492789096, accessed 26 December 2017.

Rosdol, A., (2007), Are OFCs leading the fight against money laundering? *Journal of Money Laundering Control,* 10(3), 337–351.

Ross, S. and Hannan, M., (2007), Money laundering regulation and risk-based decision-making. *Journal of Money Laundering Control,* 10(1), 106–115.

Rubinstein, A., (1982), Perfect Equilibrium in a Bargaining Model *Econometrica*, 50(1), 97–109.

Ruggiero, V. and South N., (1995), *Eurodrugs: Drug use, markets and trafficking in Europe*. London: UCL Press.

Ryder, N. (2008). The Financial Services Authority and Money Laundering: A Game of Cat And Mouse. *The Cambridge Law Journal* (3), 635–653.

Sandulescu, M., (2014) Reconciling the anti-money laundering duties and commercial objectives of the bank. In Van Duyne P.C., Antonopolous G, von Lampe K, Maljevic A., Markovska., A. (Eds), Corruption, Greed and crime money: Sleaze and shady economy in Europe and beyond. Nijmegen: Wolf Legal.

Sandulescu, M., (2016), Compliance duties and bankers at work. Coping with tensions. In P.C. van Duyne *et al.*, *Narratives on organised crime in Europe. Criminals, corrupters and policy*. Oisterwijk: Wolf Legal Publishers.

Sathye, M., (2008), Estimating the cost of compliance of AMLCTF for financial institutions in Australia. *Journal of Financial Crime, 15*(4), 347–363.

Sathye, M., and Islam, J., (2011), Adopting a risk-based approach to AMLCTF compliance: the Australian case. *Journal of Financial Crime*, 18(2), 169–182.

Savona, E.U. (ed.), (1997a), *Responding to money laundering. International perspectives.* ISPAC, Harwood academic publishers.

Savona, E.U., (1997b), *European money trails 1: Interactions between E.U. regulations and money laundering activities in Europe: Italy*: TRANSCRIME, December 1996. *Trends in Organized Crime, 2*(3), 32–36.

Savona, E.U. and Riccardi M., (*Eds.*) (2015). *From illegal markets to legitimate businesses: the portfolio of organised crime in Europe.* Final Report of Project OCP – Organised Crime Portfolio (HOME/2011/ISEC/AG/FINEC/4000002220).

Savona, E.U., and Riccardi, M. (Eds.), (2017), *Assessing the risk of money laundering in Europe*. Final Report of Project IARM (www.transcrime.it/iarm). Milano: Transcrime – Università Cattolica del Sacro Cuore.

Schneider, F., (2005), Shadow Economies around the world: What do we really know? *European Journal of Political Economy*, 21(3), 598–642.

Schneider, F., (2006), *Shadow economies and corruption all over the world: what do we really know?* (Working Paper No. 0617). Department of Economics Johannes Kepler University of Linz.

Schneider, F., (2008), Money laundering and financial means of organized crime: some preliminary empirical findings. *Paolo Baffi Centre Research Paper No. 2008-17*.

Schneider, F., (2010), Turnover of organized crime and money laundering: some preliminary empirical findings. *Public Choice,* 144(3/4), 473–486.

Schneider, F. and Buehn, A., (2013), *Estimating the size of the shadow economy: methods, problems and open questions.* Studien/pfuschneu/2013/ShadEcMethods_October2013.doc. Retrieved from http://www.econ.jku.at/531/

Schneider, F. and Enste, D., (2000), Shadow economies around the world - size, causes and consequences. Retrieved from Washington: http://www.imf.org/external/pubs/ft/wp/2000/wp0026.pdf

Schneider, F. and Windischbauer, U., (2008), Money laundering: some facts. *European Journal of Law and Economics,* 26(3), 387–404.

Schneider, F., Buehn, A. and Montenegro, C.E., (2010), New Estimates of the Shadow Economies all over the World. *International Economic Journal,* 24(4), 443–461.

SEC News Digest, Issue 80-71 at 3 (10 April 1980), available at https://www.sec.gov/news/digest/1980/dig041080.pdf

Sharman, J.C., (2008), Power and discourse in policy diffusion: anti-money laundering in developing states. *International Studies Quarterly,* 52(3), 635–656.

Sica, V., (2000), Cleaning the Laundry: States and the Monitoring of the Financial System. *Millennium: Journal of International Studies* 29, 47–72.

Simon H., (1972), 'Theories of bounded rationality' chapter 8, pp. 161–176 in McGuire, C. and Radner, R. (eds.) *Decision and organization*, North Holland Publishing Co.

Sittlington, S., (2015), *What are the Factors that Influence the Effectiveness of Anti-Money Laundering Policy Implementation in the UK: Exploring Money Laundering Crime and Policy?* PhD thesis, University of Northumbria at Newcastle. Northumbria University: Newcastle.

Sittlington, S., and Harvey, J., (2018), Prevention of money laundering and the role of asset recovery. *Crime Law and Social Change.* https://doi.org/10.1007/s10611-018-9773-z

Soudijn, M.R.J., (2014), A critical approach to trade-based money laundering. *Journal of Money Laundering Control,* 17(2), 230–242.

Spapens, T., White, R., van Uhm, D. and Huisman, W., (Eds.), (2018), *Green crimes and dirty money*. London: Routledge.

Sproat, P.A., (2007), An evaluation of the UK's anti-money laundering and asset recovery regime. *Crime, Law and Social Change,* 47(3), 169–184.

Sproat, P.A., (2009a), Payback time? To what extent has the new policing of assets provided new assets for policing? *Journal of Money Laundering Control,* 12(4), 392–405.

Sproat, P.A., (2009b), To what extent is the UK's anti-money laundering and asset recovery regime used against organised crime? *Journal of Money Laundering Control,* 12(2), 134–150.

Steinko, A., (2012), Financial channels of money laundering in Spain. *British Journal of Criminology,* 52, 908–931.

Stessens, G., (2000), *Money laundering: a new international law enforcement model.* Cambridge: Cambridge University Press.

Stessens, G., (2001), The FATF Blacklist or non-cooperative countries or territories. *Leiden Journal of International Law*, 14, 199–208.

Strafer, G.R., (1989), Money Laundering - The crime of the '90s. *American Criminal Law Review,* 27(1), 149–207.

Suendorf, U., (2001) *Geldwäsche: Eine Kriminologische Untersuchung.* Neuwied: Luchterhand.

Takáts, E., (2011), A theory of "crying wolf": the economics of money laundering enforcement. *The Journal of Law, Economics, and Organization,* 27(1), 32–78.

Tanzi, V., (1983), "The Underground Economy in the United States: Annual Estimates, 1930-80" *IMF Staff Papers*, 30(2), 283–305.

Tanzi, V., (1996), *Money laundering and the international financial system*. Washington: International Monetary Fund.

Taylor, I., (1992), The international drug trade and money-laundering: Border controls and other issues. *European Sociological Review*, 8(2), 181–193.

Thomas, J., (1999), Quantifying the black economy: "measurement without theory" yet again? *The Economic Journal*, 109(456), 381–389.

Tijhuis, A.J.G., (2006), *Transnational crime and the interface and the interface between legal and illegal actors. The case of illicit art and antiquities trade.* Nijmegen,: Wolf Legal Publishers.

Tijhuis, A.J.G., (2009), Who is stealing all these paintings? In. Charney, N. (*Ed.*), *Art and crime. Exploring the dark side of the art world.* Santa Barbara (Ca).

Tinbergen, J., (1962), *Shaping the world economy: suggestions for an international economic policy* Twentieth Century Fund, New York.

Titcomb, J., (2015), Banks fined £3.7bn for rigging foreign exchange markets, The Telegraph, 20 May, http://www.telegraph.co.uk/finance/newsbysector/banksandfinance/11617964/Banks-fined-3.5bn-for-rigging-foreign-exchange-markets.html (accessed 6 January 2018).

Tranfield, D., Denyer, D. and Palminder, S., (2003), Towards a Methodology for Developing Evidence-Informed Management Knowledge by Means of Systematic Review *British Journal of Management*, 14, 207–222.

Tsingou, E., (2005), Targeting Money Laundering: Global Approach or Diffusion of Authority? In: Krahmann, E. (ed.) *New Threats and New Actors in International Security*, pp. 91–107. Houndmills: Palgrave Macmillan.

Tsingou, E., (2017), New governors on the block: the rise of anti-money laundering professionals, *Crime, Law, Social Change*, 27th November. 1–15 https://doi.org/10.1007/s10611-017-9751-x

Tversky, A. and Kahneman D., (1974), Judgment under uncertainty: Heuristics and biases. *Science* 185(4157), 1124–1131.

Ulph, J., (2010), 'confiscation orders, human rights, as penal measures' *Law Quarterly Review*, 126(April), 251–278.

Unger, B., (2007), *The Scale and Impacts of Money Laundering*. Cheltenham, UK: Edward Elgar.

Unger, B., (2013), Can Money Laundering Decrease? *Public Finance Review*, 41(5), 658–676.

Unger, B. (2017). European parliament directorate general for internal policies policy department a: economic and scientific policy *Offshore activities and money laundering: recent findings and challenges* study for the PANA committee IP/A/PANA/2016-04 March.

Unger, B., and Ferwerda, J., (2008), *Regulating Money Laundering and Tax Havens: The Role of Blacklisting*. Tjalling C. Koopmans Research Institute, Utrecht.

Unger, B. and van der Linde, D. (2013). *Research Handbook on Money Laundering*. Cheltenham: Edward Elgar Publishing.

Unger, B., Rawlings, G., Siegel, M., Ferwerda, J., de Kruijf, W., Busuioic, M., and Wokke, K., (2006), *The amounts and the effects of money laundering*. Report for the Dutch Ministry of Finance, February.

UNODC (2011): *Estimating illicit Financial flows resulting from drug trafficking and other transnational organised crime*. Research report. Vienna.

UNODC, (2016), Publications Report, Vienna. https://www.unodc.org/unodc/en/publications-by-date.html

US Commission on Organized Crime Report of 1984 Executive Order 12435—President's Commission on Organized Crime July 28, 1983 available from http://www.presidency.ucsb.edu/ws/?pid=41647

Vaithilingam, S., and Nair, M., (2009), Mapping global money laundering trends: Lessons from the pace setters. *Research in International Business and Finance,* 23(1), 18–30.

Van den Broek, M., (2015). *Preventing Money Laundering: A legal study on the effectiveness of supervision in the European union.* (Doctorate), Utrecht, Den Haag.

Van Duyne, P.C. (2013), Crime money and financial conduct. In E. Unger and D. van der Linde (Eds.), *Research handbook on money laundering.* Cheltenham: Edward Elgar.

Verdugo Yepes, C., (2011), *Compliance with the AML/CFT International Standard: lessons from a Cross-Country Analysis,* IMF Working Paper WP/11/177, Washington: IMF.

Verhage, A., (2009), Power-seeking crime? The professional thief versus the professional launderer. *Crime, Law and Social Change,* 51, 399–412.

Verhage, A., (2011), *The anti-money laundering complex and the compliance industry.* London; Routledge.

Verhage, A. and Ponsaers, P., (2009), Power-seeking crime? The professional thief versus the professional launderer. *Crime, Law and Social Change,* 51, 399–412.

Vold, G.B., (1958), *Theoretical Criminology,* New York: Oxford University Press.

Von Lampe, K., van Dijck, M., Hornsby, R., Markina, A., Verposte, K., (2006), Organised Crime is…findings from a cross national review of literature. In P.C. van Duyne, *et al., The organisation of crime for profit: conduct, law and measurement,* Nijmegen: Wolf Legal Publishers.

Vruggink, J.C., (2001), *Gepakt en gezakt. Invloed van de ontnemingsmaatregel op daders.* Leiden.

Walker, J., (1995), *Estimates of the extent of money laundering in and through Australia. Paper prepared for the Australian Transaction Report and Analysis Centre.* September, Queanbeyan: John Walker Consulting Centre.

Walker, J., (1998), Modelling Global Money Laundering Flows. from http://www.johnwalkercrimetrendsanalysis.com.au/ML%20method.htm

Walker, J., (1999), How Big is Global Money Laundering? *Journal of Money Laundering Control,* 3(1), 25–37.

Walker, J., and Unger, B. (2009). Measuring Global Money Laundering: 'The Walker Gravity Model'. *Review of Law and Economics,* 5(2), 821–853.

Walter, I., (1989), *Secret money. The shadowy world of tax evasion, capital flight and fraud.* (3rd edition ed.). London: Unwin Paperbacks.

Walsh, A., (2015), Is the Opaque World of Corporate Monitorships Becoming More Transparent? *Bus. L. Today* (December), www.americanbar.org/publications/blt/2015/12/08_walsh.html (accessed 18 December 2017).

Waris, A., and Abdul Latif, L., (2014), The effect of tax amnesty on anti-money laundering in Bangladesh. *Journal of Money Laundering Control,* 17(2), 243–255.

Wechsler, W., (2001), Follow the money *Foreign Affairs,* 80(40), 40–57.

Weinstein, A.K., (1988), Prosecuting attorneys for money laundering: a new and questionable weapon in the war on crime. *Law and Contemporary Problems,* 51(Winter), 369–386.

Welling, S.N., (1989), Smurfs, Money Laundering, and The Federal Criminal Law: The Crime of Structuring Transactions. *Florida Law Review,* 41, 287.

White, L. and Barly, S., (2016) *StanChart faces extension of U.S. money-laundering vigilance,* Reuters, 2 September, https://www.reuters.com/article/hsbc-stanchart-compliance-idUSL3N1BD4EA, accessed 18 December 2017.

Williams, P., and Baudin-O'Hayon, G. (2002) Global Governance, Transnational Organized Crime and Money Laundering. In: Held, D., McGrew, A. (Eds.), *Governing Globalization. Power, Authority and Global Governance*, pp. 127–144. Cambridge: Polity Press.

Witgenstein, L., (1922), *Tractatur Logico-Philosophicus. Logisch-philosophische Abhandlung*. London: Kegan Paul.

Wolfteich, P.G., (1988), Making Criminal Defense A Crime Under 18 U.S.C. Section 1957. *Vanderbilt Law Review,* 41(4), 843.

Yaniv, G., (1999), Tax Evasion, Risky Laundering, and Optimal Deterrence Policy, *International Tax and Public Finance,* 6(1) 27–38.

Yeandle, M., Mainelli, M., Berendt, A., and Heal, B. (2005) *Anti Laundering Requirements: costs, benefits and perception*. City Research Series (no. 6).

Young, M.A., (2013), The exploitation of offshore financial centres Banking confidentiality and money laundering. *Journal of Money Laundering Control,* 16(3), 198–208.

Zdanowicz, J.S., (2009). Trade-based money laundering and terrorist financing". *Review of Law and Economics,* 5(2), 856–878.

Index[1]

[1] Note: Page numbers followed by 'n' refer to notes.

P.C. van Duyne, J.H. Harvey and L.Y. Gelemerova, *The Critical Handbook of Money Laundering*, https://doi.org/10.1057/978-1-137-52398-3

www.ingramcontent.com/pod-product-compliance
Lightning Source LLC
Chambersburg PA
CBHW071729030326
40576CB00005B/412
* 9 7 8 1 1 3 7 5 2 3 9 7 6 *